AUSTRALIANS AT WAR

AUSTRALIANS AT WAR

Peter Cochrane

ABC
BOOKS

Commonwealth Department of
Veterans' Affairs

This book accompanies the television series 'Australians at War'
produced by Beyond Productions Pty Ltd for the Department of
Veterans' Affairs in cooperation with the Australian War Memorial.

Published by ABC Books for the
AUSTRALIAN BROADCASTING CORPORATION
GPO Box 9994 Sydney NSW 2001

Copyright © Text Department of Veterans' Affairs 2001
Written by Peter Cochrane

Copyright © Photographs Australian War Memorial, Steven Siewert,
Palani Mohan, Brendan Read, Bluey Thomson, Andrew Meares

First published April 2001

National Library of Australia
Cataloguing-in-Publication entry
Cochrane, Peter, 1950- .
    Australians at war.

    Bibliography.
    Includes index.
    ISBN 0 7333 0917 8.

    1. South African War, 1899-1902 - Participation, Australian.
    2. World War, 1914-1918 - Participation, Australian. 3.
    World War, 1939-1945 - Participation, Australian. 4.
    Korean War, 1950-1953 - Participation, Australian. 5.
    Vietnamese Conflict, 1961-1975 - Participation, Australian.
    6. Australia - History - 20th century. I. Australian
    Broadcasting Corporation. II. Title.

994.04

Designed by Ingo Voss
Set in 11/13.5pt Caslon 224 by
Midland Typesetters, Maryborough, Victoria
Colour separations by Pageset, Victoria
Printed in Singapore by Tien Wah Press

5 4 3 2 1

Acknowledgements

Les Murray, 'Visiting Anzac in the Year of Metrication' from *Selected Poems:*
The Vernacular Republic, Angus & Robertson, 1976. Reproduced by permission of Les Murray.

Bruce Dawe, 'Homecoming' from *Sometimes Gladness: Collected Poems 1954 – 1978*,
Longman Cheshire, Melbourne, 1978. Reproduced by permission of Pearson Education Australia.

Extract from *Nasho*, Michael Frazer, Aries, Melbourne, 1984.

Remembrance Day Speech, 11 November 1993 presented by Paul Keating.
Reproduced by permission of the Department of Veterans' Affairs, Canberra.

Norman Lindsay, The Australaise. Reproduced by permission of Barbara Mobbs, Literary Agent, Sydney.

Cover images, clockwise from top
Private H. H. Ball and Private E. Jay of 17th Infantry Brigade, Melbourne 1943 (AWM 140021);
Flight Lieutenant Viv Shearn, No 77 Squadron, RAAF, South Korea 1953 (AWM JK0649); HMAS *Sydney*,
Vietnam 1968 (AWM P1539/20); Iroquois helicopters, Vietnam 1971 (AWM P02866.030); Lieutenant
Cathew holding Major McLaurin's horse, Egypt 1915 (AWM J02783);
Matron E. J. Gould, Sister Penelope Frater and Miss Julia Bligh Johnston of the NSW Medical
Corps in South Africa (AWM A03962); unidentified RNZAF Load Master sitting on rear ramp
of a RNAZF C130 aircraft, Darwin 1999 (AWM P03184.025)

Page ii
Men of the 2/4 Commando Squadron hoisting an Australian flag,
Sadau Island, Borneo, April 1945 (AWM 090925).

Page vi
Crowd in Martin Place, Sydney, celebrating the news of the
signing of the armistice, 11 November 1918 (AWM H11563).

Front endpaper
Hand and medals of Harry Newhouse, who served at Gallipoli. © Steven Siewert,
The Last Anzacs, Gallipoli 1915, Allen & Kemsley Publishing, Sydney, 1996

Foreword

In this centenary year of Federation, as we look back across the first 100 years of our nation, we Australians cannot but be moved by the number of times our fellow countrymen and women have been prepared to lay down their lives or to encounter injury, danger or hardship in the armed service of their country.

Indeed, even as the Commonwealth was born at the commencement of 1901, Australian troops were in the field in South Africa. Within half a generation they would be subjected to the awful carnage and suffering of World War I.

At Gallipoli, in the Middle East, France, Belgium and elsewhere, on land, at sea and in the air, our Australian volunteer soldiers earned a wonderful reputation for their tenacity, resourcefulness and courage in adversity. That reputation was maintained and enhanced by their sons and daughters in later wars and conflicts.

Today Australia is an active participant in the United Nations Organisation. Since 1947, only two years after the formation of the UN itself, our defence force personnel have served under its flag in many areas of the world in the cause of peace.

Looking back over the past century, there would scarcely be a household in Australia that has not been touched in some way by our nation's involvement in war or conflict.

Australians at War, encompassing as it does a television documentary series, this book, a website and educational materials for school children, forms one of the highlights of the Centenary of Federation celebrations. It helps us look back to those wars and conflicts in which Australia has participated and see again, perhaps with fresh eyes, the service and sacrifice of our servicemen and women and civilians, and discern how those experiences have helped contribute to the development of our nation.

As Governor-General of our country and Commander-in-Chief of the Australian Defence Force, I am honoured to write this foreword. We Australians are rightly proud of the history and the traditions of our armed services and of the quality and standards of our defence personnel – standards that have been based and built upon those that their forebears forged. It is a great heritage and one that is not solely theirs, for it belongs to all Australians.

I commend this volume to the reader, encouraging you to delve deep into its contents. Here you will find recorded many of those experiences that have contributed to what makes us Australian.

Sir William Deane

Contents

Preface

At Mouquet Farm on the Western Front in 1916, the Australian war correspondent, Charles Bean, buried his cousin Leo who had been killed in a storm of shrapnel. Later he received a letter full of heartbreak from Leo's bereaved parents in Hobart, Tasmania. Bean pinned the letter from his Uncle Ted and Aunt Amy inside his diary so it was with him always, a reminder of how 'a chance scrap of metal, flung at random on the hillside in front of Mouquet, drives its course right through to the furthest end of the world.'

A piece of shrapnel and a letter. These two objects could not be more different from one another nor more alien and yet, at Mouquet Farm in 1916, they were bound together in tragedy - the one unseen, bloodied, deadly, a worthless scrap of metal, rust, then dust; the other stained in tears, a poignant keep-sake to be treasured and preserved for generations to come. So it is that all events of war are woven into the lives of those at home, and so it is that all weapons of war can inflict pain everlasting a world away from the site of battle.

Early in the process of researching and writing this book, of wrestling with the big question – how best to tell the tale – I realised that the shrapnel and the letter could be my guide. My story must not only follow the campaigns and the battles in conflicts across a century, it must also link them to life at home. Australians at War must be the story of the nation in wartime. The experiences of Australian servicemen and women, from the Boer War, which began in 1899, through to the INTERFET presence in East Timor today, are placed in this wider setting.

In the chapters that follow the narrative is carried along by a number of recurring themes – the ordeals and achievements of Australian forces, conscription, the war economy, women in wartime and opposition to war; the press and propaganda, bereavement and commemoration; and those living links between the trenches and life at home: the war correspondents and photographers, war artists and documentary film-makers.

The story shifts from battlefront to home-front and back again. There is also movement from the grand preoccupations of military history, such as generalship, logistics and the politics of war, to the irreducible intensity of individual experience, of ordinary people in extraordinary times. In other words, the emotional dimensions of the story are no less important than the strategic or the political ones. The details of everyday life – of men in combat or of women in munitions work – matter as much as the panoramic perspective. The shrapnel and the letter are testament to that.

In the course of this work I have relied on the advice of numerous scholars with specialist expertise in military, political and social history. These colleagues and friends most generously shared their knowledge, though I must declare that I am solely responsible for the research and writing and, as such, responsible for any inadequacies of interpretation and dramatisation.

I am particularly indebted to those who read the entire manuscript for me, piecemeal, as the chapters came into the world. To Robert Darby, Phillip Deery, John Hirst, Richard Reid, Suzanne Rickard and Peter Stanley, thank-you for staying the distance. Others have lent their expert advice on particular chapters. For this assistance I am most grateful to Joy Damousi, Jim Davidson, Peter Edwards, Shirley Fitzgerald, Bill Gammage, David Horner and Craig Wilcox.

Bob Pounds at the Department of Veterans' Affairs was a most helpful reader when the manuscript was in its final stages. Thanks also Kerry Blackburn at DVA, to Bill Fogarty and Ben Evans at the Australian War Memorial and especially to Rowena Lennox for her excellent copy-editing. Others who helped along the way were Margy Burn, Tim Bonyhady, Stephen Foster, John Iremonger and Vince Munro.

My greatest debt is to the little team that came together at ABC Enterprises to create the visual splendour of this volume and the variety of its exposition, extending as it does beyond the written word to maps, prints, posters, paintings and photographs. It was always my intention that the illustrations, in whatever form, would be more than decoration. They are an integral part of the story. For that reason I became a member of the production team when the writing was done, and together we worked intensely through one chapter after another, weaving the textual and the visual strands together.

There is not a page where this meeting of word and image has not been talked over, debated and cordially resolved, despite the pressure of strict deadlines. My heartfelt thanks to this team – to Ingo Voss for his elegant design, to Jill Brown who is a very special editor, and to Matthew Kelly for his commitment to the project from start to finish.

Peter Cochrane
January 2001

1

UNKNOWN, UNTRIED

1899 – 1902

On 3 July 1899, more than three months before the outbreak of the Boer War, British Secretary of State for the Colonies, Joseph Chamberlain, sent secret cablegrams to colonial governments in Australia requesting a 'spontaneous' offer of military support for British policy in southern Africa. Chamberlain was a forward imperialist, an enthusiast for the spread of empire. He was bent on British supremacy over all of southern Africa and was prepared to use force if necessary. His pretext was wrapped in the language of high ideals. Colonial backing would underpin the just cause he was fashioning for the British government.

I N those days what is now known as the Republic of South Africa included two Boer states ('Boer' was the Dutch word for farmer) and two British colonies. The British held Cape Colony in the south and Natal in the east. The Boers, descendants, mostly, of Dutch colonists, had trekked north to escape British rule and set up their own colonies of Transvaal and Orange Free State. These frontier communities were landlocked, thinly populated outposts where the Bible remained more important than the balance sheet, and Calvinism complemented the continued enslavement of blacks.

In the mid nineteenth century it seemed that the British and Boer states in southern Africa were facing a similar, if separate, future: they were small farming communities, poor, illiterate and provincial by European standards, undercapitalised and seemingly with little chance of trading their way to riches. After the Transvaal War of 1881, in which British forces had been decisively defeated at Majuba Hill, an uneasy coexistence prevailed. But in the mid 1880s gold was discovered in the Transvaal. Cecil Rhodes, a British freebooter backed by mercenaries, had already found a fortune in diamonds at Kimberley and dreamed of extending the empire from Cape Town to Cairo. It seemed all southern Africa was a treasure chest waiting to be unearthed.

Rhodes had subdued the Ndebele and the Mashona and with the help of the railway had extended his political control of a huge pool of cheap African labour and land to the west and well to the north of the Boers. A great southern empire was complete, save for what was now the region's most important economic asset—the Transvaal. In London the interested section of the stock exchange was called the Kaffir Circus, 'kaffir' or 'caffre' being a corruption of the Arab term for pagan. High society was in raptures over the new El Dorado promising the chance to be richer still,

It seemed all southern Africa was a treasure chest waiting to be unearthed.

Seven men of the 2nd South Australian (Mounted Rifles) Contingent, Breaker Morant third from left, *previous page*.

At sea, a kangaroo taking a drink on board a troop ship bound for the South African war, *opposite*.

Employees of De Beers Company sorting diamonds, Kimberley, South Africa, c.1900.

Members of the second draft of the First Tasmanian Contingent on board the SS *Coogee* prior to embarkation for South Africa. Launceston, Tasmania, 18 January 1900.

It was not until the war had clearly turned against the British in 'Black Week', December 1899, that fervent jingoism spread through the colonies and silenced most open discussion.

A warrant officer with his wife and children in the city park, Launceston, Tasmania, prior to a farewell parade on 27 October 1899, *opposite*.

while the popular press encouraged those with no prospects to revel in the fantasy too. The Boers, caricatured as backward, brutal and dirty, were in the way. Sections of British society were working themselves into a fit of hysteria.

By the 1890s there were large numbers of Englishmen mining in the Transvaal and some Australians too. The miners were immigrants who paid taxes yet could not vote or hold civil office. The Boers called them 'Uitlanders' (foreigners). Rhodes and Chamberlain insisted that the Transvaal government of Paul Kruger extend the vote to these transients and in effect cede political control to the English. It was around this insistence that sufficient pretext for war was mounted. Behind the question of votes and citizenship was a simple matter of power: 'Our supremacy in South Africa and our existence as a great power in the world are involved in the result of our present controversy,' Chamberlain told Sir Alfred Milner, his High Commissioner in Cape Town. By October 1899, Chamberlain had his war—the Boer army hit first, invading the Cape—and he also had offers of military support from the Australian colonies. But these offers had not come easily.

When Chamberlain's secret cablegrams arrived in the colonies, the governors sounded out the commanders of the colonial military forces and the politicians. Imperial officers all, the commanders were keen; the politicians less so. The militia forces of the six colonies totalled nearly 19,000 men, though 70 per cent of these were in New South Wales and Victoria. They had a good opinion of themselves, they were eager, mostly, but they were untried. The radical press called them 'feather-bedders' and 'swashbucklers', 'lemon-slicers' and 'tent-peggers'. The motives of the New South Wales contingent that went to the Sudan in 1885 were evident again in 1899. They were an untested force, anxious to prove themselves. A few militiamen saw this test of their masculinity as a measure of nationhood, but it was opinion makers, press editors and other pundits who dwelt on that link.

At first, the general public and the politicians were not as enthusiastic as the militias. Premiers with vivid memories of the depression of the early 1890s worried about who would pick up the bill, the electoral consequences of a budget deficit and the remoteness or relevance of southern Africa. They even questioned the need for Australian forces, for it seemed to be a David and Goliath affair. Surely the Boers were just inflated toads and easily stepped on. Like the Sudan in 1885, it might be all over by the time they reached South Africa. Neither Victoria nor New South Wales was ready to leap into this one. It was not until the war had clearly turned against the British in 'Black Week', December 1899, that fervent jingoism spread through the colonies and silenced most open discussion. Australians started to imagine themselves more isolated than ever, should the British be driven from South Africa. Until that time there was at least some debate and the war came and went in the press, conceding column space to the tour of Darling's cricket XI, the coming federation referendum or the Dreyfus case in France. For a time there was far more upset in the colonies about poor Dreyfus and the evils of French politics than there was about the rights of Uitlanders.

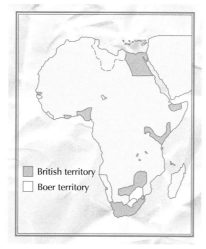

British territory

Boer territory

British Imperial Africa, 1899

Australian soldiers in a YMCA hut decorated with flags and a 'Welcome' sign, South Africa, c.1899.

Some of us are willing—wilfully, blindly, eager, mad! —to cross the sea and shoot men whom we never saw and whose quarrel we do not and cannot understand. Our cry is 'For England!' or 'Blood is thicker than water!' and so we seek to blind and deceive ourselves as fools who are unanimous in their eagerness to sacrifice right, justice, truth.

Henry Lawson,
October 1899

It was even possible to hear a voice of calculated reason. In the New South Wales parliament, Billy Hughes, scarcely imagining his future as a tub-thumping imperial patriot, pointed to the lack of information available to judge the merits of the cause. He said the Uitlanders were mere sojourners in another country and should live by its laws or go home. British workers in German bicycle factories didn't have the vote and who got upset about that? No-one. Hughes was no less a believer in the British empire for all this. He was sharp enough to know that one stumble before a lesser enemy could cost the empire dearly.

Across the land, in Coolgardie, Western Australia, the Labor member appealed for caution on the grounds of white brotherhood. The Boers were fellow Christians, fellow Europeans and fellow pioneers. From Sydney University, G.A. Wood, professor of history, wrote to the newspapers to tell people they had a choice: they could lend their weight to a piratical empire or to an empire of high ideals. Wood saw pirates at work in southern Africa, rootless, emancipated men to whom all flags were flags of convenience, treasure hunters whose first principle was greed. He was tapping a deep vein of imperial history, linking himself with forebears such as Fox, Bright and Gladstone, men who had stood against unjust wars. In the NSW parliament, the young, eloquent Labor tyro W.A. Holman took a similar line and then lost control of his tongue. He raged against swindling speculators such as Rhodes, against British bullying and against soldiers who would kill Boers for no more reason than a bit of target practice. When asked whom he wanted to win, the British or the Boers, he said the war was so unjust he hoped for a Boer victory. Later he qualified that comment and retreated. For a time there was only uproar.

These voices, cautious or not, were outweighed by those supporting 'Empire right or wrong', by anti-Boer propaganda and even, it seemed, by the laws of social evolution. As the Melbourne *Age* put it, if the Boers 'had the right to take the land from the natives in the interests of a semi-barbarous settlement, [then] Great Britain has the same right to supercede the Boers in the interests of a higher civilisation'. As the pressure for a commitment built up, so the cautious and the doubters subsided. A member of the South Australian parliament used poetry to satirise their acquiescence.

As for the war, I go agen it,
I mean to say, I kind of do—
That is, I mean, that being in it,
The best thing is to see it through.

By October 1899, legislatures around the country were giving their blessing to intervention in southern Africa. Such was the shift of mood that within months Holman was pushed off a public platform in Hobart and 'roughly handled' as the Tasmanian Governor put it, while Professor Wood came close to dismissal from Sydney University. These attacks were symptomatic. Around the country there were campaigns and 'witch-hunts' against so-called 'pro-Boers' and 'traitors'. In Victoria at South Wandin, raspberry-pickers voted to half drown any picker with pro-Boer

Two Australian soldiers, their bed rolls on the ground. A white South African boy stands to attention holding a rifle and bayonet, South Africa, c.1900.

'We must face the fact,' wrote the young journalist Winston Churchill, who had been captured at Ladysmith in Natal, 'that the individual Boer, mounted in suitable country, is worth from three to five regular soldiers.'

sympathies and not to pick for unpatriotic growers; in Natimuk in the same State, there were street fights with the German citizenry. In New South Wales at Broken Hill, the German Club was stormed by stone-throwing hardliners.

Across the Indian Ocean, on the veldt in southern Africa, the spring rains had come. There would be good forage for the Boer ponies. The Boer farmers were ready to fight. One of them said: 'God and the Mauser rifle will see the Transvaal through.'

There were about 15,000 men in the eight Australian contingents that went to South Africa (allowing for those who enlisted twice), plus a very small number of women who went with the ambulance units. Once the colonies had committed themselves to the war, the War Office made it clear that only token forces were wanted. Infantry was preferred, commanded by no-one above the rank of major, which meant that these units could be tacked onto imperial regiments and more or less forgotten. It was the symbolism of being there that mattered most to London, not the numbers.

Fewer than 1,000 members of these colonial forces were in South Africa for the first disastrous months of the campaign, which culminated in Black Week in December 1899 when the British lost or surrendered thousands of troops at Magersfontein, Stormberg and Colenso. 'We must face the fact,' wrote the young journalist Winston Churchill, who had been captured at Ladysmith in Natal, 'that the individual Boer, mounted in suitable country, is worth from three to five regular soldiers.'

Lord Roberts arrived in January 1900 to take supreme command and rescue the situation. Roberts' only son had been killed at Colenso, his body brought back by the Natal Indian ambulance team with whom Mahatma Gandhi was serving. Roberts was 68 years old and a military hero: as a young man he had won the Victoria Cross (VC) during the Indian Mutiny (1857–58); he had commanded troops in the Second Afghan War in the late 1870s where he established a reputation for burning villages as a punitive measure. He was commander-in-chief of British forces in Ireland when he was suddenly called to South Africa in 1899. Horatio Herbert Kitchener, aged 49, was sent with him as a stand-by should Roberts' stamina fail or the loss of his son overwhelm him.

Men of 3rd Troop, D Squadron, NSW Imperial Bushmen.
D Squadron acted as bodyguard to Lieutenant-General Lord Methuen.

Our worst nuisance are the ostriches, they eat our soap and clothes, and steal the horses' forage and pick up anything bright that is going about, we fed one the other day on a box of unexploded sparklets and then ran him about hoping he would explode, but had no luck.

Lieutenant Colonel
Percy R. Ricardo,
1st Queensland
Mounted Infantry

All volunteers, not just colonials, had civilian ideas about privileges and discipline. They would not tolerate attempts to turn them into regular troops

Private William Thomas
Dartnall, aged 15 years,
5th Victorian Mounted
Rifles Contingent.

Men of 3rd Troop, D Squadron, NSW Imperial Bushmen.
D Squadron acted as bodyguard to Lieutenant-General Lord Methuen.

Roberts was resolute and ready to change strategy. The British were facing the 'scourge of the modern high powered rifle', the .276 Mauser being the standard Boer weapon. It could kill at 2,000 metres. They were also facing an enemy who refused to be bound by what Sir Alfred Milner called the 'recognized rules of civilised warfare'; they would not stand still and be shot. Frontal attacks on concealed Boer positions were no way to victory. The British forces needed much greater mobility.

South of the besieged town of Kimberley, Roberts prepared a huge army to march on the Boer capitals, first Bloemfontein in the Free State, then Pretoria in the Transvaal. There would be a new emphasis on sharp scouting and constant flanking movements. Good horsemen were needed and the Australians were generally good horsemen, though they were not as valuable as the South African colonials who rode well, were familiar with the terrain and had some knowledge of indigenous languages. For the men of the first contingents, the chance to put their skills to the test seemed likely when, in January 1900, the various colonial units were combined into one Australian Regiment. These hopes were dashed for there was no fighting to be done at that time, just bickering among the colonial officers over appointments and privileges, while the rank and file whinged about the inglory of 'guarding the jam'. They did take the time to remove all insignia and badges of rank from their uniforms, in deference to Boer marksmanship. The Western Australians even jettisoned their blue jumpers and blue putties so they too could fade into an indistinguishable sea of khaki.

There were many other things to whinge about. All volunteers, not just colonials, had civilian ideas about privileges and discipline. They would not tolerate attempts to turn them into regular troops—attempts they resisted by evasion and humour and, occasionally, by outright disobedience. The Australians sized up their own officers with as much scepticism as they did British officers. The gulf between themselves and the British officer class was an issue, but not a major one. A poor officer was a danger to them; an abusive officer, an affront. The rank and file took exception to both and judged officers first on their merit in the field, not their nationality. Poor leadership was one issue among many. The groaners protested about inappropriate duties, pay levels, the quality of remounts, lack of overcoats and blankets, lack of recognition for deeds of bravery, attempts to prolong their enlistments or to keep them at the front beyond their term. One British officer, a junior cavalryman whose name was Douglas Haig, thought that the colonials were more trouble than they were worth, a strain on resources, expensive compared to regulars and poorly trained.

The Australian Regiment did not last. It was a rather sorry exercise in nationalism, jaundiced by inter-colonial rivalries and outclassed by the enchantment of brigading with imperial troops, a classic expression of the colonial cringe. Roberts opted for mobility. He converted the regiment into five companies of mounted infantry and he made mounted infantry of the second contingents, which arrived from Australia in February. These new units were tacked on to imperial formations. They practised bareback on transport mules while waiting for their mounts and for the move on the Free State capital.

To the east, in Natal, a cautious General Buller had lost the battle of Colenso and failed, three times, to relieve the besieged township of Ladysmith. To the west, General Methuen had blundered and now General French was charged with the relief of the besieged people of Kimberley, Cecil Rhodes among them. Rhodes was threatening to surrender if they didn't hurry up. It was a horse-killing dash, the kind of ride that the colonials thought 'glorious' and resented missing. Just one squadron of NSW Lancers was in the vanguard and behind the Lancers, merged into the imperial ranks, were two companies of Queensland Mounted Infantry. A.B. 'Banjo' Paterson, a correspondent for the *Sydney Morning Herald*, was there too. They heard Lord Roberts, 'Bobs' as he was known, tell them in paraphrased Shakespeare: 'You will remember what you are going to do all your lives, and when you have grown to be old men, you will tell the story of the relief of Kimberley.'

As French's cavalry raced for Kimberley, Roberts' army moved off, an invasion force of 45,000 troops, 4,000 carts and wagons, 10,000 mules, 9,600 oxen and a contingent of black attendants all moving east, away from the Western Rail line

War correspondents in camp, Colenso, Natal, 1900.

Lord and Lady Roberts drove by in an open carriage one afternoon. He is a little 'red faced man' as Kipling describes him and looks quite a little figure beside his wife who is much taller than he.

Trooper Walson Steel, 1st NSW Mounted Rifles

Paterson on the Ride to Kimberley

Banjo Paterson's poem 'With French to Kimberley' conjured up 'long, lean Walers' on the glorious ride to the besieged township. In a metre reminiscent of Macaulay's patriotic ballads, Paterson described how men had come from the far reaches of the empire to be part of General French's advance. At this stage he saw the war as a measure of racial unity and a mark of racial triumph:

His column was five thousand strong—all mounted men—and guns:
There met, beneath the world-wide flag, the world-wide Empire's sons;
They came to prove to all the earth that kinship conquers space,
And those who fight the British Isles must fight the British race!
From far New Zealand's flax and fern, from cold Canadian snows,
From Queensland plains, where hot as fire the summer sunshine glows—
And in the front the Lancers rode that New South Wales had sent:
With easy stride across the plain their long, lean Walers went.
Unknown, untried, those squadrons were, but proudly out they drew
Beside the English regiments that fought at Waterloo.
From every coast, from every clime, they met in proud array
To go with French to Kimberley to drive the Boers away.

First published in the *Sydney Morning Herald*, 29 September 1900

Lieutenant Frederick William Bell VC, 6th West Australian Mounted Infantry. Bell was awarded the Victoria Cross for bravery in the Transvaal, 15 May 1901.

that linked the southerly reaches of the Cape with Kimberley and Mafeking, also beseiged. The march to Bloemfontein produced an unexpected bonus. Within days the forward units of Roberts' force had trapped General Cronje's 6,000-strong army at a place called Paardeburg Drift on the Modder River. A terrible ten-day seige followed and the Boers were forced to surrender. Paardeburg was the second last major set-piece battle of the war (Diamond Hill was the last) and Australians played little part in it, being occupied with the convoys or patrolling elsewhere.

At Paardeburg it was the Canadians, in battalion force, who won favourable comment from Lord Roberts and whose prime minister, Laurier, waxed lyrical about how this battle had revealed the Canadian as a gifted fighting man. But the Australians would not be outdone. Most of them were patrolling further to the south, in the Colesburg area. In skirmishes earlier in 1900, notably at Slingersfontein and Pink Hill, they had shown themselves to be sometimes good scouts and sometimes bad, to be reckless and heroic, to be dogged in spite of the odds and foolhardy at times. The opinion makers at home— editors, politicians, bards and self-appointed recruiters—who measured glory in battles fought and honour by the cavalry charge, saw in these encounters what they wanted to see.

After the battle of Pink Hill, where 95 Australians took heavy casualties (six killed and 23 wounded), the Australian newspapers were ecstatic. Pink Hill was a defeat and a retreat but it was also a confirmation. The Australians had held a kopje, a rocky outcrop a hundred metres high. They held for two hours and then covered the evacuation of 100 British troops. Major G.A. Eddy had walked among the Australians apparently fearless, encouraging them and directing their fire, until he was shot through the head and killed. The Melbourne *Argus* called for a 'beautiful and stately monument' to the fallen. The Adelaide *Advertiser* found the highest military qualities in the episode. And the English writer, Conan Doyle, who went to South Africa as a volunteer doctor, said what many Australians wanted to hear: 'In all the scattered nations which came from the same home, there is not one with a more fiery courage and a higher sense of martial duty than the men from the great island continent.'

Johnnie Boer

Boer leader General Petrus Jacobus Joubert having breakfast with his soldiers, Newcastle, South Africa, 1900.

Men fight all shapes and sizes as the racing horses run,
And no man knows his courage till he stands before a gun.
At mixed-up fighting, hand to hand, and clawing men about,
They reckon Fuzzy-Wuzzy is the hottest fighter out.
But Fuzzy gives himself away—his style is out of date,
He charges like a driven grouse that rushes on its fate;

You've nothing in the world to do but pump him full of lead:
But when you're fighting Johnnie Boer you have to use your head;
He don't believe in front attacks or charging at the run,
He fights you from a kopje with his little Maxim gun.

But after all the job is sure, although the job is slow,
We have to see the business through, the Boer has got to go.
With Nordenfeldt and lyddite shell it's certain, soon or late,
We'll hunt him from his kopjes and across the Orange State;
And then across open flats you'll see the beggar run,
And we'll be running after with our little Maxim gun.

Banjo Paterson, first published in the
Sydney Mail, 17 February 1900.

After Paardeburg, Roberts' army trekked east to Bloemfontein, on the Central Railway, with some 14,000 Boers in disarray ahead of them. Most of the 1st NSW Mounted Rifles had joined the army in the aftermath of the battle when the air was still a haze of artillery smoke. They had missed everything: the charge to Kimberley, because their horses were done in; then Cronje's destruction, because they were too long in Kimberley enjoying the ginger biscuits and cake that Englishwomen cooked up for them when they arrived with the supplies. 'God

One of the Australian Bushmen astride a Cape pony.

Some of our fellows were out sharking horses from other regiments last night. They got a couple. They docked their tails, hog maned them and cut 'NSW' into their hair with a pair of scissors. I guarantee their owners will not know them when they see them.'

Private James C. Cripps, 1st NSW Mounted Rifles

knows we relished it,' wrote Trooper W.A. Steel in a letter to his sweetheart, Gerty. More imperialist than nationalist, and happy to be in partnership with nobility in war, Steel headed his letters: 'With the Army of Lord Roberts.'

Steel and the other horsemen of the 1st NSW Mounted Rifles caught up with Roberts on the battlefield of Paardeburg. They camped among dead horses and sheep, unexploded shells, cartridge cases, tons of torn iron and the remnants of wagons. 'The stench was overpowering,' Steel told Gerty, 'the men haggard and weary, the ambulances full, the heat great. I had no meat for two days and only biscuit and coffee.'

This great encampment now included the second contingents from Australia. They had come up from Cape Town and were integrated into four mounted infantry brigades under four British colonels, while a squadron of Australian Horse and the NSW Lancer squadron were brigaded with the regular cavalry, alongside units such as the Scots Greys and the Inniskillings. Some took great pride in that association. Far away in London both race and nation were coming together—colonial delegates, parleying with Chamberlain, were finalising a constitution for Australia. At

Paardeburg there was also unity with the chance of distinction. Possibly now the Australians would be better used, at least as scouts and guides. But those who hoped for military glory were soon disappointed. The advance to Bloemfontein was unrelenting and largely uneventful. The men were hungry and tired, their horses, on a half-ration of oats, were starving and exhausted. One general called the Australians 'good horsemen

A trooper leaves his dead horse on the trek to Bloemfontein, early March 1900.

There is no forgetting the carts that rumbled through the street, loaded with those stiff, blanket-shrouded shapes which had been vigorous men—the dwindling squadrons, the crowded sick tents, the unfed, unwashed, unhappy men who filled them, will never cease to linger in one's memory.

J.H.M. Abbott,
1st Australian Horse

A nurse confers with a surgeon at Orange River Hospital, sometime in 1900.

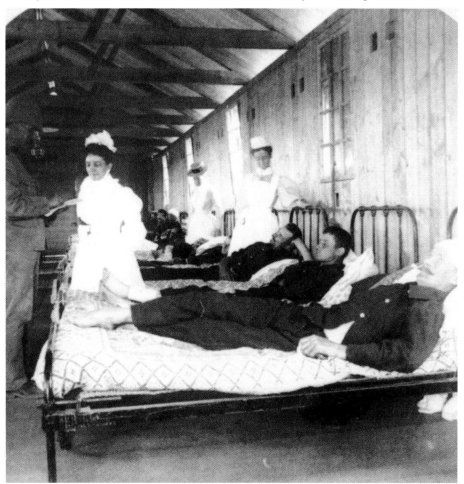

but bad horsemasters'. At least one trooper lay awake at night waiting for the transport corporal to fall asleep so he could steal a helmet of oats for his mount. Tobacco juice was used to rid the mounts of ticks. Banjo Paterson was pained by the suffering and wastage of these animals—40,000 of them came from Australia and most died a cruel death on the veldt before the war's end, ridden to exhaustion or shot by the enemy. Still, Paterson's poems celebrated the 'glorious rides' for the good of the empire.

The ride north was imperilled. Disease was travelling with this grim imperial host. Dead horses and human waste in the Modder River at Paardeburg had infected the army and completed its incubation by the time Roberts reached Bloemfontein. His troops entered the undefended city and then took rest on the black-soil plain, which reminded Trooper Steel of the 'rolling downs' of the Bathurst region in New South Wales.

At first, camping was both spectacle and bliss. As far as the eye could see, lines of horses and tents covered the plains and the lower reaches of the kopjes, while at night camp fires twinkled like stars come to ground. Then it rained. It rained for a month. Many ordinary soldiers were without tents. They made temporary bivouacs from blankets, improvising as best they could with rifles and bridle-reins as supports. They slept on flooded ground as enteric fever (typhoid) spread through the camp, and dysentery, pneumonia and rheumatism spread with it. The rats arrived. Men lay among these scampering, sodden, delighted things, like pigs in a sty. The better read Australians were reminded of the Crimea.

Hospitals in Bloemfontein filled to overflowing, so, too, did the cemeteries. New ground had to be broken beyond their perimeters. The State House where Sir Alfred Milner had met with presidents Kruger and Steyn a year before was now the principal hospital, every nook and corner filled with disease-stricken soldiers and the wounded remnants of earlier battles. The black-soil plains had become an expanse of pulverised slime under the feet of man and beast. The troops sank wells looking for disease-free water. One thousand soldiers died. Conan Doyle called it 'the greatest misfortune of the campaign'. The able men, counting on their good fortune, shivered, scratched and starved. They were there for seven weeks. That was about twenty funerals a day, one nurse observed.

They left that pest-hole early in May 1900, aiming for Johannesburg and Pretoria. Roberts' ailing army of the centre, reinforced and some 50,000 strong, now included 2,500 Australians and a contingent of Africans for digging trenches and graves, cooking, sewing, shepherding the livestock and a host of more menial tasks. The army advanced on a front that was 80 kilometres wide, kicking up a great cloud of dust that seemed to stretch to the horizons. It was hot and dry by day and very cold by night.The troops were advancing on a scattering of some 30,000 Boers who would no longer stand and fight. The tedious and unheroic guerrilla phase of the campaign would soon begin, a phase in which the enemy, putting a greater value on living to fight another day, relied on fast movement and stealth, deadly interventions and hasty retreats.

The Australians were again reorganised. Most of them were now brought together in the Imperial 1st Mounted Infantry Brigade under Major General E.T.H. Hutton, a former British commanding officer of military forces in New South Wales and a soldier bound to play a big part in shaping Commonwealth forces after the Boer War. Thus absorbed, the Australian contingents were used wherever and however the imperial staff thought best, usually under British command. No-one called them

Hospitals in Bloemfontein filled to overflowing, so, too, did the cemeteries.

'My God, Australian Sisters . . .'

Three nurses of the NSW Army Medical Corps who accompanied the Second Contingent to South Africa. Sister Penelope Frater (centre) is holding her Queen Victoria chocolate box.

Nurses with the NSW Army Medical Corps were in Bloemfontein during the typhoid epidemic. They went on to Johannesburg with Lord Roberts' army and there presented their papers to the Principal Medical Officer who groaned and said: 'My God, Australian sisters, what shall we do?'

By that time, Australian nurses were familiar with the prejudice against any woman who dared intrude into the British military system. Only a very small number of female nurses were part of that system. The arguments against them were numerous and dubious: wounded men preferred male orderlies, war was no place for women, convalescents could not relax in their presence, some cases were unsuitable for female nursing and, of course, there was the problem of 'flirtation'. 'Petticoat outfits,' said an English officer, 'blasted menace.'

The South African experience did much to end this nonsense. About 1,400 female nurses were with the British in South Africa, and of these about 100 came from the colonies. Some 60 came from Australia, though hundreds volunteered. In 1899 nursing was a profession in its infancy. Among the 60 Australian nurses there were forceful women who believed that military nursing would advance their cause. Others who sailed for South Africa wanted adventure and travel. One of them thought military nursing would be all efficiency, running on 'greased wheels' from firing line to base hospital. She was in for a rude shock. Patriotism drew them too, for they were generally well-educated women from the Protestant middle class, the daughters of professional, landed and commercial gentlemen, women who would gladly follow the flag. Queen Victoria sent her soldiers and nurses in South Africa a box of chocolates each. Some soldiers traded them or gulped them down but most, like the nurses, treasured the box as a valuable souvenir and consumed the chocolates at dignified intervals.

Most nurses were sent as part of small colonial units, fourteen from New South Wales, six from South Australia, nine from Victoria and eleven from Western Australia. Another fifteen to twenty paid their own way. All save the NSW unit were on the British army payroll. They landed in Cape Town where Kipling was distributing plug tobacco to convalescing Tommies. The nurses were soon distributed across the zones of war. The SA and NSW units arrived in Bloemfontein as the typhoid epidemic took hold. They helped turn public buildings into hospitals. The State House was converted and held 60 beds in its auditorium. Most of the casualties were typhoid cases. 'Lately I have taken to cleaning the mouths of the worst typhoids,' wrote Gertrude Fletcher who was alarmed at so many mouths stiff and caked with sores. 'By the time I have finished doing twenty or thirty tremulous pairs of lips, the same number of quivering tongues, with the teeth, gums, and palates accompanying them, I am nearly as tremulous as any of them. It is the most trying piece of work I have ever undertaken.'

Janey Lempriere was nursing a man, 'quite mad,' she thought, with a gangrenous cheek. He cried for help every time he heard footsteps. 'The night before he died, he asked me to kiss him,' she wrote.

Western Australian nurses were in Natal following the relief of Ladysmith. The Victorian nurses chose to go with the Victorian Bushmen's Contingent to Rhodesia though they were warned it was no place for women. One of them, Julia Anderson, was left on a farm with an officer suffering pneumonia. She lived in a clay hut with a mushroom-shaped roof made of reeds. The few drugs she had soon ran out, but her patient numbers increased as passing troops discovered her 'facility' and dropped off sick and wounded men. Over an eight-week period she had 30 patients with pneumonia, double-pneumonia, concussion, malaria and dysentry, and not one death.

When the war ended the Australian nurses came home, some via England and most on hospital ships, nursing all the way. Only Fanny Hines, who was with the Victorian nurses, was left behind. She was buried in a cemetery in Bulawayo beneath a cross erected by her fellow sisters and the Victorian Bushmen. William Dobbin, one of the Bushmen, wrote home to the Minister of Defence saying she was 'beloved by all'. Another wrote of her in his diary entry for 31 August 1900: 'Sister Hines died in Bulawayo a real good girl I guess it was over work did for her . . .' He was right. Sister Hines died of pneumonia, following exhaustion and lack of nourishment. She had been left alone with as many as 26 patients at a time, and no relief. She had stuck to her task.

mercenaries and most of the soldiers were pleased to be brigading with fabled imperial units. They wore a large 'A' sewn onto the left side of their helmets and since they made up nearly half of Hutton's brigade, they still hoped to make an impact as a national force. Hutton thought that they were 'fine looking workmanlike men' and that they embodied all that was best in the young and vigorous manhood of thecolonies, though they seemed to him 'ignorant of their own value'. He prayed to God for 'discrimination and the insight to know when and how best to utilize such grand material'. He was sorely grieved when his fighters rarely had a chance to fight: 'We must kill and slay if our superiority as a race is to be established over that of the Dutch in South Africa,' he wrote.

With the Boers largely out of reach, the march on Pretoria was, as Conan Doyle put it, more 'geographical than military'. The *Times History of the War in South Africa* compared the advance with that of a man-of-war, with Boer forces 'parting like the waves of the seas but gathering again as the enemy moved on'. But the flanks were many times harassed by Boer raiders and the Australians played a part in chasing them off, killing them where possible and plundering their farms. They were the 'eyes and ears of the invasion,' wrote L.M. Field in *The Forgotten War*, always scouting, 'forming protective screens for artillery, infantry and the supply columns'. But at night they came back to the safety of the main force. Occasionally a Boer unit engaged in cannon duels with this force and scouts rode back to ground freshly won, littered with dead horses and the enemy dead, the air still tinted with artillery smoke (the haze left by 'smokeless powder' fired in large quantities) and the effects of shell bursts all around, dismembered body parts, great pools of dried blood crawling with ants, a head three parts off, vultures in the trees and darkness coming on.

The 6th Regiment of NSW Imperial Bushmen running to remount after firing a volley, Mafeking, 1900.

We cleared the country by burning all the farm houses; and the poultry fell to the victors.

Tasmanian officer

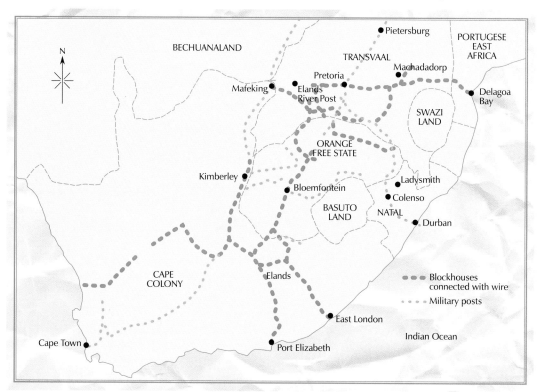

The systematic zoning of the latter stages of the Boer War

A NSW Imperial Bushman and his makeshift shelter, 1900.

There was not enough food. The men were rationed a couple of hard biscuits, half a tin of 'bully' (beef) and a measure of coffee, without sugar, per day.

It was a cruel march for many reasons. Men, asleep in the saddle, tumbled to the ground. Infantry dragged bloodied feet, their boots reduced to scraps of leather, dust and sweat like a paste on the skin. Horses, starving and exhausted, dropped by the way. The mounted infantry lost an average of one in five horses. The colonials among them covered more ground than most and sustained even higher losses. The de-horsed mounted soldier was soon as big a problem as sickness and disease. Men were lice-ridden, ragged and dirty. When they could, they washed their bodies with sand and gravel for want of soap. It was rumoured that Madame Melba's brother was influential enough to secure a pass home the instant he found he was 'lousy'. But the doughty Colonel Tom Price of the Victorian Mounted Rifles stressed the levelling merit of lousy-ness: 'Why . . .,' he shouted, 'I'm lousy, the Padre's lousy, Lord Roberts is lousy and the dear old Queen would be lousy too if she were here.'

There was not enough food. The men were rationed a couple of hard biscuits, half a tin of 'bully' (beef) and a measure of coffee, without sugar, per day. The horses, mostly remounts railed to Bloemfontein and badly abused on the trains, did it harder still. The great encampment that only weeks before had dazzled colonial eyes, quickly disintegrated into a ragged hoard of scavengers. The euphemism was 'commandeering'; the reality involved the looting of Boer farms leaving a land plucked of all life save the women and

Taking the heavy guns across the Vet River during Lord Roberts' advance on Pretoria, *left*.

Warrant Officer Herbert Arnold, DCM, regimental Sergeant Major, 1st Australian Horse, *below*.

Location unknown; however, General Buller used observation balloons along the Tugela River in his attempts to relieve Ladysmith, c.1900.

What a multitude of sins that word 'commandeering' covers! What we call at home thieving, looting, burglary, and horse-stealing, is all called commandeering here, and is very much in fashion.

William Henry Barham, 1st NSW Mounted Rifles

Location unknown; however, General Buller used observation balloons along the Tugela River in his attempts to relieve Ladysmith, c.1900.

children who stood stoically or tearfully, helpless, it seemed, while Boer grandfathers, husbands, sons and neighbours watched and waited from afar, ready to come down wrathful upon any isolated or vulnerable fragment of the enemy. The Boer women were fighters too. A small number fought alongside their men. A few colonials paid dearly for thinking that those left behind were passive. The girls had to be watched for they would send signals with their sunbonnets. Once a stout, elderly Boer woman was caught on the roof of her home waving a tablecloth. Another time two Australians stepped from a cottage where they had accepted a cup of tea and 40 Boer horsemen shot them down.

From farm gardens the looters unearthed potatoes, harvested cabbages and artichokes with their bayonets and stuffed their haversacks full. They picked fruit trees clean, strung strangled fowls to their saddles and packed eggs into their horses' nosebags. They seized grain and stock; they uprooted fences and hacked outhouses to pieces for firewood and then raided the African kraals for food and sometimes for women. Substantial homes amid groves of cyprus pines or eucalypts had the colonials talking about 'Dutch squatters'. The more frequent little farmhouses seemed not unlike the selectors' abodes back home, save for the thatched roofs that were common on the veldt. They pondered the similarity between this frontier and their own.

The journey took a terrible toll on Roberts' victorious army, the Australians included. The NSW Lancers and the Australian Horse were reduced to a ragged remnant. Of the 520 men of the Queensland Mounted Infantry under Colonel Ricardo, only 192 arrived safely in Pretoria, the rest were sick or wounded or walking, carrying their saddles, and way behind the main force. When the NSW Mounted Rifles paraded in Pretoria, 80 men out of 600 were fit to turn out. Some were dead, some had transferred to the better paid mounted police, the rest were sick or wounded or, according to one officer, 'scattered all over South Africa having lost their horses and fallen behind'. These scattered elements are now part of a peripheral history of countless background scenes, unrecorded and leaving many questions. How did these men get back to their regiments? Who did they encounter in that foreign land and by what means and what inner resources did they survive along the way?

Roberts, on the other hand, was centre stage in the enemy's capital. The field marshal's place in the imperial pantheon was secure. He was the gentleman architect of victory and a few months later he went home to an earldom and an Order of the Garter, leaving the 'clean-up' to Kitchener. Never, in the mythology, did 'Bobs' share the infamy associated with the devastation of a land and a people that had in fact begun under his leadership and was formed as policy before his departure. When it became clear that the Boers would persist against all odds, the assault on the

Lord Roberts in Pretoria. The black armband on his left sleeve is a mark of mourning for his son, Fred, who died after being wounded at the battle of Colenso.

A NSW Imperial Bushman in camp, possibly adjusting hobbles, *above*.

A small group of Australian soldiers cooking a meal.

Private Herbert Webb Anderson, 5th Victorian Mounted Rifles.

Lieutenant Charles Henry Brand, 3rd Queensland Mounted Infantry.

All the men were allowed to loot and Methuen's Tommies are adept in the art. Australians also did not require to be initiated to a great extent in the profession . . .

Captain David John Ham, 3rd Victorian Bushmen

British and colonial troops parade in the municipal square, Pretoria, possibly for a flag raising ceremony to mark the capture of the town.

civilian population was stepped up, not by Kitchener but by Roberts, in his final months as commander-in-chief. The policy of commandeering turned into one of scorched earth. Chamberlain was well aware of precedents. In December 1899 he had suggested the possibility of going through the Orange Free State as Sherman's troops had gone through Georgia in the American Civil War, destroying everything.

With Pretoria occupied by imperial forces it seemed the war might be over. Instead a new kind of war, a war of attrition, began. All over the country Boer *commando* were running, hiding, stalking and ambushing. Paterson chose to ride with General Ian Hamilton to the eastern Transvaal where many thousands of Boer resistance fighters were still active, but Hamilton's horse fell on him and shattered his shoulder blade. Sir Archibald Hunter took command and on they went. Roberts chose to drive east, to chase the Boer army of Louis Botha into Portuguese East Africa and to sieze the temporary seat of Boer government at Machadodorp on the way. Now Roberts' armies were spread far and wide. There were columns to his south rounding up the *commando* of Christian de Wet who were attacking his supply lines and communications. Columns were sent to Mafeking and the western Transvaal. In Rhodesia, further north, the British South Africa Company did not know what to fear most, an uprising of blacks or a Boer invasion. The company needed protection too. Across the continent British troops were in Natal and Swaziland. The vastness of Roberts' pacification campaign called for more colonial horsemen and these were on the way. The British government had learned that colonial mounted units from Australia were very useful. By now it knew that to ask was to receive. Early in 1900 it asked again, specifying a need for good shots and able riders. The requirement was not trained soldiers, not even part-timers like the militia, but good bushmen. The third contingents and those that came after, the fourth, fifth and even sixth contingents, were scattered across southern Africa as much by intent as by the misfortunes of war. They were nearly all volunteer bushmen, hand-picked for the job. Some of the contingents brought a mascot with them—a dingo, a sheep-dog, a black swan, a possum or a wallaby.

Efforts to raise third contingents began in January 1900 and by March they were on the Indian Ocean having been seen off by substantial crowds though nothing like the massings for earlier departures. What was sustained throughout 1900 was not the crowds but the unsightly spectacle of colonial premiers and other prominent people in Australia falling over themselves to outdo one another, acting in effect as 'recruiting sergeants' to the War Office, jumping to attention when calls for more men came from Chamberlain or Kitchener, or when they read of other calls in the *Times*.

There was no shortage of pent-up local enthusiasm to serve the empire, nor of incompetents who made better skilled men take riding and shooting tests in their name, or had patrons sign a form endorsing skills they did not have. But the selection trials were thorough and the men passed were nearly all fair to good horsemen, reasonably accurate shots, and fit. They also shared a degree of indifference to military discipline and, like the Australian Imperial Force in 1915, they were above average height, old enough to have some bush 'savvy' and young enough to be what British authorities wanted most—men with dash. General French called them 'The Wild Men'. During the 1890s writers such as Henry Lawson and Banjo Paterson, and journals such as the *Bulletin* and the *Boomerang*, romanticised the men of the bush. The Boer War made them a national icon.

With the utter destruction of his crops, the removal of every single head of stock throughout the country and the transfer of his womenfolk—the Boer must climb down from his untenable position and accept the inevitable.

James Cue Ryan, Victorian Imperial Bushmen

Captain D.J. Ham at the Siege of Eland's River

On 4 August 1900, a force of 2,500 Boers surrounded a stores garrison at Eland's River in the western Transvaal. About 500 colonials were defending the garrison and 300 of these were from Australia, mostly Bushmen. One of the Australians was a horse breeder and militiaman from the town of Hastings in Victoria, Captain David John Ham. The defenders at Eland's River took a pounding. In the first two days 2,500 shells were fired into the camp. Nearly all of the 1,500 horses, mules and oxen were blown to pieces. The Boers wanted the stores, so the battle was reduced to rifle fire with occasional shelling. The siege lasted for twelve days, then a relief column arrived and drove off the enemy. After the siege, Captain Ham wrote his account of the battle from under a wagon:

> A shell struck Trooper Bird's leg, severing it and hurtling it with force against me—the shell passed through the side of Norton taking his arm off, and continuing, took the woodwork off Smith's rifle and passed on splintering the rocks and covering us with dirt. I gave a look at the poor fellows and Norton begged me to shoot him.

Ham wrote of lying behind a mere 6 inches of cover because adequate defences had not been prepared, of hearing 'the whistle of bullets just like a hive of bees swarming, splashing and splintering the rocks', and of shells shattering into fragments, imperilling all their bodies. He saw oxen falling by the hundred, picket lines torn away, reins snapping, horses careering in madness. He sent a 'blackfellow' to cut the rest of the horses loose but a shell blew the man's legs off.

Their one artillery piece choked. Ham wondered more than once if his survival was a miracle. A shell fragment had cut his face, another had taken off the back of one hand, but otherwise he stayed well. He had never been been under fire and was pleased to note a lack of anxiety and a sense that he would come out 'perfectly safe'. The agonies of the horses distressed him most:

> I shall never forget [that] and the scenes of horses swinging their legs, some of them off altogether, some crawling about on their stumps or with their entrails dragging on the ground can only be seen to be realised.

Ham's 'Cobby bay' horse lasted until the third day. A chestnut and another bay called 'Old Kruger' were also alive that day but all three were dead by nightfall.

At night they buried the dead men. The doctor took off another portion of Trooper Bird's leg. One man with a spinal wound took another seven bullets while lying in the hospital tent. Ham and the men around him worked to entrench themselves. They dug for their lives. They used dynamite. They dug into rock. Bayonets substituted for picks and shovels. Water ran out. In the dark some of them ran a gauntlet of bullets to the river. They did this night after night. The ration was a quart of water per man per day. Unshaved, begrimed, powder-smoked, they laughed at how much like Boers or beggars they looked.

By day it was very hot. Their ground ran with gore from the putrefying beasts. Snipers kept up an almost constant fire. One man received a bullet upward through his arm, shoulder and jaw. He spat it out of his mouth with the words 'Oh Christ' and then slumped to the ground. By night men shivered in their 'rabbit holes', with shells coming in just enough to prevent sleep.

When it was over and the Boers had gone, Captain Ham walked to the enemy trenches to take a look. In one place the cartridge cases were knee deep. Kitchener had arrived with overwhelming force. The Boers had lifted the siege and disappeared into the hills. Their senior commander, Jan Smuts, acknowledged the defenders: 'Never in the course of this war did a besieged force endure worse sufferings, but they stood their ground with magnificent courage.'

Private Harry B. (the Breaker) Morant, taken just before he left for South Africa with the 2nd Mounted Rifles of South Australia.

An Intelligence nigger named Magato, Has been singing a sad obligato, And begs to complain He suffered much pain By being struck with a squashy tomato.

Breaker Morant, Bushveldt Carbineers

One of these dreamers was Harry ('Breaker') Morant, a bushman and Bulletin poet who hoped to make his fortune in southern Africa and then retire to England.

Most of the bush volunteers came in officially organised contingents from Australia, but several thousand also joined irregular South African regiments with fanciful names such as the Bushveldt Carbineers or Brabant's Horse. Some worked their own passage to the war, some were sojourners at the Cape, some came from England and some simply transferred after touring with an earlier contingent. They were happy to be soldiers; the pay was good and prospects seemed full. Many dreamed of their own farm in Africa, replete with black servants and the fruits of the land for the taking beneath a Union Jack. One of these dreamers was Harry ('Breaker') Morant, a bushman and *Bulletin* poet who hoped to make his fortune in southern Africa and then retire to England. His bush persona was less powerful than his longing to be an English gentleman.

Morant was a non-commissioned officer in the South Australian Second Contingent and was part of Roberts' drive on Pretoria. He was paid out on 31 July 1900, went to England, became engaged (though he was already married to Daisy Bates), then returned to South Africa and joined the Bushveldt Carbineers (BVC). They were located in the northern Transvaal, a wild, fever-ridden region where the violence between warring white men was matched by warring between Shangaans and Motyabyis. The two wars were enmeshed. The British used men from each tribe whenever they could. There was a rule against the use of 'armed natives', but the BVC made its own rules. Armed with assegai, axes, sticks, iron bars, pistols, revolvers and occasionally an elephant gun, the Africans could be effective. They were indispensable as guides and a vital source of intelligence, which earned some of them income as well as the label 'intelligence niggers'. The indigenous people were not long dispossessed and anxious for revenge against Boer invaders. Taking their revenge beside British invaders, a few could see the irony of their actions. Most were pragmatic, seeking accommodations in a field of limited chances.

That field was violent but it was also abundant. The colonial bushmen wanted for little. There were baboons, monkeys, jackals and other small game in the hills, as well as wood and water and 'plenty of niggers to fetch them'. On occasions black women made grass huts for the Carbineers. The arithmetic stacked up too: 'We lived like fighting cocks for about two shillings a week per man,' Trooper J.S. Silke recorded in his diary. Silke had brought horses to South Africa for trade. He joined the BVC for six months at 7 shillings a day (the Imperial Yeomanry on the veldt received 4 shilling and 6 pence). The pay drew more volunteers to these far fringes of European settlement. They were meant to be an occupation constabulary, to integrate, placate and pacify, to come to

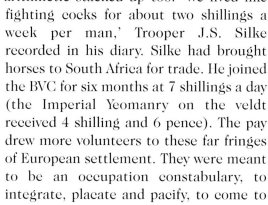

British soldiers guarding alleged 'Kaffir spies', c.1901. Both sides used black Africans to gather information about enemy activity.

Captain Edward Charles Tatchell (second from right) and Private Verne Krodstedt (extreme right),
of E Company, 5th Contingent of Victorian Mounted Rifles, bartering with black South Africans for some eggs, c.1901.

Burning a Boer farmhouse.

Many a murder went unseen, many a report simply met indifference at higher levels, but the evidence against Morant and a loyal offsider came together.

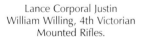

Lance Corporal Justin William Willing, 4th Victorian Mounted Rifles.

know the place and even to settle there in time. But in effect they lived like bandits. Brabant's Horse was called the Brabanetti for good reason. The term for all such units was 'Scallywag Corps'. They lived by supplementing rations with plunder, making good use of stills found on enemy farms and even raiding their own convoys for rum. They harried the Boer, in Morant's words, 'like bloody cattle dogs' and, in line with unofficial policy, they killed prisoners.

It became a war of vendettas. For the BVC, things went badly wrong in August 1901. Boer fighters were desperate for the most basic requirements—boots and clothes. They stripped the BVC dead and when they killed Morant's best friend, Captain Percy Hunt, at Duivels Kloof, they gave his body a kicking and took his clothes. Morant's revenge was to shoot and have shot the next Boer prisoners to fall into his hands, a German missionary, who witnessed the killing of Hunt, and probably the missionary's black servant boy as well for he was never found. Others who were brought in or surrendered at the time were also murdered by BVC men. Private Silke's diary suggests great unhappiness with revenge gone out of control.

Nothing would have been known of this little pocket of war crimes but for the diligence and persistence of one man who compiled the necessary evidence, and the fortuitous timing of the evidence with international controversy over British cruelty in southern Africa. The one man was Captain Frederick Ramon de Bertodano, a graduate in law from Sydney University who may have met Morant, years earlier, at the Sydney Hunt Club or at polo games near Windsor on the outskirts of Sydney. De Bertodano was responsible for intelligence in the area and he would not let news of cowardly murders rest. He was particularly distressed at the murder of the missionary and so was the German government. Many a murder went unseen, many a report simply met indifference at higher levels, but the evidence against Morant and a loyal offsider, Veterinary Lieutenant Peter Handcock, came together. It was clear that a junior subaltern called George Witton was also guilty. Witton's death sentence was commuted to life imprisonment, but he was freed in 1904. Morant and

Handcock were shot at dawn on 28 February 1902, because the case against them was legally adequate, because other 'Scallywags' needed reining in and because Kitchener was suffering controversy throughout Europe over the brutality of his campaign.

In Australia the daily press condemned Morant and Handcock, insisting their barbarity was the exception among colonial soldiers. Later they were reassessed, as romantic heroes and scapegoats of empire. They were murderers on a frontier where murder was routine, and they stand out merely as digits in that dismal fraction who pay the price for war crimes.

Nothing was heard of the case in Australia until after the executions, in part because colonial correspondents for the major dailies had all disappeared in the middle of 1901. One of them was dead, shot by a Boer. One was a physical wreck after the siege of Ladysmith, and the rest, including Paterson, had left for Australia. Paterson was particularly disappointed. He was distressed by the war against women and children. He had seen women frantically rescuing their most treasured possessions from doomed homes as men sat on horseback with their firesticks, waiting for the order to burn.

A new phase of the Boer War was underway. The set-piece battles were over. In the wild country the Scallywags were doing their work. On the veldt, the British army was operating as the French had operated in Algeria for half a century. Great columns, numbering in the tens of thousands, with steam tractors pulling tonnes of supplies behind them, travelled out from secure garrisons with secure lines of supply. The new phase was marked by long periods in the saddle, the infantry trudging, a lack of any real fighting and a 'guerrilla war' in which the civilian population was the main target. There were engagements, even small battles, for the Boers would not give up, a fact that made Kitchener even more bitter and cruel, but soldiers were occupied mainly with commandeering.

Disillusion

Unlike the soldiers, Banjo Paterson was free to depart when he pleased. From South Africa he went to London where he was offended by the hostility he encountered towards the Boers. His own attitude had changed from one of contempt to respect. His contempt was now directed at the jingoism and bigotry of the British press. He published a satirical poem, a parody of Kipling, called 'Concerning the African War'. It appeared in a radical English newspaper called *Reynolds' Weekly*. It was reprinted in the Melbourne paper *Tocsin* and then in the Sydney *Bulletin*.

Concerning the African War

Now listen to me and I'll tell you my views concerning the African war!
And the man who upholds any different views, the same is a rotten pro-Boer!
(Though I'm getting a little bit doubtful myself, as it drags on week after week:
But it's better not to ask questions at all—let us silence all doubts with a shriek!)

And first let us shriek the unstinted abuse that the Tory Press prefer—
De Wet is a madman, and Steyn is a liar, and Kruger a pitiful cur!
(Though I think if Oom Paul—as old as he is—were to walk down the Strand with his gun,
A lot of these heroes would hide in the sewers or take to their heels and run;
For Paul he has fought like a man in his day, but now that he's feeble and weak,
And tired, and lonely, and old and grey, of course it's quite safe to shriek.)

And next let us join in the bloodthirsty shriek, Hooray for Lord Kitchener's 'bag'!
For the fireman's torch and the hangman's cord—they are hung on the English flag
In front of our brave army!

The Australian Officers were in part victims at least of their ignorance of Military Law and of the brutal homicidal carelessness or worse of the Kitchener gang in appointing blacksmiths, drovers and what not as responsible military officers in disturbed districts.
Bulletin, 12 April 1902

Trooper John Waddell, NSW Citizens' Bushmen, killed in action at Eland's River, Transvaal, August 1900.

Boer prisoners in a barbed-wire compound near Ermilo. Their sleeping quarters have ends made from sods of earth with canvas or corrugated iron roofs.

The British are collecting all the Boer women and children from the farms and taking them to the nearest town where they will be properly looked after. They will not only be properly fed, but they will be safe from the attacks of African blackfellows which they have had to put up with since their husbands have not been there to protect them.

Private Harold Targett, NSW Imperial Bushmen

Holding the reins of two horses, Lieutenant N. McGregor of the 3rd NSW Bushmen stands by a simple battlefield grave on a treeless plain. The cross is made from packing case timber, Western Transvaal, c.1901, *opposite*.

As the months passed, the soldiers commandeering for their own provisions started to sweep the land clean, leaving nothing for the Boers. Columns advanced on wide fronts, razing everything. Farms were burnt to the ground as routinely as chickens were throttled and fence posts uprooted for firewood. Women and children were relocated in concentration camps, for their own good it was argued, and they began to die in alarming numbers. Twenty-six thousand civilians, mostly women and children, died from the horrendous conditions in the concentration camps set up by Kitchener. This disaster was to embroil him in controversy in European newspapers where nations went to war in print, drawing on their respective versions of history to find other nations guilty of barbarities that they could never commit.

There is no doubt about Kitchener's barbarity. In the Sudan he had a defeated emir dragged through streets in chains, a halter round his neck, and whipped as he went. The Mahdi's tomb was desecrated and his skull souvenired by Kitchener. In the opinion of the young Winston Churchill, Kitchener 'behaved like a blackguard'. But he was also a modern general and, though he died in 1916, he was a twentieth-century man. His leadership was a choreography of systematic zoning, scorched earth, concentration camps, searchlights and vast intelligence networks, all with attention to diplomacy and the management of news. The railways were cordoned off with barbed wire and protective garrisons. Tracts of southern Africa were zoned and each zone was systematically fenced in with barbed wire and fortified 'block-houses'. Columns then advanced on wide fronts and attempted to drive Boer remnants to the wire.

Australian troops played a part in the final phase of war in which the Boers somehow continued to be elusive. Some performed poorly, but many matched the expectations that surrounded the bushman–soldier. At Mafeking, 100 Australian soldiers arrived as the siege was lifting. They missed most of the fighting but were in time to join an advancing force of Fusiliers. They broke formation, took the lead and charged the Boers with no regard for their own safety, reins adrift, firing and shouting as they galloped. They would have all been killed had the enemy not been in disarray, said one Fusilier.

At Zeerust they charged fleeing Boers, pulling them off their horses as they retreated. At Eland's River, not far from where the garrison had been besieged, they refused an order to surrender and held a kopje against a superior force, with 6 men killed and 22 wounded in the process. But mostly the Bushmen on the veldt spent their time in ways that did not fit their ideas of the heroic military scenario. Nearly half of Kitchener's army, about 100,000 men, were doing duty guarding railway lines and fortified trains fitted with giant searchlights and sometimes carrying Boer captives in a wagon ahead of the engine. Still more soldiers were covering the country in barbed wire. The sick, the wounded and the stragglers numbered in the tens of thousands. The rest were organised in fourteen immense columns, capturing, punishing, scorching and, as the *Times History* put it, 'running down with an infinity of toil the broken handfuls of Boers who fled before them or hid in their very midst'.

An Australian soldier on horseback with African straw houses in the background.

The war had become a tale of unheroic action, diminishing numbers (mostly through sickness), disillusionment and a widely shared longing for home.

The war had become a tale of unheroic action, diminishing numbers (mostly through sickness), disillusionment and a widely shared longing for home. In July and August 1900, the 1st NSW Mounted Rifles were chasing de Wet's *commando*. They began with 650 horses, lost them all and could obtain only 130 more. Roberts' legions then left Pretoria for Komati Poort. The New South Wales men were left behind, waiting for miserable, mule-like remounts from Argentina. Then they were chasing de Wet again. One of their officers wrote home about his fear of mutiny.

The imminence of mutiny, or at least the talk of it, is well documented in letters and diaries and even in public controversy. In July 1900, John Hubert Plunkett Murray was with the 1st NSW Mounted Rifles at Roodevaal. Murray was an Oxford-educated, Sydney-based lawyer, a big man who had won the English amateur heavyweight boxing title in his university days. He was named 'John Hubert Plunkett' after his father's great friend, a champion of liberal Catholic concerns in early New South Wales. Initially Murray was a bitter opponent of the war, yet he enlisted and commanded a troopship to the Cape in January 1900. By July he was on the veldt. 'The war seems likely to be interminable,' he told

Troopers C. W. Cone and U. Whitty, 3rd NSW Mounted Rifles.

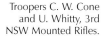

Men of the 2nd NSW Mounted Rifles crossing the Bronkhurst Spruit (River) in 1901.

his wife whom he called his 'Darling Old Tab'. 'No-one seems to do any fighting but the Mounted Infantry and occasionally the artillery; the 12th Lancers absolutely refused to charge when we met de Wet, though ordered three times to do so . . .'

De Lisle, the brigade commander with the Lancers, wrote later of his shame: 'as they had no intention of risking anything, they were not much use to me . . . finally I collected 16 Australians who charged the position with the greatest boldness to set an example to this cautious regimen . . . I always looked back on this fight with the greatest shame, for there I saw for the first time, a gallant Regiment held back and put to shame before our Colonials.'

Murray was not much keener than the 12th Lancers. He was clear about his military needs when he told Tab that all he wanted was one battle, 'and then the white winged dove [of peace] can come along as soon as he likes'.

One year later, in July 1901, Lieutenant Frederick George Purcell, a fourth contingent man, was patrolling beyond Pretoria. His unit was charged with stealing cattle from the Boers. But when the Boers came at them, his men reminded him that they were a Cattle Ranger Corps and would not fight. 'I had to retire and return to Pretoria without any stock,' he wrote to his sweetheart back home in Yea, in country Victoria.

A few weeks before Purcell's men failed him, mutinous talk became public controversy. While camped at Wilmansrust in the eastern Transvaal, a contingent of 350 5th Victorian Mounted Rifles was overrun by a Boer *commando* unit. Sentries failed, men panicked, the camp was reduced to a frantic shambles and in ten minutes it was over. Nineteen Australians were dead, 41 were wounded and those who had not fled into the darkness were prisoners. One of the British generals, oblivious to the fact that these were raw recruits, called the survivors 'white livered curs'. In turn, there was open talk of mutiny which resulted in court martials with three Victorians condemned to death. The sentences were commuted to gaol terms but there was serious embarrassment at home, a great deal of denial, cheers for 'the doughty 5th' and misgivings about British military justice. National pride had collided with imperial loyalty.

The war was going sour for many reasons. Some men imagined a desk job in Pretoria would be more exciting than life in the field. Others found the prospect of again being in combat simply terrifying. Among these were men who could not forget the sight of their own comrades upon the field of battle, bound to the ground in their own blood, agonised with pain or stilled by death. Others simply could no longer bear the invisible presence of the enemy in what had become a sniper's war.

Shots from Mausers came like bolts from the blue, shattering the quietness of the vast veldt and dealing death at random. The strongest nerves could shatter too, but the majority were able to hold or hide their nerves. They did their time and were keen to go home. For those who wanted more adventure, the Boxer

Lieutenant Frederick George Purcell in the uniform of the Victorian Mounted Rifles.

We have a very poor lot of officers, a few good men.

Trooper Jack Waddell, Citizens' Bushmen's Contingent

Lord Kitchener is presented to veterans of the Boer War by Colonel James Rowell who had commanded the 4th Imperial Bushmen's Corps in South Africa, Adelaide, c.1909.

Frontispiece of an album in the form of a photographic collage, put together by a NSW Imperial Bushman. Inscriptions include 'Bridge at Colenso', 'War Balloon', 'Long Tom', 'Majuba', and 'Shells fired into Mafeking'.

News of an unheroic war came through letters from the front, which appeared first in the radical press and occasionally in the major dailies.

Frontispiece of an album in the form of a photographic collage, put together by a NSW Imperial Bushman. Inscriptions include 'Bridge at Colenso', 'War Balloon', 'Long Tom', 'Majuba', and 'Shells fired into Mafeking'.

Rebellion in China was calling. Murray was perhaps typical. He was in command of five soldiers and a Hottentot and was seeing a good bit of the country, but he found the work very unpleasant not least because he was continually surrounded by weeping women. In September 1900 he wrote home again, telling Tab that his principal pastime was 'burning farms and laying waste to the country generally. My particular job is cattle-lifting and collecting Boer farmers who are all being sent to Pretoria as prisoners,' he wrote. 'I hate the whole business but I shall have to see it through.' And he did.

The men of the first contingents were released from duty in October 1900, without pressure to stay on and despite the need for more soldiers in the field. Milner had told Chamberlain of their war-weariness and discontent. He advised they be released with cordial thanks. From then on, men came home in large numbers as their terms expired. The first contingents returned to wildly enthusiastic crowds. A man boasted he had been kissed by 300 ladies. The streets were lined with flag-waving children and windows bearing pictures of 'Bobs' and Baden-Powell. Australians were federating but they were still British in their turn of mind. Over time the crowds at these homecomings dwindled. The novelty wore off, as did the enthusiasm for embarkations.

People at home sensed something of the gloom and doubt about the war that was common among the troops. News of an unheroic war came through letters from the front, which appeared first in the radical press and occasionally in the major dailies. On 24 August 1901, the *Daily Telegraph* ran a letter from a sergeant of the 5th contingent, headed 'Looting and Burning of Farm Houses'. But anti-war feeling, widespread though it was, was still no match for the most powerful voices in the land and the majority fell into silence rather than opposition. In Britain, the eye-witness journalism of Emily Hobhouse and the writings of W.T. Stead and others fuelled a passionate debate over the charge of war by 'methods of barbarism', but that debate had no counterpart in Australia. When Professor Wood and W.A. Holman launched an Anti-War League in Sydney in January 1902, the masses did not rally. Notably, the league's first meeting appointed Victor Daley and A.G. Stephen (from the *Bulletin*) to run a literary committee aimed at 'the dense ignorance' of the general public whose feeling about the war seemed to lie somewhere between apathy and antipathy. When the war ended in May 1902 everyone was relieved. The numbers are uncertain but possibly 1,000 Australians had died in the conflict, including men who fought in South African or British units, and counting those who died of illness or disease and the 43 who were reported missing. Six Australians won the VC, including James Rogers, a Victorian who won the award while attached to the South African Constabulary. Lesser awards were spread about extravagantly by an imperial administration once keen to keep men in the field.

Three Australians stand over the grave of their comrade, Trooper Nathaniel Horsfall of the 5th South Australian Imperial Bushmen. Horsfall was mortally wounded near Lindley in January 1902.

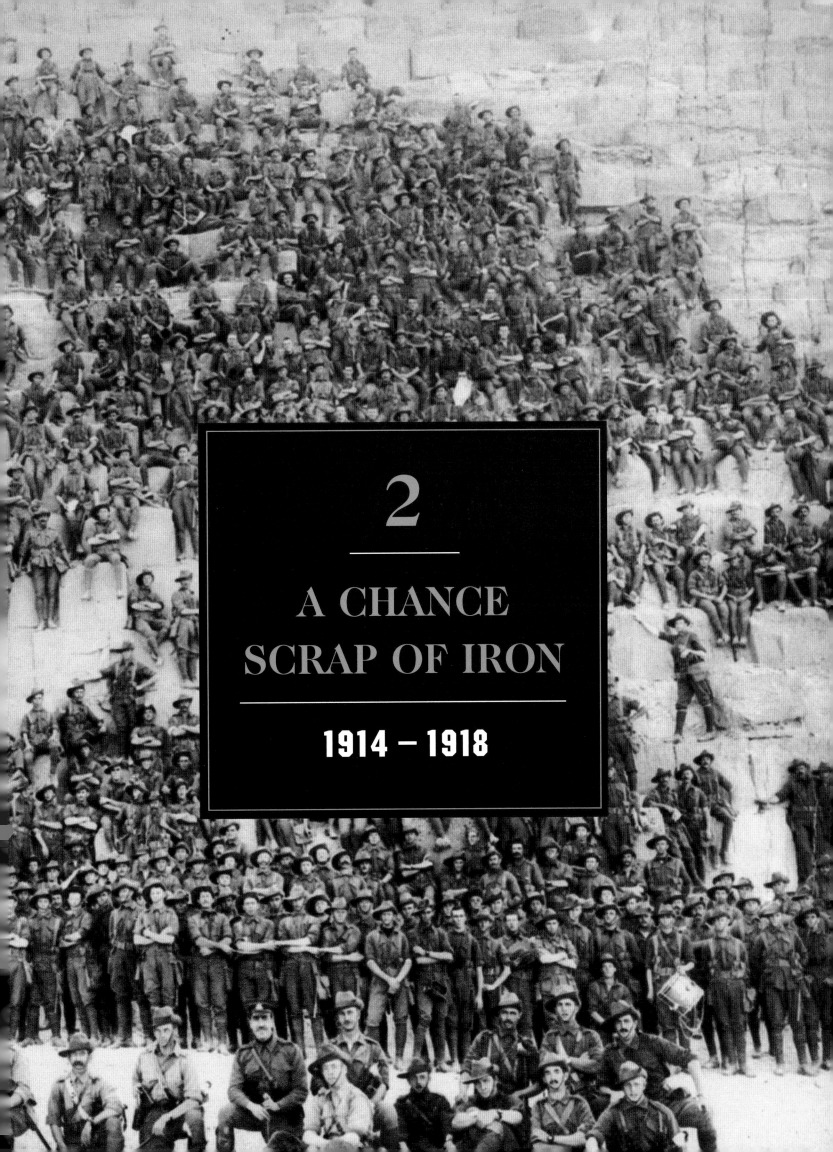

2

A CHANCE
SCRAP OF IRON

1914 – 1918

The European Powers on 3 August 1914

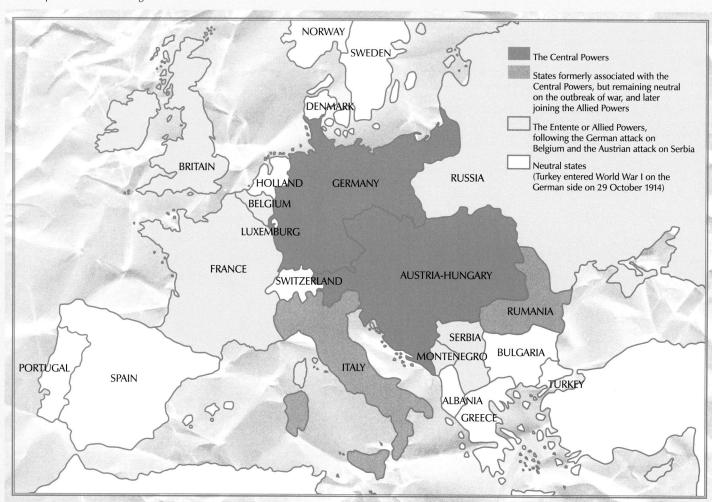

The Central Powers

States formerly associated with the
Central Powers, but remaining neutral
on the outbreak of war, and later
joining the Allied Powers

The Entente or Allied Powers,
following the German attack on
Belgium and the Austrian attack on Serbia

Neutral states
(Turkey entered World War I on the
German side on 29 October 1914)

NORWAY

SWEDEN

DENMARK

BRITAIN

HOLLAND

GERMANY

RUSSIA

BELGIUM

LUXEMBURG

FRANCE

SWITZERLAND

AUSTRIA-HUNGARY

RUMANIA

SERBIA

MONTENEGRO

BULGARIA

PORTUGAL

SPAIN

ITALY

TURKEY

ALBANIA

GREECE

Adapted from Martin Gilbert, *Atlas of the First World War*, Dorset Press, London, 1984

Banjo Paterson was with the first convoy to leave Australian shores for the war that was later called the 'Great War'. He was 50 years old. Many Boer War veterans volunteered to fight again. Paterson had reacted to the news of conflict with relish. His withered arm did not stop him obtaining permission to travel as an 'honorary veterinarian' on a troopship carrying men and horses, and some nurses too. But his real intent was journalism. Again he would write about Australia's triumphs and disasters if only he could get an accreditation.

P ATERSON was one of many Australians who believed that nations were born on the battlefield. War was a serious game, a test of manhood, the measure of a people. The Boer War was at best a prelude to the real thing, and now the real thing had begun. 'It is our baptism of fire,' rejoiced the *Sydney Morning Herald* on 6 August 1914, three days after war was declared.

In England, the Foreign Secretary Edward Grey was prophetic: 'The lamps are going out all over Europe,' he said, 'we shall not see them lit again in our lifetime.' An awful progression was underway, from big-power bullying in the Balkans to an all-or-nothing war for global pre-eminence, the first of its kind, the culmination of the imperialist era—decades of jockeying by European nations for supremacy on one continent after another. It was a war to be waged not for limited and realistic objectives, but for unlimited ends. Here was a terrifying potential and no-one, not even the prophetic Englishman, Grey, was prepared for it. No-one could grasp ahead of events the full impact of unlimited means in modern warfare, of waste and horror beyond measure, of battle so vast and vile it would stain every ideal for which it was waged.

In Australia the forebodings were few and mostly unheeded. Prescience failed altogether. There was some anti-war sentiment when King George V declared war against Germany on 3 August 1914, but the Governor-General, Sir Ronald Munro-Ferguson, thought the response was one of 'indescribable enthusiasm and entire unanimity throughout Australia'. He was close to the mark.

The government initially offered a force of 20,000 men for service anywhere, ready to sail within four to six weeks. In command was Major General William Throsby Bridges. Bridges was an austere, Scottish-born Australian who emigrated with his family when he was eighteen, joined the roads and bridges department of the New South Wales civil service, served in the Boer War and rose in the militia. In 1911 he was appointed the first commandant of Duntroon Military College in Canberra; and he was Australia's first general.

1 November.
Red-letter day in the history of Australia: first big fleet put out to sea.

3 November.
Sacred day: Melbourne Cup. Not much chance of hearing what won. Lifebelt parade. I am to collect the nurses and see that they get into the boats to which they are allotted.

4 November.
Horses are very drowsy. My horse goes to sleep and falls down.

A.B. 'Banjo' Paterson, diary, November 1914

Officers and men of the 11th Battalion, 3rd Brigade, AIF on the steps of the great pyramid of Cheops, Mena, Egypt 1915, *previous page.*

New recruits moving through the Army camp lines, Liverpool, NSW 1914.

Trooper R. Glenister
(Footscray, Victoria),
1st Division, AIF, Mena
Camp, Egypt, April 1914.

*1915. Australia's entry
into the Company
of Nations—no finer
entry in all history . . .
to have leapt into
Nationhood, Brotherhood
and Sacrifice at one
bound . . . what a year.*

Captain F.B. Stanton,
14th Battalion

It was Bridges who decided on the name Australian Imperial Force (AIF) in opposition to some officers who wanted their army to be free of imperial links. The Canadians and New Zealanders chose 'Expeditionary' rather than 'Imperial', but Bridges wanted a name to emphasise the inseparable cause of nation and empire. He convinced the government to offer Britain a complete infantry division, a complete light horse brigade, and three brigades of artillery. He wanted Australians to fight as an entity and not to be dispersed in small units among British regiments, as had happened in the Boer War. As commander he would be responsible to the Australian government and his army would be a distinctive national force, somewhere in the imperial battle formation. The Great War was to be a proving ground, Australia's first big national enterprise.

While recruitment went ahead at a great rate, the first engagements were a tiny sideshow in the Pacific. A small expeditionary force of Australians and New Zealanders was charged with seizing German colonial possessions to the north: German Samoa, Nauru, the Carolines and German New Guinea. The main objective was the destruction of the radio network on these islands, a strategic enemy asset. This was achieved against a minimum of resistance. At Bita Paka, in New Guinea, a small German garrison fought, fled, then surrendered—40 white soldiers and 110 New Guineans in all. The Australians set up an administration that continued after the war and lasted until Papua New Guinea's independence in 1975, save for the Japanese occupation in World War II. The battle cruiser *Sydney* was home in time to escort 1st Division troopships out of Australian waters on 1 November, Paterson's 'red-letter day'. A week later the *Sydney* crippled the German raider *Emden*. It was an easy victory for the *Sydney* was superior in size, speed and firepower, and it was received with jubilation in Australia. It was the Royal Australian Navy's first win at sea.

Some on board those troopships thought they were heading for a glorious picnic. Most believed that, picnic or not, they would be training first in England. But the great training camps on the Salisbury Plain were already full and the Australians found themselves disembarking in Egypt to train there, in preparation to defend the Suez Canal against the Turks and, as it happened, to invade Turkey at a place called Gallipoli.

In Egypt, the Dominion troops were placed under the command of Lieutenant General William Birdwood, a dapper, little British officer, recently arrived from India. He approved the acronym ANZAC for the newly formed Australian and New Zealand Army Corps. Previously it had been a telegraphic code name used by his staff in Cairo. Now it was a force designation. Soon Anzac also had a geographical meaning—a mark on a map, the name of a small, bloody beach-head in Turkey. After that it

Landing at 8 am,
25 April 1915. Part of the 4th
Battalion with mules for the
26th Indian Mountain Battery.

A view of the Supply Base, south end of the beach at Anzac Cove, 26 April 1915.

Anzac Beach. Troops and stores on the beach with boats in the background and some men bathing.

The Gallipoli campaign was a gambler's dream concocted by the War Council in London, aiming for maximum return from minimum investment.

became a national symbol, its commercial use proscribed by Commonwealth legislation.

The Anzacs were based at Mena—a tented camp near the pyramids—where they trained hard, oblivious to a new kind of warfare being waged in Europe that made many of their manoeuvres obsolete. They knew little or nothing of grenades, periscopes, howitzers and the lethal effect of the machine gun. They took liberal leave and used it in the bazaars, bars and brothels of Cairo, just a tram ride away. There was enough violence and racism in their swagger and cheek to make the local people, whom they called 'Gyppos', fearful at the sight of the slouch hat. English literary men who saw them responded in a different manner. The poet John Masefield, in Egypt with the Red Cross, wrote: 'For physical beauty and nobility of bearing they surpassed any men I had ever seen.' Compton McKenzie compared them to an Ajax or Achilles, 'to something as near to absolute beauty as I shall ever hope to see in this world'.

The Gallipoli campaign was a gambler's dream concocted by the War Council in London, aiming for maximum return from minimum investment. The original idea was Winston Churchill's. The First Lord of the Admiralty proposed a naval assault on Turkish defences in the Straits of the Dardenelles, a demonstration of British naval power so decisive that Turkey would quickly surrender. The rewards were many. Turkey's negation would secure the Suez Canal. The capture of the Dardenelles would open a maritime supply route to Russia through the Black Sea. The Balkan states might rally and a new allied army march up the Danube to attack the Central Powers (Germany and Austria-Hungary) from the east. Compared to the futile carnage on the Western Front it seemed to be a promising option. It was a disaster. Turkish minefields and concealed artillery batteries crippled the British fleet.

McKay's Ridge, Gallipoli. Ninth Battery gun in action during the Turkish offensive of 19 May 1915.

The army's role in this operation was to occupy territory subdued by British naval guns. When the navy failed, the plans quickly changed. To salvage the situation a Mediterranean Expeditionary Force was hastily assembled, made up of British, Dominion, French and Indian formations, 70,000 men in all, including the 20,000 Australians training in Egypt. The plan was imaginative and near impossible. Kitchener thought the invasion force of 70,000 was about half what was needed. The artillery situation was skimping to near the same degree. Another man with a withered arm was given command of the combined army—Sir Ian Hamilton, a reactivated old general and a professional soldier who had seen action in the small frontier wars of the nineteenth century, served in India and headed one of Lord Roberts' armies in the Boer War. In 1915 he was on rearguard duties, organising defences in England, when the call came.

In the early hours of 25 April this new allied army made landings at various places on the Gallipoli peninsula, the British main force landing at beaches on the southern tip, the Anzac force further to the north. The Anzacs landed, mistakenly, at Ari Burnu a kilometre away from their intended site. They found themselves on a narrow front facing a steep range of hills that were only lightly defended. Royal Navy charts were not accurate enough to land them to plan. Two companies of Turkish soldiers (about 160 men) were still able to take a heavy toll as men regrouped on the beach and charged into this rugged country. Some small groups made audacious gains but they could not hold their positions. By mid morning Turkish reinforcements had rushed in. The battle raged, front lines swaying back and forth, neither side able to win through. By the end of the day, the stalemate that marked the entire campaign had set in. The Catholic chaplain, John Fahey, buried men whose confessions he had heard that morning.

The sailor in the stern was hit first, then another fell across me; then an oarsman dropped his oar and fell to the bottom of the boat... it was horrible... you just had to sit there and wait for your bullet.

John Fahey, Catholic chaplain, 11th Battalion

A despatch rider galloping from Suvla Bay to Anzac Cove to avoid being sniped, Gallipoli 1915.

Gallipoli Peninsula

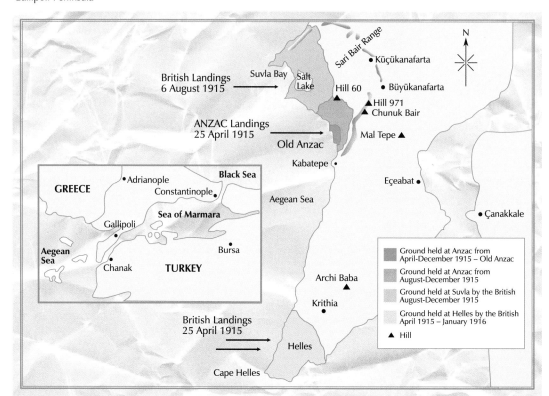

Adapted from *A duty clear before us*, Commonwealth Department of Veterans' Affairs, Canberra, 2000

Major General Sir William
Throsby Bridges, KCB CMG,
Commander of the AIF,
mortally wounded on
15 May 1915 at Gallipoli.

The Anzacs secured a beachhead of about 160 hectares within a perimeter of less than 2 kilometres, at the cost of 620 dead and many more wounded. 'How we longed for nightfall,' wrote one of them, 'How we prayed for this ghastly day to end!' They were there for eight months, clinging to their slender perch above the coast, like sea-birds on a cliff.

That night, on the hospital ships off the coast, Australian nurses dealt with the human wreckage. The patients were pale in the flickering ships' lights and the blood, in that light, so dark it seemed black. Hundreds were lifted on board from barges strewn with bodies. Sister Lydia King had 250 patients to look after with the help of one orderly and an Indian sweeper. 'Shall not describe their wounds,' she wrote in her diary on 26 April, 'they were too awful.'

Paterson's War

Banjo Paterson did not stay in Egypt. He vacated his position, took a transport to England and used his contacts in London so that he was sent to Lady Dudley's hospital in Wimereux in Boulogne. Lady Dudley was an unstoppable Quaker, the estranged wife of a former Governor-General of Australia, who ran what some called a 'petticoat outfit'—staffed mostly by uppercrust ladies—for wounded men and convalescents. Her hospital drew a number of Boer War veteran medicos and a bevy of postgraduate medical students from England, keen to learn and practise military medicine.

The would-be correspondent drove an ambulance to and from the rail terminus, bringing in wounded men over cobbled roads, 'jolting their wounds and shattered bones'. Paterson did not stay long; he was not successful in gaining a correspondent's billet and

so, in June 1915, took a ship back to Australia. He became a captain in the army's Remount Section and was soon back in Egypt. Horses were brought in from all over the world. They had to be tamed and schooled and made ready for the Australian Light Horsemen in Sinai and Palestine. 'A remount officer is like a Field Marshal,' Paterson wrote, 'he has no hope of promotion and no friends whatever in the army.'

His remount labour was arduous and monotonous and far from where he wanted to be, with the Light Horse, watching, writing and reporting the war. He knew the work he did was important, because horses were the key to the advance into Palestine, but he found no inspiration in it. The lines he penned for the Anzac magazine *Kia Ora Cooee* might have come from any canteen scribbler.

Anzac, the landing 1915
George Lambert, c.1920

Soldiers (Gallipoli Series)
Sidney Nolan, 1959

News of the Anzacs' feats did not reach Australia until 29 April, when the newspapers carried congratulations from the First Lord of the Admiralty and King George. On 3 May long casualty lists appeared but no account of how they were caused. The people waited and wondered. On 8 May a dispatch from Ellis Ashmead-Bartlett, an English war correspondent, was printed in full. It gave a glowing account of the Anzacs' heroism and celebrated their fighting qualities. It was perhaps more influential than any account thereafter in establishing the tradition of the Anzac landing. People carried it with them, mailed it to relatives and read it again and again.

The editorials crowed that a nation was born. 'The Glory of It', announced a *Sydney Morning Herald* headline, while the *Argus* claimed that Gallipoli was 'destined to be our most enduring national tradition'. Now it all made sense, as if there were some invisible hand at work shaping events. Classical allusions thickened the description. The Anzacs had made their name on ground rich with heroic significance, mythical and real. They had crossed waters once sailed by Jason and the Argonauts and swum by Leander to visit Hero. Nearby, Ulysses had embarked on his odyssey and Achilles had slain Hector outside the fortress of Troy. The Anzacs had joined the pantheon. 'Thank God, I am an Australian. Boys, you have honoured our land,' wrote a young Ballarat schoolteacher. Her letter to the editor was reprinted in newspapers around Australia.

For a time both sides believed they could win by charging the enemy's trenches and overwhelming the occupants. These charges were mostly small-scale operations,

Diggers in a trench at Walker's Ridge, Gallipoli. The Light Horseman smoking in the background and the Private in the foreground were father and son, thought to be Ernest and Ron Cavalier respectively.

On 3 May long casualty lists appeared but no account of how they were caused. The people waited and wondered.

A crowd of soldiers on the beach watch a Turkish Staff Officer mount his horse after negotiating an armistice to bury the dead, Gallipoli, 21 May 1915.

Simpson and the donkey with wounded soldier. Private John Simpson Kirkpatrick served with the 3rd Australian Field Ambulance. He enlisted under the name John Simpson.

'They walked and looked like kings in old poems.'

but on 19 May the Turks, now mightily reinforced, launched a massive offensive. The man with the donkey, John Simpson Kirkpatrick, died that day, along with many of his comrades, but the Anzac lines held. By noon there were 10,000 Turkish casualties, including 3,000 killed. Australian losses were 628, with 160 killed. The day after there were unofficial truces along the front line to allow both sides to bring in the dead and wounded, and after that a formal truce was arranged to bury the dead, putrefying in the summer heat. In no man's land, Turks and Anzacs exchanged photographs, cigarettes and other tokens, then went back to war.

British officers did not take in the lesson of 19 May. They launched similar offensives in May and June at great cost and small gain. By then the summer heat had arrived. Men went about half-naked and swam in Anzac Cove. They fell ill in great numbers from dysentry, diarrhoea and paratyphoid. Water was scarce, sanitation poor. 'Whenever the gentlest wind moved, clouds of dust rose from the torn and eroded ridges, laden with the stench and infection from thousands of untended corpses which became hosts to millions of flies.' Engorged, the flies spread disease to everything they touched. By the end of July, 200 men a day were being evacuated sick. Those who remained had lost the glow that made English writers wax lyrical about them. 'They walked and looked like kings in old poems,' Masefield wrote. Not any more. 'Thin, haggard, as weak as kittens, and covered with suppurating sores,' wrote a medical officer on the peninsula.

In August, five fresh British divisions landed at Suvla Bay to the north, establishing a third beachhead but failing to go further. At the same time Australian, New Zealand and Indian forces launched the battle for Chunuk Bair, a high point north east of Anzac Cove in the Sari Bair ranges. It began as a night operation, a pincer movement, with plans to win through in the early light. The New Zealanders were to attack from the south, while a combined force of Australians, Sikhs and Ghurkas led by Brigadier General John Monash was to march north along the coast, move inland and attack from the west. By first light the New Zealanders had almost reached Chunuk Bair but were too weak to go any further after heavy fighting. Monash's force, confounded by inadequate maps and the confusions of darkness, was lost and exhausted. They were strewn along nameless, unfamiliar gullies. They could hear Australians to the south launching attacks aimed at drawing Turkish reserves away from Chunuk Bair. There was fierce fighting at Lone Pine and the Nek. At Lone

Wounded and Missing

Vera Deakin, daughter of the former Australian Prime Minister Alfred Deakin, returned home from Europe just before World War I broke out. She was a graduate of the Melbourne Conservatorium of Music and had been studying singing and cello in Berlin and Budapest. Her uncle by marriage was Norman Brookes, a Wimbledon champion and after the outbreak of war an Australian Red Cross commissioner in Cairo. Vera Deakin wrote to Norman, offering her services and soon she was on her way to Egypt.

Once there she wasted no time setting up the Australian Red Cross Society Wounded and Missing Enquiry Bureau, an organisation that provided information about soldiers to worried families. Deakin described the bureau as 'a buffer between the over-anxious relatives and friends and the tired but cheery man who would sooner fight all day than write a letter'. By the end of the war the helpers in the bureau, now located in London, had written many letters and made over 10,000 enquiries on behalf of anxious relatives in Australia. She was awarded the OBE for her work.

One of her self-styled duties was writing to prisoners of war (POWs) and one of her POWs was a prisoner of the Turks in Mesopotamia, an airman who later wrote of his experience in a book called *Guest of the Unspeakable*. He was Captain Thomas White of the Australian Flying Corps. The correspondence between Thomas White and Vera Deakin became very important to both of them. They met for the first time in 1919, were engaged within six weeks and married when they returned to Australia.

Turkish and Australian dead on the parapet of a Lone Pine trench.
In the foreground is Captain Leslie Morshead, 2nd Battalion.

Men prayed, scratched messages to loved ones and pinned them to sandbags, shook hands and took their positions.

Pine the Australians prevailed but only after three days of savage, close-quarter battle, with 80 officers and 2,197 men from six battalions killed. Seven VCs were awarded at Lone Pine. At the Nek there was not even the slightest chance of triumph.

The Nek was a narrow plateau that fell sharply away on either side north-east of Anzac Cove. There was room on this plateau for just 150 men abreast. On 7 August the

Soldiers making bombs from jam tins at a spot called the 'bomb factory' near Anzac Cove. The old tins were filled with fragments from Turkish shells and small lengths of barbed wire.

Nek was set for battle but everything went wrong. The support and cover fire promised did not eventuate, communications between the front-line and brigade staff broke down. Watches had not been synchronised. Artillery support ceased at 4.23 am. The men of the 8th and 10th Light Horse, foot soldiers in this campaign, were to charge at 4.30 am. This was the most gallant and hopeless charge of the entire campaign, for in those seven minutes the Turks regained their positions and their composure, fired a few short bursts to clear their machine guns (they had five), their riflemen took aim and they waited.

At 4.30 am the first line went over the top, charged across open ground and was butchered. Another line of men filed into the trench and waited for death. Few in the assault lines could doubt the outcome. 'Boys, you have ten minutes to live and I am going to lead you,' cried one of the officers. Men prayed, scratched messages to loved ones and pinned them to sandbags, shook hands and took their positions.

In a gully below, the official Australian correspondent Charles Bean was limping along in the half light with a bullet in his thigh and without his spectacles, which were lost in a fall. He heard the roar of Turkish fire and instantly knew the meaning of that seven minutes. Three lines went over at short intervals, three terrible bursts of fire. Then a longer silence. There were moves to halt the fourth line, but it was

A barge with wounded from Anzac Cove alongside the hospital ship *Gascon*.

We did not even have a bath tent as water was so short, and as well the centipedes were very bad! Our hair used to be full of burrs, and in the end many girls cut their hair short. It saved a lot of trouble.

Nurse Louise Young, Lemnos Island, 1915

A game of cricket played on 17 December 1915 to distract the Turks from the evacuation preparations of allied troops. Shells were passing overhead while the game was in progress.

too late. The fourth line was ordered to attack, and again Bean heard the roar of machine guns and rifles, no single shot discernible, just one roar, like standing at the base of Niagara Falls. Then silence. Bean limped on to a casualty clearing station knowing that his wound was nothing.

A little after 5 am at the Nek, 234 Light Horsemen lay in a huddled mass in a space not much larger than a tennis court. For an hour or two there was faint movement. A hand clawed at a water bottle, an arm reached up to the sky, then returned to the ground. The sun rose high; all movement ceased. The dead lay motionless in the quivering heat. 'Most were still there in 1919,' wrote Bill Gammage in *The Broken Years*, 'their bones whitening the ridges to observers half a mile away.'

Hospital ships ferried wounded men to the Greek islands of Lemnos and Imbros, and also to Malta; some were shipped as far as Alexandria, more than 1,000 kilometres away. On Lemnos, Matron Grace Wilson and her staff of 96 Australian army nurses worked in a tent city that was No. 3 Australian General Hospital. In her diary she described the inefficiency, and the lack of adequate equipment and supplies that hampered the care of the wounded:

9 August—Found 150 patients lying on the ground—no equipment whatever—had no water to drink or wash.

10 August—Still no water . . . convoy arrived at night and used up all our private things, soap etc, tore up clothes [for bandages].

11 August—Convoy arrived—about 400—no equipment whatever . . . Just laid the men on the ground and gave them a drink. Very many badly shattered, nearly all stretcher cases . . . Tents were erected over them as quickly as possible . . . All we can do is feed them and dress their wounds . . . A good many died . . . It is just too awful . . .

The failure of the August offensive forced the allies to rethink. Hamilton was sacked. He had rarely left his ship to venture onto the peninsula. His dispatches to the British government were full of literary flourishes and laced with good humour. He was plainly out of touch. The operation was bogged down and going nowhere, and Hamilton was indulging his literary pretensions. The troops deserved better. They had little faith in British generals, though Birdwood was something of an exception. He was a frequent visitor to the front lines, good for a yarn and not unpopular. He knew that the seasoned incumbents had no desire to fight. Sick and exhausted, they held as best they could, but more than ever they were yielding to illness and they no longer endured in silence. Their grumbling grew as morale declined, made worse by the arrival of snow.

Waiting for news from Gallipoli. A crowd outside the *Argus* newspaper in Melbourne late in 1915.

We put in most of the day in the Wassa and explored most of the joy houses but didn't do any business with them. The Aussies have got these people bluffed alright. I don't think there is any place on earth where a man can go into a house of this character, do almost as he likes and walk out without cashing up or getting 'flattened out' but these people fear the Aussies more than they fear God.

Private T.J. Cleary,
17th Battalion,
Cairo, 1916

In December 1915, the Anzacs were swiftly evacuated. Australian casualities during the campaign were 26,111. Of these, 362 officers and 7,779 other ranks were killed in action, died of wounds or succumbed to disease. In 1916 almost as many died at Pozières in seven weeks as died in those eight months on the peninsula. And though it was a ghastly campaign, Gallipoli did not present the sustained terror of the Western Front. The invasion was never likely to achieve its objective and possibly its finest moment was the last retreat, the near-perfect, casualty-free evacuation of troops masterminded by Brigadier General Brudenell White. One of the chaplains, an Anglican, wanted to stay behind to ensure the graves were respected, but permission was refused.

Gallipoli was a secondary affair in military terms yet a defining moment for Australian national consciousness. The gallantry of the Anzacs' failed adventure registered at home. Official endorsement backed popular sanction. A year after the landing at Anzac Cove, there were ceremonies in all Australian states celebrating 'Anzac Day'. In London it was celebrated in Westminster Abbey by King George and Queen Mary. An enduring national tradition was born.

The AIF returned to Egypt to rest and retrain, to harass and intimidate the poor 'Gyppos', to re-equip and to absorb reinforcements from Australia. The infantry divisions were doubled, from two to four, and sent to France in March 1916. The Light Horse, mounted at last, stayed in Egypt to fight the Turks in what became known as the Palestine Campaign.

The Light Horse in Palestine was under the command of General Harry Chauvel, a man of the land, a militiaman and professional soldier who had led contingents of the Queensland Mounted Infantry in the Boer War and

Lieutenant Hugo Throssell, VC in Wandsworth Hospital, London. Recovering from wounds received at Gallipoli.

Australian Light Horsemen watering their horses at a well in the desert. At left, wearing a feathered hat, is Major-General Harry Chauvel, Katia, Sinai, Egypt, August 1916.

commanded a fiercely contested sector at Gallipoli. In Egypt he chose to stay with the Light Horse rather than go to France with the infantry. In Sinai and Palestine the Light Horsemen patrolled constantly, skirmished occasionally, and fought major battles against the Turks at Romani, Magdhaba and Rafa, always hampered by sand, heat and the logistics of water supply for men and horses. In March 1917, British forces came up against the Turkish line stretching from Gaza on the Mediterranean to Beersheba, 43 kilometres inland. This was the strongest Turkish position in the Middle East, the gateway to Palestine.

There were two failed attempts to take Gaza and Light Horse units were involved in the first of these. Light Horsemen had stalked on foot into labyrinthine territory, thick with prickly pear hedges and mud huts, on the outskirts of Gaza. In that hide-and-seek entanglement they took ground in fierce hand-to-hand fighting. But south-east of Gaza, the British infantry, fettered by poor planning, a late start and want of water, was forced to retire after fighting for much of the day. The limits of water supply meant victory would be swift or lost, and here it was not swift enough.

For a time the Light Horse took their failure badly, but there was growing faith in the new British commander, General Allenby, who spent months building up his resources, planning for superiority in numbers, equipment and proficiency. Guns, aeroplanes and ammunition arrived in unprecedented quantities. Allenby constantly visited his troops in the field. He turfed his own staff out of headquarters at the Savoy Hotel in Cairo and moved them to Rafa, close to Gaza, at the far end of a railway line the British had recently completed, a line that stretched from the Suez Canal across Sinai and into Palestine. Allenby won the Light Horsemen over.

Like most Australian troops, the Light Horse had experience of good and bad British officers. They knew the cost of incompetence and laziness and the meaning of obsession with parade-ground etiquette. In March 1916, Turkish forces had overrun the English 5th Yeomanry Brigade at posts near Romani, causing more than 350 casualties. English officers had fled ahead of the resistance. The Anzac Mounted Division

Palestine 1917

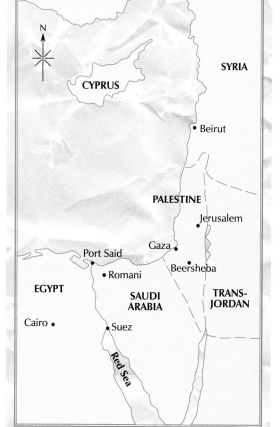

General Allenby, 1917.

Aboriginal serviceman Private Harold Arthur Cowan. Cowan was a well-known footballer and boxer in the north coast region of New South Wales.

The charge was underway at full gallop across open ground.

rode to Romani to relieve the Yeomen still fighting. They found the officers' abandoned supplies of 'beer, soda water, whisky, gin, champagne cooling in buckets of water, unopened letters, golf balls, sticks, and links, dressing tables, chamber pots, camp stretchers, carpets, cake, and tinned food'. But they knew these 'Lords of the Retreat' were no measure of the British officer class whose casualty rate in the war was fearsome.

On 31 October, Allenby's forces struck. Three British infantry divisions attacked the western approaches to Beersheba. Then horsemen swept forward, seizing roadways east of the town and smashing Turkish outposts. A careful orchestration of artillery, aerial bombing and men on foot and hoof, went on through the day, but by mid afternoon Beersheba was still in Turkish hands. Want of water was again threatening to decide the outcome. Many horses had been without water for days. The wells of Beersheba had to be seized.

With some troops as yet unused, Chauvel took the initiative. Two hours before nightfall, he decided to send in Brigadier General William Grant's 4th Light Horse Brigade. 'Put Grant straight at it,' was the order. 'It' was the town's southern defences where there was no barbed wire. The brigade had been scattered to confound German bombing planes. Now it came together. The two leading regiments were the 4th from Victoria and the 12th from New South Wales. Behind a ridge about 8 kilometres south-east of Beersheba, they drew up in three

Australian soldiers stand among the ruins of a pumping station blown up by the Turks before the Light Horsemen captured Beersheba, Palestine, November 1917.

One iron and eight wooden crosses erected by
Light Horsemen over the graves of fallen comrades.

*A captured
German officer
paid the Light
Horsemen a great
compliment: 'They
are not soldiers at
all,' he said, 'they
are madmen.'*

Men of the 53rd Battalion
waiting to don their equipment
for the attack at Fromelles,
19 July 1916. Only three of the
men shown here came out of
the action alive and those three
were wounded, *opposite.*

Lieutenant Eric MacKellar
(left) and Captain Francis
Comins, a dentist attached
to the 3rd Australian Light
Horse Ambulance, Palestine,
1 September 1917.

lines, with about 500 metres between each line and some 5 metres between each horseman. Instead of lance or sabre they carried their long bayonets in their hands.

Just on sunset, the attack force of about 500 moved off at the trot. They cleared the top of a ridge, Turkish gunners sighted them and opened fire, and the charge was underway at full gallop across open ground, towards the enemy still some 6,000 metres away. Men and horses were shattered as shrapnel and machine gun fire caught them in the first flush of the charge, but the speed of the assault carried most of them through. Watchful British batteries shelled enemy outposts on the horsemen's flanks and the foremost riders were soon leaping the forward trenches, dismounting and battling, with bayonet and rifle, as more horsemen hurtled past them and on, into the town.

The combat was brutal and shortlived. The entire exercise was over in an hour. Beersheba had fallen and its wells were intact. Men and horses drank deeply. Nine big guns and more than 1,000 prisoners were in Australian hands. Casualties were low—31 Australians killed, 36 wounded. The pace had been too fast for the Turkish gunners to adjust their range and fire of all kinds had been mostly too wild and high. A captured German officer paid the Light Horsemen a great compliment: 'They are not soldiers at all,' he said, 'they are madmen.'

The fall of Beersheba cracked open the Turkish defensive line. It was now outflanked and would soon be rolled back from east to west. On 6 November 1917 the Turks abandoned Gaza and began a retreat northwards into Palestine, pursued by Chauvel's Desert Column. Jerusalem fell in December.

After the war, the desert campaign took on a powerful mythical quality. For sheer horror and human cost, the fighting there did not match France. But it was fighting that favoured the mounted horsemen, giving some scope to individual skills and spirit. The fighting at Gallipoli was still more uncomplicated by the mechanisation of modern war. Both theatres gave rise to legends focussed on the ingenuity and dash of the nation's manhood. In the popular memory shaped by literature, film, journalism and school history lessons, Lone Pine and Beersheba loomed larger than Pozières or Bullecourt in France, though the casualties hardly compare. Of Australia's 60,000 dead in World War I, 45,000 occurred on the Western Front.

The Palestine campaign had a valuable propaganda effect. It was a sequence of victories with occasional setbacks, but the setbacks were nothing compared to the success of Chauvel's Light Horse. Wartime photographs of Anzacs crusading in the Holy Land added to the romance. The campaign was readily included in the newborn legend of Australian fighters. But its propaganda value was more immediate, for dashing victories in Palestine helped offset horrendous news coming from the Western Front in France.

The Western Front 1916

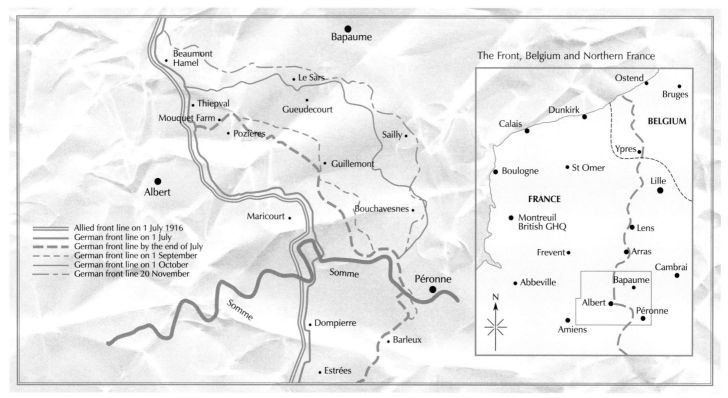

Adapted from Martin Gilbert, *Atlas of the First World War*, Dorset Press, London, 1984

They lived like rats behind sandbagged parapets and intricate webs of barbed wire.

Australian gunners with a 9.2 shell preparatory to loading a 9.2 inch BL Howitzer. Possibly at Pozières, c. 1916.

The Western Front was a parallel line of defensive trenches and fortifications that stretched from the Belgian coast to the Franco-Swiss frontier, leaving a fraction of France and Belgium in German hands. There was to be no great change in these two lines for three and a half years. Millions of men faced each other across the killing fields. They were entrenched, they were immured in tunnel networks, they lived like rats behind sandbagged parapets and intricate webs of barbed wire, bordering a no man's land of shell craters, shreds of trees and human flesh, pulverised ground, earth red with rust and wet with blood, the litter of mad infantry charges, the dead and the dying, black flies and maggots and whitening bones.

They endured days and sometimes weeks of artillery bombardment—an opening barrage might be 1 million or 2 million shells. They followed their own artillery across the scarred earth and, win or lose, took fearful casualties. Modern, mechanised warfare was astoundingly inept. Its generals were chess players with more power to sacrifice their own, and lay waste upon others, than ever was assigned to an evil spirit or a vengeful God. At Verdun in 1916 the Germans tried to break through the allied front. Two million soldiers fought it out over four months, for a million casualties. To counter, the British launched an offensive near the Somme River that cost them 420,000 dead. If this was the Great War, then Great could only mean more terrible and traumatic than any before. Into this war, early in 1916, came the Australians.

Their first months, in a nursery sector, were tranquil enough. The Australians manned their parapets, watched dogfights in the air above them, patrolled a little and took to their burrows when the shelling started. They were then used as raiders, perilous night work, in small teams in which each man, like a football team, had a job to do—demolition, collecting booty, taking

Men of the 53rd Battalion at Fromelles minutes before launching their attack, 19 July 1916.

prisoners, killing, building defensive barriers and looking for mine galleries. As at the Nek, when the artillery failed, whether by minutes or metres or both, the raiders met the most awful barrage of machine gun fire. The Australians quickly gained a reputation as effective soldiers, but outcomes here were shaped by forces above and beyond them.

At Fromelles on 19 July, the 5th Division was entrusted with a feint to draw German reserves away from the Somme, 80 kilometres to the south. The action was totally misconceived, drawing no enemy from that direction; the artillery performed poorly and thousands of Australian and British troops were slain by machine gun fire as they threw themselves against a waiting enemy. The fighting went on through the night. When dawn came the 5th Division was wrecked. Nearly half its number, 5,553 men, were casualties; some battalions had almost disappeared. Allied trenches were packed with wounded men. An Australian general, 'Pompey' Elliott, met the survivors with tears streaming down his cheeks. From no man's land the cries for help were incessant, but neither side would permit a truce. One man risked a note in his diary: 'Wounded in arm and leg. Going to try to crawl back to trenches tonight.' Another man who had been blinded stumbled around for several days before someone shot him.

Near the Somme, the butchery was on a grander scale and went on for months. Late in July 1916, the Australians were part of a 32-kilometre wide offensive in which they were to seize a heavily defended high point in the German line, a pulverised waste that once was a village called Pozières. The 1st Division went into battle on 23 July, following an enormous bombardment. They jog-trotted past limp British corpses strung on barbed wire and drove the Germans before them, taking all but one of the objectives set. They won about 1,000 metres of ground, an extraordinary

From no man's land the cries for help were incessant, but neither side would permit a truce. One man risked a note in his diary: 'Wounded in arm and leg. Going to try to crawl back to trenches tonight.'

I look round me at my damp rat-hole the sides and roof of which are lined with sand bags . . . halfway up in the corner a cluster of poison mushrooms or toadstools peer down at me. The centre one a little taller than the rest seems to nod at me as it sways and trembles to the concussions.

Private, D.B. Hartford, 51st Battalion, Pozières

Will Dyson

Will Dyson made his name as a radical *Bulletin* cartoonist in the 1890s and went on to greater fame drawing for the London *Daily Herald*. His socialism was not challenged when the war broke out This was a war to line the pockets of the capitalists and militarists and there was nothing in it for the workers but death. Dyson's arms dealers were odious fat ogres and his captions stung with savage irony. His *Kultur Cartoons* collection was published in 1915 with an introduction by H.G. Wells and circulated to some acclaim in England and Australia.

But Gallipoli stirred Dyson's nationalism and he changed. In 1916 he received permission to cross to France to 'interpret in a

series of drawings, for national preservation, the sentiments and special characteristics of our Army'. He was commissioned a lieutenant in the AIF, a war artist, and with C.E.W. Bean he was a founder of Australia's war art program.

Bean thought that Dyson captured 'the weary detached way in which men come out of the trenches'. Dyson described them as 'ghosts of men . . . moving like chain gangs dragging invisible chains'. He focussed on the daily grind rather than on the fighting—on the exhaustion, boredom and fatalism. His men are undramatic but enduring. His pictures tell of torment and tenacity.

Australian soldier wearing his souvenir German helmet while shaving after the battle of Pozières in 1916.

God was really good to us. There were only four killed. Our hospital is now a total wreck. Our tents were dug down three feet into the ground and sandbagged and even then they are riddled.

Sister Elsie Grant,
No.3 Australian Casualty
Clearing Station,
somewhere on the
Western Front

Private Edward James Powell,
13th Battalion, AIF, died aged
17 of wounds, Pozières,
14 August 1916.

achievement. Then they fought their way towards Mouquet Farm, 'inch by inch', with far away generals insisting on every one of those inches. They won another 2,000 metres.

The penalty for success at Pozières was a concentration of shelling upon them that lasted for 3 days, a merciless, almost continuous pounding. 'They dug trenches; the guns obliterated them. They crouched in holes; the guns found them and blew them to oblivion.' Some went mad and galloped into the hail, screaming; some broke down and cried like children; one of them was talking to a dead man on a stretcher. But most held their quivering nerves. 'We were nearly all in a state of silliness and half dazed but still the Australians refused to give ground,' wrote Archie Barwick, a farmer from Woolbrook, New South Wales, who was with the 1st Battalion.

Charles Bean found his way to this front line by following trenches peopled with dead men. When he reached the 19th Battalion he found soldiers 'battered almost to the edge of insensibility'. He went on into the 12th Battalion lines where, miraculously, he met his cousin Leo Butler from Hobart, a gentle giant who asked Bean to write to Uncle Ted and Aunty Amy and tell them their son was fine. That night Leo Butler's left leg was blown off and the other mangled beyond repair. He died two nights later. Bean saw to it that Leo was buried, a rare privilege at that time. Later he was comforted by letters from Ted and Amy, which he fastened to his diary. 'I have left these letters in the diary,' he wrote, 'because they show the way in which a chance scrap of iron flung at random on the hillside in front of Mouquet drives its course right through to the furthest end of the world.'

After four weeks the 2nd Division took over at Pozières, knowing its torments would be similar. Later the 4th Division relieved the 2nd. The remnants of the 1st Division—again about half of them were gone—came out of the lines in a terrible state. It seemed impossible that a mouse could have lived through that bombardment, but a human fraction had survived: 'They looked like men who had been in Hell,' wrote a sergeant, '. . . drawn and haggard and so dazed that they appeared to be walking in a dream and their eyes looked glassy and starey.' This was success.

The British generals now had another problem—a deluge of psychological casualties shuffling to the rear. Freud coined the term 'war neurosis' to describe the troubled soldiers he observed, but 'shell shock' soon became the common label. The generals tried to ban its use. They thought it was a refuge for cowards. 'Nervous disorders' had been a problem at Gallipoli, too, but in France the flood of mental

Deniliquin, New South Wales 1906. Mrs Mabel Powell and her seven children. Edward James is on the far right, sitting on the chair.

casualties seriously threatened numbers at the front. Minds were dissolving. Men wept and raved and went about with their mouths wide open. They shook like leaves, babbled, cried like children and called for their mothers. Manic cases raced into no man's land. They charged their own lines, they charged the enemy. Morbid cases just wandered, seemingly in slow motion, not fearless but oblivious. Others were so broken they were immovable, like stone. Some lost all power in their legs, some crawled about on all fours, some were found hiding in dugouts, shaking and shivering. Those who could still talk might try to bribe their way out with money or rations. One shook uncontrollably and hummed 'The Lord is My Shepherd' over and over. They ducked, winced, shivered, twitched, cringed, mumbled, read their Bibles and soiled their trousers. 'I met three officers out in No Man's Land the other night,' wrote Lieutenant J.A. Raws at Pozières, 'all rambling and mad. Poor Devils.'

Raws struggled with his own nerves as did most men at the front. Soldiers wrote about the struggle in diaries and letters, their sense of control slipping away, their pride in winning the inner battle, their fascination or horror or even their relief when someone else's nerves gave way—for it was not them. They pressed on, suffering more or less in silence, the sweats and panic attacks, the nightmares, the loss of concentration, the barely perceptible neurotic mannerisms. They could not know what was later understood—that many who kept the lid on their nerves would lose the inner battle after the war.

Raws did not live to go home, but his letters at Pozières reveal the common view that mental disorder was a failure of character and manhood. In a letter to his brother, he advised: 'Only the men you would have trusted and believed in before proved equal to it. One or two of my friends stood splendidly, like granite rocks around which the seas stormed in vain . . . But many other men broke to pieces.' Official policy endorsed this way of measuring a man and the treatment of shell shock victims was mostly suspicious, unsympathetic and designed to avoid 'wastage'—to get them back to the trenches.

In seven weeks of fighting at Pozières, the AIF lost 6,842 dead and 17,513 wounded or gassed. Bean wrote of the site where the village windmill once stood. It was 'more densely sown with Australian sacrifice than any other place on earth'. Back in Australia, the tally resounded in the referendum over conscription marked for

At a steady walk, it was awful, the uncanny feeling of death eating at ones entrails and the gasping of the men trudging behind you, the thunder of the shells, and the fires from the dumps showing ghostly through the gas smoke, a bluish vapour hanging like a pall.

Captain A.G. Thomas, 6th Battalion

They ducked, winced, shivered, twitched, cringed, mumbled, read their Bibles and soiled their trousers.

During the Somme offensive in February 1917 stretcher bearers place a wounded man on a light rail trolley for the trip to the rear.

Civilisation was at stake. Women were in peril— mothers, wives, sweethearts, sisters, babies.

The Prime Minister, the Rt Hon. W. M. Hughes, pleading for conscription in Martin Place, Sydney during the 1916 campaign.

October 1916, and it changed the attitudes of Australians in the field. The folly of British strategy was now measured in rivers of blood. Offensives made up of numerous small-scale attacks on narrow fronts allowed the Germans to concentrate their firepower and reek a terrible cost whatever the outcome. This was made worse by incompetent British generals, none more so than the man in charge of the Australian divisions, General Sir Hubert Gough. Gough used troops as one would use a battering ram. Bean wrote of the Anzacs' hatred of these tactics and their aversion to serving under Gough, which dated from the Somme.

There was a new bitterness towards the British high command, and the concept of duty among Australian soldiers was laced with a sharper sense of irony and pared down to a few essentials—self-pride, mateship and hatred of 'the Hun'. To some extent, higher ideals and wider allegiances fell away. 'It was a monstrous sacrifice,' wrote Bill Gammage, 'which tumbled the romances and grand illusions of the past into the dust, when they rarely rose again. After the Somme, the world would never be the same.'

The slaughter in France was also testing ideals in Australia. The Labor Prime Minister, William Morris Hughes, returned from a tour of England as the 2nd Division began ploughing its way towards Mouquet Farm. The diminutive Hughes was described as a 'terrier', an 'alley-cat', a 'little Caesar', a 'fiery particle' and a 'hurricane force'. He was a cantankerous, bullying, righteous and fearless autocrat. In England, he stole the show. He told the English people it would all be worthwhile, the war had 'plunged civilisation into an inferno, which saturated the earth with blood'; it had also brought the British race together, and the sacrifice would purge and purify the world. The *Times* said he was 'sweeping the Empire with his eloquence'. The Women's Social and Political Union wanted him on the War Council. The German press called him 'the darling of the imperialists and jingo agitators'. Hughes revelled in the praise. He sailed home convinced of the need for conscription.

Australians were soon bitterly divided on conscription. A long-held belief in volunteers fighting abroad, enshrined in the Defence Act of 1903, was now fortified by the grand achievements and sacrifices of the Anzacs in foreign fields. Compulsion smacked of militarism. The country began to split into two camps. Hughes focussed on the figures—voluntary enlistment was falling short of the British requirements. In August 1916 the War Office called for urgent reinforcements to rebuild Australia's five divisions in France. It wanted 32,500 men for September, and 16,500 per month thereafter. In August voluntary enlistment had dropped to a new and alarming low of 4,144.

A battle of ideals was underway. Conscription raised issues of civil liberty and the morality of compelling men to kill. It fired tensions between labour and capital that were already smouldering. It roused deep divisions of religion

Private Martin O'Meara of 16th Battalion. During heavy fighting at Pozières in 1916, he repeatedly ventured into No Man's Land to retrieve wounded soldiers and was himself wounded on three occasions. For his actions he was awarded the VC.

and race for the Irish Catholic community who saw the British army as an oppressor in their homeland. These were to be the most bitter and divided years in Australian history.

The Yes campaigners appealed to King and Country, to mateship and manhood, to destiny, democracy and decency. Protestants said God was for conscription as surely as He was in heaven. They conjured images of a Teutonic dark age should the war be lost. 'We will be like sheep before the butcher,' warned the fiery particle. Civilisation was at stake. Women were in peril—mothers, wives, sweethearts, sisters, babies. Both Yes and No campaigners used the emotive meanings they saw in womanhood. The Yes supporters made the unviolated purity of Australian women their trump card. In Norman Lindsay's posters, brutish Huns despoiled them. The No supporters saw women not so much as likely victims but as people with a decision to make. The pacifists of the Women's Peace Army, formed in July 1915, used a campaign song that was so successful the government banned it. The song was called 'I Didn't Raise My Son to Be a Soldier'. A poem called 'The Blood Vote' was just as powerful:

Why is your face so white, Mother?
Why do you choke for breath?
O I have dreamt in the night, my son
That I doomed a man to death.

The No vote campaigners included a majority of the political and industrial labour movement and a sizeable fraction of the Roman Catholic community led by Archbishop Daniel Mannix in Melbourne, though Mannix was alone among the Catholic archbishops. The others favoured conscription. Mannix was perhaps the only man in

The failure of conscription is a bitter blow to the honour of Australia. It disgusts one to think of the craven hearted citizens who voted against the measure.

Trooper Pelham
Steane Jackson,
11th Light Horse, AIF

A touring recruiting train at the railway station with some of the town's people, Wallumbulla, Queensland 1916.

A welcome cup of tea at the Australian Comforts Fund tent in Longueval, France in December 1916.
The attendant shown in the picture, Private A. Gunn, was killed when the Town Hall in Bapaume was blown up.

Menin Gate at Midnight
Will Longstaff, 1927

Ypres
John Power, c.1916

Battle for Menin Road, 1917
H. Septimus Power, 1917

The Drover
George Benson, 1919-20

the country who could match Hughes for resolve, inflammatory language and self-promotion. He was remorseless in his criticism of Britain and the empire after the crushing of the Irish rebellion in Dublin in 1916, and the execution of its leaders by British firing squad. He was stirred by matters of race and faith but much that he said resounded with working-class feeling against the rich and powerful. He called the war a 'trade war'; he condemned the profiteers; he told his vast audiences that the burden of war fell heaviest on the battlers. Trade unionists who felt this weight agreed.

Trade unionists argued that conscription was part of the class struggle. They saw no equality of sacrifice, just profiteers making a bundle while poverty spread among working people, and spread it did. The real value of wages plummeted between 1914 and 1919. Unionists imagined a future Australia, its working men spent on the battlefield, turning to coloured labour. The war could be the end of White Australia. They agreed with the Yes campaigners on just one thing: everything that mattered was at stake. Conscription, the No campaigners argued, was a monstrous deception. Even the referendum question was a trick. The 'C' word did not appear. Voters were simply asked to approve a government power to require men to serve overseas.

The referendum was lost by the narrowest of margins. The Governor-General, Sir Ronald Munro Ferguson, wrote to the Colonial Secretary, Bonar Law: 'For the moment the anarchist and most ignorant section of society has shown itself more powerful than all the rest, and that in a community which is in the main the most irresponsible, self-confident and inexperienced in the Empire.' Hughes was full of anguish. 'We have lost by a head,' he told journalist Keith Murdoch, 'Ah! That head. How very little yet how much.' He was especially angry at the soldiers who voted No. Forty-five per cent of the AIF was against conscription and the heaviest No vote was from men at the front. 'I can hardly forbear to rail at the Anzac vote which could and it would have pulled us through.' His letter rambled on and he concluded: 'I am very fit. Mirabile dictu! I've done enough to kill three men these last twelve months yet I'm better than when I started.'

After defeat, Hughes was remade anew. The outcome of the vote split the Labor Party. Hughes, shameless, did not resign as expected but led his followers out of the party room to form a breakaway Labor government and then joined with Liberals in January 1917 to create a Nationalist Party government. The Senate forced him to the polls in May 1917 but against most predictions he won a smashing victory in both houses. He had to change electorates to save himself, for West Sydney, which he first won in 1894, did not want him again. But in Bendigo he won a grand majority.

Ambulance man at Bernafay, France carrying soldier suffering from trench foot, December 1916.

One Anzac Corps obtained all its objectives and took 3,900 prisoners. The other Anzac Corps took all its objectives and met the Prussian Guards whom they had met at Pozières on the Somme. This Corps took no prisoners.

British communique after Broodseinde Ridge, 1917

The 'C' word did not appear. Voters were simply asked to approve a government power to require men to serve overseas.

Reinforcements of the 1st Division, detrained at Dernancourt on the Somme, December 1916.

Allan Benson McDougall,
16th Reinforcement,
12th Battalion, AIF, killed in
action, Mouquet Farm,
4 September 1916.

Sergeant George P. Cross,
MM (Military Medal),
13th Battalion, AIF, killed
in action at Bullecourt,
11 April 1917.

Barbed wire entanglements constructed
by the German army, France 1917.

This was wartime; the shameless schemer was also a ferocious fighter and that was enough to hold him high in the polls. The referendum vote was a vote against conscription, not against vigorous prosecution of the war.

In the streets, recruiting was more frantic than ever. Some loyalists seemed on the edge of hysteria. The labour press called it the 'sooling on business'. The gentle bush-worker and poet John Shaw Neilson was 44 years old, frequently lame with a dicky knee and so near-sighted that at times his eyes were almost useless. When he went to an oculist for stronger glasses he was told there was nothing wrong with his sight. The oculist thought he was trying to dodge the war. White feathers fluttered from envelopes; rejected volunteers wore a badge to save them from abuse; state governments changed German place names in honour of British generals—in South Australia, Blumberg was changed to Birdwood and Kaiser Stuhl to Mount Kitchener; there were internment camps for 'enemy aliens'; Lutheran schools were shut down; and there were prohibitions on speaking the German language.

The trials on the Somme were followed by the worst French winter in 40 years. Over 20,000 Australian soldiers were evacuated suffering trench foot, frostbite and exhaustion. Boiling tea froze in a minute; bread would not break or slice; and water, arriving in solid blocks, was chopped up with an axe to fit in billies. Beyond the billets and the burrows, those still alive were dark targets against a white background. 'The world seemed a perpetual round of pain, misery and death,' wrote Bill Gammage, 'and men seemed condemned to endure ceaseless travail, till their souls were deadened, and they resigned their course on earth to the whims of a malicious fate.' Grim submission to that fate was now tempered by the most pathetic hopes: 'If I get out of it with a leg and an arm off I'll be perfectly satisfied,' wrote a cashier from Glebe Point in Sydney, 'so you can understand what it is like.'

The Germans were worn out too. In February 1917, they began a retreat to a stronger and shorter string of positions called the Hindenburg Line. The British High Command was eager to follow up and break through with the British 5th Army. On the right of that army the Australians followed the yielding enemy, out of Bapaume and a kilometre beyond. Soon the Hindenburg Line was visible in the far distance, its parapets protected

Australians playing 'pitch and toss' in the support line near
Noreuil, during the fighting at Bullecourt, April 1917.

Opening packages from the Australian Comforts Fund.
Members of the 13th Battalion at Ribemont, France 1917.

by vast lines of barbed wire upon a million broken acres. Deep in this barbed-wire country were a number of fortified villages, which the Australians captured in April, revealing a new professionalism to match the keenness that had made their reputation. But one of these villages was called Bullecourt and here neither keenness nor professionalism could transcend the bungling of high command and the efficiency of German resistance.

Waiting for their orders, soldiers heard news of United States intervention. A new ally was coming. But on the Russian front, an ally was lost. The revolution had taken hold and the Russian army was disintegrating. At night, Australian and British officers argued about the meaning of the revolution. Some welcomed an end to brutal Tsardom, hoping for democracy; Charles Bean was one of these. Others shuddered at the thought. Soon they were talking about renewed mutinies in the French army and signs of rebellion in their own ranks.

Gough's plan to break through at Bullecourt exhibited masterly ineptness. Over protests from Australian commanders, it went ahead. The plan unfolded in such a way that artillery support for the Australians did not eventuate, and tank support, an innovation in itself, was a fiasco. The tanks were to substitute for artillery in wire-cutting operations, but they failed. Thousands marched into machine gun fire without cover of any kind. Somehow they breached the wire. Some units even broke into the Hindenburg Line. They did the near impossible and broke into the line without an artillery barrage. But they were nearly obliterated, 80 per cent of them killed, 1,170 captured. The fugitive remainder had to turn and flee across the firing zone. 'The word came "Throw everything away. Hop over the top and run for it",' wrote the remarkable George Mitchell. 'But I was not going to abandon my Lewis gun . . . I walked to the barbed wire . . . I heard the bullets as they hailed all around. I saw the dead, wounded and dying as they lay huddled everywhere . . . I did not even desire to run.' His brigadier watched as Mitchell, Lewis gun on his shoulder, strolled back to his line. His courage, calmness and sheer good luck won him an immediate Distinguished Conduct Medal (DCM) and later a commission. Bullecourt was a German military success but, with the feats of George Mitchell and a few audacious others, Australians remembered it as a triumph of their soldiers' willpower.

In May 1917, the offensive was resumed on a 25-kilometre front manned by 16 divisions. Mutinies in the French army threw added pressure on the British, Canadian and Australian portions of the line. On the northern tip of the attacking front, the Canadians broke through at Vimy Ridge and made of that battle what Australians made of Gallipoli. In the centre, British troops also broke through and in the south, the Australians fought for Bullecourt again at a cost of 7,000 casualties.

Sergeant Guy Hamilton Cotter, 23rd Battalion, AIF, killed in action at Bullecourt 3 May 1917.

An Australian sleeping in his trench shelter in the
second line of trenches during the fighting at Bullecourt.

*The Australians
had been butchered
and gassed, even
shelled by British
artillery at times*

Sister Pearl E. Corkhill, MM
(Military Medal), AANS
(Australian Army Nursing
Service). Her Military Medal
was awarded for bravery
under aerial attack at the
No. 38 Casualty Clearing
Station, France 1918.

The blood letting at Bullecourt sapped the strength
and morale of the AIF. Faith in British command sank to
a new low. Some Australian divisions were withdrawn for
rest and refitting. The new 6th Division, training in
England, was disbanded to replenish these battered
ranks. Other divisions fought on as part of a new
offensive in the north.

Haig's objective in the north was to turn the German
flank from the Ypres salient, occupy the Belgian coast
and capture the enemy's submarine pens, but the
Germans held the surrounding high ground, notably
Messines Ridge. The 3rd and 4th Divisions fighting with
British divisions in General Plumer's 2nd Army took the
ridge in June at another bitter price, 6,800 casualties.
But Plumer was regarded as a 'methodical planner,
careful with the lives of soldiers', and Messines was
recorded as one of the great set-piece victories of the war. Victory clearly made a
difference to morale. The Australians had been butchered and gassed, even shelled by
British artillery at times, but overall Plumer's step-by-step plan had worked and the
ridge mattered strategically.

The 1st Australian Tunnelling Company was part of this victory. It had worked
with other mining units through 1916, tunnelling its way towards Messines Ridge.
Some of these men had practised their trade at Gallipoli. They were part of two
battalions of hand-picked miners, formed under the Professor of Geology at Sydney
University, T.W. Edgeworth David. In 1917 they took over the work of the Canadian
tunnellers and reached their destination in time to be part of Plumer's plan. The
Germans were now perched on a minefield. After 2,200 allied guns laid waste to an
area about 13 kilometres by 9 kilometres, the mines were detonated, 1 million
pounds of TNT, at that stage the largest man-made explosion in history. It blew the
top off sections of the ridge as a prelude to the battles that followed. The fight for
Messines Ridge was over in a day yet the human cost was still immense.

Nurses who came to France wearing bonnets with trailing ribbons were now
wearing tin helmets and bearing up to horrors that matched anything in the trenches.
At least 2,139 Australian nurses served abroad between 1914 and 1919, some of these
in Casualty Clearing Stations (CCS) on the Western Front. At the No. 2 Australian
CCS near Messines Ridge, 21 nurses awaited the outcome. They were told the
casualties were light. In the first eighteen hours, 2,800 patients were admitted. Sister
Mimie Proctor was a recent arrival: 'it was a nightmare,' she wrote, 'blood, blood,
blood everywhere, and suffering, God forgot us, I am certain . . .' In another ward,
Sister Ada Smith worked for 'droves of dying men . . . nearly all headcases and
unconscious or else raving in delirium, and pulling their bandages off'. She was in a
'moribund' ward where few of her patients would live for more than an hour or two.

Bombs nearly killed Sister Alice Ross-King while she was working in the chest and
abdominal wards. The concussion threw her to the ground. She picked herself up,
checked on her patients, then fell into a bloody crater on her way to the pneumonia
ward tent. She got to the tent only to find it collapsed:

*Though I shouted nobody answered me or I could hear nothing for the roar of planes and
the artillery. I seemed to be the only living thing about . . . I kept calling for the orderly to
help me and thought he was funking, but the poor boy had been blown to bits . . .*

When the tent was up again, she set about getting a delirious patient into bed:

I had my right arm under a leg which I thought was his but when I lifted I found to my horror that it was a loose leg with a boot and a putty on it. One of the orderly's legs which been blown off and had landed on the patient's bed. Next day they found the trunk up a tree about twenty yards away.

Sister Ross-King was one of four sisters to win the Military Medal for her heroism in that sector that night. Yet after the war nurses' names were not recorded on war memorials for they were not 'combatants'. They were excluded from the heritage of battle. To many of them it seemed unjust.

Torrential rain then turned the offensive into even more of a nightmare. The extraordinary thing was how well the Australians fought in spite of demoralisation

The 'legs' are in the next ward and they are so funny, [they] show off how they can hop on one leg and frighten the heart out of me going past them. If they should fall they come down on their stumps.

Sister Queenie Avenell, Southall, England

A Place to Remember

Corporal Ernest Lionel Bailey, 51st Battalion and later Australian Corps Salvage, AIF, tagging battlefield trophies for the Australian War Museum at the Hoograaf Collecting Depot, Belgium, October 1917. Accidentally killed on 17 May 1918 while handling a German stick grenade.

After Bullecourt, Charles Bean was exhausted by his labours. For posterity he was recording, in carefully gathered detail, the trials of the ordinary soldier in the field. He was on yesterday's battlefield, taking notes, instructing his cameraman about what to photograph and directing his draughtsman to take measurements and draw plans of the whole area. He was a feverish worker and a brave man, but he started to feel very old, worn out by his strange job, watching history being 'made', watching through a telescope as men were flicked aside like tin soldiers on a war game table.

Bean took a few days leave and went to Oxford where he again met John Masefield and discovered the poet laureate still remembered the men he had seen in Egypt. 'He thinks these magnificent men ought to be sent back to Australia at once as it is a tragedy to have the young race killed off—he would rather let the old race die,' wrote Bean. Masefield was now so disillusioned with events that he wondered if England needed a revolution too. They talked on while Oxford men, the officer class on leave from war, played cricket. The air pulsed with a faint, continuous undercurrent. It was the artillery in France.

The following year, in May, Bean and Masefield were at Pozières, surrounded by the wreckage of battles past. They found a sign, 'Centreway', made by Australian soldiers. It recalled a fashionable Melbourne shopping arcade. They freed it from a tangle of wire and Bean kept it, not as a memento, but as an item for a national collection.

At Gallipoli, Bean had noticed Australians collecting relics of the war. National recognition and praise had heightened their sense of history. Some collected for trade, swapping shell cases for cigarettes provided by sailors on Anzac Cove which, at times, was a little marketplace with supply lines reaching all the way to curiosity stalls in London streets. But many collected for posterity, and Bean was taken with the idea of collecting not for curiosity, trade or even nostalgia, but for civic purpose—to ensure the memory of grand deeds in the cause of empire and civilisation and, above all, to commemorate Australian achievement.

At Pozières, where the true meaning of modern warfare had shattered what was left of Bean's romanticism and scythed away his simple faith in deliverance, he was seized with the need for a national museum, a place to hold the written records of Australia's part in the war along with the relics of triumph and tragedy, a place for the sacred relics of heroism and sacrifice, a place to remember.

In May 1917, an Australian War Records Section was established at AIF headquarters in France. That date is recognised as the beginning of what became the Australian War Memorial. The British were preparing for their own national museum. Their plans now clashed with Australian intentions. They wanted Australian relics. The Dominions had only just gained possession of their written military records as formerly they went to the War Office in London. A tug-of-war now began over the most unique and irreplaceable trophies. Would a British museum do justice to the Australian contribution to war? Bean and others thought not. The national identity which underwrote the Australian War Memorial in its fledgling days, before it even had a name, was sharpened by the rivalry over relics. The relics would come home to Australia and the record would be as complete as could be, not just unit diaries, old guns and an ironic street sign, but photographs, paintings (the output of the war artists who began work in France in 1916), film, maps, memorabilia, and private records too.

Telling the tale of what Australian men and women had done in the Great War became Bean's life work. He wanted to ensure the dead and their deeds would never be forgotten. Many years later he wrote of how this obligation gripped him: 'I have often thought that many a youngster when he was hit out there on the Passchendaele heights—during the last few minutes of his life, when . . . he knew that the end had come—must have thought to himself: "well at least they'll remember me in Australia."'

1917 was the worst year of the war for Australian casualties: 55,000 in all, 38,000 at Passchendaele alone.

I hate the curse of military life . . . with my intensest hatred . . . If I shall live I shall stand by the red hot socialists and peace cranks to stop any further wars after this one, but while I am at it I will fight like only one facing death can fight.

Private G.H.J. Davies,
36th Battalion, 1917

Private Archibald Patterson Elliot of the 9th Battalion, AIF, wounded at Pozières and Bullecourt, then killed in action in the Messines sector, 22 December 1917.

'Over The Top', composite photograph by Frank Hurley, France 1918. The margin photo shows Australian troops leaving their trench for an attack, France 1918. This was one of several photographs used to create the composite photo.

and anger in the face of the terrain, the weather, the bad generals and other difficulties. Absence without leave was now a serious problem in all Australian divisions as exhausted men 'literally melted away to the rear'. The official correspondent called it temporary desertion.

All manner of nervous states afflicted the ranks. Rates of nervous disability among the field artillerymen were high and otherwise sound men in the lines commonly went shaky for a time. Still, the Australians won victories at Menin Road, Polygon Wood and Broodseinde Ridge. The victories lifted their spirits, only to have them dashed again at Passchendaele where the battlefield was a quagmire. Shelling had completely destroyed the drainage, so the water could not get away. There was never a chance of success. Bean called the plan a 'great bloody experiment' and a 'huge gamble'. 'They don't realise,' he wrote of the British command, 'how desperately hard it will be to fight down such opposition in the mud, rifles choked, LGs [Lewis guns] out of action, men tired and slow . . . Every step means dragging one foot out of the mud . . . I shall be very surprised if this fight succeeds.'

1917 was the worst year of the war for Australian casualties: 55,000 in all, 38,000 at Passchendaele alone. The futility of this final fling in the Ypres campaign was reflected in horrific statistics—35 Australians killed for every metre of ground seized. Among the survivors the most potent memories were of men drowning in mud, unreachable, their cries followed by the most awful silence; the living were racked with guilt and sadness.

One witness to this horror was Frank Hurley, a recent arrival who had joined the AIF on his return from Antarctica. He was an official photographer and was given the honorary rank of captain. Hurley had been on expeditions to Antarctica with Mawson (1911–13) and Shackleton (1914–16). His reputation as adventurer and cameraman was made before he went to war. On the Western Front he clashed repeatedly with

Charles Bean over his photographic methods—Hurley had a habit of combining several photographs in one for dramatic effect. One of the most famous photographs of an Australian infantry attack at Zonnebeke measured 6.5 by 4.5 metres and used twelve different negatives. His diaries are a vivid, anguished complement to his photography. At Zonnebeke he wrote:

Another shell killed four and I saw them die, frightfully mutilated in the deep slime of a shell crater. How ever anyone escapes being hit by the showers of flying metal is incomprehensible. The battlefield on which we won an advance of 1,500 yards, was littered with bits of men, our own and Boche, and literally drenched with blood . . . It almost makes one doubt the very existence of a deity—that such things can go on beneath an omnipotent eye.

For Hurley, fate was in complete control and there was no point dodging shells. Soldiers saw him taking extraordinary risks to get images of action, shell bursts in particular. They called him the 'mad photographer'.

Bean thought Hurley's pictures were forgeries because he made composites, sometimes with an awesome sky or shell bursts added for dramatic effect. Hurley argued that his compositions were not distortion but compensation for the limits of his equipment. He claimed his composites allowed him to depict the real drama of battle, which his cumbersome equipment had been unable to match. For Bean it was a matter of honest recording, a crucial issue for the man planning a national museum of war. For Hurley it was a matter of artistry to match the events. On battlefields of blood and gore, the recorders of war were arguing about what is real and what is accurate, what is historical and what is not, and where does one cross the line. It was no academic matter, for these men were makers and custodians of popular memory.

The criticism of his work stung Hurley, so much so that he departed for the Middle East to record the feats of the Light Horse. Hurley went off to sandstorms and blinding heat; Bean stayed on in the quagmire.

After the Ypres campaign, 'Pompey' Elliott, the general with tears in his eyes, wrote of the Australian soldiers' morale: 'The difficulty once was to restrain their impatience for action . . . now we find men clearing out to avoid going into the line at all.' The home-front seemed to match this downward spiral, with a descent into division and bitterness.

Hughes' re-election in May 1917 had been a landslide victory. In the electoral returns, as though reading tea leaves, he saw contrition: traditional conservatives who had voted No had returned to the fold. The Irish might have cooled down too.

Ypres sector, Belgium. Dead and wounded Australian and German soldiers in the railway cutting on Broodseinde Ridge, 12 October 1917, *top.*

A mule team with supplies, struggling to get out of the mud in the Ypres sector, 17 October 1917.

Soldiers of the 21st Battalion line up to vote in the second conscription referendum, Vaulx-Vraucourt-Bullecourt sector, 29 April 1917.

The casualty rates told another story. Cynicism spread. War-weariness was everywhere, especially among working people whose hardships were acute.

Showing a sign to a civilian to help him decide. Australian soldiers on a recruiting drive.

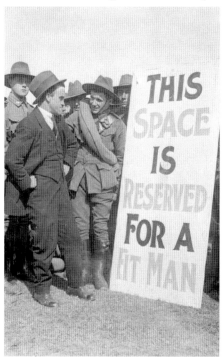

He called another referendum for December. But Australians were fast losing their enthusiasm for a war that seemed to have no end. Censorship meant the newspapers twisted and glossed every murderous encounter on the Western Front. The casualty rates told another story. Cynicism spread. War-weariness was everywhere, especially among working people whose hardships were acute. The revolutionaries of Russia were not alone in turning to radical ideas.

In mid 1917 Labor Party branches around Australia passed resolutions blaming the capitalist economic system for the war and demanding a negotiated peace. In August the greatest strike in Australian history began with railway and tramway workers in New South Wales, then spread to lorry drivers, miners, wharf labourers and seamen. Thousands of loyalist strikebreakers and vigilantes backed by the police broke the general strike. The union leaders were charged with conspiracy and their protest crushed. But the strike was no oddity. It was the spectacular sign of a new malaise—confusion, anger, polarisation and civil disorder spreading through Australian society. The Governor-General's dispatches to London in 1917 were grim: 'One can only hope,' he wrote, 'that things are so black that the better elements of society will be drawn together in a fight against the Powers of Darkness.' The King's private secretary read the dispatches and the newspapers with alarm: 'The socialistic element [in Australia] seems to be asserting itself as much as it does at the present time in Petrograd,' he wrote.

The second conscription campaign was even more venomous than the first. Loyalists composed The Anti's Creed, which read in part:

I believe that men at the Front should be sacrificed . . .
I believe that treachery is a virtue . . .
That disloyalty is true citizenship . . .
That desertion is ennobling . . .
I believe I'm worm enough to vote NO

The No supporters were just as manipulative. One of their broadsheets claimed that conscription would decimate what was left of Australian manhood and force the women to marry 'Chinese, Japs and Hindoos'.

Women were more than ever part of the campaign. Yes and No supporters knitted socks and parcelled up essentials for men at the front. In Melbourne the women of the Women's Peace Army, led by Adela Pankhurst, held street demonstrations to protest about the price of bread and other basics, to stir worries about lost manhood and coloured labour, and to insist on a negotiated peace. One of the demonstrations turned to riot, and Pankhurst and others were arrested. In a furious letter to Keith Murdoch, Hughes mentioned new, draconian legislation to crush all opposition and 'that woman': 'Adela Pankhurst is making herself a d——d nuisance and I really don't know what to do with the little devil. I hate punishing women, but fear

Women working for the Australian Comforts Fund, Melbourne Town Hall.

Australia alone fought the war without recourse to conscription, but the price was a bitterness and division that continued to mark the social fabric long after the war had ended.

I shall have to deport her.' In 1920, Pankhurst was a founding member of the Communist Party of Australia, another sign of the times.

When the votes were counted the No majority had increased considerably among civilians and the soldiers abroad. In public Hughes was bold and cheerful, but in his now regular, confessional letter to Keith Murdoch, he was perplexed. How to explain the soldiers' majority No vote? He did not know. What of war-weariness? He was contemptuous of the 'war-weariness of a people who have escaped all the consequences of this awful war!' All? He blamed the Sinn Feiners and the socialists and the 'selfish and sentimental vote of the women'. Women seemed to be a symbolic centre of all the passions of war, whether as spartan mothers or selfish mothers, sweethearts, sentimentalists, feminists, pacifists or rebels. 'Some day when I see you . . .,' wrote Hughes, 'I can pour out the anguish and anger seething within me.'

The whole country was seething. In Armidale, in northern New South Wales, a Protestant dentist discussed the referendum result with a Catholic patient who said he was a No voter although he had volunteered several times. The dentist told him conscription had been defeated by the 'three Cs: the cowards, the c—— and the Catholics.' A week later they exchanged insults and punches outside the Armidale Post Office. In the court case that followed the second 'C' was referred to as a 'very vulgar reference to women'. Of all the belligerent nations, Australia alone fought the war without recourse to conscription, but the price was a bitterness and division that continued to mark the social fabric long after the war had ended.

In 1917 the morale of Australian troops reached new depths and the rate of monthly court martials for desertion, 'temporary desertion' and other breaches of discipline reached new heights. Desertion was a feasible option for the Diggers, for their army alone had no death penalty. In July, when the Ypres offensive was underway, the number of Australians in military prisons in France was, proportionately, four times that for British and other Dominion soldiers. After Ypres, the disparity was even greater. Australians and Canadians were worn out by their

Captain R. L. Henderson, MC, AAMC, Regimental Medical Officer, 2nd Battalion, AIF, died of wounds received at Bullecourt in 1917.

The ruins of Villers-Bretonneux, May 1918. View from a window of the South Chateau, then occupied by a light trench mortar battery.

The Australian Corps was ordered south to the old Somme battlefield, to stem the German onslaught across that voracious graveyard.

repeated use as 'shock troops' and by the treadmill of battle after battle. Some commanders doubted the capacity of their troops to go on. But the men still at the front were dogged. They fought on and their reputation in these extreme times won them a great reward.

In November, the Australian divisions were brought together for the first time as a unified Australian Corps headed by General Birdwood. Commanders in the field had long argued that the Australians fought better and their morale was higher when their divisions were joined together. The troops were also rewarded with rest following the disasters of Passchendaele. They were moved to the quiet Messines sector in mid November and remained there, retraining and refitting, though raiding and patrolling as required for several months.

In the winter of 1917–18 the strategic situation was changing for the worse. The Russian front had disintegrated, freeing German divisions for battle to the west. After the enormous losses of the Ypres offensive, British forces were stretched thin. Now they gave way. The line at the Somme around Péronne was lost, then Bapaume, and more ground after that. The Australian Corps was ordered south to the old Somme battlefield, to stem the German onslaught across that voracious graveyard. When the Australians arrived, they found the British forces, exhausted. But the German troops were tired and depleted too, their artillery and logistic support running thin. Even their successes were accompanied by disspiriting realisations—flooding into British back areas they found food supplies and equipment they could only envy.

The Australian divisions came into the line and made an impact. From Hébuterne to Hangar Wood, they ground the Germans to a halt. At Villers-Bretonneux, a village east of the vital rail junction at Amiens, the 13th and the 15th Brigades drove the enemy back. It was a night battle that began on 24 April and carried on into Anzac Day, a ferocious, dog-pit entanglement with few prisoners taken. Between 21 March and 7 May the

Private William John Bottomley, 21st Battalion, AIF, killed in action at Mont St Quentin, 1 September 1918.

Australians took 15,000 casualties, but their victories were telling. They much preferred this more open warfare: 'We fight in open fields,' wrote Lieutenant Harry Chedgey, 'among hedges and farm houses and dig trenches all over the country. We have got right away from fixed trench warfare.' Chedgey was a 26-year-old solicitor from Arncliffe in New South Wales.

Allied planning now looked to counterattack. The British munitions industry was churning out more shells, machine guns, Lewis guns, rifle grenades and trench mortars per division than ever before. Tanks had been redesigned and were now an effective weapon. A new sound-ranging system for pin-pointing enemy batteries meant that British guns could range more accurately onto their target. Australian commanders knew that keenness and high morale were no longer decisive in battle. There were a few novices who still wanted a shining adventure; there were veterans whose determination was unruffled and many others, full of trepidation, but still ready to do their duty. Late in the war a few still felt God was watching over them; most believed they would die. They saw their ranks thinning, then replenished, then thinning again. It was merely a matter of time. They pressed on. So long as men went forward and did their job proficiently, doggedly, that was enough. It was hardware, particularly the number of big guns and superiority in their application, that would be decisive. The circumstances now favouring victory made the spirit of individual soldiers even more irrelevant than before.

Yet these spirits had been lifted by rest and new leadership and soon they were lifted by more victories. In May, Birdwood took command of the British 5th Army and General Monash took over the Australian Corps. Monash was a Scotch College – Melbourne University graduate with degrees in Arts, Engineering and Law, a civil engineer by trade and a gifted staff officer who showed what could be achieved with precision coordination of tanks, aeroplanes, infantry, artillery and supply. He combined a host of tactical innovations into a standard battle drill and applied to every stage of battle the cool, rational, systematic approach that he had used when building bridges before the war. He was the quintessential general of modern

Miss Evelyn Chapman, the first Australian 'lady artist' to visit the battlefields, at work in Villers-Bretonneux, 15 July 1918, with the remains of the town's church in the background.

Late in the war a few still felt God was watching over them; most believed they would die. They saw their ranks thinning, then replenished, then thinning again. It was merely a matter of time.

Corbie, France, 3 July 1918. English, American and Australian troops lunching in a wood near Corbie, the day prior to the attack and capture of German positions at Hamel and Vaire Wood.

Lieutenant General John Monash presenting decorations to members of the 4th Australian Infantry Brigade on 20 July 1918 after their success in the battle of Hamel.

Every 20 paces or less lay a body. Some frightfully mutilated, without legs, arms and head and half covered in mud and slime . . . The terrain had become one great slough. One dares not venture off the duckboard or he will surely become bogged, or sink in the quick-sand-like slime . . . God knows how those red-tabbed blighters at headquarters (60 miles from the front) expect our men to gain such a strong position when they have to drag themselves through the mud.

Frank Hurley,
Broodseinde Ridge, 1917

warfare, utterly methodical and professional (contrary to the qualities celebrated in the Anzac legend), a man with 'petrol in his veins and a computer in his head', as one of his biographers later wrote. Monash was mindful of history and comparisons that might favour him at posterity's inquisition:

My command [he wrote] is more than two and a half times the size of the British Army under the Duke of Wellington, or of the French Army under Napoleon Bonaparte, at the Battle of Waterloo. Moreover, I have in the Army Corps an artillery which is more than six times as numerous and more than a hundred times as powerful as that commanded by the Duke of Wellington. I have besides arms, services and departments not dreamt of in his day, all of the highest scientific complexity.

The grandness of his command was complemented by the good fortune of his appointment—just six weeks before what Charles Bean called 'the turning point of the Great War'. On 18 July 1918, thirteen French divisions and four American divisions attacked the Germans at Soissons. The enemy was driven back and the German offensive abandoned. Germany itself moved closer to collapse and

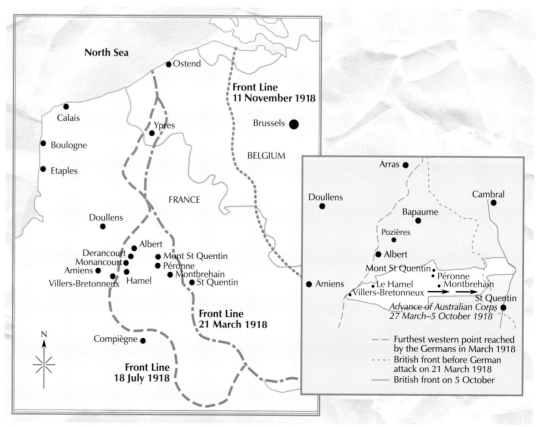

The Western Front 1918

Adapted from *Beaucoup Australiens ici*, Department of Veterans' Affairs, Canberra, 1999 revolution. French and American troops provided a setting for Monash's skills that could not have been better.

Monash was criticised for rarely going to the front (Bean, the romantic, was contemptuous), but he was undoubtedly a better planner than he was a leader in the field, as some soldiers knew from forays with him at Gallipoli. He took command of Australian troops at a time when they had already established a reputation as outstanding fighters. He played to and planned for their strengths and never made light of the special qualities they brought to the battlefield.

Monash's innovative thinking on the grand scale was matched by his soldiers' innovations at the tactical level. It was they who devised a style of fighting called minor aggressions whereby patrols, acting on their own initiative, and without artillery cover, infiltrated the German lines without warning and overwhelmed one position after another, killing and wounding, occupying ground, gathering in 'Fritzes' by the twos and threes, expropriating machine guns and shattering morale among the enemy. Another term for these sorties was rather ironic—they were called peaceful penetration. Stealth followed by aggression was the mark of this work.

George Mitchell was in the Somme area at the time. He had won a Military Cross at Dernancourt and was now leading penetrating patrols with morale lifting success:

Aboriginal serviceman, Private William Reginald Rawlings MM. The Rawlings family from western district of Victoria has among its descendents the boxer Lionel Rose and soldiers of World War II, Reginald and Harry Saunders. Rawlings was killed in action on 9 August 1918 during the capture of Vauvillers, France. His friend Harry Thorpe, another Aborigine who also won the Military Medal, was killed on the same day. They are both buried in the Heath Cemetery, Harbonnières, France.

We advanced cautiously through a wheat crop, and then crawled through the long grass. There was a little MG [machine gun] fire. A few flares were coming over. We crawled on and on. At length I found a deep comfortable shell hole . . . Listening we heard coughs, click of rifle bolts and the sound of picks and shovels . . . Sergeant Halliday and I worked forward through the grass . . . [then] squirmed back to the rest of the party. I got them ready. We all stood up together and gave rapid fire on to the party in front . . . silence. Not a leaf stirred. We crouched down in our shell hole. Still no answer. So I sent them off in the direction of home.

On the parade ground the Australians were casual and indifferent; on the battlefield they were now professional and uncommonly deadly. There were times when they captured townships without Monash even knowing. The town of Merris was one of these; the village of Chipilly was another. At Chipilly, an English regiment had been held at bay by machine gun fire for two days. A squad of six Australians arrived, stalked the machine-gunners and killed them, then cleared the village, captured about 300 prisoners, called up the English regiment and returned to their own battalion. This was a remarkable feat, but at the time success was with the Australians wherever they appeared.

These small-unit tactics were interspersed with small-scale offensives—at Hamel and Amiens—where victories were won by conventional battle, precisely executed. Hamel, on 4 July 1918, was over in 93 minutes: 775 men were lost, 1,472 prisoners were taken, two big guns were seized along with 171 machine guns and 26 trench mortars. On 12 August, Monash was knighted in the field by King George V.

The final British offensive began on 8 August. Two Australian squadrons, part of the Australian Flying Corps formed in December 1915, were now in the air above the Western Front as British, Canadian, French and Australian divisions swept through German lines south of the Somme. In five days of fighting they advanced about 10 kilometres and discovered that many German soldiers could fight no more. This day, 8 August, was a black day for the German army and a turning point in the war. Allied spirits were lifting.

At this time success was with the Australians wherever they appeared.

Women waiting for returned soldiers at the Anzac Buffet in Hyde Park, Sydney.

The Australians were ordered back into the line on 5 November but six days later Germany signed an armistice and the killing was at an end.

A wounded AIF soldier is welcomed home at the Anzac Buffet in Hyde Park, Sydney, *opposite.*

Anzac Day in Melbourne, 1919. Some of the women's complement taking part in the march.

The Australians pressed on with their minor aggressions and some major ones. In a stunning assault, the 2nd Division overran a German strong-point at Mont St Quentin, said to be impregnable. They were 'yelling like a lot of bushrangers' to make up for their depleted ranks. The preparations and preliminary battles had gone on all night. Aided by a formidable artillery bombardment, they fought their way through thick entanglements of wire and trenches, across open slopes and finally across a canal at the foot of the mount, before charging upwards. The storming of Mont St Quentin took place at dawn. Some rated it the finest movement in the war. With this stronghold disarmed, the 5th Division was able to assault Péronne to the south. The enemy was now in full retreat.

Monash and his veteran divisions played a vital part in the final, victorious assault on the Hindenburg Line. After a week of fighting, the Australians broke through the line near Beaurevoir and were then relieved by US troops. Success did not come without a price. Almost 27,000 of them had been killed or wounded in three months since 8 August. Eleven out of 60 battalions were disbanded for want of men and not one battalion could muster a quarter of its number. Some were down to less than 100 men. They were ragged and limp, pallid and sick. One soldier described his mates with an understanding that drew on his own wasted condition and a tenderness that was comradeship:

Their eyes had the fixed stare common in men who had endured heavy bombardments, and they had the jerky mannerisms of human beings whose nervous systems had been shocked to an alarming degree. So tired, so dead beat were they that many of them, when opportunity offered, slept the heavy drugged sleep of utter exhaustion for twenty-four hours on end. Their faded earth-stained uniforms hung loosely from their bodies which had lost as much as two stone in as many months. Sheer determination and wonderful esprit de corps had enabled these gallant fellows to work . . . when physically they were done.

The Australians were ordered back into the line on 5 November but six days later Germany signed an armistice and the killing was at an end. The final phase had been a stunning turn of fortune for the allied forces. The Australian troops' run of victories garnished their reputation.

The troops were relieved more than elated. There was not much rejoicing at the front. About 120 soldiers enlisted to fight the Bolsheviks in Russia, which they did, briefly. Some units of the Light Horse stayed on to help crush the Egyptian national revolt in 1919. The rest were shipped home through 1919 and 1920, their repatriation overseen by Monash with the same efficiency and coordinating powers he had used in war.

The soldiers came home to a divided nation suffering from poverty and soon after from disease, for one of the troopships almost certainly brought the influenza epidemic that killed 12,000 Australians. The labour movement was uncommonly radical and bitter, its outlook transformed by the conscription referenda and class war on the home front, and by the bloodbath in Europe and the revolution in Russia. Conservatives were full of panic. The term 'Bolshevism' was now a coverall for everything from revolutionary agitation to strikes, 'loose morals', jazz,

Crowds throng a Sydney street under a 'Welcome Home' banner to greet a cavalcade of returning soldiers, 1918.

modernist art and the 'new woman'. 'The Bolsheviks are out to destroy every man who owns a cottage and uses a toothbrush,' screamed one editorial. The artist Lionel Lindsay, Norman's brother, hoped fervently that Australia might escape from 'all the revolutionary manias of a rotted world'. Many now shared his fearful isolationism. The soldiers' organisation, the Returned Sailors and Soldiers Imperial League of Australia (RSSILA), took a firm stand for caution, conformity and loyalty, but most returned men did not join, preferring to slip quietly away from all things military, many unable to speak of what they had done and seen. A fraction of these men became socialists, among them Hugo Throssell VC, who took his own life in 1931. 'Pompey' Elliott took his life that year too and it was the year that Monash died. The premature wastage of the soldiers was out of all proportion to their numbers. It was called burnt-out Digger syndrome because so many died in their thirties and forties.

Some of the saddest cases were those who came home with mental disorders. Officially 4,984 AIF men were discharged for psychological trauma, but thousands more suffered from the delayed effects of the fighting. These were men whose 'evil hour', as the soldier-poet Siegfried Sassoon put it, came after the war 'in the sweating suffocation of nightmare, in paralysis of limbs, in the stammering of dislocated speech'. The evil hour revealed many other symptoms, too, ranging from complete withdrawal to tempestuous and violent outbursts to suicidal tendencies. Some went bush, some became a morbid, defeated presence at home or in an asylum. Others terrorised their families with violence threatened and real. Wives and children, streets and neighbourhoods, lived with this presence, the signs of war's ruination affected every community.

Many others battled with the question of how to go on, how to live with the catastrophe of this war. It was a problem shared by soldiers and civilians alike. If family extends to aunts and uncles then every second Australian family was bereaved

VC winners and recipients of other high awards for bravery on parade at the Anzac Day march, Melbourne 1927.

Sir Ross Smith, DFC AFC (pilot) and Lieutenant Mustard, DFC, in their Bristol Fighter, Palestine 1918. After the war Smith and others pioneered the air industry in Australia and became major celebrities.

Three hundred thousand left these shores to fight and 60,000 died—one in five. Almost one in two were wounded, and many who did get back to Australia died before their time.

by the bloodbath of 1914–18. Three hundred thousand left these shores to fight and 60,000 died—one in five. Almost one in two were wounded, and many who did get back to Australia died before their time.

Before the war's end, memorials began to transform the Australian landscape. All over the country, committees were formed to raise a local monument to those who served and those who died. Obelisk, stone soldier, avenue of honour, clock tower, memorial gates, honour boards—these were some of the forms the memorials took. More than half the eligible white, male population had enlisted and they were memorialised and honoured in services around the country.

At Goombungee on Queensland's Darling Downs, Rose Martyn, Aboriginal mother of Charles, killed near Ypres, stood apart at the back of a white crowd united in its grief. She was alone and in tears and she was comforted by no-one. Between 400 and 500 Aboriginal men had joined the AIF and most of these had fought overseas.

At Katanning in Western Australia, a humble stone soldier stood on a pedestal naming 263 dead sons and brothers and friends, one in five of the town's male population. Some of them had been in the charges at the Nek on 7 August 1915. The war memorial movement was a shared quest to find the right way, materially and spiritually, to honour the soldiers and deal with grief. 'I do not know where the body of my boy lies,' said one mother standing in an avenue of honour in King's Park, Perth, in 1920, 'but his soul is here.' Across the country, people came together at memorial unveilings, and they came again in the following years to deal with bereavement beyond measure and to put to rest the ghosts of memory.

Modernists claimed the so-called Great War enabled them to expose what the American poet Ezra Pound called a 'botched civilisation'. A new, raw language of dislocation, paradox, irony, anger and despair in poetry, prose and the visual arts developed.

Fitting an artificial limb in the limb-fitting department, No. 2 Australian Auxiliary Hospital, Southall, England, May 1919, *left*.

Rehabilitation services. Display of work turned out by AIF men in Weymouth, England, April 1919, *below*.

Crowds in Martin Place, Sydney, celebrating the signing of the Armistice, 11 November 1918. In later years this day became Remembrance Day.

It snapped the ties to a discredited heritage. The modernists' work expressed a rejection of all that had gone before. They claimed the Great War was a great divide. But modernism took hold more in Europe than Australia and both there and here powerful continuities carried into the peace after 1918. For many the pursuit of meaning and the need to grieve called for solace that was both patriotic and sentimental, for an idiom archaic and softening, tailored to postwar sensitivities. The urge to find purpose in this massive slaughter was powerful and people found an appropriate language of loss in traditional values, and classical romantic and religious forms, which had the power to help the grieving. They drew on a literary inheritance which included the King James Bible, John Bunyan's *Pilgrim's Progress* and Sir Arthur Quiller-Couch's *Oxford Book of English Verse*. They drew on Rudyard Kipling and Laurence Binyon and the words of town mayors, vice-regals and patriotic generals. The search for meaning went on long after the end of the war.

Some went searching for the dead through spiritual mediums. Spiritualism was not new but the war gave it a new following. In a Melbourne lounge room in April 1920, Charles Elmore went in a trance and, watched by his friends, began to write a message:

> *We wish to bring thoughts of love and peace to the thoughts of the bereaved mothers especially . . . in regard to the fate of their boys . . . Those whom they fought against . . . and in hatred slew, they now meet on grounds of brotherly love.*

Later in the 1920s, thousands acquired a mass-produced copy of Will Longstaff's painting *Menin Gate at Midnight* in which ghostly armies of the afterlife rise from a field of poppies by the Menin Gate memorial at Ypres.

Military portraits took on a new importance too. Those families with no photo of their lost son in uniform could now find a retouch artist who painstakingly painted a uniform, complete with medals, onto a photograph of the loved one.

Critics did speak out, angered by the economic and human cost of war. But criticism was mostly called off on days of ritual remembrance. Those who said war memorials were a plot to deceive, an architecture for more war, could accept that they were also sites for mourning. Leftist opposition was compromised by a sadness that crossed political trenches to a truce point in between, and also by the belief that right had prevailed, though some reckoned the carnage was so terrible on both sides it was hard to know who had prevailed.

The commemoration of war and the cult of the Anzac became a civic religion, the faith at the heart of Australian nationalism. It was not an all-is-forgiven faith. A decade after the war the conscription referenda of 1916–17 still coloured popular memory and commemorative ritual was mostly controlled by anti-Labor people. The idea that the No vote was a kind of desertion that caused many deaths at the front was a judgment that excluded Labor men from Anzac Day and Armistice Day ceremonies every year. Hugo Throssell spoke out against the war on a commemorative platform in 1919. He was never invited onto another one. The Yes voters could have it both ways, for their beloved AIF, being an all volunteer force, could be celebrated as an army of singular purity. Even when the divisions of wartime faded, this fact remained to be cherished by following generations.

Wedding portrait of Lieutenant William Hamilton MC, 26th Battalion, and Miss Hilda Sole, 24 November 1919.

Lieutenant John Scott, Croix de Guerre with Palm, 4th Divisional Artillery. Dungog, 1922.

A bronze plaque in Belgium in honour of the soldiers of the 5th Division who fought in France and Belgium from 1916 to 1918.

3

BUSINESS
AS USUAL

1939 – 1941

After the allies' victory in 1918, World War I was described, yet again, as the 'war to end all wars'. German militarism was sidelined, seemingly crushed. The triumphal nations, worn by the agonies of war, were exalted by the prospects of peace. The League of Nations held its first assembly in 1919 after the signing of the Treaty of Versailles. Delegates promised a new era of cooperation and harmony between the nations of the world. They spoke for millions when they called for world disarmament. For a short time there were a few promising signs.

ONE of these signs was the Washington Treaty of 1921. The treaty required Britain, the United States, Japan and France to scrap a portion of their fleets and set limits on naval rearmament. It was hailed in Australia as a 'magnificent achievement'. There was hardly any grumbling when Australia's navy was counted as part of the British fleet and a local sacrifice was required. The battle cruiser HMAS *Australia* was scuttled in waters beyond Sydney Heads.

The Washington Treaty seemed to confirm that Australian suspicions of Japan were unfair. Japan had been an ally during the war, playing a part in the escort of Australian troopships to the Middle East and taking no advantage of British weakness in the Pacific. Even before the war ended there was talk of a 'Pacific community of nations'. There were business people, scholars and a handful of politicians in Australia who imagined a future in which prejudices might be replaced by real knowledge of that mysterious conglomerate they called 'Asia'. One sign that some Australians wanted to be Asia literate was the appointment of James Murdoch to a lectureship in Oriental Studies at the University of Sydney in 1917. Murdoch tramped all over Japan in the 1880s, he had written novels set there and had already published two celebrated volumes on Japanese history with a third to come. He helped to introduce the teaching of Japanese at Fort Street High School in Sydney and though he died in 1921 there were others to carry his cause. In educated circles it was not hard to find believers in a new Pacific era, in mutual understanding for the sake of peace, prosperity and profit.

But there was an underside to the coming of Pacific enlightenment. Unknown to the general public, James Murdoch was brought home from Japan by the Department of Defence. His public appointment at the University of Sydney drew attention away from his job at the Royal Military College, Duntroon, where he was teaching Japanese. In military circles, and in the Pacific Branch of the Prime Minister's Department, there was a wary cynicism about Japanese intentions.

Sixth Division, 2nd AIF, troops departing for the war, Sydney, January 1940, *previous page*.

2nd AIF recruits at Puckapunyal Camp, Victoria, probably on their way to a meal, December 1939, *opposite*.

HMAS *Australia* during her ceremonial scuttling under the terms of the Washington Treaty, *below*.

Chinese labourers coaling HMAS *Sydney*, using wicker baskets slung between each pair of men, Singapore, 1925.

Hughes was certain that 95 out of every 100 Australians would reject the idea of racial equality. Australia was a 'white man's country'.

Before the end of World War I the Japanese were claiming German territory in China and the Pacific. Through the Treaty of Versailles they obtained control of the Marshall and Caroline Islands, bringing Japan's sphere of interest closer to Australia. By that time the Japanese navy was the third most powerful fleet in the world. Billy Hughes thought the Japanese had designs on New Guinea, formerly German territory, which the Treaty of Versailles had ceded to Australia. At the League of Nations meeting in 1919 the Japanese pushed for a 'racial equality' clause in the Covenant. Baron Makino, the Japanese delegate, sought a private audience with his implacable opponent, Billy Hughes. The Baron was 'literally wreathed in smiles, and beslobbering me with genuflexions and obsequious deference,' wrote Hughes, who told the Baron he would do all in his power to defeat the equality clause. No matter how mild or inoffensive the wording, Hughes was certain that 95 out of every 100 Australians would reject the idea of racial equality. Australia was a 'white man's country'.

Racial equality, even a toothless statement of principle, needled Hughes' deepest fears that Japanese traders and spies would swamp New Guinea and Japanese immigrants would soon be building matchstick-and-paper houses from Darwin to Hobart. Hughes stood his ground in the League of Nations. He marshalled the racial bias of the European delegates and he won the day—the vote went against the Japanese. 'White Australia' was safe. The ancient mystique of Japan—the temples and shrines, the lantern-lit tea-houses, the fabled geishas gorgeously adorned, the so-called 'enchanted Japan'— carried no weight with Hughes. Nor did it carry weight with the hard heads in the Department of Defence—they wanted to know what Japanese munitions factories and shipyards were up to and they wanted a strategy for Australia's security.

An amphibious aircraft, a Supermarine Seagull V (Walrus), about to be launched into flight by a catapult mounted on HMAS *Australia* (II), c.1937.

In 1923 they got one. The League of Nations was high on principle but low on power. Salvation lay in empire. The British government began construction of a massive naval base on Singapore island. The Singapore strategy became the cornerstone of imperial defence in the Far East. It was a continuation of the blue-water school of thought that colonial governments had accepted in the nineteenth century, the idea that as long as British ships controlled the seas, outposts of empire such as Australia would be safe from invaders. Colonial politicians, and Commonwealth politicians after them, had their faith reinforced by cost savings. The Royal Navy ruled the world; local forces would deal with minor attacks and raids. After the immense cost of World War I, the Singapore strategy had great appeal to Australian governments keen to rein in defence expenditure. An imperial system of defence was cheaper and far more feasible than self-reliance. The element of bluff might just keep the peace for the mere presence of this gigantic, allegedly impregnable naval base would surely deter Japan or other would be predators.

Australia's military advisers were not so trusting. As the 1920s progressed, their doubts grew stronger. In 1928 World War I veteran Harry Chauvel spoke out. At that time he was Chief of the General Staff. He said Japan could overrun the Singapore base in less than six weeks. There was a great weakness in the Singapore strategy—it depended on a British promise to send a sizeable fleet there within six weeks of any emergency. Was six weeks fast enough? And if the British navy was tied up with war in European waters, what then?

When Japan invaded Manchuria on 18 September 1931 the rumblings grew louder. The Japanese talked about 'spheres of influence'. The following year was worse. In Germany the Weimar Republic dissolved into chaos. Hitler's National Socialists had become the largest party in the Reichstag, swept to power on a wave of hope and hate, backed by thugs, army generals and industrialists. At the Versailles peace conference in 1919, vast payments were imposed on Germany as 'reparations' for the cost of the war. A 'war guilt' clause, making Germany solely responsible for the conflict, was written into the treaty. These humiliations were a gift to German nationalism and ready-made for Hitler's manipulation. If reparations were supposed to keep Germany weak and meek, their effect was quite the opposite. In 1932, Billy Hughes, now a back-bencher, returned from a European tour sure that war was imminent, certain that Britain was no longer the undisputed mistress of the seas and worried that Australia might be left alone to face a Japanese invasion.

One year later, Lieutenant Colonel Vernon Sturdee, Director of Military Operations and Intelligence, spelled out a grim scenario. He said the Japanese would act too quickly for Singapore to be effective. Australia might be caught helpless:

They [Japanese troops] would all be regulars, fully trained and equipped for their operations, fanatics who like dying in battle, whilst our troops would consist mainly of civilians hastily thrown together on mobilisation with very little training, short of artillery and possibly of gun ammunition.

The army and the air force were in a state of atrophy. The more cherished navy, the senior service, was also in need of renewal. Australia's future was in the hands of Joe Lyons, an ex-Labor man like Billy Hughes. Lyons was leader of the United Australia Party and Prime Minister from 1932 until 1939. His government was torn

View over 8-inch guns of HMAS *Canberra*. Jervis Bay, NSW, August 1935, *top*.

Night firing of a 4-inch gun aboard HMAS *Australia* (II), c. 1935.

The Royal Navy ruled the world; local forces would deal with minor attacks and raids. After the immense cost of World War I, the Singapore strategy had great appeal to Australian governments keen to rein in defence expenditure.

between the desire to believe in the Singapore strategy and growing doubts that it could guarantee its own security, let alone Australia's.

The army and the air force wanted funding for defence against full-scale invasion but financially that was out of the question. The Great Depression had terrified politicians. They were haunted by the twin spectres of economic collapse and social chaos. They believed a budget deficit would send the economy into another tail spin. They were more frightened of deficits and inflation than they were of the Japanese. Rearmament was to be financed from the budget surplus or not at all. A modest rearmament program began in 1934. The navy was favoured so it could play its part in the Singapore strategy. The army and the air force were funded to handle defence against light raids.

Rearmament also included a munitions program to boost the number and capacity of weapons and ammunition factories around the country. In this sphere Australia was surprisingly well placed. Since 1919 programs for economic development had fostered secondary industry including the industries needed to wage war: metals refining, engineering and metals fabrication, machine tools, chemicals, electrical equipment, communications and so on. Tariff protection and industrial development were defence preparation in thin disguise, insurance against the failure of imperial defence.

Cadet Midshipmen, Flinders Naval Depot, Victoria, 1939.

Much of the technical and scientific expertise needed for defence supply was in private industry but the state played a big part too, with public enterprise in electricity, railways, aircraft engineering and the powerful Munitions Supply Board established in 1919. Big overseas companies such as ICI and GM were forced by tariffs to produce locally so that, as war approached, they too became part of the solution producing high-speed tool steel needed for gun forging, armour-piercing shells, armour plate, anti-aircraft guns and a range of explosives.

As the 1930s progressed the rearmament program grew.

As the 1930s progressed the rearmament program grew. Army and air force argued that the emphasis on the navy was wrong. Within the government there were critics who said not enough was being done. In 1935 Billy Hughes published *Australia and War Today*, a broadside against complacency and appeasement thinking. Outside parliamentary ranks others were ringing alarm bells. Essington Lewis of BHP doubted the efficacy of the Singapore strategy—he had been to Japan in 1934 and seen militarisation for himself. Professor Stephen Roberts, a historian at the University of Sydney, sounded warnings on radio, in the press and in his 1937 book *The House that Hitler Built*. Journalist Keith Murdoch, who had become a press baron and a knight, blamed Joe Lyons' wife Enid for the restrained pace of rearmament. Sir Keith called her 'an ardent, even a belligerent pacifist'.

The Labor Party was divided too. The isolationists washed their hands of trouble abroad; Australia must keep out of it. The left wing organised a popular front against all manifestations of European fascism and protested against book, theatre and film censorship in Australia. But many Labor Catholics saw communism as the main enemy and were soft on fascism for that reason. Some actively supported Franco's Falangists in Spain and Mussolini's Blackshirts in Italy. When John Curtin took over from James Scullin as Labor leader in 1935, what he sought was unity. He dodged the big issues abroad to avoid splitting the party and focussed on Australia's sorry state of defence. Curtin supported one of the important arguments in Hughes'

RAF Station Pembroke Dock, Wales, September 1939. Australian airmen working on a Sunderland aircraft soon after the formation of No.10 Squadron. The Sunderlands of No. 10 and No. 461 Squadron flew patrols over the Atlantic Ocean protecting Allied convoys against German submarines and bombers for the duration of the war, *opposite*.

Front page of the *Sun News Pictorial* (Melbourne), 2 September 1939, announcing the outbreak of war.

Troops of the 6th Division, 2nd AIF, Advance Party gather in the doorway of a train, prior to disembarking, Melbourne, December 1939, *right*.

For the first time since 1918, defence was a major public issue in Australia.

We'll do all the work and all the killing:

Scum, scum, the militia may kiss my bum.

AIF poem, anon., c. 1940

book—the need for more spending on the air arm to build it up to parity with the Japanese carrier-borne strike force.

Curtin was prophetic enough to say that Singapore was a forlorn hope, which was becoming clearer by the minute. In 1935 Lyons and his Attorney-General, Robert Menzies, were in England for the silver jubilee of George V and an Imperial Conference. The jubilee celebrations were enchanting; the conference was depressing: in the event of war with Germany there might be no 'fleet to Singapore'. At the Imperial Conference in 1937 the wording was slightly different and the meaning more troubling: the fleet would probably not be available for the Far East. In Europe, Germany had flouted the Treaty of Versailles by occupying the Rhineland; the Rome-Berlin Axis had been proclaimed in 1936; the democratically elected Spanish Republic was under siege from Franco's forces; and, nearer home, Japan had seized Peking and Tientsin.

For the first time since 1918, defence was a major public issue in Australia. Fear of budget deficits and economic depression was lost in visions of Australia standing alone against the Japanese with Britain preoccupied in Europe. In 1938, the economic wisdom of the day gave way to the largest rearmament program yet, the fifth in five years. The aim was the highest possible degree of self-reliance in the shortest possible time.

Lyons died suddenly in April 1939 so Robert Menzies was Prime Minister when Britain declared war on Germany on 3 September 1939. Australia followed. Menzies' declaration of war against Germany was made without reference to Cabinet and there was no dissent in parliament when it was discussed after his radio broadcast to the nation. It was unthinkable that Australia, or any other Dominion, would abandon England. On both sides of parliament there were worries about Japan, but Japan seemed bogged down with war in China. British advisers insisted there was no Japanese threat to Australia and that Australian troops should go to the Middle East and then to Europe.

But the tension between local and imperial defence requirements did not dissolve. From the beginning Australia followed a policy of maintaining two armies, one a volunteer force eligible for overseas service, the other a militia confined to Australia. The volunteers of the 2nd AIF labelled the militiamen of the Citizen Military Forces 'koalas' (not to be exported or shot). They also called them 'chokos', a term derived from George Bernard Shaw's play *Arms and the Man* (1898), in which a soldier who will not fight carries chocolates in his pack instead of ammunition. The names were derisive but militiamen undercut the derision by happily adopting them.

At higher levels there were more serious tensions and conflicts. Australia's tiny Staff Corps, the career soldiers, must have wondered if, like the horse, they too were obsolete. Throughout the inter-war years they were subjected to inadequate funding and delayed promotion. The nation's attachment to the part-time, citizen-soldier, strengthened by the AIF's performance in World War I, was a millstone for them. Young officers who had served in France were still unit adjutants to the militia ten years later. Some of the best officers left, joined the Indian or British army, or simply went back to civilian life. Those who stayed more or less marked time for two decades. Regulars, however capable, fell outside the aura of the citizen-soldiers. A great gulf emerged between the two, and their bickering, squabbles and outright hatreds hampered military leadership till the end of World War II.

The citizen-soldier who sneered loudest at the Staff Corps was Henry Gordon Bennett, an AIF veteran with a formidable record as a front-line commander. He was wounded in the first attack on Lone Pine on 6 August 1915 but returned to the fighting before he could be evacuated. In 1916, at the age of 29, in France, he became the youngest brigadier-general in the British empire. Bennett was a prickly, argumentative, cantankerous character. In the inter-war years he mixed a business career with citizen-soldiering and anti-Labor politicking, sometimes on radio. He told listeners in 1932 that the federal election was a choice between 'a British democracy or a Moscow dictatorship'. But he kept the toughest criticism for officers in the Staff Corps and published his views about their shortcomings in newspaper articles in 1937. These views were so disruptive he was censured and silenced by the Military Board.

When the war broke out Bennett was the senior citizen-soldier on the army list and expected the top command in any expeditionary force, but he was overlooked. The top job went to Thomas Blamey, Monash's collaborator in 1918, a soldier whose talent for command won him support at the highest levels of politics when it counted. Blamey was one of the regular officers who had lost confidence in

Australian troops waving farewell as their ship leaves Port Melbourne docks, September 1940.

The citizen-soldier who sneered loudest at the Staff Corps was Henry Gordon Bennett, an AIF veteran with a formidable record as a front-line commander.

Volunteer Aboriginal soldiers, at No.9 Camp, Wangaratta, Victoria, December 1940.

Saying good-bye, Sydney, 13 September 1940.

Government concerns about Japanese intentions in Asia were suppressed. Priority went to helping England in its coming hour of need.

soldiering as a profession in the inter-war years. In 1925, aged 41 and with a young family to support, he left the army to become Chief Commissioner of the Victoria Police Force. It was a stormy reign that ended, sensationally, in 1936 after he got offside with the press and both sides of parliament. He scandalised the high-minded with his eye for a fetching woman, his head for hard liquor and his open flouting of Victoria's restrictive liquor laws. In 1936 he misled the press, trying to cover for a senior officer wounded in a shoot-out. He had been knighted in 1935 but in 1936 he was drummed out of the Police Force on a pension of £5 per week. One of those sorry to see him go was Jim Cairns, a 22-year-old detective in Blamey's Criminal Investigation Branch Shadowing Squad who would, one far-off day, lead the biggest anti-war movement Australia had ever seen.

Blamey was shunned and out of work. But with the drift towards war, some people in high places wanted him back in the army. Australia would soon need a commander-in-chief. Critics said he was too fond of the bottle. The same thing had been said of Ulysses S. Grant, Lincoln's commander in the American Civil War. Lincoln's retort was playful—he wished all his generals would drink the same whisky. That was the point, said the Commonwealth treasurer Richard Gardiner Casey, one of Blamey's strongest advocates, arguments about the man's private life were irrelevant. His powers of organisation and leadership were undeniable. Menzies, along with AIF veterans Casey and Sir Henry Gullett, and also Frederick Shedden, the powerful Secretary to the Department of Defence, all wanted him; so, too, did some of the top commanders from 1914–18, White and Gellibrand among them. Other candidates were lobbying but Blamey's lobby won the day—the short, stoutish Blamey took command of the new AIF. He was, his first biographer wrote, 'physically as far removed as a man could be from the "typical Digger" of poetic and journalistic tradition—the lean, lounging, hard-bitten fellow with a sardonic aphorism forever on the tip of his tongue. This hardly mattered since most of the men he was to command also bore astonishingly little resemblance to the popular image.'

When Blamey rejoined the army as Commander, his call for urgent attention to local defence was not heeded. The staff heads of Australia's navy, army and air force were all British officers who owed a higher loyalty to their services in Britain. Government concerns about Japanese intentions in Asia were suppressed. Priority went to helping England in its coming hour of need. 'If Britain can be defeated, we

'The Sentinel'

After he lost his job as Police Commissioner, Blamey took part-time work with radio 3UZ. His weekly fifteen-minute broadcasts in which he used the pseudonym 'The Sentinel' focussed on Australia's unreadiness for war, the dangers of German expansionism and the inevitability of a Pacific war against Japan. The managing director of the *Argus* newspaper, Errol Knox took up his call to spread the word. Knox was an AIF veteran. He asked Blamey to supply military detail for a futuristic invasion novel to be written by one of his journalists. Instalments of the novel were serialised in the *Argus* in 1938 and the book, *Fool's Harvest*, by Erle Cox, was published in 1939. Some of the story-line was supplied by Blamey. It included a sneak attack on Sydney Harbour, battles fought in Newcastle and Port Kembla, capital cities overwhelmed, a bush resistance by Australian fighters and, ultimately, the United States coming to the rescue.

The Strategic Mediterranean and Africa, December 1940

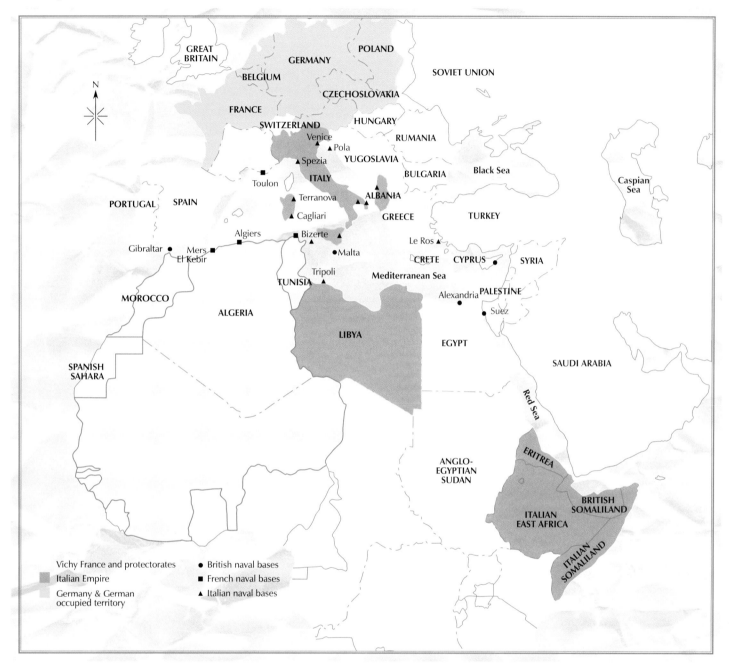

cannot hope to survive alone,' said Menzies. There was some deliberation in the War Cabinet, but first the navy, then most of the air force and then the 6th Division, the volunteers of the 2nd AIF, were placed at the disposal of the British High Command. The navy would go to the Mediterranean; the air force to England; the 6th Division to Egypt, then Palestine, then North Africa.

The popular mood in 1939 was not that of 1914. The experience of World War I had diluted enthusiasm. Australians watched a progression towards war in the 1930s—Japanese soldiers marauding in China, the Italian subjugation of Abyssinia (Ethiopia), the defeat of the Republicans in the Spanish Civil War, the German seizure of Austria and Czechoslovakia, and German demands on Poland. In 1938 newspapers reported the flight of Jews from Germany. Australia pledged to take in up to 15,000 refugees. Cinemas began showing anti-Nazi propaganda films. The sinister intentions of the Nazis were slowly dawning on the people of Australia.

Apprehension and a sense of duty had replaced excitement and a sense of destiny.

When war was finally declared the mood was subdued. Apprehension and a sense of duty had replaced excitement and a sense of destiny. The *Sydney Morning Herald* had called World War I 'our baptism of fire'. In 1939, its editorial was teacherly and sombre: 'It is Britain's war and our war because it is a war to save for the world those principles of justice and freedom upon which our civilisation has been built and which, when they are attacked by force, we must defend by force.'

Those seized by urgency called for self-sacrifice, emphasising the need to curtail theatre and sporting fixtures. But there was not much urgency around—the shows went on and sports continued to be played. The Anglican Canon Hughes, President of the Victorian Cricket Association, explained why it should be so: he could not imagine Hitler or Stalin (equally the enemy in 1939) 'doing the things they had done if they played cricket'. In public Prime Minister Robert Menzies backed these continuities. He seemed intent on a cheery optimism as if his long-held belief in appeasement might still come good. His call for 'business as usual' was a phrase he would live to regret.

Behind the scenes there was more worry about Japan than Germany. Despite British reassurances, both Menzies and Curtin worried that Japan might turn on Australia. For that reason the government did not leap with enthusiasm into the raising of an expeditionary force for service abroad. For a few weeks the emphasis

Japan: the Wild Card

In 1940, the British army had been chased from Europe, most of its equipment abandoned, and England was under siege. The prospect of Japan entering the war was a nightmare. The conclusion was simple: Japan must be conciliated, it must be kept out of the war for as long as possible. While the United States was imposing tighter restrictions on iron and steel exports to Japan and planning for an oil embargo as well, Britain and Australia were trying to organise concessions for Japan in China. American opposition prevented this, but Britain still bowed to Japanese pressure to close the frontiers between China, Burma and Hong Kong, thus further isolating the embattled Chinese. In August 1940, Australia's first Ambassador to Japan, the former Chief Justice John Latham took up his post in Tokyo. The posting lasted just one year, a year in which Japanese intentions became clearer by the day.

On 27 September, Japan signed a Tripartite Pact with Germany and Italy, in which the newcomer to the imperial stage was allotted both the responsibility and the spoils of the Far East and all three signatories agreed to fight the Americans should they enter the war. The Japanese government then sought special rights to oil supplies in the Netherlands East Indies. It was granted air and military bases in French Indo-China which was run by the Vichy government and supported Japanese slaughter in China. Perhaps the Vichy regime in Indo-China saw that Japan was seeking equality with the European powers and capitalising on their vulnerability, a practice those powers had been perfecting for centuries.

But where to strike first? In the Japanese High Command there was a bitter struggle over strategy. The Imperial Japanese Army favoured a northward thrust, a war against the Soviet Union, to be launched from Manchuria. The navy wanted to strike south. The navy won out. In April 1941, Japan signed a Neutrality Pact with the Soviet Union. With an American-led embargo on Japanese oil supplies, seizure of the oil fields in the Netherlands East Indies

became a priority. In July the decision was taken. It would be a war against the Dutch, the British and the Australians and against any colonised people who sided with them. The Japanese had already tried to manoeuvre the Americans into a neutral corner. Their overtures had failed. America too would be an enemy. On 21 July, Japanese troops moved into southern Indo-China. The British and the Americans responded by freezing all Japanese assets held in British and American banks.

At the highest levels in Australia, apprehension had grown sharply since June 1940 when the British government told Menzies 'we cannot spare a fleet for the Far East at present'. The need for home defence and for more troops in Singapore now seriously conflicted with the commitment to support England's struggle and the fight to hold Egypt and the Suez Canal. Australia's perpetual dilemma was never sharper—a small power that could not survive without powerful allies, a government torn between home defence and British military priorities. Where should the military effort fall—on pre-emptive action for the defence of Australia or the salvation of Suez, on self-help or support for great and powerful friends?

In 1940 and 1941, the Menzies government tried to strike a balance by raising a larger home defence force, by sending three RAAF squadrons and two brigades from the 8th Division to Singapore, by retaining the rest of the 8th Division for forward defence positions in Timor and Ambon, and by keeping the weight of AIF commitment in the Middle East. It was a precarious balancing act that still left Australia's defences fearfully thin, which was all the more worrisome as Japan's intentions became clearer. But when Curtin took over the reins of power it was again 'business as usual'. He too put faith into conciliating Japan as did Evatt, his Minister for External Affairs. He did not recall troops from the Middle East. That happened only with the threat of imminent invasion. Curtin, too, was caught in the perpetual dilemma.

Bardia (action leading to the fall of Post 11)
Ivor Hele

*Australian troops disembarking at
Alexandria after the evacuation of Greece
Ivor Hele, 1942*

*Study for Australian troops disembarking
at Alexandria (John Dowie),
Ivor Hele, 1942*

*Study for Australian troops
disembarking at Alexandria
Ivor Hele, 1942*

was on building up the home militias and retaining men in reserved occupations. One major general quipped that the restrictions were so severe only stockbrokers and the unemployed could enlist. Although Menzies is remembered as an Anglophile and devout servant of empire, within weeks of the declaration of war he was being attacked by ardent empire loyalists for dragging the chain and deserting England. His imperial loyalty was complicated by a competing imperative—Australian security. There was a duality of attachment that the men and women of Greater Britain could not always balance—King and country, nation and empire, race and region—and that their public did not always understand.

Menzies was also stalling to obtain a better deal from Britain and troops were a bargaining chip. He wanted a signed contract for the wool clip for the duration of the war, which he received. He also obtained favoured agreements for metals, meat, dairy products and sugar and after that he held out for verbal assurances over wheat.

In the meantime the *Sydney Morning Herald* turned on him, rallying patriots to the cause of an expeditionary force. Letters to the editor supporting the *Herald*'s line suggested a groundswell of imperial loyalty. The formation of a 6th Division was declared on 15 September, but there was no announcement that it would be sent abroad until the end of November and it took almost that long to decide to call the new division a 2nd AIF. Even the promotional possibilities of tradition, the valorous overtones of an acronym, seemed forgotten. For a time the government labelled it a Special Force, as if disguising its purpose. Finally the AIF was cleared for service overseas.

Painting by Norman Lindsay of a working man rolling up his sleeves and getting ready for action. Published in the *Bulletin*.

The men here are getting disgusted with the slowness of the Empire to do something definite, and talking of going home to their jobs soon . . . They will take some holding if they are left in this camp much longer.

Private D. Wall, 2/4 Battalion, letter, c. December 1939

The decision to send 20,000 men to fight in far-off lands was also divisive.

The decision to send 20,000 men to fight in far-off lands was also divisive. Some called it 'theatrical', a face-saving exercise. Others now said home defence was being sacrificed for imperial adventures. There were people on the left wing of politics who were cynical about fighting for any system that had failed so badly in the Depression years preceding the war. A wider spectrum of people spoke of the 'phoney war' or at least sensed it was not yet all-out war and consequently wondered if a country so far away from the conflict should be involved. Some intellectuals, and many in Labor's ranks, thought that 'phoney war' was a phrase with real meaning. Doubts about the war in both England and Australia were often doubts about the leaders, Neville Chamberlain in England and Robert Menzies here. Both were long-time advocates of appeasement. Menzies carried the added burden of the catchy sobriquet 'Pig-Iron Bob' after his insistence, in 1938, that trade in strategic metals to Japan must continue, despite warnings that the metals might return as bombs. Mistrust spread across the traditional parliamentary divide. Britain was at war with Germany at sea, but there was, for more than six months, little fighting on land and in the air. Neither France nor Britain stood in the way of Germany and Russia as they divided Eastern Europe between them. Was this real war?

Not until the shattered remnants of the British Expeditionary Force were evacuated from Dunkirk in May 1940 did the 'phoney war' seem to be over. All-out war against Germany began. At that point Prime Minister Menzies must have pondered the wisdom of 'business as usual', for having in that breath dismissed the war so casually, how could Australians now be martialled for self-discipline

Flight Lieutenant Desmond Sheen receives the Distinguished Flying Cross (DFC) from King George VI, London 1940. Sheen was a former Canberra public servant who joined the RAAF in 1936. He was one of a small number of Australians who served with Fighter Command in the Battle of Britain.

and sacrifice? The nation was riven by differences. Nationalists wanted home defence; imperial patriots wanted Anzacs fighting beside British soldiers in Europe or the Middle East; some trade unionists rejected involvement altogether, fearful that Britain was manoeuvring to turn Germany onto 'socialist Russia'; a few pacifists believed it was going to be a shabby re-run of 1914–18; many citizens were apathetic and indifferent.

The summer of 1939–40 was a hot one, post-Christmas sales were a bonanza for retailers, and Donald Bradman made his 90th century and 34th double century at the Melbourne Cricket Ground in front of a vast crowd. In Europe, combined British casualties by land, air and sea were less than the British road toll. It was hard for Australians to believe the empire was in mortal danger. Many wondered if this was just another in a long line of European catastrophes that had come and gone in the 1930s and whether their comfortable spectatorship might not continue. The indifference was made worse by complacent reading of the progress of the war: J.V. Fairbairn, the Minister for the Air, returned from a tour of France saying the Maginot Line could not be breached by any German army he knew of. When the German Army crashed through Norway, with the help of the local Nazi leader Vidkun Quisling and others, the armchair strategists writing for the press declared the invasion was a colossal blunder on Hitler's part and his downfall was imminent. Early in April 1940, Neville Chamberlain declared that 'Hitler had missed the bus'. After Norway fell people said he must have caught a taxi instead.

Perhaps some Australians thought the war would just fizzle out. There were those who still believed a negotiated peace was possible; and more than a few thought Hitler's defeat was a battle or two away. Among the conservatives, Hughes was closest to the mark when he spoke of a 'supreme crisis'. The problem was facing up to it, as the young John McEwen, Minister for External Affairs, revealed with his delusional comment on the withdrawal from Dunkirk: 'The British troops have been driven into the sea, it is true,' he said, 'but the sea is the natural element of our race.'

The Battle of Britain

In the spring of 1940, German forces overran Norway, Denmark, the Netherlands, Belgium and France. The Maginot Line was bypassed with ease. After Dunkirk, the war in Europe was effectively over for a time. Britain stood alone against Hitler, who was now intent on an invasion across the channel. In May and June, nearly 1,000 RAF planes were lost. Just 500 fighter aircraft and two battle-ready divisions stood between the Nazis and London. From mid July to September the Battle of Britain raged. Australian flyers fought in it and Australian citizens followed it with a strange mixture of detachment, admiration for the British people and anxiety.

Combat Report of Flight Lieutenant S.C. Walch, No. 238 Squadron RAF.

Some 450 Australians were serving in the RAF as the Battle of Britain began. Twenty-two were in Fighter Command and 14 of these were killed in the skies or died as a result of these air battles. The elite squadrons of Fighter Command flew Spitfires and Hurricanes, dubbed the Heavenly Twins, fighter planes that were light, fast, manoeuvrable and a match for the Messerschmidt 109s. From mid July to mid September, outnumbered RAF flyers outflew the Luftwaffe. They destroyed some 800 German aircraft and after Eagle Day, the climax of the battle on 15 September, they were still in command of the skies over England.

The RAF squadrons flew with extraordinary courage and skill, but their losses were fearsome. In the end it was industry that was decisive. British factories were turning out fighter planes at the rate of 500 per month. Germany's production rate was 140 per month and German losses were unsupportable.

On 17 September, British cryptanalysts deciphered a Wehrmacht order cancelling the invasion plans. In their place, Hitler ordered his bombers to attack industrial and then civilian targets—the big cities. Churchill retaliated in kind. The Battle of Britain was followed by the Blitz bombing of English and German cities. Modern warfare was evolving—outcomes in the air were decided in factories on the ground, and civilians in their tens of thousands were targets for destruction.

Members of No. 5 Course, Empire Air Training Scheme, meet English entertainer Noel Coward at Essendon aerodrome, Victoria 1940.

While the army's appeal suffered from popular images of the mud in France in 1917, flight had become the most glamorous symbol of modernity in the inter-war period.

Recruiting rates picked up in response to the crisis. The 20,000 men needed for the 6th Division had responded slowly. That quota took three months to fill. Then Europe's agonies and England's peril made an impact. By March 1940, 100,000 men had volunteered for service; by July, with the Battle of Britain underway, a 7th and 8th Division had been formed with men to spare. More than two-thirds of these volunteers wanted to be airmen. While the army's appeal suffered from popular images of the mud in France in 1917, flight had become the most glamorous symbol of modernity in the inter-war period. Record-breaking flyers, men and women, were accorded Hollywood status as heroes, daredevils and celebrities. The aura of flight drew so many volunteers that many a would-be pilot had to settle for the second option and ended up in the army.

What to do with the air force was another difficult question. Britain could manufacture more warplanes than it could man and the Dominions could man more than they could make. In October, Menzies agreed to a British proposal for an Empire Air Training Scheme (EATS), which in effect turned the Royal Australian Air Force (RAAF) into a training arm of Britain's Royal Air Force (RAF). EATS pooled the air training resources of New Zealand, Australia, Canada and Britain. Over a five-year period Australia sent about 26,000 airmen to England as part of this arrangement. Supporters celebrated a scheme whereby men from several nations might combine to form the crew of a Lancaster bomber for a night raid over Germany. But again controversy emerged from the tension between imperial and home defence priorities. The agreement turned over the operational control of Australia's air forces to another power. When Japan threatened Australia in 1942, about 40 per cent of the RAAF's training effort was tied up in preparing pilots for the air war over Europe, while Australian industry had belatedly shifted manufacture away from trainer aircraft to fighters and bombers. Later in the war, British enforcement of the agreement kept thousands of airmen from the fight against

General Wavell salutes 6th Division, 2nd AIF, troops, 9 June 1940.

Gaza War Cemetery, Anzac Day, 1940. Sergeant Gent of the Postal Unit kneels beside his brother's grave. His brother was killed at Deir Senied in December 1917.

In June the Italians entered the war at the high point of Germany's success in Europe.

General Sir Thomas Blamey (right) with General Giffard on arrival in Palestine, 9 June 1940.

Japan. The lesson of the global conflict of 1914–18, that the identity of Australian forces must be retained, not absorbed indiscriminately into a much larger, British war machine, was lost in the EATS agreement.

In February 1940 the 16th and 17th Brigades arrived in Egypt. The 18th Brigade, completing the 6th Division, was in Britain, having been re-routed on the high seas. It was many months before the 18th made it to the Middle East. The two brigades in Egypt were sent on to Palestine by 'Archie' Wavell, commander of British forces in the region. Wavell did not want the Australians 'running riot around Cairo' as he believed they had in the previous war. The New Zealanders, their discipline in better repute, trained at Maadi in Egypt. Both forces trained hard for months, some Diggers using pieces of wood as substitutes for rifles.

In Palestine there were many reminders of the deeds of the First AIF. At Beersheba soldiers dug out derelict Turkish trenches for use in a training exercise, trenches the Light Horse had galloped over in 1917. At Gaza they visited a cemetery where Australian soldiers lay buried, their headstones emblazoned with the AIF insignia of the Rising Sun. Some of the nurses accompanying them made posies for the graves. There were 49 nurses at 2/1st Australian General Hospital (AGH) at Gaza Ridge. Sergeant Gent from the Postal Unit sat beside the grave of his brother, killed in 1917.

In June the Italians entered the war at the high point of Germany's success in Europe. Like a vulture, Mussolini came in late, for what seemed to be easy pickings. There were half a million Italian troops in Libya and Abyssinia. The one-eyed Wavell— he'd lost the other eye at Ypres in 1917—had about 86,000 troops at his disposal. On paper the odds looked very poor, but only the battlefield could test the odds.

Blamey was in Palestine by late June, facing an entirely unexpected situation. The 6th Division might have to fight the Italian army in North Africa. It was still short of

Lady Blamey comes to Palestine

Blamey's firmness with the British did not win over all his commanders, either in Palestine or at home. He mixed his bull-like energy for desk work and his formidable stands on this or that with a dissipating life that included the fine wines and rich foods of select restaurants in Haifa, Tel Aviv and Jerusalem, and 'short-lived intimacies with accommodating women', to

quote his first biographer. His gout recurred, his girth filled out, and he developed leg ulcers from lack of exercise. There were times when the troops wondered if the 'Old Man' had gone home. His critics grew in number. Sam Burston, the Assistant Director of Medical Services with the 6th Division, spoke to him frankly and told him to get into shape or he would soon be back in Australia. Blamey took the advice. He called in a masseur, adopted a better diet and set about restoring his fitness. And he pressed to have his wife join him, despite the rule banning 'womenfolk' from travelling with officers or men. Menzies broke the rule, partly to keep Blamey on the straight and narrow. Lady Blamey flew to Palestine.

Trooper H. Archer puts finishing touches to the kangaroo symbol on a captured Italian Carro Armato M13/40 Medium Tank, Tobruk, 23 January 1941.

battle equipment and Britain was in no position to supply the Australians. In the desperate exit from France the British had abandoned a vast arsenal. Australia, in fact, was busy sending rifles and ammunition to Britain in 1940. An emissary was rushed back to Australia to plead for weapons and munitions. Some Italian units were now inside the Egyptian border. There was pressure from the highest levels, from Churchill, Wavell and others, to put units of the 6th Division into British formations.

Blamey had a charter set down by the Australian government to resist this. The charter required him to prevent the fragmentation and dispersion of the AIF. The fight for the AIF's integrity in World War I had been hard won only late in 1917. A formidable commander was required, one who could not be duchessed by the smooth tongue of Anthony Eden, the British War Minister, or cowed by the bluff and pique of British commanders. Again and again Blamey told the British that the AIF was a single unit, not to be dispersed without his clear consent, and for now there was no consent. The 6th Division was not ready to fight and would not be dismembered. Blamey used the stand-off to press for equipment for the defence of Egypt. For a time he held sway, but in the longer term the tension between national and imperial priorities saw Australian forces scattered across the globe—in the Mediterranean, Syria, Libya, England, Malaya, Timor and New Guinea.

The Italians crossed the Egyptian border but did not press on. They dug in along the coast, as if stunned by the news of Mussolini's failed invasion of Greece. In December the British Western Desert Force, along with an Indian Division, drove them back into Libya. The AIF was fit and ready. The 6th Division, led by Major General Iven Mackay, now joined the chase.

Mackay had been a citizen-soldier since 1913. He was a company commander at Gallipoli, was twice wounded at Lone Pine, evacuated to England and then rejoined his battalion in France in time for Pozières, Mouquet Farm, Bullecourt and more. He fought through until the bitter end. In peacetime he lectured in Physics at Sydney University and he was principal of Cranbrook School when the war broke out in 1939.

Major General Iven Mackay, August 1941.

At Bardia some 40,000 prisoners were taken and 25,000 more at Tobruk, along with vast quantities of equipment and munitions.

The troops called him Mr Chips. He was a shy, temperate, sometimes pedantic man, and a stickler for discipline, a methodical, clinical planner and a fearless commander.

The 6th Division fought the first Australian land campaign of the war and, unlike Gallipoli, it was a military success. Mackay's notebooks reveal that his planning was meticulous. It extended to notes on daylight intensity and plans to curtail looting after victory:

0635 hours, the shadows of motor cars could be seen
200–300 yards away motor cyclists visible at 300 yards
0645 hours, object much more distinctly visible.
0650 hours, fair general light
Points to guard against:
Scattering of troops from gullies into small parties
All units down to sections must be kept in strict control by leaders.
Guards must be put upon all stores, etc. No looting to be permitted,
especially chianti or spirits.
Deception: work up some ideas . . .

Mackay was determined this beginning would not be a shemozzle like the Anzac landing in 1915. Very little went wrong this time. It was a brief and sometimes brilliant campaign. The 6th Division seized the heavily defended fortresses at Bardia and Tobruk, before sweeping on to Benghazi, all in the space of a month. At Bardia some 40,000 prisoners were taken and 25,000 more at Tobruk, along with vast quantities of equipment and munitions. There were kangaroos painted on the turrets of 127 captured Italian tanks. The grim odds on paper had proved not so bad on the battlefield as the Italian army was poorly led and equipped with obsolete weapons, although some units fought bravely and well. Ivor Hele's painting, *Post 11*, is testament to that. One hundred and thirty Australians died taking Bardia alone.

Radio Rome called the Italian defence of Bardia 'an epic of legendary grandeur' and told a story of a few gallant Blackshirts holding out against hordes of brutal Australians. From Mackay's reticent standpoint, the assault was a 'satisfactory military achievement', and his assessment acknowledged the role of British gunners and tank crews who supported the Australians. Propagandists would talk up the

Australian infantrymen advancing during the dawn attack on Bardia, 3 January 1941.

Wounded Australians at the 2nd Australian General Hospital, El Kantara, reading of their deeds in the local paper, 10 January 1941, after the battle of Bardia, *opposite*.

Australian troops move up to Tobruk's front line, August 1941.

Congratulations flowed in from the King and from Churchill. In London the Daily Express described the Australians as the 'cream of the Empire troops and the finest and toughest fighting men in the world'.

I have just been reading some Australian papers . . . It makes me mad to see pictures of race meetings featuring fit and healthy looking little bastards in civilian clothes sitting in grand-stands at home without even a look of shame on their faces . . . May their dirty little souls rot.

Captain G. Laybourne Smith, 2/3rd Field Regiment, letter to wife, 4 February 1941

national achievement; Mackay recognised the multi-national contribution. Menzies cabled 'We are all proud of you'. Congratulations flowed in from the King and from Churchill. In London the *Daily Express* described the Australians as the 'cream of the Empire troops and the finest and toughest fighting men in the world'. The Washington *Times Herald* carried the headline: 'Hardy Wild-Eyed Aussies Called World's Finest Troops.' *Life* magazine reported 'big rowdy Australians who carry horseplay to terrible lengths in war'.

In Bardia, there was revelry. One Digger galloped through the streets on the back of a white horse. He was dressed in an Italian admiral's uniform and waving a sword. Such men never did the hard fighting, said Mackay, who quickly put an end to the picnic atmosphere. The next objective was Tobruk. There the quiet schoolmaster ordered his troops to 'go in hating', to use the bayonet until the enemy 'prayed for mercy'.

Some were praying for mercy before the Allied land troops arrived. The resolve of many Italian units was weakened by advance attacks from air and sea. The RAAF,

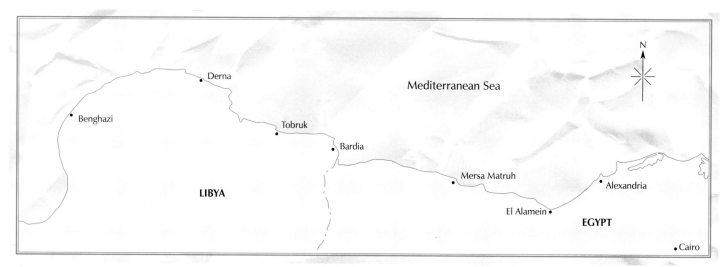

North Africa

armed first with antiquated biplanes called Gladiators, then upgraded to Hurricanes in January 1941, was involved from the start of the desert war. Its fighters moved constantly, leapfrogging the ground troops, maintaining a presence over the battle-field, bombing, strafing and protecting infantry and tanks.

The topography also favoured combined combat operations with the RAN as the key Italian positions, along with lines of communications and roads, were all on or near the coast. Under the command of Captain Hector Waller, the navy's Inshore Squadron of gunboats, destroyers and minesweepers was able to bombard these locations ahead of the land attacks and it was at the shoulder of the fast-moving battle front as it raced across the top of Africa. There were many other tasks for the navy: night offensive patrols, protecting supply ships, water carriers and oil tankers, destroying the enemy's sea-borne supplies, regularly landing fresh water and, crucially, maintaining the sea lanes to keep supplies up to the battlefront.

This strip of coastline across the top of northern Africa, encapsulated the navy's role throughout the Mediterranean: advance and support bombardments and anti-aircraft cover, supply and transportation by sea in the face of continuous and heavy enemy attack from the air, from submarines, from motor torpedo boats, from mines and from shore artillery. This agenda was all the more remarkable because the RAN was no modern exemplar of war craft. There were two heavy cruisers (*Australia II* and *Canberra*) dating from the 1920s, three modern light cruisers (*Sydney*, *Hobart* and *Perth*), and four sloops, only two of which were ready for sea duties. The destroyer force was made up of five almost obsolete vessels of World War I vintage, all five on loan from the Royal Navy, which had intended to scrap them. These were

Sapper A. Bower at 2nd Australian General Hospital, El Kantara, 10 January 1941.

Post 11

Ivor Hele was a successful oil painter when he enlisted in the AIF and went to the Middle East as a private in the Intelligence Section. There he was transformed into Lieutenant Hele, war artist, and told to 'go and paint the bloody war'. About 40 artists in all were appointed to portray World War II and Hele, an Archibald Prize-winner in the 1930s, was one of the first. He was given a truck, paints, brushes and other equipment and sent to the Western Desert where one of his most powerful images was the painting he called *Post 11*, from the attack on Bardia. Like much Australian war art, its emphasis is not primarily on battle but on the portrayal of suffering and comradeship—soldiers salvaging a life from the human wreckage. His men, alive and dead, are uniformly bull necked, square jawed and angular, too uniformly so to be real. But the painting is still powerful. The placement of the fallen beam is suggestive of crucifixion and the chaos of human bodies inside the post is claustrophic. The post has become a tomb.

Bardia, like Tobruk, backed onto the sea. Its landward defences were a semi-encirclement of block-houses, minefields, barbed wire and a deep anti-tank ditch. The plan of attack involved a diversion at the southern tip of the perimeter. While the main attack came from the west, Lieutenant Colonel Godfrey's 2/6th Battalion was to engage the heavily defended strongpoint known as Post 11, on the far side of a wide, deep gorge called Wadi Muatered. The attack called for defiance of long odds set by topography and savage Italian resistance. The Australians had to clamber their way down one side of the Wadi, an almost perpendicular drop of some 200 metres, cross the valley floor through barbed wire, then climb up the steep northern side under heavy fire and storm the Post, embedded in rock. This they did.

It was believed that the post held some 30 to 50 men with perhaps two machine guns and several light Breda automatics. In fact it was a little fortress in its own right defended by two field guns, more than 40 machine guns of varying types, mortars, anti-tank guns and a reserve of 325 rifles.

Platoons of the 2/6th assaulted the post in waves. The Italian gunners poured shellfire into the valley. Machine gun and rifle fire ricocheted in all directions from the rock walls of the Wadi. Sergeant Jo Gullett, a platoon commander, was one of the Australians who came out wounded: 'We stormed their first line of trenches with 50 riflemen, and most of us fell there. The rest of us went into the centre of the position, but only a handful of us reached it and we were not able to hold it. When there were only three of us left, all wounded, we came out. The other two carried me.' And so it went on.

The war correspondent Chester Wilmot wrote that the Italian commander of Post 11 had greatly admired the courage of the Australians and conceded that their assault on that first day very nearly succeeded.

A Breda gun crew on HMAS *Perth* after a full day fighting off German fighter planes, c. 30 May 1941.

Stuart, *Vendetta*, *Vampire*, *Voyager* and *Waterhen*. Several ocean liners had also been requisitioned. All were put at the disposal of the Admiralty in November 1939, and most were operating in the Mediterranean soon after.

The conditions in which the RAN performed its Mediterranean duties varied enormously. There were sunny days when the sea was exquisite shades of green and blue; there were grim grey days inside a northerly gale, and there were days of fierce southerlies when blinding sandstorms whipped the decks and men could only function wearing protective clothing and sand-goggles. In the Mediterranean winter ships routinely slammed into heavy weather, diving and corkscrewing their way forward, with a great green wash crashing over the forecastle. On the upper decks lifelines were rigged; men wore sea boots, oilskins and sou'westers, while below the mess decks were aswirl with clothes and gear hurled adrift on surges of sea water.

There were also quiet days in captured ports when sailors went 'rabbiting' for valued enemy weapons (Breda guns, for example), ammunition and souvenirs.

There were, of course, better times. In the warmer weather there were the chances to swim in the sea, or to eat giant meals in the cafes of Valetta (Malta) or Alexandria, meals that dwarfed the rations on board, which, from an Australian point of view, were somewhat 'English' and meat-shy. The café sector in Valetta was nicknamed the Gut. There were also quiet days in captured ports when sailors went 'rabbiting' for valued enemy weapons (Breda guns, for example), ammunition and souvenirs. By contrast there were busy nights at sea when gunfire, star shells and anti-aircraft flares lit the surrounds with vivid flashes. A diarist on *Waterhen*, during the advanced bombardment of Bardia, recorded the experience of enemy air attacks in which mines and bombs and torpedoes were dropped. The entry is dated Christmas Day.

Torpedo attack by aircraft. 3.30 pm attack by 24 bombers escorted by 18 fighters. First salvo missed Waterhen 40 yards clear on starboard side. Chakla near missed and leaking. Many soldiers killed on shore. Great dog-fight by Gladiators, several bombers and Italian fighters shot down by our fighters. Last Italian fighter escaped from two Gladiators by a vertical dive from about 8,000 feet and made off at sea level (a good effort). 7.15pm torpedo attack by aircraft turned away by fire from Waterhen's main armament. 9 pm left Sollum on patrol to westward of Bardia.

That night *Waterhen* intercepted the *Tireremo Diritto* and sank it after removing '24 men, one Fascist officer and a dog'. By 5 February, Tobruk harbour was in British and Australian hands, taking in over 1,000 tons of supplies from Hector Waller's Inshore Squadron each day. At Derna, further west on the line to Benghazi, fuel ships under the squadron's protection were off-loading 150 tons of petrol per day.

'Pambo' Morrison, driver to the Photographic Unit, comes across a welcome addition to the larder—a beehive in a Syrian garden, 3 June 1941.

The desert offensive was filmed, on land and sea, by war cameramen with the Department of Information's Cinematographic and Photographic Unit. The unit had been formed in 1940, on the recognition of the importance of film as propaganda. It was a vital link with the home-front, bringing Australians closer to their men in battle than they had ever been before, albeit from the safety of a seat in a cinema. Imaginations could now be fed with film footage. The newsreel was an established fixture on cinema programs when war broke out. It was usually about eight minutes long and though it occasionally broke important stories, it was mostly light-weight in subject matter and screened for entertainment. But the war changed expectations. The public wanted to see what they read about in papers and heard about on the wireless. Newsreel companies were keen to profit from the new demand for a visual war, while government was keen to control content in the national interest, to ensure newsreels were effective as propaganda—stirring, rallying, heartening and in no way subversive or demoralising.

Control was easy in Australia because the newsreel companies could not fund a film unit abroad, so the Department of Information (DOI) funded the films using distinguished photographer and cameraman Frank Hurley, the much younger Damien Parer and others. To the general public the war newsreels came to them courtesy of familiar names—Movietone and Cinesound—but the reality was that DOI's photographic team did the fieldwork, they were wartime pioneers of a tradition of government film-making that led to the formation of the Commonwealth Film Unit, then Film Australia. Films were sent back from the battlefront, vetted by the DOI, then passed on to the newsreel companies for editing, embellishing (with archival footage) and screening.

Hurley, the 'mad photographer' from World War I was appointed as head of the Photographic Unit by the new head of DOI, Sir Keith Murdoch. They had met in France in 1916. Acquaintances in one war became opportunities in another. Hurley's appointment was an entrepreneurial masterstroke. His reputation as an Antarctic photographer, his earlier war record and his inter-war film-making adventures in remote regions (a 1921 film was called *Pearls and Savages*) gave him great popular standing. But he was a hard man to work with.

Hurley had a flair for antagonising companions. He gave his men a curfew hour; for a time he addressed his soundman only through their driver, a former snake handler called 'Pambo' Morrison; he warned Parer off all 'heroics'; and seemed to want him confined to Palestine where nothing was happening. Ever the one man band, he was also intent on covering the land offensive with just one assistant. That freed Parer to be on HMS *Ladybird*, a British warship, for the bombardment of Bardia. On land and sea the tiny Photographic Unit followed the 6th Division charge across the Western Desert.

Damien Parer holding
cans of film, Middle East,
February 1941.

Hurley had no chance of filming the start of the battle because it was 5.30 am and the light of the grey dawn was too poor. He had one camera to film a 27-kilometre battle front. The best he could do was to move from one gun emplacement to another, filming the frantic work and the tension of the artillery duels. He filmed some of the infantry going through the wire on their way to what 'Tubby' Allen called fighting nearly as savage as that on the Western Front in 1917, and then he covered the massing of Italian prisoners—a beautifully judged camera pan—showing a line of captives reaching to the far horizon. In theatres in Australia audiences cheered this scene.

Meanwhile, Parer had a 'marvellous ten days with the fleet'. He wrote his parents a long letter all about it, describing some of the action:

My first taste of actual warfare came when we had been bombarding the coastal defences for a while and the Italian shore battery turned on us . . . they were pretty good shots and shrapnel hit the ship from two bursts. We only had one casualty . . . There were several air raids during the day and the following days. The Italians mainly aimed for a larger ship that was with us so I was able to get a marvellous shot of a stick of bombs falling about her. None hit thank God—the Italians fly at a great height keeping in formation and drop their bombs in a dead straight line. Considering their great height they are really pretty straight—but haven't much courage—they don't dive bomb.

In Australia, Ken G. Hall of Cinesound amplified Parer's footage with library shots of shell bursts, knowing his audience would appreciate the dramatised result. The DOI insisted on 'authenticity' but had no problems with these patriotic embellishments.

Parer joined Hurley as the army marched on Tobruk. Hurley now realised he could not cover the land battles alone. At Derna, on the way, Parer followed C Company commanded by Captain Ralph Honner of the Western Australian 2/11th Battalion. But the climax of the attack was at night, and unfilmable. In the town, the next day,

The Australian press
camp, the night before
embarkation for Greece.
The correspondents are
checking travelling rations.
Kenneth Slessor is on
the far right, smoking.
Egypt, 23 March 1941.

Parer introduced himself to Honner, little knowing that they would meet again in far more desperate circumstances in New Guinea the following year. Honner had already witnessed Parer's readiness to share the dangers of the soldiers and admired him for it. He agreed to re-enact the advance into the town for the cameras, but the problem this time was soldiers hamming it up, dancing about, laughing and prodding one another in the back with their bayonets.

The Western Desert offensive came to a halt after Tobruk and the Photographic Unit was soon busy following Mr Menzies around as he toured the troops on his way to London. When the unit arrived in Alexandria, the cameramen took a rest. Suddenly they were joined by the government's official correspondent, Kenneth Slessor, and by journalists Chester Wilmot and Gavin Long. Something was on.

Australian troops depart Alexandria, Egypt, en route to Greece, 1 April 1941.

Churchill hoped a good fight might rally Yugoslavia and Turkey into the alliance against Germany.

The Western Desert offensive was cut short by a controversial piece of Churchillian strategy—the result of frantic liaising in London and Cairo—to send an Allied force across the Mediterranean to defend Greece against a German invasion. Britain had promised assistance to Greece against any aggressor, and Greece was the last surviving ally of the British Commonwealth. This small nation had fought resolutely against the Italians and was ready to fight again, even though a portion of its political leadership and officer class was, at best, uncritical of Nazism. Churchill hoped a good fight might rally Yugoslavia and Turkey into the alliance against Germany. He was also thinking about the United States, which was still an onlooker to the war. The sight of Britain abandoning a small and resolute ally would hardly shift the isolationist lobby in Washington. But if the political repercussions of abandoning Greece were too great to contemplate, it was still an almighty miscalculation in military terms.

Blamey was told that Menzies had consented and Menzies was told Blamey was consulted. Each was allowed to think the other had accepted the Greek venture. Yet both had misgivings about the campaign, Blamey in particular, for he could see that political reasoning was paramount and military thinking subordinate. An operation, which key people believed was a forlorn hope, was put together in haste and effected with deception. The reality, when it was discovered, soured relations. Churchill treated the AIF as a chattel to do with as he pleased. He sacrificed the confidence of Australian and New Zealand politicians for a short-term advantage.

A dispatch rider of the 1st Signals Corps outside a small Greek taverna with patriotic graffiti on the walls.

The village of Elosson after it had been bombed by the Germans, April 1941.

Britain paid a high price in North Africa for the Greek venture. The offensive there was halted as plans for Greece were thrashed out.

A narrow mountain road near Mt Olympus, April 1941.

One commander acted on his doubts about the Greek venture. Horace 'Robbie' Robertson was a Gallipoli and Palestine veteran, a winner of the Distinguished Service Order (DSO) in 1916, a professional soldier between the wars, a dashing commander of the 19th Brigade in the Western Desert and an undisguisedly ambitious man. At Tobruk he refused to take the surrender offered by an artillery colonel who was dressed for the occasion in a decorative uniform splashed with medals with a sword at his hip. 'Throw him back, throw him back,' Robertson ordered. 'Nothing below admirals and generals for me today.' Afterwards he souvenired the personal flag of General Bergonzoli, nicknamed 'Electric Whiskers', the most famous of the Italian desert commanders. At a Benghazi hotel, in the presence of Menzies, Shedden and Blamey, he dined out on tales of his recent exploits. In public Blamey dressed him down: 'Robertson, you are not to give the impression that you alone are fighting the war,' he told him. When the Greek campaign came onto the agenda Robertson took himself off to hospital to have his varicose veins treated. Another officer told him to get better quickly or he would miss the campaign. That was the idea. 'Greece is going to be a disaster,' he said. 'I'm not going to Greece.'

Britain paid a high price in North Africa for the Greek venture. The offensive there was halted as plans for Greece were thrashed out. Had the offensive continued on to Tripoli and beyond, North Africa might have been secured. Instead, North Africa was lost and had to be won again. The 6th Division was withdrawn from the Western Desert as a German general, flushed with success in France, was landing, unmolested, at Tripoli. He was Erwin Rommel. His Afrika Korps soon reversed the Allied gains in the region and besieged the 9th Division at Tobruk.

General Wavell's order of battle for Greece revealed that the fighting would be done mainly by Dominion troops while supply and line of communication duties were left to British soldiers. Yet Blamey was overlooked as commander, as was Major General Bernard Freyberg, VC, the great New Zealand commander. Maitland Wilson, a British general, took command. 'Jumbo' Wilson disliked Australians intensely and Australians returned the dislike. Blamey thought him lacking upstairs ('the grey matter is not quite adequate'). In his diary, Menzies wrote of him as 'tall, fat and cunning'. In Cairo, Wilson had said to Menzies: 'We have had a lot of trouble with your chaps over here you know.' To which Menzies replied: 'I understand the Italians have found them quite troublesome too.'

'Lustreforce', the fighting force for Greece, was to consist of the 6th and 7th Divisions (AIF), a New Zealand division, a Polish brigade, and possibly two British

Greek soldiers welcome Australian troops, Athens, 1941.

'Bloody George', Brigadier George Vasey, 1941.

The Australians and the New Zealanders received a rapturous reception in Greece. Crowds lined the streets and cheered.

armoured brigades, a total of 100,000 men. Fifty-eight Australian nurses went with the AIF. The force was always going to be small, ill-balanced and desperately short of tanks and aircraft cover, but when the 7th Division, the Polish brigade and the second British armoured brigade were withdrawn for duty elsewhere, the shortages and imbalances were made even worse. The Australian War Cabinet was worrying about plans for evacuation before the troops had landed. And so was Blamey. A slender fighting force was being sent to another land to face overwhelming forces—anything up to 27 German divisions was possible. As it happened, ten divisions rolled into Greece through Yugoslavia, while in the air 80 British planes faced a Luftwaffe force of 800. Only at sea were the defenders stronger.

The Australians and the New Zealanders received a rapturous reception in Greece. Crowds lined the streets and cheered. Diggers sat with Greek soldiers, drinking in sidewalk cafes. In the countryside, as they moved north, the Australians were welcomed by peasants—some soldiers slept in beds hastily made up in barns and cottages. Women with children by their sides hastily repaired the roads as convoy after convoy rumbled through village after village.

Even as the troops moved into northern Greece, British command was planning a pullback. The British official history is blunt in its summary: 'The British campaign on the mainland of Greece was from start to finish a withdrawal.'

By 9 April, a thin Allied line was spread across northern Greece. Mackay's forces were on the western end of the line around Vivi. They were astride the road running south from Monastir straight through Greece. His scratch force consisted of 'Bloody George' Vasey's 19th Brigade, the 2/1st Australian Anti-Tank Regiment, the New Zealand Machine Gun Battalion, the 1st British Armoured Brigade, the 1st Rangers

Lieutenant General Sir Thomas Blamey, Lieutenant General Sir H. Maitland Wilson and Major General B.C. Freyberg VC of New Zealand. Greece, 1941.

On 12 April, when the German onslaught began, Blamey announced the formation of the Anzac Corps, the reunion of Australian and New Zealand divisions.

Bombed and machine gunned for over an hour in the pass before reaching our destination. Absolutely rooted.
Lieutenant W. Dexter, 2/6th Battalion, diary, 20 April 1941

Sister M. Hammond (foreground) with Sister M.A. Crittenden resting in a cemetery while avoiding air attack, Argos, Greece, 24 April 1941.

(British infantry) and three artillery regiments in the charge of Western Front veteran Brigadier Edmund Herring. It seemed to Mackay that these mountain ranges, 5,000 to 7,000 metres above sea level, were a natural stronghold and, with adequate supplies, could be stoutly defended. But for troops fresh from the desert, the freezing weather and the terrain—snow, sleet, mud, slippery rocks, deep ravines and gullies—were the first test. The weather kept the Luftwaffe out of the skies for a time, but it also meant men came out of the lines with frostbite in a matter of days. At a forward observation post, 3 kilometres south of Vivi Pass, the Photographic Unit met up with the 19th Brigade: 'What the bloody hell are you fucking bastards doing here?' roared the camera wary George Vasey.

On 12 April, when the German onslaught began, Blamey announced the formation of the Anzac Corps, the reunion of Australian and New Zealand divisions. Part of his proclamation read: 'The task ahead is not nearly as desperate as that which our fathers faced in April 26 years ago.' But the pullback had already been ordered and the fighting in retreat, on widely separated fronts, was desperate. Many an Anzac did not know of the proclamation until the campaign was over. Some, taken prisoner, only learnt of it after the war.

Mackay's trouble was too few forces over too wide a front, no possibility of defence in depth and no reserves. The retreat continued. To the east, more Anzac forces were falling back through mountainous country well above the snowline. At the toughest pinches, small donkeys loaded up with equipment were lifted and carried forward by four men. After three days, the entire Anzac Corps was in a new position—the Olympus–Aliakmon line. The line seemed strong and was reinforced by fresh troops not long disembarked. But the weather was fine and the Anzacs experienced the Luftwaffe for the first time. They took a hammering from the air, the Greeks on their left flank gave way and the retreat was on again, this time over 200 kilometres. The Messerschmidt 109 was a formidable machine. It could inflict immense damage on ground forces and civilians trapped on roads, running across fields, hiding in olive groves or crouching beside tombstones in cemeteries. In a broadcast on his return home, Chester Wilmot, the ABC correspondent, lamented their unchallenged reign: 'At no time during the campaign was there anything like adequate support in the air for the force which had been sent to face the world's most powerful army on the ground.'

In deep, mountain passes where German tanks were punching forward against rearguard units

Emergency loading at night, Perth
William Dobell, 1943

Member of AWAS, Sergeant Frazer
William Dargie, 1943

Operation in a field hospital, New Guinea
William Dargie, 1944

trying to hold, some of the fiercest fighting of the campaign took place. There were rumours that the Australians had refused to take prisoners and the Germans were retaliating in kind. Kenneth Slessor confirmed the rumours, but censorship prevented him using the information. Further south, the Luftwaffe attacked again, this time bombing and strafing convoys bumper to bumper on narrow roads. Freyberg and Mackay both determined to set an example. They moved among the rearguard battalions at the height of the air attacks. Their bravery did not fail to make an impression. Mackay seemed untroubled by the danger, whenever and wherever it came. While others went to ground or hurled themselves into slit trenches, Mackay walked about, calmly surveying the scene. Some men watched him from ground level, peeping out under tin hats.

The nurses were also in retreat. On 16 April medical teams, including five physiotherapists and 49 nurses, were moved further south to Kephissia, not far from Athens, where they set up in several houses and a nearby hotel. Sister Margaret Barnard wrote about the scene in her diary after Allied casualties were trucked in:

Australian nurses of the 2/6th Australian General Hospital, Greece, 1941.

All was a total shambles! The corridors were lined each side with patients on mobile stretchers, and the wards were crammed. Many of the patients [were] still clad in their soggy battle dress, from action in snow country to the North . . . Supplies of all sorts desperately short—no linen—very little medication of any sort, and even food in short supply. One ward with at least twenty amputation patients—some multiple—and not a tourniquet anywhere. At least every second night a convoy of 300 would come in.

The nurses heard the continual scream of air-raid sirens, and the sound of anti-aircraft fire and bombs exploding in the near distance. German mastery of the air was unchallenged while the German army gathered overwhelming forces. On 18 April, the day the Greek Prime Minister, Koryzis, committed suicide, Field Marshal List noted in his diary that his enemy, the Anzacs, would soon be annihilated. That enemy had now taken up positions on a third, shorter line stretching from Thermopylae to the Gulf of Corinth. Here, 2,500 years before, Leonidas and his 300 Spartans had blocked the advance of Xerxes' Persian army and saved democracy. Australian men who, as young children, had read of this battle in their school readers, now stood to arms on the same ground. The ancient legend stirred Churchill into flights of imagination. Perhaps the Anzacs could hold out for a fortnight, or even three weeks? At best they could hold out for a few days. But on the Thermopylae line the Anzacs were digging in. Mackay's force was to cover one of only three passes to the south—the Brallos Pass. There Bloody George Vasey barked his famous order: 'Here we bloody well are and here we bloody well stay.'

Everything was lovely until thirty feet above the trees the air became black with planes . . . and they gave us the doing of our lives. Before a man could move every vehicle in my troop was on fire. True we saved one gun but nothing else.

Captain Laybourne Smith, 2/3rd Field Regiment, letter to wife, 8 May 1941

Field Marshal List noted in his diary that his enemy, the Anzacs, would soon be annihilated.

Victory in Syria

In the middle of 1941, while the North African campaign continued to ebb and flow, British policy makers decided to invade Syria, a French mandate with an administration allied to the Vichy government. The aim was to secure the region, preempt a German invasion and deny German access to key oil supplies. Australian troops, ships and a squadron of the RAAF were committed to the invasion. The 7th Division, and a few units from the 6th, contributed more than half the total troop number and suffered nearly two-thirds of the casualties in five weeks of fighting that were much harder than anticipated. But the successful outcome was a welcome reversal after the failures in Greece and Crete. Oil was a strategic resource of immense importance. The total production of Middle East oilfields in 1940 was a mere 5 per cent of world output, but that oil was essential to Britain's capacity to wage war in the region, and equally important was the necessity to deny access to the enemy.

Members of the 6th Division Signals resting against a camouflaged truck during their retreat through Greece, Brallos Pass, 18 April 1941.

Just two months before these men were unstoppable, celebrating victories in Bardia, Tobruk and Benghazi. Now they dug in, ready to fight and die. They had no idea that orders were on the way for their evacuation and departure from Greece. When the orders came, pride was a casualty, but there was relief, too, for many were exhausted. Mackay chopped up his valise, his rubber bath and his tin trunk. 'No bloody German will have these,' he said.

In Australia, on Anzac Day eve, the Acting Prime Minister Arthur Fadden told the Australian people that it was over: 'Despite the heroism of the new Anzacs, and despite the heavy losses which have been inflicted on the enemy, there is no ground for hoping that the fighting in Greece can, or will, take any turn to our advantage . . . We are now seeing the last stages of a most gallant rearguard action, and it would be foolish to regard it as anything else.' On Anzac Day the *Sydney Morning Herald* declared that the new Anzacs had shown the 'unconquerable strain' of their forebears.

Yet the home front was still not on a war footing; at best it was partially mobilised. The *Herald* declared there was something 'shamefully incongruous' about the way people were at ease, enjoying a holiday, while the Diggers were fighting for their lives abroad. At Tobruk the novice 9th Division was besieged by Rommel. The 9th had orders to hold at all costs. The grimness of the situation was evident when all nurses were ordered out. They were shipped out of Tobruk harbour on a moonless night. Their ship ploughed the perilous bomb alley on the sea run to Alexandria.

The evacuation from Greece was underway. Over five successive nights, British and Australian navy ships and other makeshift carriers plucked the troops from assorted southern beaches. One senior officer told Chester Wilmot: 'You can best help the AIF by getting out now, and trying to tell the truth about what happened here.' Some stayed behind to hold the Germans back until death or captivity. Others who had been cut off in earlier fighting made their way through Turkey or the Greek islands to Crete and North Africa. They hid in olive groves, goat pens and cemeteries and Greek peasants took great risks sheltering them in their homes. Some of the nurses left, but Matron Katie Best was told that 40 of her nurses must stay. Matron Best told her nurses that those who volunteered to stay behind would almost certainly be taken prisoner. Then she asked them to write their name on a slip of paper, together with the word 'stay' or 'go'. Not one sister wrote 'go'. The nurses moved back into their hospital. Some had dressed for the evacuation. Now they dressed for captivity. They donned their Sunday best, their scarlet capes and white caps, and they put on their tin hats. The Luftwaffe was coming, and they worked on. Then a decision was taken to evacuate them too. At a beach near Megara they took a merchant ship for Crete. It was Anzac Day 1941.

Australian soldiers at a Regimental Aid Post in the Brallos area, 16 April 1941.

Such a feeling of relief I don't think you could imagine and we were all giggling like a lot of kids over the beer and cocoa the ships officers gave us.

Captain C. Chrystal, 2/4th Battalion, letter to parents, 2 September 1941

Sixth Division Signals men on board HMS *Wryneck* on the way from Greece to Crete, Mediterranean Sea, Anzac Day 1941.

Water sprays into the air from a near miss during a German bomber attack on HMAS *Perth*, Crete, c. 21 May 1941.

All the cigs we had we 'ratted' off dead Fritzes but most of us smoked grass or grapevine leaves rolled up in any paper we could get, or a pipe made from bamboo.

Private L. Williams,
2/11 Battalion, letter,
3 November 1941

Of the 17,125 Australians who fought in the Greek campaign, 320 were killed, 494 wounded and 2,030 became prisoners of war. The defence of Crete went just as badly. A composite force of Britons, Australians and New Zealanders, supported by Cretan fighters, was overwhelmed after a brief resistance against great odds. Over 16,000 troops were evacuated by the navy, which suffered terrible punishment from air attack during the rescues. Three battalions of the 6th Division were wrecked, 274 Australians were killed and 3,102 became prisoners of war.

Between those killed or captured and those who got away, there was another category—the fugitives. On Crete several hundred Australians lived off the land, eluding German patrols, after failing to get a boat off the island. One of them was Reg Saunders, an Aboriginal from Portland, Victoria, a soldier with the 2/7th Battalion, 6th Division. Saunders fought in numerous savage encounters in Greece and Crete before he took to the mountains where, in groups of two or three, Australians, Greeks, Britons and New Zealanders survived as best they could. They preferred to steal food rather than take the help of the villagers as German forces were executing anyone suspected of aiding them. Many villagers died doing just that. For 11 months Reg Saunders was a fugitive on Crete, known to both the locals and the occupying Germans. He was the only black soldier hiding in the mountains. He finally got off the island on 7 May 1942, and went on to fight in New Guinea where his brother Harry was fighting on the Kokoda Track with the 2/14th Battalion, 7th Division.

By April 1941 military realities were beginning to sink in on the home-front. The Mediterranean theatre was a debacle. Within a month, Britain was on the edge of disaster. The evocative and moving phrase 'brave little England' came into vogue in newspapers and magazines. An intense affection and loyalty now surged into the hearts of thousands of Australians. In the months to come they would follow the trials of the beleaguered British people, stalwart, proud, fierce, before the 'Frankenstein monster' (Menzies' phrase) of fascism. The King and Queen stayed on in London through the Blitz, touring the rubble-strewn neighbourhoods and hospitals and venturing to other devastated cities in their kingdom. In England and

Somewhere at sea, September 1940. Sergeant Reg Saunders.

Tomorrow and tomorrow and tomorrow

Although war news was heavily censored, it was impossible to conceal the fact that the Greek campaign was a disaster. The realisation made a strong impact in Australia. The writer and pacifist Marjorie Barnard wrote to Nettie Palmer on 22 April 1941. 'When I think of the war . . . My heart is molten with grief and anger,' she wrote. 'There's one thing which keeps twisting in my mind like a corkscrew—that 1st battalion AIF was 75 per cent unemployed men. I'm going to write a book.' She did, and the book was one of the most challenging Australian novels of the 1940s, *Tomorrow and tomorrow and tomorrow*.

A futurist account, the novel looks back from the twenty-third century to tell the story of Australia from the 1920s until the destruction of Sydney in the later stages of World War II. Because of its controversial subject matter, the novel was heavily censored in wartime before it was finally published in 1947, and only in 1983 did the full text become available for the first time.

Australia, royal fervour was renewed in these desperate times. The Australian press celebrated the virtues of British character and race. If the war was to produce a great upsurge of Australian nationalism, it is also true that it revived a love of England that has rarely been equalled for its intensity.

This new phase in the war brought new tensions. Wartime paranoia lead to attacks, both verbal and physical, on German and Italian residents of Australia and on Jewish refugees. Italian fruit shops took a hammering. In some suburbs police closed them down as they had become focal points for trouble. Australians lived in an insular country and sustained long-held prejudices and fears of foreigners whom they defined negatively as non-Britons. There was a thin but virulent strain of anti-semitism that was most evident in the *Bulletin*. As huge formations of German planes bombed English cities, and as news of fighting in North Africa reached Australia, particularly the heroic resistance of the 9th Division at Tobruk, suburban paranoias grew. As in World War I, there was talk of changing place names. There were demands for the internment of 'aliens', there were whispering campaigns about 'Nazi sympathisers', wild rumours of public utilities threatened with sabotage and calls for the sacking of German and Italian workers. Sackings followed.

Worst of all, there were attacks on Jewish refugees who were double victims, having fled from persecution and who were now bewildered by the provincial ignorance and meanness they were encountering in this new land. One letter to the *Bulletin* suggested the Jews might have brought trouble on themselves: 'May there not be more than a grain of truth in Germany's statement that these people by their sweated labour, employer and employee alike, had brought down the standard of living to a race of slaves.'

There were demands for the internment of 'aliens'.

Wounded allied prisoners of war at a German POW hospital in Athens, 1941.

Some ex-servicemen were anxious to protect public utilities from sabotage. Many were keen to help the war effort in any way they could. They felt an obligation to do their best again. They began to rally to the causes of beleaguered 'little England', to preventive action in Australia, and to the defence of Australia should events come to that. They began to drill in public places, to make speeches and take sombre oaths at cenotaphs. The government quickly formed the Volunteer Defence Corps (VDC) to recognise former AIF men, give them purpose, and rein in the spontaneous formation of private armies around the country. The VDC was given a charter: 'to preserve law and order, protect public utilities and prevent subversive activities by aliens or disaffected persons'. There was not a lot to do. The organisation struggled on, but many members dropped away. Some kept busy as air-raid wardens teaching air-raid precautions, but the general public for the most part did not take them seriously. It was inconceivable that a bomb could fall on an Australian suburb.

A significant number of women felt sidelined too. Not content with the traditional work women did in World War I, their keenness to do more was expressed in a poem published in the *Sydney Morning Herald* in June 1940:

We want to do more,
To help win this war,
Than sit with our knitting.
This business of sitting
While Hitler is hitting
Our men is a bore.
WE WANT TO DO MORE

Quite spontaneously, women's auxiliaries formed, but unlike the ex-servicemen, whose energies the government sought to channel, the women were ignored. They pressed on regardless, intent on learning new skills and working in areas outside of knitting, food preparation and first aid. They drove trucks, ambulances, bread carts and motorcycles. They learnt morse code and other forms of signalling to free up men to enlist; they learnt aircraft maintenance; they designed and made their own uniforms, disregarding the government's refusal to recognise them; and they formed the WANS (Women's Australian National Services) to coordinate all the new groups working in areas that were formerly off limits to women. Their patron was Lady Wakehurst, wife of the Governor of New South Wales. They made it plain that if the government ever allowed women to enlist, they would be ready. Women's magazines began to change, portraying the new work possibilities as attractive options.

Not all women were adventurous in this way. Many were more comfortable with work in the traditional areas such as fund-raising. There was still plenty of knitting required, including polo-neck sweaters and scarves for RAAF men. Some continued to knit socks even though machine-made varieties were now the norm. But the greatest demand was for canteen staff, as there was now a large standing army based permanently in Australia (the militia), and women found new work preparing and serving food to troops on leave.

A sheep station near Bethungra, NSW, September 1941. The weekly sewing bee for the men at war, *top.*

Women at work on 'Killara', a sheep station near Stawell in Victoria, sometime in September 1941.

These changes in the labour force were signs of a war economy slowly taking shape. The war economy was like a jigsaw puzzle barely commenced, with most pieces still to be put in place, to fit smoothly and efficiently into the overall picture of production, a picture which in turn fitted into a larger jigsaw—that of the Allied war economy. Australians had only ever known war as a distant thing. Unless their own land was in great peril, they would not readily accept increases in taxation, directives telling them where to work or cuts in living standards— the social and industrial unrest of the previous war was testimony to that.

For the first two years of World War II, the home-front was saved from real severities. In Britain, in 1941, war expenditure was 52 per cent of national expenditure and though rationing spread the burden, hardships were many. In Australia things were different. War expenditure had risen from 1.4 per cent of national expenditure in the year before the war, to 15.3 per cent by June 1941. Living standards had barely changed. The contrast was stark on New Year's Eve 1940. In Australia there were illuminations, dance bands and fireworks—rockets soaring into the air, star shells dissolving into exquisite patterns high in the night sky. Britain was blacked out for protection against night squadrons of Nazi bombers.

Menzies' slogan in the September 1940 election was 'Labor Fiddles while London Burns'. He scraped home with the barest majority and within his own party his downfall was being plotted. Many thought he was the fiddler. Parer's impression of Menzies in the Middle East was that of a tourist intent on shooting his own home movies. Parer filmed Menzies filming. But Menzies had at least laid the groundwork for a shift to a war economy earlier in 1940. In the week of Dunkirk, late in May, he appointed Essington Lewis Director-General of Munitions. Lewis had the face and the build of an old prize fighter. He was 59. As managing director of BHP, the 'steel master', he was already linked to the aircraft, shipbuilding, heavy engineering and munitions industries. The *ABC Weekly* reported that he had 'the driving force of a battering ram and the energy of a steam hammer' but he was so retiring no-one could find a photograph of him. On his desk at BHP was the sign 'I Am Work'.

AUSTRALIAN COMFORTS FUND

A poster issued by the Australian Comforts Fund.

The Prime Minister, Robert Menzies, filming an oil tanker burning in Tobruk Harbour, February 1941, *left*.

Essington Lewis, Director General of Munitions, August 1940, below.

A recruiting poster showing women of the armed forces, a nurse and a factory worker.

A woman using an electrical riveting gun in the assembly of a Beaufort tail plane in the Department of Aircraft Production's Beaufort Division, Fairfield, Victoria, 1942.

Lewis was given powers that, in Menzies' words, were 'as wide as the sea and as high as the sky'. Overnight he became an industrial tzar. The entire economy jumped to his dictates. If he declared that boots or balaclavas or bottled lolly water were munitions, then munitions they were. He had direct access to the War Cabinet and the chiefs of staff of the armed services. He could compulsorily acquire any tools, factories or buildings he required, anywhere in the land. His powers represented a wholesale invasion of industrial routine that, some said, was preferable to a wholesale invasion of Britain, or Australia.

Before the war, Australia produced a range of arms and munitions and this productive capacity, though underutilised in 1940, was still useful in equipping the militia and the 6th Division, and in supplying Britain after its huge losses in France. Australia shipped 30,000 rifles to Britain in 1940, a year in which Britain itself produced only 81,000 rifles. By June 1941, Australia's supply role had stepped up. Anti-aircraft guns were shipped 'Home' along with 100 million rounds of small arms ammunition and 182,000 mortar bombs.

Lewis had drawn together talented industrialists and civil servants into a round table of directors who now ran all branches of war production. He made a chemical engineer and senior munitions man his Deputy Director-General; he made a former Victorian Railways Commissioner the Director of Aircraft Production; the Managing Director of GMH was appointed Director of Ordnance Production; a large Sydney manufacturer got the job of overseeing gun ammunition; an ICI man got explosives supply; a New Zealand trained geologist with a background in BHP got materials supply; a military engineer became Director of Machine Tools and Gauges; a Melbourne accountant and businessman was made Director of Finance; and J.B. Chifley, a former Defence Minister in the Scullin Labor government, a one-time locomotive driver, got the job of Director of Labour.

In the first six months, the output of munitions nearly quadrupled. The first Bren machine guns to be made in Australia were completed five months ahead of schedule, and a country that had never made a weapon larger than a machine gun could now produce a 25-pounder made up of 5,000 components, only one of which came from outside Australia. It was a hurried transformation, but the industrial basis for war had been laid before 1939, and much of the skill and knowledge needed was available. The shift to a total war footing was underway when the Pacific War began.

The war economy created even wider opportunities for women. About 1,000 women were employed in defence industries in September 1939. That number had risen to 71,200 in December 1941. The *Australian Women's Weekly* had at first assumed that women's role would not be much different from that in the last war: 'Men must fight and women must work so that peace may come again. Mouths must be fed, beds made, socks darned . . . The majority serve best in keeping the family cheerful and happy, in keeping the doors of the home bolted against uncertainty, panic or nerves.' But by mid 1940, an *AWW* reporter was glamorising women's work in the munitions industries:

> *From them all I gained a picture of Miss Munitioneer . . . She is surrounded by the whirr of machinery, her pretty face set in intense concentration (her hair and complexion just so) and her deft fingers capably, ceaselessly engaged on some small part of the enormous and complex job of munitions making . . . They really feel that they are doing something tangible towards helping to win the war . . . Pretty brunette Winifred Atkinson . . . gave up a good job at a confectionary factory. 'I could go back there and I like it. But I have a brother overseas. I feel somehow I'm helping him.'*

Work for women in munitions led into an even more exclusively male bastion—the armed services. Women still figured in recruiting posters as passive symbols of higher virtues (love, family, motherhood) and as potential victims in war. There was a poster that took their moral power one step further. The 'Mister, here's your hat' poster was a slightly kinder alternative to the white feathers of World War I. But by mid 1941 such stereotypes were under challenge. Women were at last winning access to the workforce, and to the services.

Menzies' four months in London (January–May 1941) had been an eye opener. He observed Churchill's total domination of the War Cabinet, he toured the ruins of various cities and he even experienced a night of Blitz. He also took note of British women, in vast numbers, contributing to war work of all kinds, including work in the services. The door was opened to Australian women when the government offered them 250 positions in the RAAF. The positions were for wireless and teleprinter operators. A Manpower officer thought the change would please everyone. 'Men are seldom satisfied with these duties and invariably try to transfer to other duties,' he wrote. 'These duties can be competently carried out by women.'

Recruitment was a serious problem. Some recruiting drives turned into virtual circuses to win signatures for the AIF. In country towns mobile recruiting units worked all day long, with a sergeant interviewing likely candidates while a van cruised up and down the main streets playing patriotic songs and calling for recruits over a loudhailer. In Orange, New South Wales, the recruiting team organised a picture show and community singing and then brought on 'Don Athaldo' who lay on

Pressing .303 cartridge cases at the Small Arms Ammunition Factory, Footscray, Victoria.

Work for women in munitions led into an even more exclusively male bastion—the armed services.

Lands Department Clerk, Leo Gibney, applying to join the Air Training Corps, Melbourne, October 1941.

A flight of WAAAF aircraftwomen at the No.1 School of Technical Training, RAAF, West Melbourne, 1941.

The women's pay was inferior to men's, but many women were earning more than they had ever earned before.

a bed of nails while another burly man broke rocks on his chest with a sledge-hammer. When it was over, Don Athaldo showed the audience the punctures on his back and declared that was the number of recruits he wanted.

In August 1941, while exhausted Australian troops at Tobruk were still under seige and RAN ships ran bomb alley to bring them water, food and munitions, Percy Spender, the Minister for the Army, announced the formation of the Women's Home Army (WHA). Members of the WHA would take over in occupations ranging from cooks and clerks to mechanics and tailors, in order to release more men for enlistment. The women's pay was inferior to men's, but many women were earning more than they had ever earned before. As women moved into new kinds of required work an acute shortage of domestic servants began to trouble the rich. Domestic servants were notoriously underpaid and were voting with their feet. These changes didn't disturb the rich only. There was resistance to every female step into new territory and it was registered in the press. Letters to the editor and cartoons led the way, belittling, demeaning or sending up female workers, playing on appearances or temperament rather than on skills or leadership qualities. Changes in the workforce unleashed all manner of hilarity, insecurity, prejudice and bigotry in the black-and-white art of newspapers and magazines. If cartoons are a weathervane of public feeling, the balance of that feeling tilted clearly in the direction of unease.

After Greece and Crete, Mackay was determined that his 6th Division would be rebuilt to fight another day under his command, but the government had other plans for him. He was to return home to Australia as Commander in Chief of Home Forces. It was another sign of unease over Australia's security. Mackay was now Major General Sir Iven—he had been knighted in the field after the Western Desert offensive. Near Cairo he reviewed what was left of the 6th Division. He gave his troops a glowing tribute and reminded them of something: 'A good battalion can fight its way out of anything.'

The Tobruk Ferry Service

The Destroyer HMAS *Waterhen* takes water over her bow after she has been crippled by German dive bombers, 29 June 1941.

The forces holding Tobruk needed food, fresh water, replacement weapons, ammunition, petrol, oil, and medical and maintenance supplies. They needed to evacuate the badly wounded, send sick men out and bring new men in. All this was done via the sea, through Tobruk harbour. The supply of Tobruk was largely maintained by destroyers of the Inshore Squadron under Captain Hector Waller. Destroyers shuttled back and forth from the Egyptian ports of Mersa Matruh and Alexandria. Other destroyers from the Mediterranean fleet were intermittently involved, but the mainstays of the shuttle were the old destroyers of the RAN, which had all been built in 1917–18 and were dubbed the ancient warriors—*Waterhen*, *Vendetta*, *Voyager*, *Vampire* and *Stuart*.

Their perilous journeys along bomb alley off the African coast began in May 1941. *Voyager* and *Waterhen* made the first runs on 5 and 6 May. *Vendetta* followed on 8 May but all three were then caught up in the battle for Crete until later in the month. After that interlude the ships of the Tobruk 'Ferry Service' began a continuous shuttle, an unchanging routine, which might have been drearily repetitive had it not been so dangerous. *Stuart*'s diarist recorded the regular features of the run:

> Morning of the first day sailed from Alexandria for Tobruk with troops, ammunition and stores. Air attacks at so and so and so during the day. Arrived Tobruk in dark, unloaded and took on so many wounded, 200 troops, and ammunition empties, and proceeded to Mersa Matruh. Air raid at Matruh. Next day embarked ammunition and stores and sailed for Tobruk. Air attacks . . . Tobruk continually raided throughout stay. Air attacks on passage back. Arrive Alexandria. And then, 36 hours later, the same thing all over again.

It was an exhausting cycle with little rest or sleep for the men who rarely woke naturally. Their sleep was almost always broken by the sounds and shock of bombs and bullets. On 9 July, *Stuart*'s diarist recorded a crowded hour, not atypical, with 'heavy moonlight and dawn attacks by enemy bombers at 0508, 0509, 0512, 0520, 0521, 0535, 0538, 0607, 0616'.

The Australian destroyers made a total of 139 runs. *Vendetta* set the individual record with 39 runs in all. From the end of May until early August, *Vendetta* carried 1,532 troops and 616 tons of supplies to the embattled fortress, brought 2,951 wounded or exhausted men away, and carried prisoners of war back to Egypt.

Sometimes the sloops *Parramatta* and *Yarra* did escort duty with slow convoys but this method of supply was even more dangerous, for the round trip took 48 hours and included two full days exposed. The convoys hugged the coast on the first day for fighter protection, then, with a good offing, they pushed hard through the night hoping to approach Tobruk on a south-westerly course the next afternoon.

On one run, late in June, *Parramatta* and the British sloop *Auckland* were escorting the petrol carrier *Pass of Balmaha* to Tobruk. It was 5.50 pm when three formations of sixteen dive bombers attacked. *Auckland* emerged from a cloud of smoke, badly damaged and careering towards *Parramatta*, which took evasive action. *Auckland* was a wreck behind the mainmast, with no stern visible, ablaze yet with guns still firing. *Parramatta* closed and dropped whalers, skiffs, lifebelts and floats as the men of the *Auckland* abandoned ship. *Waterhen* and *Vendetta* received news of the attack and steamed towards the battle. As the dive bombers came in again, *Parramatta* was caught at a disadvantage for she was surrounded by men, struggling in the water. The men in the water were machine-gunned by the attacking aircraft. Nearby the *Auckland* exploded with a force that lifted her 'slowly and steadily about 6 or 7 feet in the air'. Her back broke, she rolled and sank. For nearly two hours the dive bombers kept coming, only relenting when darkness fell. *Parramatta* headed back to Alexandria with 164 survivors.

Waterhen took the damaged petrol tanker in tow and delivered her precious cargo into the harbour at Tobruk. Four days later, on another ferry run, *Waterhen* was attacked by dive bombers, holed and crippled and sunk. The 'old Chook' as the destroyer's crew affectionately called the ship, was the first of the RAN ships to be lost through enemy action.

Soon after, a British Admiral signalled Lieutenant Commander Swain, 'late of HMAS *Waterhen*'. His message stands as a reminder that war is as much a story of the ledger book, finance and debt, as it is a story of fighting: 'His Majesty's Australian Ship *Waterhen* having been sunk by enemy action, it is my direction that she is to be regarded as having been formally paid off on Monday 30th day of June, 1941.'

Waterhen was on loan to Australia from the Royal Navy, as were three other destroyers. The loss of *Waterhen* raised the question of who would pay. The conditions of the loan arrangement required the Commonwealth government to return the destroyers at some time or, if they were scrapped, to pay His Majesty's government the scrap value. The date for scrapping had long passed, the Australian government being quite happy to persist with ancient warriors beyond their prime. And there was no provision in the conditions of the loan covering the loss of the ships in war or any other circumstance, an extraordinary oversight. The Admiralty had advised the British government that, had the ship been lost in peacetime, the Commonwealth would have been billed for the scrap value. But since it was lost in war, in the Allied cause, no claim for payment would be made. When the wounded *Waterhen* sank to the bottom of the Mediterranean, she took His Majesty's invoice with her.

That evening he had four incisors removed by an army dentist and a denture fitted. In the morning he made a broadcast to Australia with a bit of a lisp. He conferred with Blamey, lunched with his daughter Jean (there were now Australian 'womenfolk' aplenty in the Middle East, following the Blamey precedent), watched Walt Disney's *Pinocchio*, then left on a flying boat. It was a habit, at that time, for Allied generals to fly around the world in disguises that were frequently as funny as they were transparent. In Athens before the Greek debacle, 'Jumbo' Wilson went about as a civilian called Mr Watt, an identity that fooled nobody. Mackay's identity was typically untheatrical. He travelled in civilian clothes under the name 'I.G.

An Australian gun crew of 8 Battery, 2/3rd Light Anti-Aircraft Regiment, in action at Tobruk, June 1941.

Mackay, Lecturer'. He had a stopover in Singapore where he conferred with British service chiefs and with Major General H. Gordon Bennett who was unhappy as always, this time because he was in command of the only idle division in the AIF and only a fraction of that division was with him. Malaya was the quiet sector. After that encounter, Mackay dined with his son, Iven John, who was an officer there with the 2/18th Battalion, destined for captivity. On 22 August 1941 he arrived in Australia to a hero's welcome. He was 'Mackay of Bardia' and 'Mackay of Tobruk'.

But Tobruk, under the command of Major General Leslie Morshead, veteran of Gallipoli and Ypres, had now been under seige by Rommel's forces for some five months. The 9th Division was trapped there, exhausted but unyielding. In the fortress, nearly 700 Diggers had already been killed and total casualties were moving towards 3,000. Mackay was astonished at the complacency he encountered in Australia. Speaking at a graduation ceremony at Melbourne University he decided to make his audience squirm. He described the AIF as the 'cream of our manhood'. He said he feared these men would look for reinforcements in vain. He spoke of 'face saving', of 'sheltering in schools and universities', while the AIF was fighting to save them all.

A week later Menzies resigned. He had lost the confidence of the people and, more importantly, of many in his party. He bowed to the inevitable, but stayed on in the Cabinet as Minister for Defence Coordination. The new leader was 'Artie' Fadden and he ruled for 40 days and 40 nights before the two Independents who sustained the Conservative government switched sides and put Labor into power. On 7 October, John Curtin became Prime Minister. Nothing much changed. The steady building of the war economy continued, the pace and trajectory set by Menzies was sustained. Australia was winding up slowly. A week after the election a bumper crowd turned up to see Skipton win the Melbourne Cup. Another week passed and Blamey was back in Australia, briefly. He accused Australians of a 'carnival spirit'. He warned those who listened to his broadcasts that Hitler's devastation in Europe would be carried throughout the world. He said Australians were like 'gazelles in a dell on the edge of a jungle'. Then he left for the Middle East. Three weeks later the Pacific was ablaze. Aggressors from the jungle were at the northern doorstep. The Japanese were coming.

So I'll pick up my Lee Enfield, and buckle my web about,

Though I'm a flamin' gunner, I'll see this business out,

If I stop a bullet I'll die without a moan,

'cos they've got me flamin' back up,

My friends who stayed at home.

Lance-Sergeant H.W. Adeney, 2/2 Field Regiment, letter to wife, 24 July 1941

Three prime ministers within two months: John Curtin, A. W. ('Artie') Fadden and Robert Menzies.

A 3.7 inch gun of the 192nd Anti-Aircraft Battery, Royal Artillery, in action during a night raid, Tobruk, 30 September 1941, *opposite*.

4

NEVER
MORE ALONE

1942 – 1945

Japanese offensive operations 1941–1942

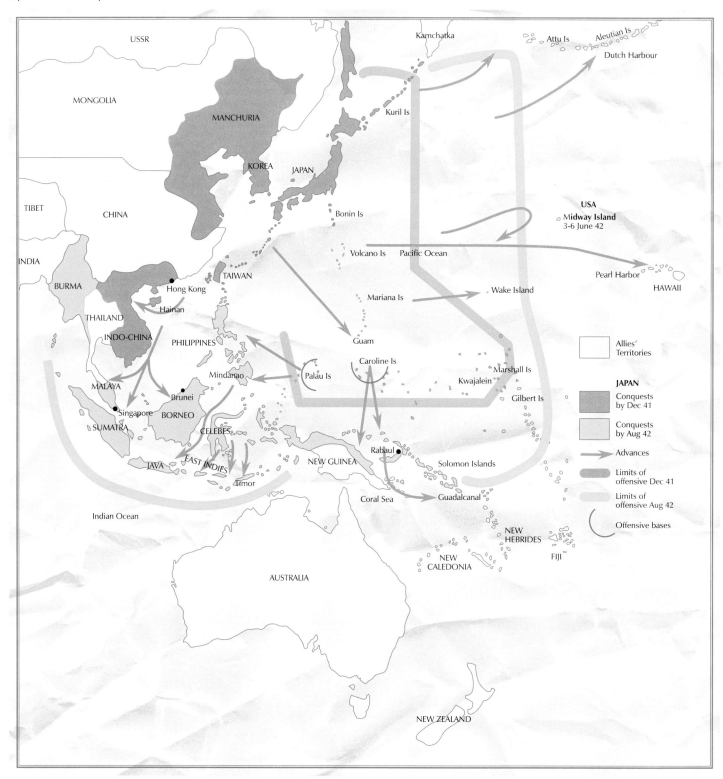

Adapted from *The Penguin Atlas of World History*, volume 2, Penguin Books, Harmondsworth, 1978

When Japan attacked the US naval base at Pearl Harbor on 7 December 1941, the war became a world war and Churchill was immensely pleased. He called it the 'greatest joy' because he believed that with the industrial and military might of the United States, Britain would be on the winning side after all. In Australia there was no such pleasure. The Japanese were racing south, triumphant over all opposition. There was talk of Newcastle being another Tobruk and Sydney another Leningrad, but there was also pessimism and panic and the terrifying thought that this could be the end of a British people in the south seas.

I N the Philippines, American troops under a reinstated retiree named General Douglas MacArthur were in retreat. Off the coast of Malaya (now Malaysia) the British warships *Prince of Wales* and *Repulse* were sunk. Those two ships were all that Britain could spare—the fleet to Singapore—and their loss was a terrible shock to Australians. Japan now had total command of the sea and control of air space over Malaya.

Australian troops on the mainland fought valiantly but were overwhelmed as were British and Indian forces. A British general described the Australian defence at Muar River as an 'epic of the Malayan campaign'. The aftermath of that battle was a sign of things to come. Captured Australians, many of them wounded, were rounded up, kicked and cursed, beaten with rifle butts and jabbed with bayonets. At sunset they were trussed up with wire and rope, led away and executed. Their bodies were doused with petrol and burned.

Possibly a million civilians and some 85,000 soldiers flooded onto Singapore island. Churchill demanded a 'last man, last round' defence of the island and the city, but Lieutenant General Percival, the British commander, sensed it was hopeless; his own failure to prepare adequate defences ensured that—artillery and aerial bombardment and starvation lay ahead with no possibility of relief. Poorly led and demoralised, discipline declined and the unity of some troops disintegrated.

The 8th Division, AIF, was short of artillery, transport, anti-armour and anti-aircraft weapons, divisional support and even machine guns. There were sections of the division that had little training either at unit or formation level. There were sections that had not even qualified with small arms. The last of the fighting troops retreated across the causeway onto the island and prepared to fight again. Combined forces, including the Australian 21st Brigade, fought a major rearguard action, but were

Australian troops of 2/7th Cavalry Regiment advance on Buna, Papua, through knee-high swamp, December 1942, *previous page*.

The USS *Arizona* explodes during the Japanese attack on Pearl Harbor, 7 December 1941, *below*.

Lieutenant General
A. E. Percival surrenders all
British forces to Lieutenant
General T. Yamashita,
Commander-in-Chief (far left),
Singapore, 15 February 1942.

*Men slumped
onto the well-kept
lawns of expatriate
mansions or sat
in the gardens of
the Anzac Club
and wept.*

Sister Elaine Balfour-Ogilvy,
one of 20 nurses massacred
by Japanese troops on
Banka Island, after the
fall of Singapore.

forced to give ground. By 12 February, the Japanese were half-way across the island and in control of the water supply, the reservoirs in the central hills. By 15 Febuary the Singapore naval base and the city, on the island's southern tip, were ensnared. Now the provosts (military police) could detect a changing mood among the troops, a mood which some of them shared. 'Most of us,' said one of them, 'had the bitter feeling that we had been sold down the river.' The provosts tried to do their job, but to no avail—the threat of being shot had little effect on hundreds of soldiers who now streamed towards the wharves, intent on escape.

There was confusion and a sense of hopelessness. As the battle continued, some 2,000 AIF men wandered around Singapore. The provosts, mobile in whatever vehicle they could scrounge, were out on shell-holed roads, trying to round them up. The situation grew so desperate that they were called in for front-line action but they were in no mood to fill in for the fraction who would not fight. The enemy closed in on the city. Resistance fell apart. There was a constant flow of deserters to the rear, some heading for the wharves, some ransacking shops for grog. Men slumped onto the well-kept lawns of expatriate mansions or sat in the gardens of the Anzac Club and wept.

It was over. On 15 February Percival surrendered. In little more than two months, three divisions of the Japanese Imperial Army under General Yamashita had conquered Malaya and Singapore, killed 8,000 Allied troops including 1,789 Australians, and turned 130,000 soldiers into prisoners of war, 15,395 of these from the 8th Division.

Simultaneous with the Allies' loss of Malaya and Singapore, the Japanese advanced east and south, through Borneo, Java, Ambon and Timor. Troops had seized Rabaul in New Britain and from there fighter planes flew across New Guinea to attack Port Moresby. Four days after the fall of Singapore, the first air raid on Darwin took place with the loss of 243 lives. There was a rush of residents southwards towards Alice Springs. A week later HMAS *Perth* was sunk in the Battle of Sunda Straits. The *Perth*, in company with USS *Houston*, had engaged a large Japanese convoy and inflicted great damage upon it, but both the *Houston* and the *Perth* were lost. The *Perth*'s Captain was Hector Waller, formerly of the Inshore Squadron in the Mediterranean. Waller was last seen on the bridge as his ship went down.

In 1939, Menzies had followed Britain to war. In 1941, two days after Pearl Harbor, Curtin declared war on Australia's behalf. The King, Curtin said, had authorised the declaration solely on the advice of his Australian ministers. It was a small step, but the first in an emotional distancing between Britain and Australia that grew greater as the Japanese moved south. On 27 December, Curtin made his now legendary call to America:

Australia looks to America, free of any pangs as to our traditional ties or kinship with the United Kingdom. We know the problems that the United Kingdom faces. We know the constant threat of invasion, we know the dangers of dispersal of strength, but we know, too, that Australia can go and Britain can still go on. We are therefore determined that Australia shall not go…

Ships ablaze in Darwin harbour after the first Japanese air raid on Australia, 19 February 1942.

Churchill was furious. He called Australians 'bad stock', but then he narrowed that abuse down to the government alone. Behind closed doors Churchill said if the Australians were going to squeal he would send them all home again out of the various fighting zones. Menzies was also upset, claiming that Curtin's call was a 'great blunder'. He seemed to think Curtin was dispensing with traditional ties when that was not the issue at all. The issue was survival. Traditional alliances could not defend Australia. Australia could not stand alone against the Japanese. Who might stand with Australia if the British could not? There was only one possible answer.

The tensions between Canberra and London increased through January 1942, as Japanese successes continued. At an Anglo-American conference on strategic planning, the Australians were excluded. The small fry, feisty ally or not, took no part in the big decisions. The big decision, now confirmed, was the 'Beat Hitler First' policy, which had been prepared in 1941. It meant that the war against the Japanese would be a holding operation—the bulk of men and resources would continue to go to Europe and the Middle East. On 23 January the accumulated resentment of the Australian Cabinet poured into a cable from Curtin to Churchill. The cable warned that the evacuation of Singapore would be seen as an 'inexcusable betrayal'. It went on:

> We understood that it was to be made impregnable and in any event it was to be capable of holding out for a prolonged period until the arrival of the main [British] fleet.

The bluntness, scratched by the pen of H.V. Evatt, Minister for External Affairs, was close to insult. Wartime realities compelled Australia to look to its own defences. In February, Curtin opposed the Churchill plan to divert Australian troops, the 6th and

There is no doubt that if there is any threat to Australia a number of us must go home. When all is said and done the brains of the Staff Corps are over here and if anything important is to be done at home some of us will be wanted.

George Vasey, letter to wife, December 1941

One day we heard there was a Jap convoy heading this way . . . Most of the boys played cards to try and take their minds off it . . . Daylight came and we wondered how long we had to live.

Private J. Armstrong,
2/21st Battalion,
POW diary

7th Divisions, from the Middle East to Burma, to prop up the defences there. A few advance units in a fast troopship had already landed in Java, destined for captivity. Before more troops could land, Curtin directed the remaining convoys home. Churchill countermanded the direction. Curtin countermanded Churchill. The contest of wills is evident in the cables exchanged.

Churchill to Curtin: 'We could not contemplate that you would refuse our request, and that of the President of the United States, for the diversion of the leading Australian division to save the situation in Burma.'

Curtin to Churchill: 'We feel a primary obligation to save Australia not only for itself but to preserve it as a base for the development of the war against Japan.'

Curtin is remembered as the leader who finally stood up for national over imperial priorities but Artie Fadden, the Prime Minister who preceded him as PM for just 40 days, had done something similar. In September 1941, Fadden and his Cabinet had stood firm behind Blamey on the question of withdrawing the besieged and exhausted 9th Division from Tobruk. The 9th had held the old fortress, and the barbed and battered country around it, for nearly six months. Churchill wanted

Perth to POW

Australian POWs, Thailand, c.1943.

When HMAS *Perth* went down, one small group of survivors managed to reach a little island in the Sunda Strait, steal a boat, stock it with a few rations and set out for Java, hoping to find the island still in Dutch hands. They arrived to find that the Japanese were in control and they were prisoners of war.

One of these survivors was Ray Parkin, Chief Quartermaster on the *Perth*, a vivid and determined diarist and, it was later discovered, a gifted writer. Parkin spent the next 15 months on the Burma–Thailand Railway, a slave labourer working with many others in conditions of squalor, brutality and near starvation. At great personal risk he kept a 'diary' on little scraps of waste paper and they, like their owner, survived.

When the railway was completed, Parkin was moved to Singapore and then shipped to Japan where he and other prisoners were put to work in a privately owned coalmine under the Inland Sea, about half-way between Hiroshima and Nagasaki. There they dug coal for the Japanese war effort in conditions that were severe but an improvement on life in the camps along the Burma–Thailand railway. After the atomic bombs were dropped, the fortunes of Parkin and his comrades changed sharply. The guards disappeared. The prisoners gorged themselves on food dropped by US planes. They fed some starving villagers. Then they were packed onto trains and eventually onto US warships and brought home, still dazed by the sudden arrival of meals and other comforts and the wondrous sense of having survived. Long after the war was over, the little scraps of paper became a book, one of three, and each one a classic: *Out of the Smoke* (1960), *Into the Smother* (1963) and *The Sword and the Blossom* (1968).

In all, more than 22,000 Australians were captured by the Japanese, the vast majority in the defence of Malaya, Singapore and the Netherland's East Indies. Of these, 8,296 died in captivity from malnutrition, overwork, disease, brutal punishment or lack of medical facilities. Of the 306 survivors from the *Perth*, 106 died in captivity. The death rate on the Burma–Thailand Railway was 35 per cent, yet in other places it was even more terrible. In camps on Ambon it worked up to 77 per cent and on North Borneo it was almost 100 per cent by 1945. The death rate for prisoners of the Germans and Italians was 4 per cent, but a small number of Australian survivors from German concentration camps witnessed the barbarity of the Final Solution. Nine RAAF men were captured and transported to Buchenwald in 1944. Pilot Officer Bob Mills was forced to collect the dead from gas chambers and to watch their emaciated bodies being fed into ovens.

Ray Parkin survived by never losing his faith in goodness, nor his delight in the wonders of nature, and by a measured sense of his own suffering. His thoughts, scribbled in pencil on those little scraps of paper, were both free of bitterness towards the Japanese and full of affirmation for the natural world. 'It is no good hating at all,' he wrote. 'That could kill you. The sight of beauty, patience coming from it, and thoughts of loving friends at home—these, I am sure, matter more.' He noted that the life of one of his mates as an orphan in Tasmania was not much better than life as a POW. He noted the brutality of Japanese officers towards their own guards, many of whom were Koreans. He softened the misery of his existence with little drawings of plants, insects and reptiles. He never stopped thinking and wondering about the big questions of existence and the minute detail of day-to-day life. And some time after he returned to Australia, he began to write. His tales of survival are distinguished by a humanity and understanding that make his trilogy a classic of wartime experience.

Parkin was lucky. He possessed an inner calm and a creative gift that allowed him to assimilate and transcend those brutal experiences. There were other survivors who, in their own way, were able to do that too, most notably 'Weary' Dunlop and Vivian Bullwinkel. And there were many who could not.

them to hold on indefinitely. This time Churchill played to Dominion vanity: surely the Fadden government would not deprive Australia of the glory of final victory at Tobruk? Fadden and his Cabinet did not fall for that one and in Cairo Blamey was told to hold firm, which he did. Blamey's final exchange with General Claude Auchinleck, the British commander, was equally revealing. 'I think you don't understand the position,' Blamey said. 'If I were a French or an American commander making this demand what would you say about it?'

Auchinleck replied: 'Ah but you're not.'

Blamey said, 'That's where you are wrong, Australia is an independent nation . . . Now, gentlemen, in the name of my government, I demand the relief of these troops.'

Curtin was backed in the confrontation over the return of the AIF by Lieutenant General Vernon Sturdee, his Chief of General Staff, who declared his intention to resign if the troops did not return immediately. Sturdee was an engineer and a professional soldier, one of numerous front-line commanders from World War I who had gone on to bigger things. He led a field company through the Gallipoli campaign and in France he had been responsible for the Anzac's light-rail system in the Somme area, another reminder that winning at modern war was as much about assembly lines and traffic systems as it was about stout hearts and fearsome sergeants. Sturdee took on the Chief of the General Staff (CGS) job after Brudenell White's death in the Canberra air crash of August 1941. Sturdee knew that the best soldiers, the seasoned fighters, and most of the best commanders were abroad. His determination put iron into Curtin's resolve.

During the dispute with Churchill, the two AIF Divisions had sailed for home before they were redirected north to Rangoon and then turned for home again. Curtin prevailed but Churchill would provide no cover. The troopships steamed south without the protection of a naval escort, imperilled for nearly two weeks. For most of that time Curtin was unable to sleep. One of his friends, Frank Green, called on him, late one night at the Lodge. At that time Canberra consisted of more paddock than city.

Home from the Middle East, a Warrant Officer Class 2 of the 7th Division arrives in Adelaide, 14 March 1942.

Struggling back to Singapore. Feet all raw and festered. But have to carry on. Living in hell. But still smiling.

Private A. Collins, 2/20 Battalion, diary, 12 February 1942

Troops of the 7th Division welcomed home as their train travels from the docks into Adelaide, 14 March 1942.

General Douglas MacArthur (light uniform) arrives at Melbourne Railway Station, 21 March 1942.

He played the invincible Caesar with an unprickable self-belief.

Steel helmet manufacture in Australia, June 1942.

There was a flimsy wire fence around the Prime Minister's residence, a sign of a nation's innocence. Curtin was standing in the garden in the moonlight when Green approached. 'How can I sleep,' Curtin said, 'when our transports are in the Indian Ocean with Japanese submarines looking for them?' It was an early indication of the fatal toll the war would take on him.

The alliance of Australia with the USA was a marriage of convenience. Australia desperately needed a powerful ally in the Pacific; the US badly needed a base for a counteroffensive against the Japanese. One US admiral said Australia must not fall because it was a 'white man's country'. But strategy, not racial affinities, determined the alliance. London agreed though there were worries there about the loss of British prestige and power in Australia. Australia became a 'strategic responsibility' of the United States. Eight days after the fall of Singapore, President Roosevelt ordered General MacArthur to leave the Philippines and proceed to Australia as supreme commander of a newly designated theatre of war, the South West Pacific Area (SWPA).

MacArthur's war against the Japanese had begun badly, much as Gordon Bennett's had in Singapore. The US general had doubted the Japanese would enter the conflict. Preparations had not been thorough. American pilots were having a leisurely lunch when 200 Japanese bombers caught their planes on the ground and wrecked the main US air force at Manila. Retaliatory bombings of Japanese airfields in Formosa were delayed for eight hours while photographic missions were flown. MacArthur was still listening to rumours of Japanese defeats when enemy troops were landing on outlying islands of the Philippines. His army fled from Manila on 24 December 1941 into defensive positions on Corregidor Island and the Bataan Peninsula. When he arrived in Australia the troops he left behind were facing defeat and captivity, and his military career was at a low point. But circumstances combined with his massive egotism to carry him onward and upward. To the crowds of Australians who gave him a euphoric welcome in March 1942, he played the invincible Caesar with an unprickable self-belief. Concealing his contempt for Australians was a more difficult role but the gifted general was also a gifted showman and he pulled it off. Crowds kept on gaping, cheering and adoring. Behind the scenes he was autocratic and dismissive. He denied the Australian generals a voice in strategy for the south-west Pacific and though he worked well with Curtin the relationship was unequal—Curtin was the junior partner.

A fraction of the enthusiasm for MacArthur was driven by bitterness towards Britain. The popular attitude to England was now more mixed than it had ever been. There had been great Allied victories in the Western Desert, legends revisited, blood allegiances confirmed. Australian heroes had fought in Fighter Command in the Battle of Britain. On the seas, the two navies were operating as one. At the siege of Tobruk, again, it was shoulder to shoulder. But there were also the debacles of Greece and Crete, and now the fall of Singapore, possibly the final straw. The word 'betrayal' was in the air. The press fostered it. Some papers played on the 'guilty men' theme, a theme which ran through Australia's military history from anti-Kitchener feeling in the Boer War, to the sense that Gallipoli was Churchill's mess, to the bungling British generals of the Western Front and now to the blundering directors of Far Eastern war policy. 'Mr Churchill may be the world's great spellbinder,' cried the *Bulletin*, 'but he has proved himself the world's worst campaign planner.' The *Sydney Morning Herald* placed Singapore among the greatest miscalculations in all British history. There were calls to take British war decisions out of the hands of failures.

The University of Sydney academic A.P. Elkin had been so worried about morale in February 1942 that he formed a team of pollsters to gauge popular opinion and, though his sample was small and his methods amateur, his results confirmed that anti-British feeling was widespread. At the highest levels, there was the worry that sheer necessity might induce love and affection: the USA might take the place of Britain in Australian hearts. Billy Hughes fired off a cable to Churchill, a warning about Curtin and others who, he said, were straying from the path of empire loyalism:

> *Some of his ministers are extremists and anti-British . . . Curtin is at best cool towards Britain. Under influence of Caucus and leagues [he] may plump for America as against Britain. The press, almost solidly behind the Government, feeds people daily with insidious pro-American propaganda . . . The Empire needs a victory.*

Hughes was a confirmed believer that popular opinion, for whatever cause, must be led by the nose. He thought Sir Keith Murdoch, the new Director-General of Information, was too pro-US. Murdoch had lowered cable rates so that US news could more easily infiltrate the local press. He financed a public relations report on how to promote American interest in Australia. In politics and the bureaucracy the war was fought by men with eyes on the prize, men keen to shape the peace as they would have it. Some would lean to a future shaped by traditional ties; others saw the prize in a new world order. But in the first months of 1942 it seemed the new world order might be German and Japanese.

Singapore was Australia's Maginot Line. When Singapore fell it seemed there was nothing to stop the enemy from invading Australia. The crisis pulled Australians together as never before. The entire country seemed to be digging slit trenches, filling sandbags, bricking up windows in public buildings, installing air-raid sirens, blacking out house windows with blinds and battens, and staking man-high rolls of barbed wire to the beaches, without much concern for pleasure swimmers on an incoming tide. Air-raid wardens were now taken more seriously. The Army Minister promised every one of them a tin hat. The first

'Mr Churchill may be the world's great spellbinder, but he has proved himself the world's worst campaign planner.'

Air raid shelter in the Botanical Gardens, Adelaide, March 1942.

casualties of this new street bureaucracy were innocent creatures. At Waterloo in Sydney, three lions, a leopard and a tiger at Cell's Circus were destroyed because they might get loose in an air raid. Travel restrictions prevented their removal to the country so they were shot.

The countryside took on immense appeal for humans too. Plans were canvassed, then dropped, for the mass evacuation of children to places outside of the cities. Refugees from Singapore arrived in Perth by the boatload, reminding Western Australians that their main cities were much closer to the once 'impregnable fortress' than Sydney. Families in Perth and Fremantle sought refuge in inland towns. There was a similar panic on the east coast where country boarding schools for wealthy children were soon booked out and real estate prices registered the flight of whole families from eastern cities. In Sydney's eastern suburbs house prices dropped sharply, while in the Blue Mountains they moved upwards. But most people had to stay put. They calmed themselves by being useful. A cottage industry in camouflage net-making started and was thought ideal for the fine, nimble fingers of women and children. At Shore Grammar School in Sydney in 1942, the boys embarked on a net-a-thon. Within a year they made 1,356 nets with nearly 1,000 kilometres of twine and almost 8 million knots.

In February the Department of Home Security released a booklet on how to behave in the event of invasion. The booklet cast civilians as onlookers who must keep out of the way and see to their safety. The popular writer of travel stories Ion Idriess, himself a Gallipoli veteran and author of *The Desert Column*, was so outraged he took his own action. He formed a People's Defence Auxiliary, which soon became a People's Army. He wrote six training manuals. He called for the government to arm the people. 'We want to fight,' he wrote, 'not cower in a dug-out in a garden.'

In New South Wales, and to a lesser extent in other states, people took to the idea; briefly, hundreds organised themselves and drilled using pretend weapons in their manoeuvres. But neither the army nor the government wanted an amateur

In Sydney's eastern suburbs house prices dropped sharply, while in the Blue Mountains they moved upwards.

A schoolboy from Ascot Vale Public School, Melbourne, displays camouflage netting made by his class, 3 June 1942, *opposite*.

The Volunteer Defence Corps, 1942, before the issue of uniforms, *left*.

Paintings of John Curtin, Lenin and Stalin in the Anglo-Soviet Unity Procession, Melbourne, 5 September 1942.

In Australia country people were talking about scorched earth before Singapore fell. The Advisory War Council approved the concept on 18 February, three days after the fall.

force deciding which bridges to blow up or otherwise getting in the way. The government moved quickly to expand the Volunteer Defence Corps to ensure that civilian enthusiasm was channelled in a coordinated direction.

The inspiration for a People's Army might have been drawn from China, where over a million people, soldiers and civilians, had already died fighting the Japanese for a decade, but racial leanings seemed to prevent Australians from recognising their de facto ally in the Chinese people. (China was to Australia what Russia was to England—a great sponge, absorbing vast amounts of the enemy's ferocious energies and munitions.) Chinese resistance tied down more than half the Japanese forces in World War II, and had it not done so the odds and the outcome in New Guinea and the south-west Pacific might have been very different. But in 1942 European events combined with European affinities, to publicise and highlight the mighty resistance in Russia. The 900-day siege of Leningrad was underway; the siege of Stalingrad was soon to begin. Millions of Soviet men, women and children died in their mighty resistance to Hitler's aggression.

One of the Russian tactics in retreat was the scorched earth policy. Crops, bridges, anything not portable and likely to be useful to the enemy was destroyed by Russian peasants and workers. In Australia country people were talking about scorched earth before Singapore fell. The Advisory War Council approved the concept on 18 February, three days after the fall. Property values became irrelevant with the spectre of a Japanese Army advancing across Australia and only a few who talked scorched earth pondered the possibility of government compensation for patriotic scorching. Cattle and sheep owners also began to plan the movement of vast numbers of stock. Committees formed to prepare for the ruination of mines, the destruction of jetties, the sabotage of roads and bridges, and the withdrawal of oil supplies, coastal craft, trucks, cars and trains.

General Gordon Bennett arrived back in Australia with views on scorched earth. He had escaped from Singapore and carried the stigma of a commander who had deserted his men. But Bennett, like MacArthur, was convinced of his destiny to command at the highest level. He did not see the escape as desertion but as duty to his country's calling. He wanted Blamey's job and once he was back in Australia he was quick to express his opinions on many things. Scorched earth, he said, was a matter for the army. Planning was good, people must be busy and positive, but the actual destruction of things must be done by the men who knew best.

The manufacture of Owen guns, May 1942.

Most of the men who knew best were in the Middle East, and they were alarmed. Some of them had been studying Japan for a decade. Australia's defence was in the hands of a poorly trained and poorly equipped militia and the AIF Divisions that were on their way home. The nation was never more alone. Isolation was imminent. Invasion was possible. In previous wars men had sailed off to adventures secure in the belief that their own country was safe and believing their contribution to empire would make it safer still. It was collective security at its simplest. Now everything had changed. Europe was burning, Russia was starving, Britain was desperate, and the Curtin government knew that Australia's fate was a secondary matter to Churchill, at least for the time being. Roosevelt agreed—priority must go to beating Hitler.

There seemed no option other than a dramatic shift in the direction of self-reliance. The Australian economy became a war economy in a matter of months with non-essential industries cut back or converted and essential industries set to work at top speed. The transformation strained human and industrial resources to their limits. Draconian powers emanating from the Manpower Directorate forced the changes through. By May 1942 the non-essential factory sector had lost about two-thirds of its labour force. There was a vast transfer of labour to munitions, weapons, ship and aircraft manufacture, to defence infrastructure around the country, and to the production of food and clothing supplies for Australian and, increasingly, US troops. The war economy program, in those crisis months, presumed a continent besieged, with traditional lines of supply cut off and almost nothing but its own resources to fall back upon. But by the middle of 1942 the Japanese had failed to isolate Australia and they had serious problems of their own. The Australian war economy was receiving machinery, materials and even petrol from the USA under the Lend-Lease scheme.

There were many technical achievements and the output of weapons and munitions, particularly the simpler lines, frequently matched the most ambitious quotas. The decentralisation of production for security purposes meant that country towns now had a greater share in the industrial effort. In Victorian towns, even motor garages were making munitions such as cartridge casings. Around Australia, men and women worked long hard days turning out the weapons and supplies of war. By September 1942, the capacity in small arms ammunition exceeded a billion rounds per year, which was sufficient to supply all Australian troops and to meet US orders in Australia. The war factories were turning out other kinds of ammunition, too, in addition to Bren guns and Vickers guns, the locally designed Owen sub-machine gun, shells, bombs, land mines and, with the highest priority, anti-aircraft guns and war planes—Beaufort bombers and Beaufighters.

The technology underpinning warfare: valves were essential for military hardware on land, sea and air.

Lend-Lease

Unloading a Lend-Lease tank from America. Melbourne docks, 20 February 1943.

Lend-Lease was a credit and barter arrangement to help finance the war. It began in December 1940 when Britain told the USA it would soon be unable to pay for any more weapons or supplies. Rearmament and war in Europe had helped to lift the US economy out of the Great Depression of the 1930s. The question was how to keep good customers shopping at the US arsenal? Lend-Lease—an exchange system allowing Britain to borrow war equipment and settle up later or pay with reciprocal aid—was the answer.

The scheme was quickly extended to include British empire nations, including Australia, and it helped to lay the foundation of a new global order in which the USA replaced Britain as the world's leading trading nation and creditor. Australia's Lend-Lease requisitions were channelled through London as the US government made no distinction between Britain and the empire. The requisitions were carefully monitored by a US Lend-Lease Mission based in Canberra and led by William S. Wasserman. There was a lot of quibbling about eligibility and Australian orders were frequently pruned by Wasserman and his team. Laurence Hartnett was the Director of Ordnance Production. He was unhappy with American pruning: 'It soon became evident,' he wrote, 'that Washington could not comprehend why we wanted to make guns and ammunition and war equipment of all kinds. After all, they considered that was their task and they'd be content to see us getting about our business of growing food and supplying troops.'

But Lend-Lease filled a vital gap in Australia's requirements for war, providing aircraft, tanks and other fighting vehicles, heavy armaments and ammunition, transport equipment such as cars and trains, machine tools, tinplate and petroleum. In return, Australia provided US troops with a range of goods and services including camp stores, hospital treatment and transport, uniforms, boots and boot repair, motor vehicles, tyres, engineers' stores, building materials, small ships, naval stores, telegraphic and telephonic materials, ammunition, weapons, medical supplies, ship, vehicle and aircraft repairs, towage and more.

The idle and the aged were a possible labour pool, but the main source of extra labour was women in the home, housewives and mothers.

The manufacture of a two pounder anti-tank gun, General Motors Factory, Melbourne, March 1942.

In some cases the lack of skills and delays in the delivery of machine tools from the US required local firms to innovate. One of these firms adapted its own machinery to produce six different types of shells from weldless tubing. By mid 1942 the new machines' output was 33,000 shells per week while slower machines at the same location were churning out 20,000 per week. At GMH the production of the 25-pounder gun, was so successful it was in surplus towards the end of the year and GMH began exporting 70 guns a month to the UK. The Owen sub-machine gun was also a great success. In 1942 war industry was turning out 500 per week to meet an army order for 100,000.

Some of the plans for the war economy far exceeded what was possible. Some of the more ambitious programs—for tank and torpedo manufacture, for example—were failures or faltered when cheaper and better alternatives became available through the Lend-Lease program. The war economy soon absorbed workers from non-essential industry but still there was a labour shortage. The idle and the aged were a possible labour pool, but the main source of extra labour was women in the home, housewives and mothers. Only traditional prejudices stood in the way of their employment and in the crisis months tradition was flung aside so that women could move into jobs that in the past had been filled by men—jobs in factories, commerce, transport and the public service. The trade union movement fretted about reclaiming these jobs for men some time in the future. If the women did good work on lower wage rates then they might become a permanent source of cheap labour. But the emergency outweighed the traditional views. As the writer and reluctant patriot Vance Palmer put it, everything familiar and loved and trusted was at stake. 'These are great, tragic days,' he wrote. 'Let us accept them stoically, and make every yard of Australian earth a battle-station.'

Bombs burst along the Port Moresby waterfront during a Japanese air raid, 24 July 1942.

The Japanese Imperial Forces advanced south with astonishing speed. Their original war plan was influenced by the need for victory in China. The aim was to cripple the US Pacific Fleet at Hawaii, overrun unprepared enemies in South East Asia, and set up a defensive perimeter, a vast 18,000-kilometre arc, running through the islands of South East Asia and into the Pacific fringe. The most valued bases were to be covered by secondary locations and each would flank or protect the others in some military way. The result was a thin cordon of isolated island garrisons stretching from the Indo-Burmese border through the Netherlands East Indies to New Guinea and New Britain, on to the Gilbert Islands (now Kiribati), then north to the Kuril Islands.

Timor

Australian guerilla in Timor with 'criado', December 1942.

In February 1942 the Japanese occupation of Dutch West Timor extended across the border into Portuguese East Timor. Combined Australian–Dutch resistance had been quickly overcome, but in East Timor a guerilla force of about 400 Australians operated against the Japanese for almost 12 months. The campaign is now part of the Digger legend and the Timorese are remembered for their loyalty to the Australians. These memories come from the first half of the campaign. The second, which was far more complex, has been forgotten.

When the Japanese occupied Dili, the Australians of the 2/2nd Independent Company took to the hills. They broke up into small groups and thereafter operated as 'hit and run' units, ambushing Japanese patrols whenever possible. The Timorese fed them, watched out for them, guided them, hid them and healed them, fought with them and even rescued them on occasions. They also watched over caches of ammunition and food supplies.

Soon every Australian soldier had a *criado*, a personal servant who carried his pack, blankets and food—everything but the soldier's weapon. In this first phase of the campaign the Japanese were largely confined to the area around Dili and the Australians had the run of the hinterland. Conditions for popular support were propitious. Many officials in the Portuguese regime, plantation owners and priests, supported the Australians. Loyal Timorese followed their lead. There happened to be a food surplus on the island, the Australians were few in number and they made no unwanted demands on the villagers. And in military action they were successful, killing some 40 Japanese for every loss on their own side. In West Timor, where the Dutch-Australian resistance was quickly overrun, the local people were not supportive at all.

In the villages, the Australians went to mass whenever they could, following the lead of a commander, B.J. Callinan, a devout Catholic. They also paid for their supplies. Early in their campaign they issued 'surats', which were government endorsed IOUs. Once radio contact with the mainland was achieved in April, they were supplied with bags of silver coins dropped from Hudson bombers out of Darwin. Pennies from heaven. The Australians were a welcome source of income.

These simple alignments were shattered in August when the Japanese, reinforced threefold and now some 18,000 strong, moved into the hinterland to clean out the Australians. They bombed the villages, seized crops, fruits and stock and brutalised Timorese women and girls. Starvation and death spread quickly and with it disillusionment with the war. Possibly there was a belief that the Australians were doomed.

As the landscape changed, with razed villages, burnt crops and bodies in rivers, and as the terror spread from one end of the colony to the other, so support for the Australians declined. The Portuguese administration was also in trouble. In August an uprising began at Maubisse in the centre of East Timor. The *Chete de Posto* (administrative chief) was killed, his hands and feet cut off. Said Callinan: 'The Chete was a good man who had looked after the natives well, and it was obvious that he had been killed solely because he was a white man.' Callinan blamed the 'anti-white man' propaganda circulated by the Japanese and this was part of it, but the Portuguese regime was exploitative, unenlightened and apathetic—not even in Dili was there running water or electricity in 1940.

The rebellion went on as the Japanese drove the Australians further east and local support fell away. By October, Timorese labour was virtually unobtainable and the movement of stores was now only possible when ponies could be acquired. Food was scarce. The local people were starving and most now wanted the Australians to leave for their presence seemed to be the cause of great strife.

It was not long before the areas where the guerillas could move freely were restricted. Exhaustion, poor diet and malaria were afflicting what remained of the 2/2nd Independent Company. The harassing activity of the first phase was no longer possible; casualties were rising fast. At Northern Territory Force Headquarters it was decided to bring them home.

The Timorese death toll in World War II is estimated to be between 40,000 and 60,000, though how many died in the rebellion or in the fight against the Japanese or under Japanese occupation after the Australians left is unknown. The Australian death toll, arising from the guerilla resistance, was 40.

A 'spotter' looking for Japanese Zeros and bombers in the sky above Port Moresby, July 1942.

But the southern onslaught was so swift and successful it made Japanese planners reassess their objectives. For several weeks after the fall of Singapore, they argued about the possibility of invading northern Australia, then rejected the idea in favour of isolating the country to prevent its use for a US-led counteroffensive. To isolate Australia, to cut off US supply lines, a string of victories was required in New Guinea, New Caledonia, Fiji and the Solomons, and had those victories been achieved the Japanese may have reassessed again. There was no plan to invade Australia but the Australian mainland was imperilled, invasion was always a possibility if the enemy continued to win.

The immediate Japanese plan was to conquer Port Moresby on the south coast of Papua New Guinea. Rabaul had fallen to the Japanese in January and was now a virtually unassailable land and sea base offering defence in depth to the key Japanese centre at Truk in the Caroline Islands. Several points in Papua were targeted, Port Moresby among them. Their seizure would mean sound defence for Rabaul and make attacks on northern Australia and the east coast of Queensland that much easier.

In the first week of May a Japanese naval convoy travelled south around the eastern tip of New Guinea into the Coral Sea, into a trap. US cryptanalysts had broken the Japanese diplomatic code and forewarned MacArthur of the coming attack on Port Moresby. The enemy ships were intercepted by a force of US, Australian and New Zealand naval vessels acting in concert for the first time.

Both sides suffered heavy losses in the battle of 7–8 May but the invasion of southern New Guinea (Papua) was abandoned and the Japanese turned back to Rabaul. The outcome had tremendous military and psychological repercussions for Australia. Although the Allies had suffered greater losses than the Japanese, the battle was called a victory. And, like the Gallipoli landing, it was instantly marked for national commemoration. Coral Sea Week was first celebrated in May 1943.

For the Japanese a string of victories was at an end. Their planned assaults on New Caledonia, Fiji and Samoa were abandoned and the attack on Port Moresby would now have to come from the hinterland. From lodgments on the north side of the island, Japanese troops would march to the Owen Stanley Ranges, seize the all-weather airstrip at Kokoda village in the northern foothills, and ascend to the Kokoda Track. If all went to plan they would pass through a dozen or more high-altitude villages, march on to Ioribaiwa and Imita Ridge, then drop seaward into the southern foothills and from there besiege the garrison at Port Moresby. There was little, it seemed, to stand in their way, save a pathetically unprepared militia force at Kokoda, the 39th Battalion, and the little garrison at Port Moresby.

The Japanese landed at Buna and Gona on 21–22 July 1942 and within a week were pushing inland, murdering missionaries, nurses and planters who failed to escape, bribing, beating and killing the tribal peoples as well as lecturing them in Pidgin Japanese and

Japanese air raids over northern Australia, 1942-1943

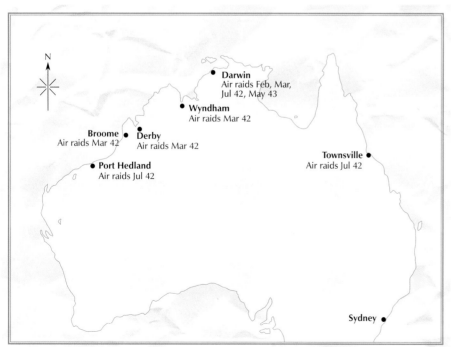

Bearded members of the New Guinea Forces, 1942.

promising them liberation. They had arrived with little knowledge of the terrain, intent on building a road across the mountains, for trucks, if possible, or pack horses, if necessary. A reconnoitring force of Japanese infantry, mountain artillery and engineers made the first forays, taking 150 horses with them. Soon all the horses were dead and the invaders knew the terrain was an awesome barrier.

The only Allied force to the north of the mountains was the 39th Battalion supported by soldiers from the Papuan Infantry Battalion (PIB). The 39th Battalion was a militia unit, 'chocos', designated never to fight away from home but, as New Guinea was a mandated territory, the meaning of home extended to the Owen Stanley Ranges and the strategic village of Kokoda. Had the village and its airstrip been fortified earlier, the entire Kokoda campaign could have been averted. The failure to prepare in New Guinea was akin to the failure in Singapore. Now Japanese Zeros were in command in the skies and there was no chance of flying troops in. They would have to cross the Owen Stanleys.

The Kokoda Track began about 40 kilometres inland from Port Moresby at a village called Llolo. From there it dropped gently for a small distance then rose to Imita Ridge where the saw-toothed peaks of the Owen Stanley mountain range came into view, filling strangers with apprehension and self-doubt. From Imita Ridge to Kokoda there was a string of villages, each a little clearing of huts and gardens, just a few hectares to the tree line where the track took up again and disappeared into

Fear and Loathing

Japanese prisoner captured late in the Kokoda campaign.

There were all sorts of misconceptions in Australia about the Japanese and their military prowess. In 1933, Lieutenant Colonel Vernon Sturdee had described them as 'fanatics who like dying in battle', but a more popular stereotype cast the Japanese soldier as short-sighted and second rate, an incompetent 'little toothy bugger with glasses', and his equipment as 'tinny' and cheap.

By the time that Singapore fell, Australian military propagandists were stressing that the Japanese were not invincible. Frightening tales circulated of Japanese fighters, of a race of merciless 'super soldiers'. In March and April 1942, the Department of Information organised a Hate Campaign in the form of radio broadcasts and posters. 'We've always despised them—NOW WE MUST SMASH THEM!' was the punchline on one poster. One of the radio broadcasts was called 'How the Japs were prepared for war'. Listeners were told 'the Japs have been educated to hate you from infancy'. A passage was read from what Colonel Hashimoto wrote in a magazine for school boys: 'The bones and blood of the despicable whites will be used by us to build the road to final glory over which it is Nippon's destiny to pass.'

Unlike the war in Europe, the Pacific War was framed as a race war from the outset, with John Curtin declaring the nation's determination to keep Australia white. Blamey called the Japanese 'vermin'. It was common to refer to them as animals and one of the broadcasts in the Hate Campaign described them as 'loathsome creeping creatures'. There was a lot of talk about 'exterminating' them. But there were also reservations about this kind of talk. When a gallup poll surveyed opinion about the posters and the broadcasts, 54 per cent of those polled were opposed to the campaign.

Very different results might have been tallied had the poll been taken in May 1943 after a Japanese submarine sank the hospital ship *Centaur* off the south Queensland coast. The ship went down before lifeboats could be launched and 268 lives were lost including those of twelve nurses on their way to Port Moresby. Public opinion was outraged. War Loan advertisements carried the slogan 'Avenge the Nurses' and MacArthur spoke of the enemy's 'limitless savagery'.

Stretcher bearers in the Owen Stanley Ranges
William Dargie, 1947

Battlefield burial of 3 NCOs
Ivor Hele, 1944

2/10 Commando Squadron wash and
clean up, Suain, New Guinea, 1944
Ivor Hele, 1944

Spitfire of the 'Grey Nurse' Squadron, Labuan,
Donald Friend, 1945

the gloom beneath the forest canopy. Its ups and downs were measured in hundreds of metres: it climbed into air so thin and cool that men gasped for breath and vomited when they stopped to rest, and it descended so sharply that soldiers with heavy packs grasped vines and saplings to save themselves from falling.

In August and September 1942, when the 39th Battalion fought along the track, it rained torrentially each afternoon and night, so the ground beneath their feet became a 'boot-sucking porridge'. Their clothes were sodden and rotting and hung off their limbs, and their Port Moresby issued half-blanket was a soaking, heavy, useless burden.

The 39th Battalion was a scratch unit thrown together in October 1941, its ranks mostly young men of eighteen and nineteen. In camp at Darley, Victoria, AIF men had attacked some of them with tin hats and the small number of AIF men who were posted to the militia battalion would not wear its colours (brown over red); they stuck with their AIF colour patch instead. The 39th Battalion troops were mostly untrained and untried, and had been destined for a passive garrison role in Port Moresby. But they arrived there as nations and islands to the west and the near north were tumbling to the Japanese and they soon found themselves in the front line of Australia's defence. While the seasoned 7th Division languished in Queensland, with High Command unsure what to do with it, the 39th Battalion, about 700 men, was given the unenviable task of checking the southward momentum of the Japanese at Kokoda.

American Engineer Units had arrived in Port Moresby. The Australians marvelled at their luxuries, which included kerosene-operated refrigerators and ice cream at mealtimes. Their emergency ration packs held dried fruits, cigarettes and chewing gum. The soldiers of the 39th Battalion trained hard but briefly. They were destined for a long march and a jungle war. Japanese Zeros were raiding Port Moresby and the men of the 39th watched their own RAAF Kittyhawks do battle in the skies above.

Corporal J. A. Canty of the 39th Battalion, AIF, just before going into action at Isurava.

The Track climbed into air so thin and cool that men gasped for breath and vomited when they stopped to rest.

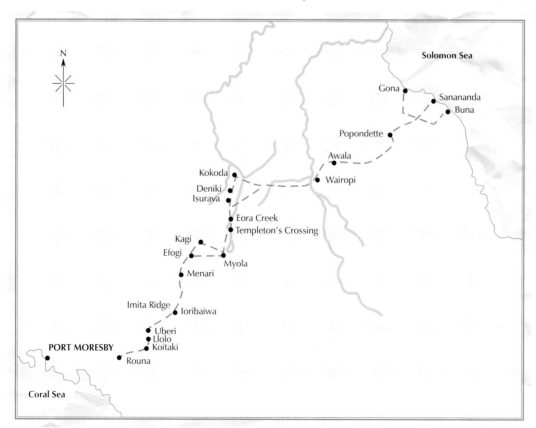

The Kokoda Track

The 'Golden Stairs' at Imita Ridge, Kokoda Track, 1942, *page 144.*

Men of the Rabaul Anti-aircraft Battery not long before the Japanese attack, December 1941.

On one of these days the Zeros dropped bombs and packages. Soldiers on the ground thought that the packages were time bombs but they turned out to be parcels of letters written by Australian prisoners of war in Rabaul.

In July, the 39th Battalion walked 120 kilometres across the Owen Stanley Ranges to Kokoda in eight days of breathless scrambling. Units were strung out over the ranges so that the early arrivals were fighting the Japanese when others were only halfway across. When they finally regrouped, eleven of them were dead including the battalion commander, more were wounded, some were sick and most were exhausted. Outnumbered by about four to one, the forward units had engaged Japanese forces in the hills around Kokoda. Now the battalion—31 officers and 433 fit men—was in retreat. It was a running battle, platoons scattered far and wide, fighting from tree to tree in the rubber plantations and the jungle, from hut to hut in nameless clearings. Some slipped and fell into deep ravines. They crashed through creeks. They carried and dragged the wounded. They left the dead and they tried to hide the dying. The Japanese had ample supply lines and reserves. The Australians had none. The Japanese had jungle green uniforms and could disappear in an instant. The Australians were wearing stand-out khaki. Guns were seizing for want of oil, ammunition was low. The 39th was introduced to Bren guns on the walk across the mountains, hurriedly instructed on their use but not their maintenance. The tricky gas valves started playing up. At the village of Deniki the remnants regrouped, waiting for lost and wounded to come in. Their numbers were down to 400 and reinforcements were far away.

Far away, the administration that had sent the 39th Battalion into this front line was stirring itself. Two battalions of the 21st Brigade, 7th Division—the 2/14th and the 2/16th—were steaming across the Coral Sea towards Port Moresby. At Llolo, high above the Port, the 53rd Battalion was setting out for Kokoda. The 53rd was another scratch outfit, mostly untrained lads, 18 and 19 years old. And half way across the mountains a new commander for the 39th Battalion, Lieutenant Colonel Ralph Honner, was hurrying northwards along the Kokoda Track.

But at Deniki the 39th Battalion was alone, save for a unit of about 30 Papuan Infantry, and for the villagers who gave them some potato tops and pumpkins before they fled. The soldiers fell back to the village of Isurava where they encountered a Signals Unit that had run a thin red wire across the Owen Stanleys and organised

Lieutenant Colonel Ralph Honner during the Libyan campaign, January 1941.

'say-again' relay stations at 12-kilometre intervals. The signallers cooked dehydrated mutton for the new arrivals and issued blankets, one to every three of the exhausted fighters. Some were too exhausted to eat. They slept where they slumped.

Nearing his destination, Honner passed through a village called Eora Creek, which was fast becoming a medical post for the sick and wounded. There were soldiers dying of wounds and dysentry. There were New Guinean stretcher-bearers and porters dying of pneumonia, lack of food and exhaustion. Honner moved on to Isurava where he found the rest of the 39th Battalion. They had dug in, using bayonets, steel helmets and bully beef tins, for there were no shovels. On the defensive perimeters he found young soldiers crouched wearily in putrid fox holes, shin deep in water, drenched through, shivering with the cold. He found gaunt scarecrows, worn by combinations of malaria, dysentry, tropical ulcers, hookworm, scrub typhus and near starvation, by the terror of battle, by the fearful demands of the character they had discovered within themselves, by the long chill vigil of the nights. Some could barely walk but Honner found them waiting to fight.

The new commander was an AIF volunteer whose war began at Bardia, continued on through the Western Desert, and then moved to Greece and Crete. His orders were to hold the enemy on the northern side of the mountains until the 39th Battalion was relieved by battalions of the 21st Brigade. Honner was slightly built, trim, not tall, mild-mannered and quietly spoken. As was so often the case,

From a Japanese diary

In the foothills below Deniki, 1,500 Japanese soldiers were massing. An officer among them made an entry in his diary. Second Lieutenant Hirano was a platoon commander and he wrote of his part in the fighting:

> Commenced a night attack at 10.20. Advanced stealthily on hands and knees and gradually moved in closer to the enemy. Suddenly encountered enemy guards in the shadow of the large rubber trees. Corporal Hamada killed one of them with the bayonet and engaged the others but the enemy's fire forced us to withdraw. The platoon was scattered and it was impossible to repeat our charge . . . The night attack ended in failure. No. 1 Platoon also carried out an attack about 0300 hrs but it was unsuccessful. Every day I am losing men. I could not repress tears of bitterness. Rested, waiting for tomorrow, and struggled against cold and hunger.

Bearers carrying wounded Australians out of forward areas, Kokoda Track, September 1942.

17 August:
Most strenuous
day of my life
heavily loaded
18 August: ditto
19 August: ditto
20 August: ditto.

Private S. Clarke,
2/14th Battalion, diary
entries for August 1942

he did not fit the myth of the Australian soldier, the rangy, wise-cracking, natural-born fighter. He was a family man and a devout Catholic. He had a degree in Arts and Law from the University of Western Australia. He was something of a linguist, a writer of poetry, a man schooled in classical mythology, and now in the art of war. He saw the war coming in 1936, enlisted and began to brush up on Spanish, French, German and Dutch as he could not be certain where he might be fighting. He was utterly professional in his approach to soldiering, a decorated commander, cool-headed, fearless but not recklessly so, and a believer that war, for all its horrors, was a paradox, in his own words, a 'fiery crucible' that degraded men and reduced them to bestiality like nothing else in this world could do, but also lifted them above this into a 'shining, faithfulness and fortitude and gentleness and compassion'. All of that he had seen with his own eyes. All of that he was about to see again.

The day that Honner took command at Isurava, the 2/14th Battalion, 21st Brigade, left Port Moresby for Kokoda. These were hardened AIF troops, veterans of

RAAF in the Pacific

RAAF ground crew of No.75 Squadron bombing-up a Kittyhawk and pilots of No.75 Squadron RAAF going out on a strafing raid, Milne Bay, August and September 1942.

Six weeks after the first Japanese air raid on Port Moresby, a Kittyhawk squadron arrived to defend the airfield, the harbour and the town. The town's anti-aircraft gunners had begun to talk about 'Tomorrowhawks' and 'Neverhawks' and 'Mythhawks' by the time No 75 Squadron flew in on 21 March 1942. A real contest in the skies began that day when two Kittyhawks shot down a Japanese bomber. In the town the relief was visible—the skies no longer belonged to the enemy. Osmar White was there: 'We onlookers fell on each others' necks, howling hysterically with joy. For miles around, men found they had business at the airfield. They came roaring up the road in lorries, cheering and laughing. They stopped, poured out of the vehicles and stood staring at the fighters with a mixture of awe and disbelief.'

The defence of Port Moresby took another dramatic turn late in August when No 75 and No 76 Squadrons played a decisive part in the battle of Milne Bay. The Japanese landed an invasion force at Milne Bay on the night of 26 August. At first light the two squadrons were in action, bombing and strafing the enemy beachhead. They attacked throughout the day, inflicting great damage on Japanese landing barges, fuel and ammunition supplies and disrupting enemy forces ahead of Australian infantry. For a week the Kittyhawk pilots sustained their intensive harassment. The fighting was so close to one of the air strips that the pilots were firing as they took to the air.

Nat Gould, a pilot with No 75 Squadron described the action:

You'd take off, pull round—because the Japs were right at the end of the strip practically—and then come back and land. And you'd always take off over their area and so you'd crouch down . . . in the cockpit under your armour plating and get out over the water and pull your wheels and flaps up, come back and strafe and then you'd come back and land over them, flat out, wheels and flaps down, no pretty landing, just push the aeroplane on to the ground, then pull your throttle off and then they'd rearm you and you'd go and do it again. And you might do half a dozen of these at ten minutes a flight.

The pilots landed on makeshift runways—1,500 metres of interlocking steel matting laid over mud. Ground crews worked frantically, amid the roar of engines and battle, to get the planes back in the air. Armourers, riggers, fitters, engineers, even transport drivers and cooks filled ammunition belts, loaded bombs onto under-carriages and muscled fuel drums into position.

The battle of Milne Bay continued for 12 days until the enemy was finally overcome. It was the first land defeat for the Japanese in the South West Pacific theatre and it is remembered as an outstanding example of army/air force cooperation.

Many RAAF squadrons were committed to Australia's coastal defence where most of the action was over Darwin. Not long after the battle of Milne Bay, however, seven squadrons based in New Guinea were formed into No.9 Operational Group and merged into the 5th American Air Force, headed by General George C. Kenney. Their targets were enemy supply lines and garrisons and their actions followed the course of the ground war in New Guinea, then moved to New Britain and the Japanese main base at Rabaul. From there Kittyhawk and Spitfire squadrons of the RAAF supported American asssaults on the Solomons and Admiralty Islands. A second task force, called No.10 Operational Group, was organised to give defensive cover to MacArthur's forces on the north coast of New Guinea, then to work with the navy and the army in the mopping up operations in the islands. The RAAF's combat deaths in the South-West Pacific area rose to 1,400.

the Syrian campaign against the Vichy French, brimming with confidence. They marched into the Owen Stanleys with 37- and 44-kilogram packs and with hopes of regular supplies at Myola where airdrops into a dry lake bed were planned. But on 17 August US transport planes, parked wing tip to wing tip at Port Moresby, were destroyed by Japanese Zeros. On 18 August, Major General Tomitaro Horii landed his all-conquering South Seas Force at Gona on the north coast. This raised the enemy force, in total, to 13,500, most of them front-line fighters, plus 700 'native slaves' from Rabaul and 170 horses including Horii's own white charger. At Isurava the 39th Battalion waited for the enemy. The 2/14th Battalion was further back along the Kokoda Track, exhausted by the absurd weight of their packs and stalled near Myola while the supply disaster was sorted out.

A Salvation Army Chaplain, Albert Moore, lights a cigarette for a wounded soldier, Menari, September 1942.

Isurava was a scattering of huts in a flat clearing to the east of the Kokoda Track. To bypass it meant tackling precipitous gradients and dense jungle, which was not an option for the Japanese. They had to command the track, to crash through the 39th Battalion. Company perimeters were all within 150 metres of a village hut. Lines of fire ranged across vegetable gardens, sugar-cane stands, scrub and untilled open ground stretching to the timberline. These were the killing fields and across them the 39th Battalion planned to take a heavy toll on the enemy.

But the enemy did not attack for nine days and while the Japanese reinforced, probed and prepared, the Australians at Isurava deteriorated. They were soaked through, they shat and shivered constantly, and they survived on a meagre ration of bully beef, biscuits and water. Finally, the onslaught came. Early on 26 August, mountain artillery and mortars pounded the village, the enemy came on, wave after wave, hour after hour, lashing one perimeter then another in a furious day-long battle. The perimeters barely held. There was frantic movement. Men, sections, platoons rushed to fill a gap, to counter enemy movement, to scamper and crash through to the wounded, to prevent outflankings, to deny high ground, to cover the streams, to stalk snipers, to raid machine gun positions. The killing fields were strewn with Japanese dead and dying. Australians were dying too. The wounded were dragged to the rear through the hail of fire. In the rear a mobile reserve rushed to a perimeter whenever the Japanese broke through. By mid afternoon, the Australians had given almost everything. They could not hold much longer. Further back along the track, near the village of Alola, the 53rd Battalion was ambushed and dispersed, judged harshly by headquarters at the far end of the telephone line and not sent forward again. The 39th Battalion was still alone. The day went on and the fanatical frontal assaults continued. The defenders concentrated a lethal fire; they went at the enemy with grenade and bayonet and bare hands. They fought on, ever more depleted and bloodied but still holding. Their commander's orders were to stand and fight and

It is the story of small groups of men, infinitesimally small against the mountains in which they fought, who killed one another in stealthy isolated encounters beside the tracks which were life to them all; of warfare in which men first conquered the country and then allied themselves with it and then killed or died in the midst of a great loneliness.

Dudley McCarthy, official historian

Overflowing, the village of Eora Creek, 1 September 1942.

A break in the jungle fighting. Diggers in the Kokoda area, September 1942.

that is what they did, praying that reinforcements were, as promised, on the way.

Late in the day the first of the 2/14th Battalion arrived, filing into forward positions to relieve the men of the 39th. Honner noted their 'splendid physique and bearing and their cool automatic efficiency', but the irony was not lost on him. A band of youthful militia had held the line. The AIF were the novices in this jungle setting. Some of them went into the forward pits straight away. The soldiers there could hardly believe their eyes. 'Where are you from? Who are you?' 'We're the 2/14th.' They looked big and confident. They wore uniforms of jungle green and they said things like, 'Move over, we'll fix this mob up'. The men of the 39th saw instantly that the new arrivals were trained. 'You're welcome to fix them up,' said one. 'Thank you,' said another.

The reinforcements continued to flow in, but the Japanese were reinforced too and retained a vast numerical superiority. Honner's men were meant to fall back to Myola to help with supplies, but Honner knew that he could not extricate the 39th without leaving the 2/14th dangerously alone. There were no more reinforcements. Honner's men had bleeding, swollen feet. They turned around and walked back into the fight. The bloody, furious battle of Isurava went on for another four days.

The Kokoda Track was now two streams of traffic, with soldiers going forward in shin deep mud and the wounded filtering back to Eora Creek in ones and twos, some on stretchers, some on sticks, a few on the backs of men with rare strength. Some men were giving up, dropping to the side of the track; others, weak and disoriented, shuffled along on broken-down legs. There were men with infected sores, shivering bodies, blood-soaked bandages and chests aching from sucking at thin air; limbless men; men scalped by shrapnel; men holed by bayonet and bullets. It was a pitiful procession. Stretchers were scarce. One man with his leg badly wounded had bandaged the wounds and now dragged himself along the track driven by the words passed down the line—'they're on us'. Another drew his gun and ordered his mates to leave him. Then he crawled into the jungle to die.

At Eora Creek, the journalists Chester Wilmot and Osmar White had arrived. Damien Parer was there too, filming the gathering of ill and maimed and wounded. Hundreds of men and bearers packed into the jungle clearing in mud up to their shins, the air smoky from fires boiling tea. The Salvation Army was there, ministering to all. Many with dysentery had cut the seat out of their trousers. 'A whole village built of pandanus and grass looked as if it were about to founder in a sea of mud,' wrote Osmar White. Piles of cracked ration boxes were strewn about half submerged, soldiers lay exhausted in the slime 'their skin bloodless under their filth'. White noticed the exhausted carriers, lines of them, 'squatting on the fringes of this congregation eating muddy rice off muddy banana leaves. Their woolly hair was plastered with rain and muck. Their eyes were rolling and bloodshot with the strain of long carrying.'

The two journalists decided to go forward towards the fighting. Parer decided to stay at Eora Creek. A field ambulance captain told him people at home did not want to see this. 'This is what they're bloody well going to see,' Parer replied, 'the complacency down there; they've got to be shaken out of it.' He was suffering from severe dysentery too, but he had to keep moving to film. Somehow he found a bit of rubber tubing. He stuck the tube up his bum and ran it to a bottle, which he fitted inside his sock and, in great pain, he continued to film.

The Australians at Isurava could no longer hold. Orders came through for a fighting retreat. Ralph Honner relinquished command to Brigadier Arnold Potts of the 21st Brigade. The Kokoda campaign became a series of desperate delaying actions as the front line held, then dropped back to the next village, held again, and so on, all the way across the Owen Stanleys until Port Moresby was almost in view. The defenders had been fed into the front line piecemeal and were never able to consolidate. Now they were paying the price, hoping that somewhere along that track they would win the time and find the ground for a decisive stand.

Behind the retreating fighters, the wounded had to be evacuated. Hard decisions were required. Men with shocking injuries were left behind, some with a suicide grenade or a gun. Others were put to sleep with a lethal dose of morphine. The stretcher-bearers again took up their living loads. 'This is a war of walking and hill climbing,' Parer noted in his notebook. 'No field guns, no petrol. If a stretcher case wants anything—a drink, a shit—the bearers will fix it.' The term 'fuzzy-wuzzy angel' was invented, and there was a new, smart-Alec quip—'no boongs, no battle'. Parer filmed much of this portage, capturing what mattered to him—the gentleness of the bearers, the fortitude of the wounded, the cruelty of the conditions.

At the village of Menari what was left of the 39th Battalion was on parade. Fifty-four of them had been killed in action and four died of wounds, 125 more were wounded, some were lost, and most of the rest were too ill to parade. About 50 of them lined up and stood at ease, their clothes rotting on their bodies, some leaning on sticks. Ralph Honner spoke to them. The AIF veteran wanted them to know that they were good soldiers, as good as he had ever known. He also mentioned the 53rd Battalion, for some of them felt the 53rd had let them down. Honner told his men not to judge harshly for in better circumstances those soldiers would have held their positions. Their leaders had failed them.

This was an extraordinary moment in Australia's military history: a near forsaken battalion, all but crucified but now redeemed, a ragged remnant, an impromptu ritual in a jungle clearing, the marking of valour, the call for compassion and understanding. Parer filmed the parade. He captured the men's faces by moving along the line of soldiers with his heavy Newman camera, a tracking shot, somewhat jerky for the camera was too heavy for this sort of work, then a 180-degree whirl to line up a shot of Honner and his adjutant. The sequence concludes with the men breaking up and waving to the camera as they walk away. One of them almost falls over. The parade was the conclusion to the documentary *Kokoda Front Line*.

Kokoda Front Line was a timely complement to John Curtin's national austerity campaign. That campaign had begun informally and badly, early in 1942. The Manpower Directorate was created in January, forcing the movement of labour from civilian to military production and launching a massive shift from non-essential to essential commodities. Curtin pleaded

You can look into the eyes of the dying and you can see they [want] to be relieved of their distress. On the other hand, the hardest thing for a doctor is to look into the eyes of a man you know is going to die but he doesn't think he is. One had a terrible throat wound and I could read hope but when I examined him I thought, I hope he can't read my eyes because there was despair [in mine].

Captain H.D. 'Blue' Steward

Members of the 39th Battalion parade at Menari after weeks of intense fighting, September, 1942.

The fear of invasion became all the more real, but the shopping spree continued until rationing was finally introduced.

The *Kuttabul*, holed by a Japanese torpedo during the midget submarine raid on Sydney Harbour, 31 May 1942.

A single breasted 'Austerity' or 'Victory Suit' made of sugar bags, with the 'Refining Company' label visible on one leg, 14 September 1942.

with Australians to cut back on consumer spending and invest in war loans. Following Britain's lead, it was decided that rationing was the best way to ensure both restraint and a fair share of goods. The idea appealed to Labor. First petrol, then tea was rationed. Then the government announced its intention to ration clothing. Curtin told his radio listeners that national survival depended on their economic sacrifices. While ration books were being printed and the rationing bureaucracy was set up, and while Australian and American sailors and airmen fought in the Battle of the Coral Sea, consumers responded to their Prime Minister's call for restraint with an orgy of buying. Shops were rushed in a nation-wide display of wilful entitlement.

Japanese midget submarines raided Sydney Harbour on 31 May, aiming to do damage to US ships. A week later the enemy shelled Newcastle and Sydney. Five shells fell on Bondi and Woollahra and the papers were full of miraculous near-miss stories. Up and down the east coast of Australia the Japanese hunted Allied merchant ships. The fear of invasion became all the more real, but the shopping spree continued until rationing was finally introduced. It seemed people were prepared to dig trenches, to black out their homes, some were even prepared to drill in bushlands on the suburban perimeter, but they did not want to go without. When they queued for their ration books in mid June, some women were shocked to find that the details printed on the inside cover included their age.

As the 39th Battalion readied to cross the Owen Stanley Ranges to Kokoda, the ration book queuers in Australia experienced the privations of wartime. But the protests were few. Out of fear and duty, people accepted the command economy. There were rumblings about inequities but breaches of the new regulations were uncommon and signs of a will to economise were many—some women handed in unused clothing coupons saying they would sew their needs from sheets and pillow cases; men put up with the charmless Victory Suit for as long as it was mandatory. Old boys donated their school sports gear to new boys at the alma mater, and mothers

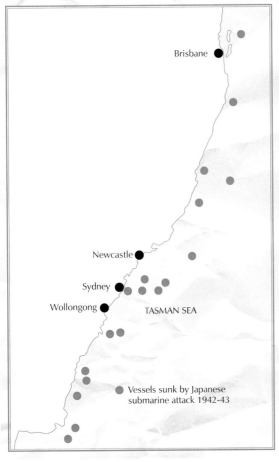

Children lining up at a wood yard to obtain their ration of firewood, Melbourne, 7 June 1942.

darned old swimming costumes for their manufacture was now prohibited—it was reckoned the prohibition would save enough material to make 500,000 knitted garments for soldiers.

The regulations on food were not as severe as those on clothing, and they came in piecemeal through 1942 and 1943, but still the rationing regime made a mark. Mainstays such as tea, sugar and meat were rationed in order to keep up food supplies to Britain and the South West Pacific Area. Rationed tea was now drunk without sugar. Butter was spread thinner, and meat was subjected to a bewildering complexity of coupon values because there were so many cuts and grades. Horseflesh appeared in butchers' windows, ostensibly as pet food, but many dog owners destroyed their dogs fearing they would not be able to maintain them. Gavin Long, the official historian of World War II, kept a record of shortages based on his own observations. In mid 1941 blankets were unobtainable; by October the list included blue bags (for washing), waxed paper for wrapping lunches, tinned tomatoes, olives and olive oil. Picture wire and key rings were also rare. The list hardly suggested great sacrifice.

In 1942 the loss of Malaya to the Japanese meant the loss of rubber supplies. Hot-water bottles disappeared from the shelves as winter came on. Long's list now included margarine and coffee crystals, rice, prunes and even potatoes for the army had first call on them. The presence of US troops in Australia raised the price of fruit and vegetables. Long was horrified at the price of oranges—sixpence each. Australians everywhere were converting their lawns into vegetable patches. In Melbourne the women of the Australian Garden Army turned a Yarra Bank flower garden into a patch that they called the Victory Vegetable Garden.

The presence of US troops in Australia raised the price of fruit and vegetables. Australians everywhere were converting their lawns into vegetable patches.

The men look on as women of the Australian Garden Army turn a flower garden into a 'victory vegetable garden', Melbourne, 1942.

There was also a sharp cutback in beer production, which resulted in a switch to spirits, more drunkenness, more public brawls, and more grumbling than the rationing of any other product seemed to generate, particularly as US soldiers' canteens were flush with it. There was grumbling about women too—men could no longer take home a bottle of beer for Mum and the girls, so Mum and the girls were coming to the hotels, forsaking dainty little glasses for handles and schooners and disturbing the male sanctuary, so said the *Bulletin*, the same magazine that was disturbed about women drilling in the scrub to fight the Japanese.

An RAAF man with his wife and baby son applying for a share in the austerity loan, Melbourne, 14 December 1942.

The Catholic church endorsed the austerity campaign as penance to accompany prayers.

Miss Joan Mair of the Australian Garden Army with some of the harvest from a Burwood garden, Melbourne, 27 September 1942.

Women outdoors, doing anything new, made the *Bulletin* very jittery.

By March 1942, the Curtin government was planning to draw these haphazard changes together under the rubric of the national austerity campaign. The idea was to provide citizens with a philosophy that had real moral power. Shopping madness, record crowds at the racetracks, unrestrained gambling expenditure and a booming black market in liquor all suggested the need to concentrate the collective mind. An advertising blitz was designed to encourage the spirit of joyful penitence. Financing the war hinged on savings and a wholehearted subscription to the war loans. As Kokoda became a battle ground, as the 9th Division prepared for battle at El Alamein in northern Africa, and as RAAF men flew their nightly sorties over Germany, Cabinet moved to limit racing and coursing by 50 per cent, to cut back on hotel hours and services, to standardise restaurant meals, to take glamour and enticement out of advertising, to restrict gossip columns to war-related functions, to ban radio ads for dress, fashion and holidays, and to permit women to go stockingless to work. On 3 September, Curtin delivered a national broadcast to rally Australians to the new £100 million Austerity Loan. 'Austerity,' he told his listeners, 'calls for a pledge by the Australian people to strip every selfish, comfortable habit, every luxurious impulse, every act, word or deed that retards the victory march.'

The Catholic church endorsed the austerity campaign as penance to accompany prayers, while newspapers and magazines gave advice on how to save and how to live cheaply without compromising nutrition. There were competitions for the best austerity recipes and the best new designs from old clothes. One woman made a twin-set for her daughter from two worn singlets, another revealed the secret of the eggless pancake. It was the world turned upside down—advertising was imploring people to save and save. Cities and towns vied with one another to raise this amount or that, and department stores encouraged shoppers to accept war savings stamps in place of change. In October a monthly sacrifice called Raceless Saturday was promulgated with track fans advised to use their free time productively, planting vegetables or renovating old clothes. But near-record attendances on the other Saturdays of the month, and near-record gambling outlays, sent a message to the government that sacrifice was a frail virtue.

Sacrificing the little pleasures such as a few hours at the races was harder now because so many people were harnessed to the treadmill of production for war and because war work was taking a toll. As the war economy built up momentum, absenteeism became a major problem. Absentees were branded deserters on the home-front, and as women were absent about twice as much as men, they took the brunt of the criticism. Moralists delighted with this failure, as they called it, saying it showed women were better suited to the home. There was little understanding of their multiple responsibilities for home care, child care and sometimes the care of aged parents. Nor was there allowance for the depressing and utterly unfamiliar industrial conditions that women often endured, nor for the hostility they sometimes received on the workshop floor. Many were used to the relative decorum of grocery stores, beauty parlours, emporiums, offices and the home. Their absence, for whatever reason, only fuelled the fervour of the Manpower Directorate, which increasingly resorted to policing and compulsion to raise the labour force required for the war effort. In April, Manpower officials began to raid restaurants, clubs, hotels, race tracks and cinema queues looking for the lazy, the unemployed and the absentees. With the help of police, they cut off all the exits then proceeded to check identification cards, which were another innovation. The minister responsible for the Manpower raids was Eddie Ward, a radical Labor man, a proponent of complete disarmament in the early 1930s and now a commissar of the new command economy. He appeared to delight in the raids on private clubs and other elite establishments. But most people were not deserters on the home-front, they were enjoying small pleasures in their spare time. One outcry in the letters column of a Sydney newspaper reminded readers of war work and its disruptions in the countryside:

I've got 10,000 sheep to look after on my property, and I haven't had a break to visit the city for two years. These Manpower blokes have taken nearly all my jackeroos and boundary riders and even the station rouseabout. I've been slaving to keep the place together almost on my own, and as soon as I reach Sydney some fellows come up and practically tell me I'm doing nothing for the war effort.

In April, Manpower officials began to raid restaurants, clubs, hotels, race tracks and cinema queues looking for the lazy, the unemployed and the absentees.

'Painting ghosts': RAAF in Europe

RAAF crew of Lancaster Bomber.
Photographed by Stella Bowen, April 1944.

RAAF personnel took part in virtually all the major bombing campaigns over Germany and occupied Europe. Through the Empire Air Training Scheme, a total of seven RAAF squadrons were raised for the Mediterranean theatre and 12 for Britain. Thousands more Australian airmen flew as part of RAF squadrons. In the Mediterranean they fought for control of the sky, flew against enemy ground forces and shipping, and supported partisan fighters on the coast of Yugoslavia. Further north, they played a major part in the bombing of Germany. Men from the Dominions provided nearly 40 per cent of RAF aircrew during the bomber offensive.

Bomber aircrews had the highest casualty rate of the three services and were the most decorated fighting men in the War in relation to their number. They were mostly young men in their twenties and they died in numbers so great that the release of casualty figures became a serious concern for the managers of propaganda and public morale. It was also of concern for the airmen, for the chances of a crew completing a prescribed set of missions were not high. One RAF pilot wrote of watching flyers arrive for a mission, no longer laughing and smiling as they once had: 'I was distressed by the tense bearing and drawn faces of the bomber crews,' he wrote. 'At that time, late in November 1943, some 80 per cent were failing to complete unscathed their tour of 30 operations. Of courage they had plenty, but there was nothing but lip-biting gloom registered on those faces.'

Their purpose was the destruction of German industry and civilian morale. These goals were pursued at immense cost. In 1942, Bomber Command suffered the shooting down of 1,404 aircraft and damage to 2,724, while doing no great harm to German infrastructure. At the same time, scientists made improvements to the instrumentation required for precision night bombing. The Mark XIV bombsight was perfected and installed in all RAF bombers; a radar navigation device, the H2S, showed densely populated areas as a glow emanating from a cathode-ray tube and specialist 'Path Finders' (fast, unarmed, wooden-framed Mosquitos) now led the bombers to the target area. The leader of the Path Finder force was Don Bennett, a young Queenslander described in the RAAF official history as 'that brilliant rarity—the almost perfect pilot, engineer and navigator combined'.

Late in 1942, the British aircraft industry began to turn out the Lancaster bomber, an unsurpassed instrument of air war. The Lancaster had a range of 4,000 kilometres with a 3,400 kilogram load. It could fly at 460 kilometres per hour at 3,500 metres. It combined great strength with manoeuvrability. Round-the-clock carpet bombing of Germany began soon after the new bomber came into service, with the RAF Lancasters raiding by night and US 8th Air Force 'Flying Fortresses' raiding by day.

In 1944, the war artist Stella Bowen sketched a group of Australians—a Lancaster bomber crew at their base in England—in preparation for a group portrait. That night they were shot down over Germany, reported missing the next day and presumed dead. 'It was terrible having to finish the picture after the men were lost,' wrote Bowen. '[It was] like painting ghosts.' A total of 3,486 RAAF bomber crewmen were killed in the skies over Europe, virtually one in 10 of all Australia's war dead for 1939–45. In all, 5,100 RAAF men died in the air war over Europe.

A woman takes home her ration of firewood, Melbourne,14 June 1942.

I have seen men standing knee deep in the mud of a narrow mountain track, looking with complete despair at yet another seemingly insurmountable ridge. Ridge after ridge, . . . heartbreaking, hopeless, futile country.

Captain F. Piggin, 3rd Battalion, letter home, 10 December 1942

But there was victory still to be assured and that required continued sacrifice, and the way to spur sacrifice was to create fear.

Behind Curtin's crusade for war focus and war finance were his own puritan inclinations, his personal belief that self-denial would improve the character of the nation, and his understanding that Australians would make real sacrifice only if they were genuinely fearful. For this reason the campaign for austerity and hard work went hand in hand with regular reminders of the constant and undiminished threat of invasion, even when that threat was gone. In June 1942, after the Japanese fleet had been routed in the Battle of Midway, MacArthur told Curtin that 'the security of Australia has been assured'. But Curtin felt he could not tell the people. Instead he told them that Australia could be lost at any time. On 3 September, as Australian forces retreated across the Owen Stanley Ranges, Curtin knew Port Moresby was at risk, but he also had news of a great victory at Milne Bay—Australian soldiers, with support from RAAF fighters, had inflicted the first decisive defeat on Japanese land forces. And he knew the secrets of the Japanese diplomatic encryptions that continued to be read by the Allied cryptanalysts—there was no plan to invade Australia. But there was victory still to be assured and that required continued sacrifice, and the way to spur sacrifice was to create fear. Curtin sensed commitment was skin deep; he worried that apathy and complacency could surface at any time. He kept on playing the fear card. He knew the war was turning in the Allies' favour, but it was still in the balance, and by mid September the desperate situation on the Kokoda Track was reason enough to be wary that the war might turn against Australia and the Allies once again. This was Curtin's own deepest fear and he would not slacken while it seemed real.

Damien Parer was fearful too. He flew back to Sydney as the battalions of the 21st Brigade—2/14th, 2/16th and 2/27th—dropped back to Imita Ridge to make a final stand. Imita Ridge was the last defensive position before Port Moresby. Parer, and the men of the 21st Brigade, were unaware that the Japanese were at the end of their resources and about to pull back. Ken Hall, the Cinesound chief, was roused by Parer's talk of Kokoda and Australia's peril. He could hear conviction in the cameraman's voice and he knew audiences would hear it too. Parer made a personal

Commonwealth Coal Commission poster urging restraint in the use of electricity and gas, *opposite*.

John Curtin, Prime Minister, *below*.

The 'Fear State'

Australian nurses arriving in New Guinea, waiting with their baggage, 1942.

With the Japanese in retreat, Australian nurses arrived in Port Moresby. The Australian war correspondent, George Johnston, reported immediate changes to the streetscapes: 'The most typical characteristic of Port Moresby has disappeared,' he told Australian readers, 'the communal showers on every street corner, alongside every fire hydrant and at most roadside camps. They have now all been screened off with hessian!'

The nurses went straight to work at the 2/9th Australian General Hospital (AGH). Hundreds of wounded, fevered and otherwise ill men were streaming in from the Kokoda Track and later flown in from the beachhead battles on the north coast. 'Stretcher after stretcher of filthy, blood-stained bodies, often in pain, and some of the extent of their wounds was unforgettable,' said one of the Sisters. There was still no penicillin (unavailable until 1944), and sulphur drugs were the only antibiotic on hand. Sulphaguanidine was used for dysentry and the troops called it 'cement'. Sulphonamide was used for infections and wounds, quinine for malaria. For the rigors of malaria and the comatose state of scrub typhus and dengue fever patients, the only remedy was constant attention and the intake of copious fluids. Between September and December 1942, the 2/9th AGH took in over 10,000 admissions, about ten per cent suffering wounds, the rest stricken with disease and malnutrition. Reg Saunders' brother, Harry, was one of these. He was a gaunt bag of bones and he had malaria too. He recovered quickly, rejoined the 2/14th Battalion at Gona on the north coast and was killed in battle on 25 November.

Over the next three-and-a-half years, Australian Army nurses served in general hospitals and casualty clearing stations throughout the territory, while RAAF nurses flew to Medical Receiving Stations (MRS) for RAAF casualties at locations that mapped the Australian and American offensives through to 1945. In some locations medical staff were so close to an uncertain front line that nurses went about their work behind armed pickets; convalescents who could walk shared guard duty at night and wards were issued with rifles. 'As I signed for the rifles I wondered about the Geneva Convention,' said Sister Helen McCallum, who was at Torokina on Bougainville late in 1944.

In February 1944, the 2/7th AGH took over from the 106th Casualty Clearing Station at Lae and remained there for another 18 months. Patients came in from New Guinea, Bougainville, New Britain, Morotai and Borneo. They were suffering from wounds, disease and psychiatric problems associated with combat stress. The preferred medical terms for psychiatric problems were 'fear state' and 'exhaustion', although some doctors used the phrase 'bomb happy'. The 'fear state' came in many forms. Most commonly, it was a state of acute alertness, startled reactions to any sudden noise, unrestrainable flight or aimless running about and shouting, or its opposite: a man curled up, trying to be invisible, frozen with fear. It was, as one doctor described it, 'a misery of apprehension and alertness' which was accompanied in sleep—if sleep was possible—with terrifying dreams. Variations on these widely shared symptoms of the 'fear state' were to be found in every theatre of war.

In the Greek campaign a signalman reported men 'cracking up' under air attack. They 'went haywire', they tried to dig holes in creek beds, they went 'bush' by day only to reappear after dark, hungry and in search of a meal. After El Alamein there were cases of terror-inspired stuttering and in New Guinea there were men who lost some powers of speech. 'He became almost speechless,' wrote Sister Elsie Ellen, 'and would communicate with others by use of the incomplete, ungrammatical speech of young children . . . He refused to leave a friend who brought him down the track to the hospital, and the latter stated that at night the patient would whimper and would not sleep till he was allowed to curl up in the arms of his friend.' At the 2/7th AGH in Lae, Sister Barbara Woodward saw men who 'ran the entire gamut of psychiatric ills, right through to manic depressives and schizophrenics. Our job was to treat them, talk to them, feed them, and send them South for, we hoped, rehabilitation in Australia, and return to civilian life,' she said. The medical 'weapons' at the 2/7 AGH in Lae were limited to tranquillisers and, later in the war, electric shock treatment.

In the field, however, the army took the view that many 'fear state' cases were curable and the cure was not subtle. For anxious novices, the best solution was battle itself. For 'failures' it was conceded that some, through 'weakness of personality' may never readjust to battle conditions, but in other cases a rifle butt jolt between the shoulder blades, or on the jaw, was reckoned to stifle sobbing and reassert control. Alternatively, a firm, open-handed left and right slap to the face could achieve a similar result. The Middle East veteran who passed on this advice to incoming officers in New Guinea assured them that the offender would later apologise and would not offend again. He had seen it work many times. Yet some months later, he chose a gentler method when a Bren gunner 'snapped' during a tense stand-off in the jungle: 'As he sobbed, I comforted him, cradling his head on my chest, he was trembling violently, then after about 20 minutes he stood up, tensed himself, thanked me and said "I'm OK now" and strode back to his position on the Bren.'

A stretcher bearer provides water for a wounded infantryman, October 1942.

appearance in the film *Kokoda Front Line*, he pleaded with Australians to understand the desperate situation so near to their shores, he contrasted the plight of the fighting men in New Guinea with the casual atmosphere at home. The concluding words were scripted carefully: 'I've seen the war and I know what your husbands, brothers and sweethearts are going through. The sooner we realise the Jap is a well-equipped and dangerous enemy, the sooner we can forget about the trivial things and get on with the job of licking him.'

There were other strategies subtly woven into the commentary. The bias in the information released by MacArthur's headquarters was shameless. Australian achievements were denigrated and ignored; American successes, even fictional ones, were constantly trumpeted as the Commander-in-Chief vied for approval and supplies in Washington. *Kokoda Front Line* was an attempt to shift the spotlight onto Australian troops. It was also a jibe at the abysmal ignorance of conditions in New Guinea, which MacArthur and Blamey shared in equal parts. When the campaign began, there was uncertainty as to whether motor vehicles could negotiate the Kokoda Track. When that was cleared up, they continued to believe in a fiction called the Gap, a crack in a hillside so narrow that a few Vickers guns could hold the entire Japanese army at bay. It turned out that the Gap was 17 kilometres wide. Enemy strength was grossly underestimated. Novices were posted at the gates of hell. Both commanders thought the Japanese were an inferior enemy in inferior numbers and they talked as if the Owen Stanley Ranges were undulating pasture. *Kokoda Front Line* exposed the harshness of the Owen Stanleys and the realities of jungle fighting. Even in the shades of black and white, it showed how khaki stood out in the jungle, making easy targets of Australian soldiers. There was not a word of criticism in the commentary. The footage did the talking.

The situation in New Guinea was perilous. MacArthur feared the loss of his own command if another battle turned against him. George Vasey described the anxiety among MacArthur's staff: 'They're like a bloody barometer in a cyclone—up and down every two minutes.' Blamey was equally fearful—the doubters were circling him. The New Guinea campaign was going badly. On 17 September, MacArthur convinced Curtin to send Blamey forward to Port Moresby. Off the record, Curtin told the General Manager of the *Herald* that Blamey was 'going to New Guinea for no other reason than to give him one final chance'. Blamey knew that. When he reached Port Moresby he was ruthless. He sacked the commander there, Lieutenant General Sydney Rowell. Rowell had foreseen the folly of the Kokoda campaign but his wisdom was overridden and now Rowell's hurried planning was paying dividends on the Kokoda Track. Blamey also sacked Brigadier Potts, whose misfortune it was to command the retreat along the track. Potts had endured every hardship with his desperately pressed troops and his leadership had won Port Moresby critical time. Ralph Honner thought Potts was the finest brigadier he had ever fought under. Blamey saw him as a convenient scapegoat.

The blood-letting paid dividends for Blamey. He had arrived in Port Moresby as the Japanese were drawing to a standstill. They had failed at Milne Bay, they were failing

Australian achievements were denigrated and ignored; American successes, even fictional ones, were constantly trumpeted.

Private H.E. Newman of the 2/33rd Australian Infantry Battalion, AIF, on patrol between Nauro and Menari, October 1942.

at Guadalcanal in the Solomons, and on the Kokoda Track they had outrun their supply lines. Australian troops were about to pursue the enemy back across the mountains just as fast as their own supply would allow.

Raising the Australian flag. Australian troops retake Kokoda, November 1942.

The yellow devils show no mercy and have since had none from us.

Brigadier J. Field, 7th Brigade, diary, 2 September 1942

Brigades from the 7th Division under Major General A.S. 'Tubby' Allen, another AIF veteran, led the pursuit. The enemy continued to fight and withdraw and fight again. These were hard and bloody encounters but at Eora Creek, where the Japanese were badly mauled, a great injustice descended on Tubby Allen. At MacArthur's insistence, Blamey dismissed him for lack of progress and he was replaced by George Vasey. Again, Blamey was the dutiful servant; again blame was passed down. For Allen's devoted soldiers there was one consolation—one fine commander, Bloody George, replaced another.

The pursuit across the mountains was dictated by the pace at which supplies and ammunition could be brought forward. There were never enough bearers to allow a brigade to advance as it would in less punishing terrain. And there were other restraints. The Australians swept purposefully and thoroughly to ensure no Japanese units slipped the net. All units were to be found and killed. Burial parties were on continual duty and the burying was retrospective. The dead from past battles were strewn in the jungle by the track. The living were drawn into dark recesses by the stench, to skeletons and bodies picked half clean by rats and other vermin.

Engineers building a bridge on the track from Kokoda to Buna, November 1942.

The horrors of a past still tangible were worst at Eora Creek. All along the way there were signs that the Japanese were starving—emaciated bodies with splattered intestines leaking grass, weeds and roots and even wood. At Eora Creek the burial parties found the bodies of Australian soldiers with steaks carved off arms, calves and thighs. There was more of this further along the track, and beyond, on the north coast, at Sanananda, Gona and Buna Mission.

At Eora Creek, the Diggers listened to George Vasey: 'The enemy is beaten,' he told them. 'Give him no rest and we will annihilate him. It is only a matter of a day or two. Tighten your belts and push on.' Those last words were meant literally. The Australians' supplies were never enough and they were moving through a serial wasteland of villages decimated, gardens plundered and destroyed. They were desperately hungry. They tightened their belts and pushed on.

On 1 November the Australians occupied Kokoda. The engineers inspected the airfield. They would have it usable in two days.

Japanese dead from suicide raid, Labuan
Donald Friend, 1945

Night Recreation at Civil Constructional Corps camps, 1944
William Dobell, 1944

One Sunday afternoon in Townsville
Roy Hodgkinson, 1942

Young and Jackson's Corner
Donald Friend, 1945

Back Home
Sali Herman, 1946

Burial party, 23 November 1942. The Japanese dead were buried five
to ten together in common graves, their steel helmets on top of the grave.

Supplies in; wounded out. Thoughts turned to fresh cooked meat, sugar, milk and delicacies such as tinned fruit. Some of the men thought the worst of the campaign was over. They were wrong. The beachhead battles were yet to come, the battles to dislodge the Japanese from heavily fortified enclaves at Gona, Sanananda and Buna. They were among the bloodiest of the Pacific War. Few prisoners were taken, most of the Japanese fought to the death and Allied casualties were high. The beachhead battles became massacres. Pinned down, the Japanese lived, fought, ate, defecated and died in their bunkers and pillboxes or on the ground nearby. They used bodies for sandbags and donned their respirators as shells churned up the stench of their comrades' rotting corpses. Battle-hardened Diggers who fought their way across that polluted ground found they could not face their food until the burial parties had done their work, buried thousands, and the sea breezes finally cleared the air. One officer said he could never again look at a picture of a romantic palm tree setting, for it seemed that everywhere the soldiers looked the palms were ringed with torn, blackening, fly-blown bodies. 'It was sickening to breathe, let alone eat,' said Ralph Honner.

Australian battle casualties in New Guinea had now reached 5,698, with 1,731 killed in action, 306 dying from wounds, 128 from other causes and 3,533 wounded. And there were over 15,000 cases of infectious diseases to the end of 1942 alone. The Japanese had landed 16,000–17,000 troops since July 1942 and some 12,000 of these were dead.

Late in January 1943 the Japanese offensive in eastern New Guinea was at an end. In North Africa, Allied forces were about to enter Tripoli, having slogged their way from El Alamein. In Russia, German troops had withdrawn from Leningrad; the 900-day siege was over. Italy was still in the war but no longer a serious problem. In February the Japanese withdrew from Guadalcanal after months of battle and immense casualties. The fortunes of the Axis powers had slumped in unison.

Few prisoners were taken, most of the Japanese fought to the death and Allied casualties were high.

Although I find this work a great strain I am grateful for the opportunity of serving these men. I do not believe there has ever been a campaign when men have suffered hardship, privation and incredible difficulties as in this one. To see these men arrive here wounded and ill from terrible tropical diseases, absolutely exhausted, clothes in tatters and filthy, long matted hair and beards . . . no description of their incredible suffering could possibly be an exaggeration . . . I have seen so much suffering and sorrow here that more than ever I have realised the tragedy of war and the heroism of our men.

Chaplain R. Smith, Salvation Army, 2/9th Australian General Hospital, letter home, 10 January 1943

Signals personnel were another kind of 'front-line'. They were invisible relay stations. Their work was long and hard, immensely stressful and unheralded.

The signals clerk at work in the Signals Office, HQ, 9th Division, Tobruk, 1941.

'Born for this Battle'

Germaine Greer was almost three years old when her father enlisted in the RAAF, late in 1941. Reg Greer, aged 40, was then seconded to the RAF and sent to Cairo. He arrived sucking salt tablets to fend off dehydration and walked the busy streets trying not to brush up against the locals as the city was in the midst of a louse-born typhus epidemic and thousands had already died. In Cairo he trained for eight weeks at 'MECCS', possibly Middle East Codes and Cypher School, an organisation which officially did not exist. Reg Greer was a signals officer, and may have played a low-level part in the top secret Ultra program that had succeeded in breaking the German codes. The Allies exploited their new knowledge of German intentions at the battlefront to spectacular effect, while putting in place a massive intelligence operation to disguise their advantage for as long as possible.

Signals officers in the Middle East worked in stressful conditions known only to themselves. Usually hidden away in anonymous, cramped, windowless settings, their job was to listen intently to the cacophony coming through their headphones, sorting and transcribing, re-encoding and transmitting enemy signals. The Ultra specialists worked for hours on end taking down and grading gibberish, then re-encoding it for transmission to Bletchley in England where it would be decoded and analysed. It then came back to them for transcription, de-coding and, in the case of Ultra decrypts, hand delivery to the field commander. Signals personnel were another kind of 'front-line'. They were invisible relay stations. Their work was long and hard, immensely stressful and unheralded. It required a cover (such as an air force identity) and complete discretion. Women were increasingly used in this work and some men derided it as just that—'women's work'. At the junior officer level, Reg Greer's station, it was possible to be engaged somewhere along the line in the transmission of immensely important information, yet never know it. It was equally possible to be privy to the most terrible news.

In mid July 1942, Reg Greer was posted to RAFHQ, Western Desert as the Allies prepared for a massive counter-offensive against Rommel. The two armies had chased each other back and forth across the north of Africa. On Christmas Day 1941, the British 8th Army reached Benghazi in the west, only to be driven back to Gazala by May 1942. At Gazala 530 British tanks were destroyed, which meant that British armour had practically ceased to exist for the time being. On 21 June, Rommel captured Tobruk, a British counter-attack failed and Allied forces dropped back to El Alamein, the last defensible position before the Suez Canal. The Axis 'Great Plan' was a German breakout through the Middle East, control of Suez and of Persian oil, and a link-up with their Far Eastern allies. All this seemed close at hand. Rommel thought he would be in Alexandria in a matter of weeks.

The British began pouring men and material into the defence at El Alamein. The 9th Division, under the command of Lieutenant General Leslie Morshead, was rushed from Palestine to Egypt late in June 1942, the Australian government having agreed to its retention in the Middle East at least until this crisis was over. The 9th Division went straight into the front line and immediately began to suffer from the incompetent generalship of the British 8th Army. Both Australian and New Zealand units took fearful casualties because the planning was mediocre or British armour failed to support them. On one occasion, Morshead sent a blistering note to British command refusing to fight again unless guaranteed that the tanks would stick with his infantry in the white heat of battle. He said his men had lost all faith in the armour and the armour needed to restore that faith. His diary entry on the same day, 29 July 1942, indicated his own frustration with 8th Army command:

No stability, a wealth of plans and appreciations! Fighting always in bits and pieces, and so defeats in detail. Formations being broken up continually—it has been difficult and unpleasant keeping 9th Division intact.

The mediocrity of British commanders at this time led to a succession of dismissals and appointments, but finally leadership in the Western Desert was settled with the arrival of Lieutenant General Bernard Montgomery on 12 August.

Montgomery was intent on a huge build-up, no more fighting 'in bits and pieces' and he assured Morshead that the armour would fight. He was a self-promoter and a charmer. He stressed his Commonwealth ties, having spent some of his boyhood with his father who was a bishop in Tasmania for a time. He wore a slouch hat for the Diggers and they warmed to him. 'Montgomery, bless him,' wrote Morshead, 'has plainly told the armour that it has to fight.'

The great build-up went on—2,100 guns and 2,518 tanks were amassed and battle plans were laid down with a decisiveness and confidence that few commanders have ever matched. Montgomery planned to make full use of the revelations provided by Ultra, and such was the top secret nature of the program that he alone had access to the signals. Information from Ultra had been available for some time but previous campaigns in the Western Desert indicate poor intelligence or failure to adequately interpret it. If Ultra did have an impact on the war in northern Africa, if it did help Australian troops, it was not until the 'last ditch'—El Alamein.

In August 1942, in Montgomery's caravan by the sea, the commander was able to show Churchill, who was on a round trip home from Moscow, a long signal from Rommel to Hitler. The signal set out the details for his final assault on the 8th Army. Montgomery called his commanders together for a briefing and a demonstration of his remarkable clairvoyance. As 'predicted', Rommel launched a desperate attempt to break through the Allied lines

on 30 August. Australian airmen were among the readied forces which repelled the attacking divisions. The Allies continued their build-up, launching their own offensive on 23 October, the second battle of El Alamein in which the 9th Division played a decisive part. Morshead told his troops they must fight on, even if cut off or surrounded. 'We must regard ourselves as having been born for this battle,' he told them.

Now Allied forces outnumbered Rommel by two to one in men, tanks and guns. Air predominance was even greater and, most telling, was the fuel factor. The 8th Army had unlimited supplies; Rommel's reserves were desperately low and, thanks to Ultra, Montgomery knew it.

The men of the 9th Division faced the main German defensive position in the north—two lines each six kilometres wide behind half a million mines. Further to the south, next to the Australians, were Scottish, New Zealand, South African and Indian divisions and Greek and Free French brigades. What followed was a bloody slogging match which lasted for 11 days. The Australians fought their way into Rommel's defences, then drove off a counter-attack led by German tanks. Then they attacked again. This was some of the most fierce and fanatical fighting yet seen in the desert, and it gave Montgomery the opportunity to push Allied armour against enemy positions further south. The 9th Division had drawn upon itself such enemy strength as to weaken Rommel in the south where the decisive breakthrough took place. By 2 November, against Hitler's orders, Rommel withdrew his forces to save what was left of them from annihilation. The war in North Africa had turned decisively. Axis casualties were 90,000, Allied 13,000. Of the latter, the grim tally in the 9th Division was 620 killed, 1,944 wounded and 130 taken prisoner. The 9th was one of 10 divisions in the 8th Army, yet it suffered 20 per cent of the casualties. Soon it would be replenished and fighting in the south-west Pacific.

Reg Greer was in Malta during the Battle of El Alamein. He had been promoted to the rank of Flying Officer, trucked out of the Western Desert and shipped to the embattled island in a submarine, its ballast tanks packed with supplies of kerosene, medicines, ammunition, mail and powdered milk. As the 9th Division went into action, he was capturing wireless intelligence from quarters set deep in the damp limestone catacombs of Valetta. In Russia the Germany army had just collapsed at Stalingrad. In North Africa it was near collapse. When Rommel retreated to Tunisia, desperate for supplies, dumping equipment for lack of fuel, Greer and others in Malta were able to pick up the signals telling the German commander of supply ships coming from Naples and Taranto. The intelligence included details of the supplies on board, date of departure and expected time of arrival. Few of these ships reached the shores of Africa.

Lieutenant General Bernard Montgomery wearing an Australian slouch hat, El Alamein, 1942.

Jerry was completely finished in our sector. What a feeling it was. The boys were laughing and joking...like a lot of kids. How good it was to feel free and alive, to be able to walk about in the daylight without the fear that was constantly in our hearts.

Private R. Anson, 2/17th Battalion, El Alamein

Lieutenant General Leslie Morshead speaking with Winston Churchill, El Alamein, 5 August 1942.

*From mid 1943
a string of
Japanese ground
positions fell in
quick succession.*

The shape of the Pacific War was also about to change. To this point the Allied armies in the Pacific had fought a war of grinding attrition, much of it borne by Australian troops. There was more of this to come for the Australians in New Guinea, but Allied forces were preparing to launch a series of breathtaking landings, airborne and amphibious attacks on Japanese strongholds in the islands of the South Pacific. These were called the Cartwheel Operations and they went well. From mid 1943 a string of Japanese ground positions fell in quick succession, while the near impregnable stronghold at Rabaul was isolated and neutralised. The bypassing strategy worked in New Guinea, too, when US forces leapt to Aitape, and to Hollandia in Dutch New Guinea. Japanese forces at Wewak and Hansa Bay were sidestepped and left to wither on the vine.

Now the Allies had the advantage of naval and air supremacy and they also had Japanese codes. Formerly, the skilled cryptanalysts at headquarters in Brisbane had deciphered the Japanese diplomatic code. In 1943 they cracked the four-digit Japanese Army code and so had accurate knowledge of the Japanese order of battle. The cryptanalysts saved thousands of Allies' lives.

While American forces prepared to sweep through the islands of the south-west Pacific, the main Australian force continued the grinding fighting in New Guinea. After defeat at the beachheads, the Japanese set about reinforcing positions further to the north-west. Late in January 1943, an enemy force of 2,500 marched on Wau intent on dislodging a small Australian garrison and seizing the airfield. The Australians tried to stop them in the jungle to the east of Wau but the five-day battle was finally settled on the fringes of the airstrip where attack and counterattack went

A Wirraway from No.4 Squadron, destroyed in a Japanese raid on Wau, 6 February 1943.

on for two days. Allied aircraft ran the gauntlet, landing in the midst of the action, off-loading fresh troops and supplies and taking on the wounded. Some Australians were shot or shattered as they left the planes and so were taken straight back on board and flown out. But over these two days the initiative passed to the Australians and within a week the Wau Valley was cleared of all enemy. Japanese dead amounted to some 1,200. The Australian losses were under 300.

Radio intercepts now revealed that the Japanese were about to reinforce Lae on the Huon Peninsula. Six thousand Japanese troops of the 51st Division put to sea at Rabaul on 28 February in a convoy of eight transports under the cover of eight

The Tojos are tough and great jungle fighters, and have given the infanteers a hard job but they have met their masters at that game.

Gunner H.C. Sunley, 2/1st Field Regiment, diary, 20 December 1942

Allied counteroffensive operations 1942–1945

Adapted from *The Penguin Atlas of World History*, volume 2, Penguin Books, Harmondsworth, 1978

*Today we are carrying
rations up to B Coy
and what a bastard
of a job. The track up
the mountains in some
places is perpendicular
and we are down on our
hands and knees, pushing
boxes and bags of rations
up a foot at a time.
Christ! The places they
pick for us to fight in.*

Corporal Jack Craig,
2/13th Battalion, diary,
1 November 1943

The *Krait*, September 1943.

Sergeant Tom Derrick,
VC, DCM, of the 2/48th
Infantry Battalion, Sattleberg,
New Guinea, November 1943.

destroyers. In the Bismarck Sea, to the west of New Britain, and then in the waters of the Huon Gulf, they were shattered by Allied air attacks. Beaufighters of the RAAF's No. 30 Squadron led the attack, followed by American B-17 and B-25 bombers, A-25 Bostons and the RAAF's No. 22 Squadron. All of the transports were destroyed, the destroyers were sunk or disabled and nearly half of the Japanese troops perished in a forbidding display of air power.

Next the Diggers fought a series of smaller actions, notably at Mubo in May and Lababia in June. As US operations began further to the north, the Australians fought major battles on the Huon Peninsula. Early in September 1943, Australian and US forces launched a combined land, sea and air attack on the enemy at Lae. Brigades from the 9th Division, home from El Alamein, launched the operation from the sea. They landed virtually unopposed to the east of the Japanese garrison. Air raids followed and then more amphibious landings brought more troops. Three battalions of US paratroops accompanied by Australian gunners were then dropped north-west of Lae, the airfield at Nadzab in the Markham Valley was secured and the 7th Division, AIF, flown in. The enemy garrison was encircled and their resistance immensely costly—about 1,500 Japanese were killed and 2,000 taken prisoner. 115 Australians were killed and 432 wounded. At the same time, at Port Moresby, a US Liberator bomber had crashed and exploded among 7th Division troops waiting for their airlift to Nadzab, killing 59 of them and wounding 92.

After Lae, the Japanese garrison at Salamaua fell to the Australians and, after that, bitter fighting at Finschhafen secured an airfield and naval base crucial to the American 6th Army's invasion of New Britain. While the battle of Finschhafen raged, an operation that was both seamless and symptomatic of the turn in Pacific fortunes was underway at Singapore. A team of Australian and British commandos, led by a British officer, Major Ivan Lyon, sailed from Exmouth Gulf (Western Australia) in a 23-metre wooden vessel called the *Krait*. There was a crew of eight and a raiding party of six. About 11 kilometres south of Singapore the raiders took to rubber and canvas canoes.

Bushcraft for Defence

Early in 1941 the War Cabinet approved preparations for the defence of the far north against possible Japanese invasion. A Torres Strait Defence Force was set up and, after the Japanese bombed Horn Island, virtually every Islander male of military age became a member: 774 men at full strength. In Arnhem Land a reconnaissance unit was also created. A force of 51 Arnhem Land Aborigines was led by the anthropologist Donald Thomson who knew the local people well, having lived with them for a number of years and earned their trust. Thomson's unit was charged with scouting duties, coast watching and guerilla operations in the event of invasion. In a report to the Director of Special Operations in 1941, he wrote of their warrior tradition and their expertise in the element of surprise. Their avenging tribal expeditions were called *miringu* raids—these could be the basis of guerilla warfare against small parties of invading Japanese.

In the nineteenth century, European settlers had been much troubled by the bushcraft and, it was widely conceded, the tactical superiority of Aboriginal resistance on many frontiers. Disease, numerical odds, horsepower and firepower had diminished these advantages, but on the last frontiers, in 1942, some warrior tradition was still intact. 'They are nomadic hunters,' wrote Thomson, 'and the men . . . live with a spear and a spear-thrower in their hands. Warfare is part of the daily life of these people—and ordeals by single combat are regularly practised . . . *Miringu* expeditions are frequently organised.'

When invasion seemed imminent early in 1942, a larger force was established to cover more territory. The North Australia Observer Unit (NAOU) was made up of volunteer bushmen including Xavier Herbert, the author of *Capricornia* (1938), a novel which explored the relationships of Aboriginal people and whites to the land and to each other. At peak strength the unit was 550 white men, who adopted the nickname 'Nackeroos', and 59 Aboriginal guides and labourers. In the event of an invasion the unit's patrols were not to resist the Japanese but were to be like shadows, hiding, scouting and reporting the enemy's movements. These men were not well-trained fighters, but as 'shadows' they could be elusive and effective.

In charge of the NAOU was another anthropologist with extensive field work in the far north, W.E.H. Stanner from Sydney University. Stanner was inspired by the example of the Boer commandos and soon the bush patrols began to look like Boers, with their beards and their tatty, faded, worn-out clothes. They worked in small, highly mobile units moving by horse, river boat or canoe, with good radio links, light weapons and the capacity to live off the land. Their area of responsibility was impossibly vast, more than 3.8 million square kilometres, from Normanton in Queensland to Yampi Sound in Western Australia, harsh country in which their effectiveness as reconnaissance units depended almost entirely on their Aboriginal guides.

In 1942 the Nackeroo patrols carried flour, tea and sugar and other basic supplies but had to rely on their environment for water and much of their food. The practical knowledge of their guides allowed them to live off the land. Almost every type of animal could be used for food and the range of useable plants was an entertainment in itself—rootstocks, fruit-bearers, seed foods, fungi, exudations and nectar, leaves, stems and flowers were all gathered to feed the patrols, to provide liquid or to cure ailments. There were inhalants for sore throats, anaesthetics for pain, liniments for

Shooting party. Men of HMAS *Moresby* with Aboriginal guides, Melville Island, October 1944.

damaged muscles, antiseptics for cuts and lesions and potions for stomach upsets, fever, bites and stings. 'You always felt safe when you had an Aborigine with you,' wrote one of the Nackeroos. 'You knew that you wouldn't starve.'

Nor would they die of thirst, for the guides found water and other thirst quenchers in many unlikely places—in the roots of trees and in the gizzards of bloated hibernating frogs. 'They just held these hibernating frogs up to their mouths,' wrote Corporal Des Harrison, 'bit a little hole in them and drank the juice straight out of the frogs' bodies.' Every Nackeroo knew there could be no reconnaissance and no 'shadowing' without these guides.

Officially the guides received 5 shillings a week 'or such lesser rate as approved by the commissioning officer of the NAOU.' This was a small fraction of what white soldiers received but even that frequently went unpaid. The guides were mostly paid in kind, in various rations and in two forms of tobacco, one called 'Nigger Twist', the other 'Nikki-Nikki'. None of the guides was called by their tribal names. Some were burdened with mission names such as Joshua and Mordecai, others were tagged for irony with names like 'Snowball' and 'Publican Charlie'. But this was not an accurate reflection of race relations within the NAOU.

In the far north, it was still of no great consequence to shoot a troublesome Aborigine and justice was so racially skewed that the law offered little or no protection to black fellas. When *Capricornia* was published there was outrage at Xavier Herbert's fictionalised account of the white violence and bigotry he knew from personal experience. Within the NAOU the subordination of Aboriginal guides to the Nackeroos was enforced at all times. Any black man who stepped out of line was knocked to the ground. But mostly the guides were treated with a respect that stemmed from the new-found utility of their bushcraft, so much so that some locals thought they got far too much respect. 'When you fellas move out, we're stuck with them blacks,' said one cattle station manager, aggrieved at the sight of white and black men eating together. The Unit began to 'move out' in 1943. Operations were scaled back from July as the Pacific war shifted northward. The NAOU was disbanded in March 1945.

A Commonwealth poster urging housewives to save food.

Delivering bread, St Kilda Road, Melbourne, June 1943.

In Singapore Harbour and at nearby Bukum Island, they attached timed limpet mines to Japanese merchant vessels, then withdrew to an uninhabited island and in a state of exhaustion waited for the explosions. The mines exploded in quick succession around 5 am on 27 September, sinking seven ships. The commandos then took to their canoes again, paddled 80 kilometres to rendezvous with the *Krait* and were back in Exmouth Gulf on 19 October.

While the Special Unit commandos were sailing to Singapore, Finschhafen had fallen and the long battle to capture Sattleberg Mountain, which dominated the area, was underway. The Sattleberg heights were not controlled by Australians until late in November but the cost in human lives was comparatively small and organised Japanese resistance was all but wiped from the land of New Guinea. Port Moresby was safe. Japanese bombing raids on Australia's far north had ceased. Combined US forces were advancing to the Philippines.

For much of 1942, the government knew that Australia's mobilisation for total war was unsustainable. The economy was overstretched and the army was too large to replenish. Labour and recruits were now hard to find. From October 1942, eight battalions were progressively disbanded. The 39th Battalion, resting on the Atherton Tablelands in Queensland, was one of these. Ralph Honner knew before his men did that they were to be split up and distributed to other units as reinforcements. He was so upset he took to drink, something he had never done before. Honner took command of the 2/14th Battalion and fought on in New Guinea until a machine gun bullet shattered his left hip joint, just missed his right hip and ended his war. He was in Queensland, learning to walk in callipers as the government battled on, trying to find labour to plug gaps in the economic front line.

Military prospects had brightened early in 1943 at about the same time that the supply of manpower and womanpower reached its limits. Australia had run out of people. Munitions was still operating as though invasion threatened, trying to produce more of everything, but the civilian economy was dangerously neglected. Of a workforce of 3.2 million, about 1 million men and women were engaged in the direct war effort—in the armed services and the munitions industries; another 1 million were employed in the provisioning of Australian and Allied troops, supplying food, clothing, transport and administrative services. The rest were trying to keep the civilian economy going.

The armed services were draining the labour supply too. The casualty rates were high in New Guinea; they were also high in North Africa, on the Mediterranean Sea and over Germany. The problem was partly solved by taking in more women. The number of women in the services grew from 20,000 in July 1942 to 44,000 in June 1943. But all three services were in constant need of more men. The required monthly intake was 10,000: 5,500 for the army; 4,000 for the air force, and 500 for the navy.

The many calls on manpower and womanpower left the civilian economy in real trouble. In the crisis of 1942, the Manpower poachers drained the civilian economy of skilled and other labour. It was underequipped and dependent on a substitute workforce, often unfamiliar with the work and the conditions. Productivity had dropped off alarmingly in some sectors; roads, bridges and buildings were falling into disrepair. Health, education and other professions were short of labour too. Agriculture and dairying were near collapse.

Still the Manpower officials wanted more war workers. As labour supplies dried up, the search for likely candidates became more intense. They raked over the clerical staff in banks and insurance firms. By June 1943, 500 bank branches had shut down. Manpower targeted the retail and wholesale trades. Manpower representatives went after labour in the miscellaneous sector—in entertainment, sport, photography, watchmaking and electrical contracting—and there they found more likely candidates, but the limits of the labour supply were fast approaching. They even investigated beauty parlours and found that only a few hundred workers could be diverted to war production unless permanent waving was abolished. Here morale was a factor. The Directorate decided that perms were essential, such was the power of fashion. Hairdressers in beauty parlours would not be diverted. Nor would the makers of ice cream. Ice cream production was deemed to be in the same essential-for-morale category as perms. While other dairy products were restricted, the ice cream makers soldiered on.

Rural production was hard hit. The land was a prime source of fit young men and by July 1942, the rural workforce was down to two-thirds of pre-war strength. Men between 18 and 45 had almost disappeared from the countryside. The men and women left behind were struggling desperately to meet the needs of the troops in Australia, to feed and provision the fighting forces in the south-west Pacific, to provide civilians with their ration quotas and to meet obligations to Europe where food shortages were becoming a critical problem. The gap between supply and

The men and women left behind were struggling desperately to meet the needs of the troops in Australia.

Members of the Australian Women's Land Army at work near Atherton, Queensland, 23 October 1943.

demand was widening. The need to increase food production was acute. The UK was much in need of Australian supplies and US troop demands were going up as the number of GIs in Australia grew to 250,000 in February 1943. Their caloric intake was now a sore point. US rations averaged 4,758 calories per day, compared with Australian rations, which averaged 3,944, and no amount of argument would persuade the US generals to lower the American level. They put the difference down to national characteristics and expected Australians to do without.

In desperation in June 1943, the Curtin government declared that food was a munition of war and so too was agricultural machinery. The government reckoned 50,000 men would have to be returned to agriculture to satisfy total demand for calories in Australian homes, in troop camps to the north and in England.

The worst hit primary product was milk. Milk production sank in 1942 when dairy farmers readily abandoned their farms for military service or war work in industry. Poor conditions on dairy farms, low returns, long hours and minimal mechanisation made dairy farmers the peasants of mid twentieth-century Australia. Some had sent their cows to the butchers without a second thought. Others left the dairy work to their wives. In their keenness to get away they defied the best efforts of the government to keep them on the land. The decline in milk production and related products, especially butter, continued into 1944. Australia's butter exports to the UK in 1943–44 were 41,700 tons compared with 109,000 tons in 1939–40, while dairy products required by US troops in the Pacific theatre were supplied in full. The UK was last on the list of priorities. The ramifications of Curtin's call to America in 1941 went all the way to English dinner tables.

Groups of civilians organised themselves in various ways in response to the crisis in agriculture. The Young Soldiers Pool consisted of shearers, and university and senior school students and was especially useful at certain times to harvest vegetables, fruit, rice, cotton and flax. Trains and buses were organised to move its members about and they were generally billeted with families. It was an ad hoc arrangement but it worked. The same applied to the Women's Land Army. Formed in July 1942, the WLA reached a peak of 4,000 permanent and auxiliary members during the 1943–44 harvest season. Some country wives did not like the idea; some farmers claimed women workers were not worth the prescribed rates of pay, but performance generally outshone ingrained prejudice. The women of the Land Army were trained in animal care and management, market gardening, dairying and the use of farm machinery. They worked on farms everywhere, tending dairy cows, pigs and poultry, growing vegetables, harvesting flax and picking fruit. They also came together in camps of 200 to 300 to pick the big crops at harvest time.

A far more unlikely set of labourers was living in India behind British barbed wire—Italian prisoners of war. In mid 1943, Cabinet approved a war immigration program to bring 10,000 Italian prisoners to Australia. Dairy farmers, fruit and vegetable growers, wheat farmers and others made good use of them. At first there were restrictions on allowing large numbers of Italians to work together but these restrictions were soon relaxed and they were engaged in rice production, timber cutting and vegetable seed growing.

From the primary industries there had been withdrawn 180,000 men, or 31 per cent of their 1939 strength; from mining 20,000 men or 28 per cent; from building and construction 160,000 or 48 per cent; from commerce and finance 115,000 or 30 per cent.

H.C. Coombs, Director-General, Ministry of Post-War Reconstruction, 1944

A horse drawn sled transports milk to save on petrol, Bendigo, Victoria, April 1943, *opposite*.

An ice-cream vendor does a roaring trade serving troops at a rail stop, Clapham Junction, Queensland, October 1943, *below*.

In 1943 the output of every major agricultural product, except wheat, was dropping further behind production targets.

Italian POWs harvesting a crop of onions at Yanco, New South Wales, January 1944.

The story of rice production stands out. In the Wakool irrigation district (in south-west New South Wales), Italian labour plus local expertise with Lend-Lease machinery plus local trucks combined to grow some 2,020 hectares of rice in 1943, 1944 and 1945. At the time it was the world's largest rice paddy and the most successful exercise in state farming in Australia's history. The Italians were congenial and hard working and there were plans to import more of them, but in September 1943 Italy capitulated. A new Italian government declared war on Germany. Those Italian prisoners already working in rural Australia continued to do so for the duration of the war, but plans for more transfers from India were dropped.

In 1943 the output of every major agricultural product, except wheat, was dropping further behind production targets. The question was who was to go short: civilians, the troops, or Britain? The answer was Britain. Britain was last on the list because the South West Pacific Area had to come first. Ever since he had called the troops home from the Middle East, Curtin was adamant about that. And the big powers in the alliance were equally adamant about beating Hitler first.

In January the top Allied leaders met at Casablanca in Morocco to determine combat priorities. The Pacific theatre was placed fifth in order of importance behind the Atlantic, Russia, the Mediterranean and the United Kingdom. For some months not even MacArthur was sure of the resources he was to have for Cartwheel. The situation impeded planning and rattled his vanity. He never reconciled himself to the fact that his war did not rank first in Allied priorities. Just twelve out of every 100 GIs overseas were under his command. When Eisenhower invaded North Africa he was allocated 15 tons of supplies per man; MacArthur was receiving 5 tons per man for the Pacific. Australian war workers were making up the difference.

But Australia's war effort had reached saturation point. Curtin knew the country could not continue to provide troops, munitions and food at current levels, let alone the levels required for the Cartwheel Operations. Something had to give. Munitions was the

Zoe Allison working a lathe, part of the process of making 20 mm shells, 5 March 1943.

obvious candidate for consolidation because the blockade conditions of early 1942 no longer applied and munitions production was in surplus. Australian munitions production in April 1943 was valued at £100,000,000 and 22.2 per cent of it was designated as surplus to current or expected needs, a surplus including hundreds of artillery pieces, millions of shells and thousands of gun carriages.

These were just the main items. There was also a heavy surplus in 3-inch mortars, mortar-bombs, .303 cartridges and other less expensive items. In that momentous January of 1943 with victories in New Guinea, North Africa and Russia, the surplus was already a problem that could not be postponed.

War at Sea

HMAS *Hobart* in dry dock at Cockatoo Island, Sydney Harbour, December 1943.

To promote the government's fourth war loan, a spectacle in the form of a munitions parade was organised in Melbourne. Shoppers lined the streets to watch the 'Miles of Munitions' parade, on 29 October 1943. The Minister for the Navy and for Munitions, N.J.O. Makin, sat on a dais in Collins Street as the hour long parade of nearly 240 trucks and floats went by, each bearing a munitions achievement from the factories of Australia.

Weaponry for the army predominated but the navy and air force featured too. Navy exhibits included mines and depth charges, lifeboats, collapsible dinghies, surfboats and flat-bottomed assault landing barges. There was a 15 ton propeller for an Australian-made merchantman and depictions on billboards of the manufacturing process for 4-inch Mark XVI naval guns, ship-mounted 40 mm Bofors anti-aircraft guns and other marine necessities such as sea markers, flame and smoke floats, and distress signals.

As the war progressed, the navy's many tasks multiplied and to meet them industry had to expand. To back up the small combat fleet (13 vessels at the start of the war), two coastal liners were armed with 6-inch guns, others were converted into infantry landing vessels and some were transformed for service into auxiliary minesweepers or victualling ships. Three Atlantic liners were converted into troopships at Sydney and several other civilian vessels became hospital ships. Of the 750 vessels dry docked at Cockatoo Island in Sydney Harbour during the war, almost half were naval vessels requiring conversion or modification, refit or repair. Around the nation, moribund ship-building centres came to life to build corvettes, frigates, replacement cargo ships, other powered craft, pontoons, life-boats and dinghies, and to provide refit and repair facilities for incoming craft. Elsewhere in industry, production geared up to supply marine engines, gearboxes, electrical switchboards, mines and depth charges, naval guns, armour-piercing shells, gun turret mountings, innovative radar equipment and even torpedos.

The RAN was building towards a peak wartime strength of 337 ships and 39,650 personnel.

When the south-west Pacific became Australia's main concern, the demands on the navy and associated industries intensified. The nation's major naval facility was Cockatoo Island. It was repairing the combat ships of Australia, Britain and the USA throughout the war. In 1943, HMAS *Hobart* reached Sydney with her stern hanging on by a thread, two propellers and shafting blown away. In January 1945, *Australia* was dry-docked there for structural repair after repeated kamikaze attacks during the Allied landings at Lingayen Gulf. RN aircraft carriers were also repaired at Cockatoo Island, as were US heavy cruisers stricken with torpedo damage. The USS *New Orleans* came into Sydney Harbour missing 46 metres of her bow. More than 100 tonnes of steel were required to fit a false bow to get the ship home to San Francisco for further repairs.

From May 1941 Australian ships in the Mediterranean were gradually redeployed to eastern waters as the Japanese threat to Australia grew. Australians had been conditioned to put their faith in sea power, but in November that faith received a hammer blow. HMAS *Sydney*, one of the navy's three modern light cruisers, was sunk by an inferior craft, the German raider *Kormoran*. The two ships met in the Indian Ocean about 240 kilometres south-west of Carnarvon. All 645 crew of the *Sydney* were lost.

The navy's war against the Japanese began soon after this devastating loss. There were more losses to come. Spread too thin and over-committed, the RAN suffered severe losses against the Japanese—three of its biggest and newest cruisers, three destroyers, two sloops and a corvette were lost in enemy action. No Japanese warship was sunk by an Australian vessel, though the RAN did sink one Japanese submarine and took part in the destruction of two others.

The RAN's achievement from 1942 to 1949 was not to be found in victorious exchanges at sea, but in the less spectacular exercise of maritime power in Australian waters and the nearby Pacific. As a small force attached to the US Navy, RAN work was primarily policing sovereign waters, protecting convoys, escorting supply ships, minesweeping, naval gunfire support, mapping (the north coast of New Guinea is an important example) and generally denying the sea lanes to the enemy, while ensuring the free movement of troops and supplies to the Allies. Later in the war, the navy played a major role in the amphibious landings and battles for New Guinea and the islands of the south-west Pacific. Total RAN deaths for the war, all ranks and all causes, numbered 2,170. Of these 1,170 died in the war against Germany and Italy, and 949 in the war against Japan.

The men of munitions were zealous about the challenge of production. Even complaints from the Prime Minister were regarded as interruptions.

But munitions was unstoppable. The department had become a power unto itself. It dealt directly with the Australian armed services and even with the US army, it was placing orders with itself to maintain continuity of production, it was touting for business in London and India, and accepting orders outside the normal supply channels—selling bulletproof plate, machine guns, fuses and ammunition to South Africa and New Zealand. It was building up a nice little export trade on the side. The men of munitions were zealous about the challenge of production. Even complaints from the Prime Minister were regarded as interruptions. Empire building in the Munitions Department was out of hand and it was at odds with the desperate need to balance the war effort. The War Cabinet decided munitions must be curtailed and consolidated so that labour could be moved to food production where tens of thousands of new hands were required.

Munitions resisted, dragged the chain, fudged the figures and misinformed the government. But the main reason why it was hard to divert labour away from munitions was the Pacific offensive. The labour saved in cutting back production of 25-pounder guns, gun carriages, mortars and small arms ammunition was now being drawn to the needs of the amphibious and airborne campaigns in the islands to the north. An island-hopping offensive put a premium on landing craft, craft maintenance, harbour and coastal patrol vessels, barges, tug boats, floating wharves and docks, and, of course, aircraft; on canned food, radio and signalling equipment; on automotive spare parts, internal combustion engines and refrigerators; and on war supplies, which ranged from bold ventures into the manufacture of Lancaster bombers and Mustang fighter planes to the making of the humble nut and bolt.

Diversion became conversion. The ammunition factory at Rocklea in Queensland was converted to aero-engine reconditioning; at Tamworth the gun primer factory switched over to food dehydration; munitions factories at Katoomba in the Blue Mountains in New South Wales and Stawell in Victoria were converted to the manufacture of clothing; shipyards along the east coast of Australia and in Tasmania switched production to the marine needs of the offensive; and nine ammunition factory annexes now took to the automatic machining of nuts and bolts with combined service orders for 21 million and 14 million respectively. This kept the annexes busy for two years.

By mid 1943 shipping lanes were open again. The UK wanted Australia to slot back into a traditional empire division of labour, to buy more guns and sell more food. The US government endorsed that but MacArthur did not. He wanted Australia to supply more troops, more war equipment *and* more food. Curtin was worried that Australia would be bled white. It was clear that Australia's commitment could not be sustained without a drastic reduction in the Australian standard of living and more regimentation. There was

Electrical welder, Mrs D. Dunlop, working in a munitions factory near Melbourne, 2 February 1943.

even talk of conscripting young single women into the services and other women into industry and agriculture, but that was considered too radical.

Australian society was already more war-geared than the US and there were doubts Australians would accept more controls. Those doubts were strengthened by good news from abroad, news of victories. The mood had changed from anxiety to optimism. As the danger abated, it became more difficult to demand sacrifices, rewards were easier to pursue and cracks reappeared in the nation's unity. One sign of this was the increase in industrial disputes, up sharply in 1943. In crucial industries—meat slaughtering and coalmining, and wharf labouring—the old pattern of conflict was back. On the wharves US troops were

. . . as I look around me and see all the equipment we have I sometimes think it can't be many more months. The Jap was beaten by us when practically all we had was rifles, but now we have so much.

7th Division artillery officer, unnamed

Fighting Fitness: the Battle of the Canteens

American servicemen waiting for ice-cream sodas, Mackay, Queensland, 1943.

In 1943, Brisbane was a small provincial capital with a population of about 330,000 and facilities to match. On the outskirts of the city, US troop numbers had built to about 90,000. The city could not cope. Everything was in short supply—transport, accommodation, entertainment and food. Shops ran out of supplies. Restaurants and hotels were packed out. The patience of hosts and patrons was strained and hospitality started to fade. Cafes chained teaspoons to the table or tied them to the handle of the sugar bowl. Superbly fit soldiers wandered the streets in a city where there was little in the way of entertainment or diversion.

There were nearly 250,000 US troops in Australia at this time, most of them in camps in the eastern states. Their interaction with locals was usually peaceable and pleasant, and the cultural encounter for many Australians was novel and fascinating. Curtin encouraged Australians to fly US flags in their front gardens. Cinemas played the 'Star Spangled Banner' after 'God Save the King' and churches held Thanksgiving services.

But Australian troops welcomed the Americans with less enthusiasm than the general public. The Americans seemed overly boastful, their uniforms smartly tailored, their pay packets far in excess of what the Diggers earned. A US lieutenant earned £63 a

month; an Australian lieutenant earned £29.15. The Americans spent freely and seemed to receive favoured treatment from taxi drivers, hotel patrons, restaurateurs and women.

The government and the opposition were anxious that these disparities could lead to trouble in the streets. They also worried that American spending would, as Billy Hughes put it, 'imperil the stability of the price structure'. American spending was creating black markets, it was warping the distribution of controlled goods, it was angering the locals and, it was said, it was attracting Australian women.

Some women found the Americans glamorous and fun; others found them loud and superficial. Some heeded the writer Alan Marshall's warning that they should think of the AIF men fighting and dying abroad and give first preference in their affections to their militiamen at home. Dating Americans was a contentious issue that raised nationalist hackles; it was also a moral issue in which women were a focal point for many Australian male anxieties.

The anxieties were exacerbated by the lack of a place to go—by the upsurge of scandalising activities in jeeps and parks and shop doorways. Parsons, journalists and some radio commentators welcomed fraternisation and socialising but frowned on dating. But the moral censure did not stop women dating, loving and even marrying US soldiers.

Many women found the Americans to be a refreshing change from Australian men. They were articulate, wise-cracking, lively, courteous, attentive and generous. Sexual jealousy and other resentments combined with the fitness and aggression of soldiers to produce street brawls and riots in every city, but in Brisbane a massive brawl earned the label battle. The numbers involved (about 3,000), the violence, the severe injuries sustained and even one death seemed to justify the name the Battle of the Canteens or the Battle of Brisbane.

Flying Officer M. E. Collard and Leading Aircraftman D. W. Sinclair at work in the RAAF's Survey and Design Unit, Aitape, New Guinea, June 1944, *opposite*.

The Australians' last battles in the Pacific cost many lives and made no difference to the outcome of the war.

sometimes unloading their own supplies. Another sign was the return of party political brawling in parliament, notably the Brisbane Line controversy.

On 7 June 1943, MacArthur confirmed the new optimism when he assured the Prime Minister that the threat of invasion had passed; Japan's defeat was only a matter of time. Three days later Curtin told the people, and soon after the government decided to divert 20,000 men from the army and 10,000 from munitions to work in food production. Food was now more important than fear. The decision was made easier by MacArthur's determination to exclude Australian troops from the main thrust north. The Americans would advance to the Philippines, then to Japan; the triumph would be all theirs. Australian troops would mop up in the rear.

The Australians' last battles in the Pacific cost many lives and made no difference to the outcome of the war. Australian forces took over from US troops in the Australian-mandated territories of Bougainville and New Britain, and in the Aitape-Wewak area in New Guinea. They also fought in Borneo, at Tarakan, Brunei Bay and Balikpapan. In the mandated territories, the Japanese they fought had already been bypassed, isolated and neutralised. In Borneo, oil was allegedly the prize but the Japanese could not ship it because they had lost control of the sea and the air. These have been called the unnecessary wars.

The final phase of fighting the Pacific War saw MacArthur sweeping on to the Philippines and then to Japan, while Australian troops were left behind to eliminate the remnants of the Japanese army. Strategic decisions resulted in the marginalisation of the Australians and first-rate troops ended up doing a low-ranked job. They knew they were mopping up and not vital to the winning of the war, Australian newspapers told them so. They had to ignore letters from their loved ones advising caution, they had to get on with the job of fighting and dying as if final victory depended on every inch of ground they seized.

But if the unnecessary wars did not count in military terms, they did have political meaning. The War Cabinet made this clear late in 1943 when it was trying to balance the economy. The military effort needed to be concentrated in the Pacific and sustained, in the words of a

Surrender

Photographers waiting for the surrender ceremony on Morotai, 9 September 1945.

A surrender ceremony took place on USS *Missouri*, anchored in Tokyo Bay, on 2 September 1945. Blamey signed for Australia and a week later the Japanese surrendered, officially, in a purely Australian ceremony. This was held on the island of Morotai in the Moluccas.

There Blamey received the surrender of Lieutenant General Teshima. Teshima was escorted to a table surrounded by a phalanx of Australian troops, seven deep. Blamey spoke directly to Teshima:

In receiving your surrender I do not recognise you as an honourable and gallant foe, but you will be treated with due but severe courtesy in all matters. I recall the treacherous attack on our ally, China . . . I recall the treacherous attack made upon the British Empire and upon the United States of America in December 1941, at a time when your authorities were making the pretence of negotiating peace. I recall the atrocities inflicted upon the persons of our nationals as prisoners of war and internees, designed to reduce them by punishment and starvation to slavery. In the light of these evils, I will enforce most rigorously all orders issued to you, so let there be no delay or hesitation in their fulfilment at your peril.

Putting a cross on the grave
of Lieutenant Tom Derrick,
VC, DCM, Tarakan,
26 May 1945.

*The war was
over. The atomic
age had begun.*

War Cabinet minute, 'on a scale to guarantee Australia an effective voice in the peace settlement'. These last battles were to show the flag in the Pacific, to reassert the colonial claim to New Guinea, to strengthen Australia's hand at the peace table and to speed the liberation of its POWs. One thousand six hundred Australians died fighting these wars and 4,377 were wounded.

The atomic cloud rises
above Nagasaki, Japan,
9 August 1945.

Germany surrendered on 8 May 1945 while Australian troops were still fighting remnants of the Japanese army in Bougainville and New Guinea and Australian engineers were trying to stem massive oil fires in Borneo. Ralph Honner was in Perth, working for the Directorate of Military Training. He had dispensed with the callipers on his legs, but could never do without a walking stick. Honner was disabled for life. The Prime Minister was another casualty of war. On 5 July 1945, Curtin died of a heart attack and a few days later Ben Chifley was appointed the new Prime Minister. The nation mourned. Curtin's death united Australia as nothing before, save the threat of a Japanese invasion. A month later the US air force dropped two atomic bombs, one on Hiroshima on 6 August, the other on Nagasaki on 9 August. The war was over. The atomic age had begun.

5

FIVE MINUTES
TO MIDNIGHT

1950 – 1966

Members of the Australian Victory Contingent in the Russian Zone, Berlin, June 1946.

In February 1945, John Curtin invited Australians to do an uncommon thing. He invited them to fly the red flag to salute the Red Army on Red Army Day. He told the people that Russian forces were closing in on Berlin. They were closer to the German capital than he was to Sydney. Curtin was speaking from Canberra. He ordered red flags to be flown from Commonwealth buildings and asked state governments to issue a similar directive. The New South Wales Premier suggested that the Russian flag might be flown if the red flag was not 'practicable'.

I N the capital cities there were Red Army Day receptions. In Sydney the Town Hall was full—the celebrations were so popular Soviet embassy staff were caught in the overflow of enthusiasts on the main steps and accidentally locked out. Amid the speeches, a message from Dr Herbert Vere Evatt was read to the crowd: 'The Australian people and their warriors salute with unbounded admiration the imperishable deeds of the men, women and children of Russia.'

The deeds may have been imperishable but the official salute was never to be repeated. This was the high point of Australia's fraternal relations with a great wartime ally. From here on the fear of Russia's global ambitions grew. The Soviet Union moved clumsily and brutally to occupy nations of Eastern and Central Europe. For many Australians, sympathy and support turned into repugnance and fear. It was becoming harder to believe the USSR simply needed buffers to insure against future invasion.

The idea that the USSR wanted to force communism onto the rest of the world became the main tenet of US foreign policy. In March 1947, President Harry Truman issued a call-to-arms that was immediately enshrined as the Truman Doctrine. He called for a new age of US intervention 'to support free peoples wherever they face attempted subjection by armed minorities'. Truman's Secretary of State, Dean Acheson found the nearest historical parallel in classical times: 'Not since Rome and Carthage had their been such a polarisation of power on this earth.' The only answer to the Soviet global plot, it was argued, was a US empire capable of exercising decisive world control.

In Australia the public campaign against communism was led by Robert Menzies and his new Liberal Party. As Opposition leader, Menzies linked the Communist Party of Australia (CPA) to Soviet ambitions. The Labor government did not agree with him. Nor did it agree with US foreign policy. Both Chifley and Evatt were sceptical of the 'global plot' thesis and cautious about the USA's global ambitions. A string of events in Australia and abroad did not help their case. In June 1948

Frozen waters.
An Australian soldier on a Korean footbridge, Han River, January 1951, *previous page.*

Anglo-Soviet Unity procession, Melbourne, 5 September 1942, *below.*

181

One of the first official RAF photographs of Berlin after its fall, May 1945.

Australian society after the war was a paradox — there was growing affluence and personal comfort alongside growing apprehension and fear.

Lieutenant General S.F. Rowell.

the Russian blockade of Berlin began. It continued for 11 months and RAAF pilots took part in the massive airlift to supply Berliners with food and fuel. Menzies said the situation was tantamount to a state of war.

At home the industrial scene was also riven with conflict. The CPA had a membership of about 25,000 when the war ended and was a powerful force in many trade unions as well as in defence-related areas. In 1947, Dr Evatt introduced legislation to protect the new Long Range Weapons Establishment at Woomera in South Australia from trade union black bans. In July 1949, Chifley ordered the army into the coalmines to do the work of striking miners. For the Acting Chief of General Staff, Lieutenant General Sydney Rowell, this was a straightforward mission: 'there is no magic,' he wrote, 'in the process of open-cut mining, least of all to a corps like the Royal Australian Engineers, skilled in the use of explosives and in handling heavy earthmoving equipment.' The strike was broken in August.

Defence spending was once again a public issue. The daily press picked up on the US lead: 'Record US Budget Shows High Cost of Staving off World War III' claimed one headline. Editorials argued that Australia was unarmed and unprepared but Ben Chifley stuck to his modest five-year defence plan. He was certain that the Soviet Union could not wage war even if it wanted to. The general public was not so sure. Australian society after the war was a paradox—there was growing affluence and personal comfort alongside growing apprehension and fear. In 1949, 65 per cent of Australians polled agreed that the USA and the USSR would be at war within five years. Later in the year Menzies was elected to power with a program that included banning the CPA. He also made Chinese communism an election issue and in his campaign speeches talked about a 'Fifth Column' of traitors in Australia. Sir Keith Murdoch agreed. The Soviet Union now had the atom bomb. China might have the bomb soon. Murdoch warned that communists were poised to destroy Australia with atomic weapons. 'The enemies of this country are 800 million Eastern Europeans and Chinese,' he said. In less than a year Australian forces would be fighting in Malaya and Korea, pitted against a communist enemy.

Dire predictions escalated with the arms race. Menzies returned from Washington in August 1950 with a $US100 million loan from the World Bank and a briefing on Anglo-American preparations for World War III. Australian troops were already fighting in Korea and the Prime Minister now fervently believed that world war was imminent. Emergency planning for a war economy, and a war mentality, began immediately.

In September, Menzies gave the first of three radio broadcasts on the world crisis. 'It is because your government has considered the facts and weighed the risks,' he said, 'that it has decided to call upon the people of Australia for the greatest effort in defence preparation . . . ever undertaken in time of peace.' His vision of the coming atomic war was apocalyptic. The atomic age had unleashed dreams of technological utopias but it had also released the darkest fears of war, fears of a past revisited, like the Great War, a scale of destruction beyond the most bleak imagination. What most concerned Menzies was the need to prepare because, unlike 1914 and 1939, Australia would have no breathing space. The nation would be engulfed instantly and mercilessly under aerial and atomic attack. The nightmare vision justified immediate action. It was 'five minutes to midnight'.

Trajectory for rockets from the Woomera Rocket Range to the Monte Bello Islands. October 1952.

In the same month, September 1950, £50 million was transferred to a defence trust account to pay for a Strategic Stores and Equipment Reserve. This amount was one-seventh of total Commonwealth income tax for the financial year 1950–51. After coal, copper, tungsten, manganese, hard fibres, oil and other war inputs were dealt with, the government turned to the 'uranium option' and plans were laid for uranium production in South Australia, with a railway line to be built from Uranium Hill in the Northern Territory to Port Pirie on Spencer Gulf. Australia was anticipating an upcoming conference in Washington, where allied supply responsibilities would be shared out. These would include uranium supplies for atomic weapons.

A test site was also required for a British attempt to build an atomic arsenal. Australia offered the Monte Bello islands in the Indian Ocean and remote country in the central desert in South Australia, the latter handed over with little concern for the Aboriginal inhabitants. Between 1952 and 1957 there were 12 atomic explosions, the first at Monte Bello and most of the others at Emu Field and Maralinga in the central desert.

In December 1950 the National Security Resources Board was created, a panel of top businessmen and public servants whose job it was to do the groundwork for total mobilisation. Soon after, a National Service scheme was introduced, requiring eighteen-year-old males to give about six months service to the Citizen Military Forces (CMF) or the Citizen Naval Forces (CNF). Most went into the CMF, did their 90 days continuous training and then trained part-time over the remainder of a three-year period.

In his radio broadcasts Menzies continued to hammer the theme of a Fifth Column in Australia's midst. When talking about communist deception he was fond

A test site was also required for a British attempt to build an atomic arsenal.

Fierce winds made life uncomfortable for the press photographers covering the atomic test activity on the Monte Bello Islands, 1952.

The remainder of the time I spent in Sydney was working in teams of two and four giving special attention to the numerous Communist representatives from the Youth Carnival and their activities in many places, including the Public Library, Museum, Taronga Zoo . . . dancing exhibitions on the street and loud speaker addresses to workers during their lunch hour period . . . Whilst at Sydney I was able to obtain the names and addresses of a large number of Tasmanians who have communistic interests and will report on them accordingly on the following form.

J.J. Webberley, Tasmanian ASIO agent in Sydney for the 1952 Youth Carnival for Peace and Friendship

RAN national service trainees, Melbourne, July 1951, *opposite.*

of quoting Lady Macbeth's advice to her husband: 'Look like the innocent flower, but be the serpent under it.' Traitors were everywhere. Radicals and critics in the public service, the schools and the universities were now watched and vetted by the Australian Security Intelligence Organisation (ASIO), which had been created in 1949 by the Chifley government. The Communist Party Dissolution Bill was passed into law in October, challenged in the High Court and then defeated in a referendum held almost a year later, on 22 September 1951. The margin for the No vote was less than 0.5 per cent. The Cold War was a heated affair in Australian public life, fuelled by the fear of atomic confrontation.

One of the government's targets was the peace movement. An Australian Peace Council (APC) was established by the CPA in 1949. The APC's membership was small but immensely energetic, ready and willing to lobby people at shopping centres, churches and factory gates, on university campuses, in clubs and on street corners. In 1952 it was behind the organisation of a 'Youth Carnival for Peace and Friendship' in Sydney, the first to be held outside Eastern Europe. There was no shortage of hostile publicity in the press. The Sydney *Sun* called the proposed Carnival 'a gigantic Soviet propaganda attack, deliberately aimed at breaking down the self-defence of the democracies'. The Menzies government was equally hostile but unable to ban the Carnival because a ban would defy the High Court's 1950 ruling that the Communist Party was a legal body. Other methods had to be found.

Visas were denied to about 100 overseas delegates and some interstate visitors were intercepted en route for questioning. ASIO and Special Branch police persuaded 25 city and municipal councils to withdraw permission for the use of town halls, sporting facilities and cultural venues booked for the Carnival. The main venue, Harold Park Trotting Ground, was withdrawn two weeks before the opening day. Hollywood Park, 25 kilometres south of Sydney, was booked as an alternative venue until the booking was cancelled. The Carnival's organising committee took its case to court and won the right to proceed, but other key venues were lost for good. The 'Grand Carnival Ball' at Paddington Town Hall was forced to reschedule to a venue in Bankstown, the symphony concert at Sydney Town Hall was compelled to go elsewhere and the Surf Carnival organised for Newcastle had to move to other shores because the local council refused access to all of its beaches. The effort that went into stopping the Carnival was a measure of the government's concern. A Cabinet paper made the point forcefully: 'The Carnival may distract the attention of many Australians away from the menace of the Communist international threat, and to that extent morally cripple the government's rearmament programme.'

In the event of atomic confrontation, it was assumed Australia's role would be to follow tradition—ground troops and air squadrons would go to the Middle East, the ground troops to be deployed as required and the air squadrons to bomb advancing Soviet forces as well as oilfields in the Caucasus. The deserts of North Africa and Palestine still figured powerfully in the minds of conservative politicians and some defence planners. Even as Australia became embroiled in conflict in Malaya and Korea in mid 1950, Menzies was noting in his diary: 'All these Asian adventures are diversions by the Russians.' By 'diversions' he meant peripheral wars to tie up 'free world' forces away from future battlegrounds in Europe and the Middle East.

The Right Honorable R.G. Casey, ex-Governor of Bengal, on his return to Australia in 1946.

Not everyone agreed. There were senior officers in the armed forces, and ministers in Cabinet, who could see that Asian unrest was overtaking plans for the Middle East. In Chifley's time as prime minister, the colonies to Australia's north were in upheaval. The Philippines became independent in July 1946; India in January 1947; after partition and much bloodshed, Pakistan was created. An independent Burma followed. Indonesia fought a war of independence against Dutch rule and communist forces had prevailed in China. Where would this end? One of the dissenters was Percy Spender, Minister for External Affairs. He was deeply concerned about the consequences of change in Asia and held a dim view of how Australia's expeditionary forces had been used in World War II. He tried to turn Cabinet against the Middle East plan, but lost out to the formidable Menzies.

Richard Gardiner Casey was another doubter. He was a World War I veteran with a Military Cross awarded on the Western Front. As Federal Treasurer in 1937–38, he dramatically boosted the rearmament program, notably to the army and air force. He served as Australia's first ambassador to the United States in 1940, he was then coopted by Churchill into the British War Cabinet and after that served a three-year term as Governor of Bengal. In 1946 he came home to Melbourne, re-entered federal politics and replaced Spender as Minister for External Affairs early in 1951.

Casey was particularly unimpressed with British efforts to quell insurgents in Malaya. As early as 19 May 1950, he told Cabinet that the situation called for 'dirt boy's stuff', for cunning to be pitted against brute force, for 'bribery, deception, whispering and underground methods generally'. He believed Australia could supply small and highly professional troops trained in jungle warfare who would require backing by effective intelligence and subversion. The Australian Security Intelligence Service (ASIS) was established five days later, for covert operations in South East Asia. Casey toured Asia in July and August, 1951 and returned more convinced than ever that Asia was no 'diversion'.

Concerns about the Middle East retained their hold on the Prime Minister and he was supported by powerful voices in the Department of Defence. But the sheer preponderance of unrest in Asia soon changed defence policy. When Menzies wrote about 'diversions' in his diary, the situation in Europe had settled into an uneasy peace, while the colonial system in Asia was collapsing. It was there that national aspirations, along with superpower anxieties and frictions, were played out to the point of war.

For Australia, the period between 1950 and 1972 became one of continuous military engagement in Asia. This was a new kind of war experience. The impact upon life at home was not so great as in previous wars. Indeed, it was comparatively

Men of No.1 Squadron, RAAF, on a jungle survival course in Malaya, 1950. Possibly at the British Army's jungle warfare training centre at Kota Tinggi.

negligible until the Vietnam War became a controversy but that too erupted in forms of protest that were new to Australia. The scale of the commitment did not disrupt or threaten the way of life at home and the number of combat troops involved was small enough to ensure that few Australians had direct, personal links to the battlefield. The tragedy of death or serious wounds in battle was also limited in its impact. Of 102,000 Australian combat fatalities this century, 100,000 occurred before 1950. Even the toll in Vietnam (504) could be expressed by one historian as 'roughly equivalent to the road toll in New South Wales alone over six months'.

The composition of the armed forces committed to battle was different too. While there was heavy reliance on militia or citizen force officers in both world wars, this reliance had diminished in the second. Planning for a regular army began before World War II was over and was realised in 1947. The military, at last, was to be run by professionals. In a nation that prized its volunteer tradition and relied on a part-time militia, whose citizens believed in the power of national character, in mateship and resourcefulness on the battlefield, this was a sharp break with military tradition. Reliance now shifted to a new ethic that combined professionalism and duty. The 'citizen armies' of past conflicts would be no more. The implications for leadership were immense. Regular officers would lead. There was no longer any room for the spirited amateurism of the citizen-soldier.

One sign of the new ethic was the regular army's attitude to conscripts. As the Defence Act permitted only volunteers to serve abroad, conscripts were seen mostly as a reserve for home defence and were not a great help in the Asian troubles. They were also a burden on regular army members, who had to find time away from their own preparations to train these novices. National Service placed a huge strain on hard-pressed regulars and was not popular with the officer class who reckoned the money could be much better spent on professionals and equipment than on reluctant part-timers. But opinion polls differed, showing the general public rated National Service highly and the government seemed to think it good for social discipline. It was the 'short back and sides' treatment, the making of men, but it did not last. The government quietly succumbed to the compelling case for increased professionalism. The scheme dwindled with intakes cut from around 35,000 per annum in 1951–53 to just 12,000 in 1958. A year later National Service was dropped.

Australia's military engagement in Asia was renewed in June 1950. The British government called for assistance in Malaya where a state of emergency had been

Australia's military engagement in Asia was renewed in June 1950.

Taking a break. Jungle survival training for Australian airmen in Malaya, 1950.

In 1950 Australia responded on two fronts to the British call for help.

Lincoln Bomber from No. 1 Squadron, RAAF, on a bombing mission over the Malayan jungle, 1950.

In-flight diet for Australian airmen, low in fat and high in protein.

Lincoln Bomber crew, No. 1 Squadron, RAAF, Singapore, 31 August 1950.

declared two years previously. A guerilla force led by the Malayan Communist Party was intent on overthrowing the colonial government. The pattern would repeat itself again and again in Asia—colonial regimes disrupted by World War II now faced communist or nationalist movements bent on an independence of their own design. The Malayan one was small in number, just a few thousand fighters with mostly outdated weaponry, some of it Japanese, and more old ammunition than new, but it had wide support in the Chinese community through the Min Yuen (masses' organisations).

After World War II, the British military administration had failed to provide minimum food rations, basic law and order, and hope through the agency of an effective constitution for the Chinese minority, many of whom lived as squatters on the fringes of Malayan life. Corruption thrived. Gang warfare was out of control. Racial tensions were high. The racial dimension was all important as most in the Chinese community were marginalised, and denied services and equality before the law. Plans for constitutional change had first promised the Chinese a realistic schedule for gaining citizenship but this had outraged the mostly Muslim Malays, and the plans were withdrawn. Suspicion and distrust reigned. Malaya was ripe for revolution, at least in the Chinese community. In 1948 three estate managers were murdered in northern Malaya and the Emergency, which would last thirteen years, was declared.

In 1950 Australia responded on two fronts to the British call for help. It sent a small team of advisers on jungle-fighting techniques, which was not well received by the British who felt they had as much experience of jungle fighting in Burma as the Australians had in New Guinea. Planes were sent too—six Lincoln bombers and a flight of Dakotas. But no ground troops were sent until 1955, so most of the vital action was missed. That took place over three years, following the assassination of the British High Commissioner, Sir Henry Gurney, in October 1951. The Dakotas dropped paratroopers, supplies and leaflets—part of the psychological war—and they picked up sick and wounded soldiers. The slow-moving Lincoln's dropped bombs to keep the CTs (communist terrorists, the official label) on the move, but to doubtful effect. Opinion in the RAAF regards these efforts, at the very least, as 'unparalleled training experience'.

In June 1950 a signals intelligence unit was also sent to Malaya as war began in Korea. The North Korean People's Army had crossed into South Korea. In 72 hours it had captured Seoul, the southern capital, and it kept going, laying waste to most resistance. The aim was to seize the entire Korean peninsula and unify the country under the communist rule of Kim Il Sung who launched the invasion with Stalin's approval.

At the end of World War II there was great hope in Korea. Brutalised by four decades of Japanese occupation—the Korean language had been banned and the Royal Archives burned—Koreans sensed an opportunity to throw off the colonial yoke. But by 1949 hope had slipped away in bitter civil war. The country had been artificially divided at the 38th parallel by the victorious new occupiers, the Soviet Union and the United States. They departed in 1949 leaving their proxies in charge on either side of the great divide. In 1950 100,000 people died as a result of the war. Korea was the Cold War's first major battleground. In three years 4 million Koreans died. Allied air power inflicted greater destruction on the resources of

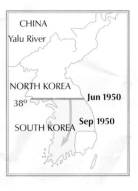

North Korean advance, 1950

United Nations advance, 1950

Chinese and North Korean advance, 1951

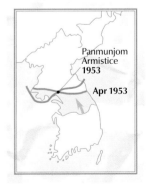

Armistice Line, 1953

North and South Korea

Air power was critical to the survival of South Korean and US ground forces from the start.

Mustangs in Korea

On 30 June 1950, four days after North Korea's invasion across the 38th parallel, Prime Minister Menzies announced that Australia would provide naval and air support to the UN Command. Number 77 Squadron had fought in the Pacific theatre in World War II, before taking part in the occupation of Japan. The squadron had been away from Australia for seven years. It was readying to return, plans for celebrations were afoot, when the news came. Within days the squadron flew its first operational mission against the North Koreans. There were nearly 19,000 more sorties before the return of peace in 1953.

Air power was critical to the survival of South Korean and US ground forces from the start. The North Koreans had quickly driven their enemy to a southern corner of the Korean peninsula, around the city of Pusan. Without allied air power in those early days, they may have driven the UN Command ground forces into the sea. Number 77 Squadron was part of Lieutenant General George E. Stratemeyer's Far East Air Force based in Japan, a front line in the Cold War stand-off. Stratemeyer could use some of his air power in Korea but fear of a Russian attack on Japan compelled him to keep strength in reserve. This placed ever more responsibility on No. 77 Squadron.

The Australian flyers were based at Iwakuni in Japan, where men and families had settled in comfortably. When No. 3 Bomber group USAF moved in, they put up signs ruling the town off limits and placed a guard on the swimming pool that Australians had built. Australian airmen pulled down

the signs, threw the guard into the swimming pool, and then rescued him because he could not swim.

The P-51 Mustang of No. 77 Squadron was perhaps the best US-made fighter in World War II. A classic piston-engine aircraft, it was ideal for what was primarily a ground attack war before Chinese jet fighters and Soviet-made MiGs, joined the fray. The airmen of No. 77 Squadron were highly trained in air-to-ground gunnery, rocketry and 60-degree dive bombing, and they were one of only eight squadrons ready for combat in those first desperate months.

Ironically, Australia's slowness to switch to jet fighters meant that No. 77 Squadron's airmen had immense experience that was used to short-term advantage. Until the MiGs entered the war in November 1950, the finesse of pilot and piston-engine played a vital role. It was one of those odd moments when circumstances rendered an outmoded technology vital if not decisive in battle, and in diplomacy. The Mustangs were attacking southbound trains, blowing up bridges, napalming fast-moving tank columns and machine-gunning North Korean troop concentrations while Percy Spender was in Washington pressing the Americans for a Pacific alliance. 'Needless to say,' wrote the official historian Robert O'Neill, 'Spender would have had little diplomatic leverage had No. 77 Squadron performed poorly.' Fortunately, the squadron's one disaster in this period—the bombing of a South Korean train carrying US and South Korean troops—was entirely due to defects in General MacArthur's target allocation system. It was an event that compelled another US

Men of No.77 Squadron, RAAF, in the snow at Kimpo, South Korea, December 1951.

Wing Commander L.T. Spence prior to take off, Pusan, South Korea, August 1950.

general to fly to Iwakuni and personally apologise to distraught Australian airmen. The Americans had adjusted their maps with north and south battle lines in the wrong places.

Number 77 Squadron was used constantly in the last-ditch defence of the Pusan Perimeter. The outdated North Korean air force was fast being destroyed, but over target areas Australian pilots met intense anti-aircraft fire. Pilots were weaving constantly to avoid ground fire, but they were especially vulnerable when dropping napalm, which required low flying, sometimes as low as 30 metres, on a straight path. The hardy Mustangs were frequently hit but mostly got home. The first Australian serviceman to lose his life in the conflict was Squadron Leader Graham Strout who was shot down on 7 July while striking at a railway line near Samchok. Strout's remains were recovered by a veteran sergeant, Tom Henderson, and an RAAF chaplain, the Reverend Esmund New. New had been a Presbyterian missionary in Korea in the 1930s. He and Henderson went into the hotly contested area, found the local people who had buried Strout, and brought his remains back for burial at the UN Command war cemetery.

Many times the Pusan Perimeter was breached with the North Koreans, on Blitzkrieg principles, pouring everything they had through the gaps. But the enemy was repulsed and the line re-established just as often. The battle to avoid annihilation reached a peak in late August. By early September, the perimeter was secure, and a new phase of the war was about to begin with MacArthur's successful landing at Inchon. That landing enabled the UN forces to cut supply lines to the beseiging North Koreans. It was a turning point in the war.

Throughout these desperate months, No. 77 Squadron flew hundreds of sorties. They left their base in Japan early in the morning, to fly a routine four missions a day over North Korean-held territory. Between missions they refuelled at Taegu, just inside the perimeter and, to the sounds of ground battle not far off, they took their place with US fighters in long queues, awaiting turn-around and take-off. 'At many stages of the battle, pilots could contact the airborne controller during the climb after take-off, receive their target and roll in for a dive-bombing pass as soon as they had gained the necessary altitude.' At the end of the day, exhausted, they flew back across the Sea of Japan to their home base.

On one of these routine days, the squadron leader, Wing Commander L.T. Spence, a veteran of World War II, was to attack storage facilities north of the battle line, in close support of MacArthur's 8th Army. Only two weeks before, General Stratemeyer had flown to Iwakuni to decorate Spence with the medal of the Legion of Merit for outstanding leadership. That night, like all others, Spence had then sat down to a heavy load of paperwork. He had been a bank clerk in earlier days in Bundaberg, Queensland, so paperwork was not new to him, but the stress must have been immense. At 6.30 am he was off again. In that way he passed his days and his evenings, until the day he flew north looking for the storage facilities near the township of Angang-ni. He was in a group of four Mustangs. He led the way with a steep dive from 180 metres and for reasons unknown was unable to pull out of the dive. His Mustang crashed into the centre of the township and exploded. Civilian casualties are unknown.

The Mustangs continued to do their work in the months that followed, but once the MiGs entered the war they were seriously outclassed and had to be replaced. Number 77 Squadron was re-equipped with British Meteor Mark 8s because adequate fighters, like the American Sabres, were not available. The men of No. 77 Squadron were not pleased. Re-equipped, yet still unable to match the MiGs, the Australian squadron was relegated to less demanding fighter-sweep and ground-attack roles for the rest of the war.

A ground crewman pumps napalm into a tank mounted on an RAAF Mustang, Korea, 1950.

The Mustangs continued to do their work in the months that followed, but once the MiGs entered the war they were seriously outclassed and had to be replaced.

Mustang aircraft of No.77 Squadron on the tarmac at Iwakuni aerodrome, Japan, 1950.

Commonwealth poster from the Korean War period to promote the popular image of Australia's fighting services.

They keep Australia strong

As I lay in the ditch the Chinese Communist Force literally ran over me after the tanks down the road.

Lieutenant James Young, 3RAR

Men of the 3rd Battalion, 3RAR, interrogating prisoners with the aid of an interpreter, Pakchon, Korea, July 1950.

North Korea than that inflicted on Japan in World War II. Seoul, the southern capital, changed hands four times in one year as two gigantic armies chased one another up and down the Korean peninsula.

With the Russians unwisely boycotting the United Nations Security Council, thus waiving their veto, the UN was able to endorse a multi-national force for Korea. The Turks sent a brigade. The French, the British, the Canadians and others were there too. Even little Luxembourg sent a platoon. They all backed the might of the US armed forces headed by General Douglas MacArthur. Memories of the Munich Agreement of 1938 were invoked. The catch-cry, popularised in the press, was that this time the invaders must not be appeased.

Australia was one of the first member states to volunteer. Like Britain, it had declined to send ground units, then changed policy. Ground force participation in the UN force was announced by the Country Party rough nut, 'Artie' Fadden, the Deputy Prime Minister, on 27 July 1950. Fadden did the honours because Menzies was in the US pressing for a World Bank loan on favourable conditions. His Minister for External Affairs, Percy Spender, was another moving force behind the scenes. Spender believed, rightly, that strong support for US policy in Korea would help lever the Americans into a security pact. It probably did. The ANZUS Security Treaty was drafted in February 1951, signed in September and though it guaranteed nothing, it made many Australians feel safer at night. ANZUS was the 'bolt on the back door' while the Menzies government planned for 'forward defence' in the Middle East.

Australia had no ready-reaction force on hand, just 3RAR (3rd Battalion, The Royal Australian Regiment), a 'half-strength battalion in Japan, under-trained [and] under-equipped', and due to go home. Number 77 Fighter Squadron was also in Japan. Within a few days it was active against the North Koreans. The navy, too, was in a position to quickly send two ships to Korean waters, but essentially the defence forces were not ready.

3RAR was boosted by a special recruitment campaign—'Join K-Force'—for service in Korea. Recruiting offices had been rushed and among the 1,000 men chosen were many with good combat records from World War II. The battalion was rapidly re-fitted, re-trained and sent to Korea in September. It was brigaded with two British battalions, designated a Commonwealth Brigade and made ready for action. By this time the North Koreans were in retreat with UN forces hot on their heels. The Australians joined the pursuit, all the way up the peninsula to the Yalu River on the border between Korea and Chinese Manchuria. Thirty Chinese divisions, more than 300,000 troops, were massed and waiting. The Chinese crossed the Yalu and drove the UN forces south. Bombastic as ever, MacArthur said the war would be over in a month and Korea would be reunited under a democratic government in Seoul, but offensive and counteroffensive continued for almost a year, until the war became bogged down in stalemate in the middle of 1951. By then MacArthur was no longer in command.

3RAR was 'blooded' in the fierce fighting of 1951. The battalion was part of the advance into North Korea. In near arctic winter conditions it was then caught up in the desperate retreat after Chinese intervention in October, and after that participated in the counteroffensive. In April 1951 the battalion held the line at Kapyong against an entire Chinese division and was awarded a US Presidential Unit Citation (a unit VC). There was more hard fighting in October when 3RAR stormed entrenched Chinese positions on the craggy ridges of Maryang San. But this was a war of rapid movement—for Australian forces there has not been one since—and the rapid movement was almost over. What followed was a 'static phase', two years of positional warfare, a 'war of trench raids and patrols reminiscent of the Western Front'. The static phase lasted until the ceasefire of July 1953.

Approximately 17,000 Australian service personnel served in Korea, including army and RAAF nurses. Total Australian casualties for those three years of fighting were 1,584, with 306 killed in action or dying of wounds, 33 other deaths, 1,216 wounded in action and 29 taken prisoner.

Australian troops stayed on in Korea to keep the peace. A phased reduction began in August 1954 when the US reduced its commitment from six divisions to two. The Australian army was now able to deploy forces elsewhere. Attention was immediately upon Malaya, once again.

The British were already pressing Australia to commit to their Far East Strategic Reserve. The strategic reserve was set up to guard against Chinese expansion and could be deployed anywhere in South East Asia. It could also be used against local insurgencies, a secondary responsibility that became its primary activity. Chief of the Imperial Staff, Field Marshal Sir William Slim, had been in Australia for talks on the defence of the region in 1953. It was clear that the US would not back the security of Britain's Far East colonial assets in Malaya, Singapore and the Straits—this would be a Commonwealth effort. Australian units were to join with forces from British and Gurkha regiments, imperial units from Fiji and East Africa, troops of the Royal Malay Regiment and also the Malayan Police.

Private N.L. Neyland, 3rd Battalion, 3RAR, carrying firewood back to camp.

Wounded soldier. Private D.G. Stewart, 3rd Battalion, 3RAR, after the attack on Sardine Hill, April 1951.

Approximately 17,000 Australian service personnel served in Korea, including army and RAAF nurses.

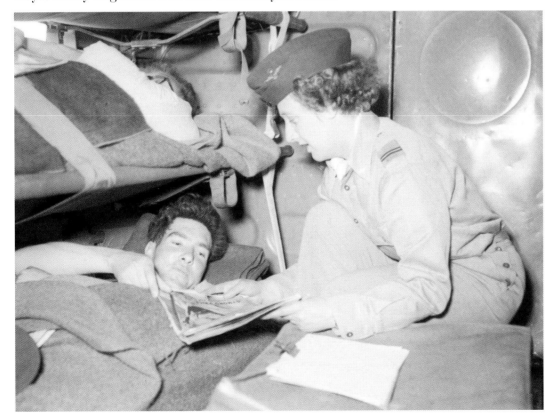

Homeward bound. RAAF Nursing Sister Helen Blair tends to one of the POWs exchanged after the cease-fire, 6 August 1953.

Men of C Company, 3rd Battalion, 3RAR, hauling a wounded comrade across a snow covered slope.

Ferguson would turn up wherever you went, whether you were humping mortar ammunition or whatever. He would always have a crack at you whenever he appeared, and you would think 'He is not a bad sort of bastard—we will do some more for him.'

Anon

Former POW, Private Keith Gwyther, on his return to Leongatha in Victoria, 9 August 1953. Gwyther was captured during the Battle of Kapyong.

Battle of Kapyong

On 23 April 1951, 3RAR was preparing to commemorate Anzac Day while friends and relatives at home were doing the same. The regiment was resting at a small village a few kilometres north-west of Kapyong, about 100 kilometres from Seoul. An invitation to attend the service and celebrations had already been accepted by the Turkish brigade encamped not far away. Songs were rehearsed, beer was laid on, a spit readied. For their commemorative wreaths, Australian soldiers gathered wild azaleas in bloom on the hillsides. That night, the Red Army launched its Spring Offensive. The valley of the Kapyong River was a natural avenue to the capital, a traditional invasion route. The Australians, stretched thin in four companies, barely had time to dig in.

North of them a South Korean Division (6ROK) was routed and the British Gloucester Regiment beseiged, to be all but wiped out the following day. Hastily the Australians reconnoitred and occupied a string of posts on high ground on an eastern range of hills above the confluence of the Kapyong River, while a Canadian battalion positioned itself on the western range, two compact strong points on a dangerously wide battlefield. From these points the defenders looked northwards across a valley perhaps 2 kilometres wide. There were villages and hamlets on the valley floor, the flats were cultivated,

and the hillsides revealed patches of low scrub amid white remnants of snow yet to thaw. The nights were still cold.

The routed South Koreans withdrew in some disorder south of the Australian positions, their trucks were overloaded and the men directionless, shedding equipment, moaning with fear and exhaustion. Men jostled for positions on anything that might carry them, even the ox carts of refugees. Chinese forward troops had mingled with this flood and were now behind Company B, rendering it encirlced. A near full moon rose soon after nightfall, illuminating the battlefield. A lone platoon of US tanks forward of Company B took the first shock as the enemy came on, down the valley. Short of infantry cover, the platoon commander was killed almost immediately. Several tanks were disabled, others were driven back. Mortars were fired into the valley upon suspected concentrations of Chinese but the enemy were lost in clouds of grey smoke before they reappeared and charged the Australian positions.

It was obvious that 3RAR was overcommitted; so too were the Canadians. There were gaps in the defences and some flanks were undefended. The Australians were spread out on the western slopes of Hill 504, eight clusters of men each some 200–400 metres across and separated by gaps of up to 500 metres. The brigade HQ was in the valley to the

Korea, 17 April 1950. Captain Reg Saunders (right), commander of A Company, 3rd Battalion, 3RAR. Saunders was a veteran of World War II and the first Aboriginal commissioned officer in the Australian army. He fought at Kapyong.

Throughout the night and through the next day fierce gun battles raged, the enemy closed in and men fought hand to hand. High ground was won and lost and won again.

rear, and the commander, Lieutenant Colonel Ferguson, was charged with preventing the spread of panic among the South Koreans while conducting this epic defence. This he did.

Ferguson was a New Zealander, a salesman and a decorated veteran of the 2nd AIF in New Guinea. 'Bravery was routine to him,' wrote one of his lieutenants, 'his battle knowledge and execution was superb.' Throughout the night and through the next day fierce gun battles raged, the enemy closed in and men fought hand to hand. High ground was won and lost and won again. Company B relinquished trenches under orders, then retook them with the bayonet. It was a night of fury. Company A took the worst of it. The charging enemy, led by grenade throwers, was mowed down. Bren and Owen guns and rifles ran hot. Reg Saunders and his men held their ground. The Chinese fell in great numbers, but they would not relent. They rushed over heaps of their own dead and wounded, across a carpet of pale and torn bodies, of ripped and ragged revolutionary uniforms unmarked by rank and dark with blood. The sounds of dying and the poses of death seemed numberless.

Casualties among the Australians were high too. In the quiet intervals, while the enemy massed before another onslaught, one man said he could hear his heart pounding like rifle shots. The dead and incapacitated reduced some platoon numbers by half. By morning Company A had nearly 50 casualties. Medical dressings and blankets ran out in some entrenchments. Number 12 Platoon called for air support and Number 10 Platoon was mistakenly napalmed, killing two Australians, igniting

ammunition and sending fire racing through the Command Post area. The Chinese lit fires too, which raced through little Australian strongholds, setting off grenades and other munitions and charring the flesh of the shivering wounded. Daylight brought one advantage—the enemy, in numbers, withdrawing over open country. It was like 'potting rabbits as they dashed hither and thither', wrote Major Ben O'Dowd. Further south down the valley the British Gloucesters were all but annihilated. 'Dead Englishmen lolled behind shattered steering wheels, and rows of holes in the vehicles showed the line of enemy machine gun fire.' It would be a long day. The Australians fought on. Ferguson, riding forward to company positions in the gun-loader's seat of an American tank, was compelled to learn how to load.

At 3.30 pm, the battalion began to withdraw to new and better positions. On the slopes forward of the company perimeters lay hundreds of enemy dead. With the help of New Zealand gunners and an all too brash and now devastated US tank company, and with the gallant Canadians who held the other side of the valley, the Australians had fought an entire enemy division to a standstill. When the survivors reached their new locations they slept. They had fought for 24 hours, outnumbered about nine to one. Thirty-two Australians were dead, 59 wounded and three were taken to Chinese prison camps. The next day was Anzac Day.

Menzies announced the Malayan counterinsurgency operations in June 1955 in the midst of a devastating schism in the Labor Party. The Split was so devastating that the 's' was capitalised and the word stuck in popular consciousness. It divided the Labor vote and kept the party out of power at the federal level for seventeen years.

Events in Malaya played a part in fracturing the Labor Party. Labor, now led by Dr Evatt, saw the insurgency as an anti-colonial revolt based on legitimate economic grievances. The party leadership also worried about a troop presence besmirching Australia's image among its Asian neighbours. The breakaway Laborites organised themselves into the Anti-Communist Labor Party. They charged Dr Evatt with being soft on Asian communism. The right-wing Catholic journal, B.A. Santamaria's *News Weekly*, voiced their fears:

> *If we refuse to fill this country with people to the full limit of its resources, we must always be on the defensive against 12 hundred million pairs of hungry eyes—not only against 86 million pairs of Japanese eyes. If it is not Japan, it will be China, and if it is not China, it will be somebody else.*

Tunku Abdul Rahman, Chief Minister of Malaya, inspects a guard of honour aboard HMAS *Anzac*, September 1956.

The forces sent to Malaya in 1955 were all regulars and they were welcomed by most Malayan leaders. The general public at home was barely interested. By the time Australian troops arrived the insurgency had been politically outmanoeuvred and its military hopes crushed. A long and gruelling cleaning-up phase was underway. The British had announced they would grant independence and Malays generally settled for a future in which the new constitution would favour them, the Muslim majority, over the ethnic Chinese who were non Muslim and strongly represented in the guerrilla resistance. But many Chinese remained neutral, prepared to wait and see what independence might bring. Popular support for the insurgency was disintegrating and, contrary to Cold War rhetoric, it had very little support from the Chinese or the Russians to sustain it.

In Australia, the ALP was also in a difficult position. When Malaya achieved independence in 1957 the first prime minister was Tunku Abdul Rahmin, Cambridge educated, pro-British and supportive of the Australian presence. The Tunku aligned his nation with Britain and the Commonwealth. Menzies' conservatives were quick to call this a vindication of their policy. They won a political victory because ALP warnings that Malaya's friendship would be lost proved wrong.

When the Emergency began in 1948 the Chifley government sent small arms and walkie-talkies, but no troops to Malaya. When Menzies was free to act, after Korea, he sent an infantry battalion, an artillery battery and supporting troops. These were integrated into the 28th Commonwealth Infantry Brigade under the command of British officers. The RAAF squadron of Lincoln Bombers, present in Malaya since 1950, became part of the Strategic Reserve in 1955 and was replaced by another squadron in 1959. Ships of the RAN patrolled Malayan waters from 1955 and one of the new fleet carriers took part in joint naval exercises there, but the navy did not figure in Emergency operations.

Men of C Company, 2nd Battalion, 2RAR, on a jungle track in Perak, Malaya, May 1956, *opposite*.

Bridge building. Sappers of 4 Troop, 11th Independent Field Squadron, Royal Australian Engineers, at Lubok Segintah, Malaya, November 1955, *below*.

Troops going to Malaya went for two years at a time and, for the first time in the history of Australian combat operations, they were able to take their wives and families with them. For some soldiers this was a surreal experience. They left their families in Penang and went for a few weeks of policing, patrolling, and possibly combat in the jungle, then returned to

2RAR and the Pipeline Ambush

Testing weapons before a patrol. Members of 2nd Battalion, 2RAR, at Lintang, Perak, Malaya, May 1956.

The Jungle Training Centre at Canungra, Queensland, was reopened in 1955 after ten years of inaction. The men of 2nd Battalion, Royal Australian Regiment (2RAR) were to undergo three months preparation there before going to Malaya. The centre would prepare the troops, physically and mentally, for the hardship of jungle warfare in a conventional war setting, similar to that of New Guinea in 1942. There was no preparation for anti-terrorist activities. The commanding officer of 2RAR, Lieutenant Colonel J.G. Ochiltree, was not even shown a copy of *Conduct of Anti-Terrorist Operations in Malaysia (ATOM)*, a British manual that contained some useful lessons.

Once in Malaya, the men were to be moved quickly from their base on the island of Penang (and the seedy attractions of George-town) to the northern and far more dangerous state of Kedah, but the move was delayed because of the federal election in Australia. Menzies wanted no setbacks for Australian troops while votes were on the line. Strengthened by the Labor Party Split, Menzies' majority in the House of Representatives rose from seven to 28.

Australian forces in Malaya waited, cast their votes, and then went into action. Their objective was to clear southern Kedah of enemy forces with constant harassment, food denial and population-control measures. This was thick jungle territory dotted with large-scale rubber plantations. Sightings were few and fleeting and exchanges rare, but patrols routinely found enemy camps, rice caches and sometimes ammunition and documents. The tracking was painstaking and there was little to show for it, just a few ragged, barefoot captives and the sight of enemy huts, deep in the jungle, going up in smoke. The frustration was palpable. The men said they were 'looking for a needle in a haystack' and worse, the 'needle' kept moving. At least one of their commanders thought failure was due to inaccurate shooting, but even with the help of Sarawak trackers and dogs following a blood trail, a wounded enemy was rarely run down. The blood trail might just disappear in the jungle. Or it might lead to a rubber plantation or a village. Local support for the guerillas was part of the problem.

Morale was low when 2RAR was moved south to Perak state. The number of kills and captures had not met expectations. Inaccurate shooting was now acknowledged, and the troop numbers killed in accidents suggested poor weapons handling too, at least by some soldiers. The operation in Perak was more difficult. The patrolling area, Sungei Siput, was 592 square kilometres of mostly jungle, with some large and small rubber plantations, tapioca and vegetable gardens tended mainly by the Chinese, and some tin-mining operations. Numerically the Chinese predominated and they were considered unreliable. The Malays and the Indians were not trusted either, nor the 2,000–3,000 indigenous people who lived in the jungle. As one historian put it: 'In the cultivated areas, therefore, it had to be assumed that a sizeable proportion of the population was actively or passively hostile.'

Some of these people, the Chinese fringe dwellers by and large, now lived in barbed-wire compounds called New Villages. These were designed to cut off local support to the guerillas. The New Villages were to provide elementary schooling and health services. They were heavily policed. 2RAR was kept busy patrolling, as well as intercepting food and other supplies going to the guerillas. Gate checks and fence checks were a lowly but necessary task. These involved body searches of workers leaving plantations and minute examination of everything leaving the village: 'Every container had to be searched, bicycles had to be dismantled in case rice or other commodities were hidden in the frame, and—worst of all—night soil buckets had to be thoroughly stirred to be certain that no tightly wrapped packages were concealed.'

Real action, on patrol in the jungle, was much preferred though far more dangerous. There were numerous near misses and minor confrontations, and on 22 June 1956 there was Pipeline.

On that day, two patrols from No. 1 Platoon, A Company were checking the jungle fringe bordering the rubber plantations of the Heawood estate. They were near a pipeline running from the Sungei Bemban reservoir. They had been this way before and the tracks they left had alerted guerillas who lay in wait for them. There were twelve Australians and 25 guerillas. The ambush began with remote-controlled landmines exploding around the Australians. Sten and Thompson machine guns laid them low. Corporal Allan was killed dashing to a better position. Private G.C. Fritz was badly wounded but kept firing his Owen gun until he died. A Bren gunner, Private L.A. Pennant, was blown off his feet and badly concussed but kept fighting. The sounds of firing drew two other patrols in the area, along with the platoon commander, Lieutenant A.W. Campbell. Numbers were now about even and small groups were darting in all directions, some retreating, some searching for vantage points, machine gun and rifle fire raking the track along the pipeline. A four-man flanking assault climbed the hillside above the ambush party and fired down with a light machine gun. The returned fire killed Private C.C. Ingra. The guerillas were dispersing but they kept shooting until Campbell hurled two hand grenades among them. Some ran for the river, others fled to the jungle. Two guerillas were dead and blood trails told of several wounded. Three A Company men were killed and three wounded. Lieutenant Colonel Ochiltree said the men had stood and fought and lost no weapons or material. But the cost was great, nothing could disguise that.

the luxury of their 'amahs' (household servants). Australian patrols were mainly in the rugged, mountainous north, areas of deep jungle, wild and isolated country leading onto the Thai border. One innovation was the use of Alsatians and Labradors as tracker dogs, though patrols routinely took Iban and Dyak men to track and to mediate for the Australians when indigenous tribes were encountered in the jungle. The Malayan work was small-scale patrolling, a platoon commander's war in which there was little scope for higher levels of command to affect outcomes.

The purpose of these patrols was to ambush and to isolate, to kill the enemy and to cut remnants or reinforcements off from the civilian populations where they might obtain food and information. There were encounters with enemy groupings up to twenty strong—fifteen Australians died in these encounters and 27 were wounded—but because Australia came in to the Emergency in its latter years such run-ins were few and far between. Enemy units had diminished in number and size. In its two-year tour (1959–61), 1RAR did not conflict with the resistance at all. But on previous tours, some encounters had been deadly.

One of the strangest complications for Australian troops in Malaya arose because the army had undergone the most radical reorganisation this century. Pentropic divisional organisation was a new battlefield structure introduced to modernise the army and better integrate it with the US forces, which had only recently switched to the Pentropic model. The Australian experiment was mimicking a US one. The Pentropic system dispensed with the British-pattern army, organised on a triangular, battalion–brigade–division formation and replaced it with a five-sided structure in which each battle group was made up of five battalions with five battle groups to a division. At the time US army personnel thought this arrangement would be better suited to the atomic battlefield. The historic commonality that had existed between the Australian and the British armies, which included organisation, equipment and operational methods, was about to be dispensed with.

An Iban tracker in slouch hat with members of 6 Platoon, B Company, 1st Battalion, 1RAR, c.1960.

One of the strangest complications for Australian troops in Malaya arose because the army had undergone the most radical reorganisation this century.

A bush camp in the jungle, Perak State, Malaya, 1960.

Well into the 1950s, the armed forces were still training and fighting with aged equipment drawn from World War II stockpiles

Behind the scenes there were also attempts to radically reform the defence bureaucracy, which was an outdated, Byzantine labyrinth that had not changed much since the inter-war years, and had been under the intensely personal control of the Secretary for Defence, Frederick Shedden, from 1937. Shedden's methods were consciously modelled on those of his mentor, Sir Maurice Hankey, and the old Committee of Imperial Defence and were no longer appropriate. In 1956, Shedden was asked to step aside to facilitate reform, but little changed, so entrenched were the old ways. It was on the battlefield, not in the bureaucracy, where something new and very different was to be tried.

The 1959 decision to change to Pentropic organisation fitted the three-year defence program announced in 1957. This was a program that made no bones about integration with the US, and caused unhappiness in British defence industries, traditional suppliers to all three Australian services. Menzies said:

Australia will standardise as far as we can with the Americans. We have decided, both in aircraft, in artillery, and in small arms, to fit ourselves for close cooperation with the United States of America in the South East Asian Area.

Switching to the Pentropic pattern also coincided with the abolition of National Service and so became a top-brass strategy to retain the funding that had been expended on training conscripts.

Pentropic organisation made cooperation with British forces in the field very difficult. Battalions sent to Malaya as part of the strategic reserve had to be reorganised along standard British lines before departure, and then switched back to the Pentropic pattern on return. In June 1961, the US army abandoned Pentropic organisation, leaving the Australian army as the world's sole practitioner of a five-sided army organisation. This absurd situation persisted until 1964 when the scheme was finally discarded, and the army returned to its traditional arrangements.

Members of 3rd Battalion, 3RAR, taking air transport into the jungle to search for Indonesian infiltrators, Sarawak, Borneo, 1965.

Pentropic was a blunder but it did help to sustain the re-equipping program that began in 1957, a program that modernised the weaponry and equipment Australian infantrymen took into the Vietnam War.

Well into the 1950s, the armed forces were still training and fighting with aged equipment drawn from World War II stockpiles or based on technology of that vintage. The press created a scandal out of this state of affairs in 1956–57, which may have hastened reform. In what one military historian has called a 'buying spree', the army obtained their favoured weapons, semi-automatic SLRs and Belgian FN rifles, and a replacement program for the navy and air force was also underway.

Three pilots, 77 Squadron
Ivor Hele, 1953

HMAS Sydney in Korean Waters, 1951
Ray Honisett, 1973-1974

Chopper lift out
Ken McFadyen, 1967

Diggers sitting on patrol
Ken McFadyen, 1967-1968

Image for a Dead Man
Ray Beattie, 1980

Equipping with Belgian rifles and US aircraft demonstrated the readiness to move away from Britain as chief supplier.

In the air, alignment with the US went more smoothly than the Pentropic experiment, though it was not without great controversy. The RAAF bought the Lockheed C-130 transport aircraft, and almost bought F-104 Starfighters, which were also American, but in the end acquired the French Mirage III fighter, which made the British even more unhappy. New helicopters came from the US. So did the controversial F-111 bombers—24 of them were ordered in 1963, they were scheduled for delivery in 1967 and did not arrive, due to technical faults, until 1973. The F-111s were a response to the growing troubles in South East Asia, particularly the 'Confrontation' between Indonesia and the new Federation of Malaysia. The Air Chief Marshal, Frederick Scherger, wanted Australia to have its own nuclear deterrent. He advocated that the RAAF acquire tactical atomic bombs but in 1958 the government warned him off the topic. Nevertheless in other areas (missiles, helicopters, air-defence systems) his pushiness in pursuing state of the art equipment reaped rewards at a time when the call on the defence forces was expected to come from one country in South East Asia or several at once—that was the fear among the jittery defence advisers in Canberra.

Air Chief Marshal
Sir Frederick Scherger.

The origins of Confrontation lie somewhere in the internecine politics of Jakarta, but they emerged for the world to see in the form of Indonesian President Sukarno's desire to frustrate Malaysian federation. Britain was eager to dispense with the territories of Sarawak and Sabah on the island of Borneo, adjacent to the Malaysian peninsula. Having them incorporated into the proposed Federation of Malaysia seemed a clever solution. Sukarno saw this as a British strategy to retain colonial power in Asia in another guise. In 1962 he adopted the policy of 'confronting' Malaysia, thus the terms Konfrontasi or Confrontation.

Sukarno was emboldened by having recently bluffed the Dutch out of West Irian (now West Papua). Now he turned on Malaysia. Confrontation was a small, undeclared war that ran from 1962 until 1966. The build up was slow but by 1964,

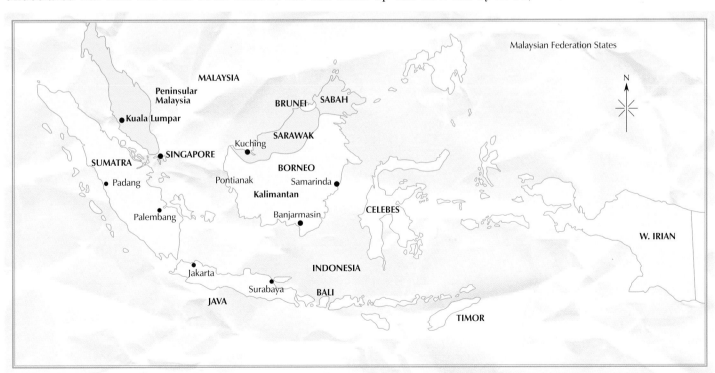

Malaysia and Indonesia, 1962

Second Lieutenant David Savage, 2SAS, with a Gurkha soldier, somewhere in Kalimantan, 1966.

Not a trace of Australian troops was to be left on Indonesian soil. Everything was to be carried out—the dead, the wounded, everything.

Operation Claret

Private Kevin Rogers, 3RAR, of WA in an observation tower on the Sarawak–Kalimantan border, May 1965.

Indonesian military incursions into Sarawak and Sabah had became frequent. There were incursions into the mainland peninsula too, but the centre of the fighting was in Borneo where the Indonesians were crossing into Malaysian territory from their own province of Kalimantan. Confrontation had become a low-level war. Fond of dramatic gestures, Sukarno labelled 1964 the 'year of living dangerously'.

Australian citizens knew virtually nothing about the conflict in Borneo and almost as little about the high-level concerns over Indonesia as a threat to Australia. From the early days of Confrontation, the British had been portraying Sukarno as a huge threat, possibly another Hitler, and were calling on Australia to commit, militarily, to the defence of the new Malaysian Federation. The US line was very different. The Americans were advising Australia to stay calm, emphasising the importance of keeping channels to Sukarno open, not isolating or cornering him and thus driving him towards the communist bloc.

Official opinion in Australia was much closer to the British point of view. Confrontation caused great alarm. Policy-making and intelligence circles in Canberra worried about a Peking–Jakarta axis and about Sukarno's growing ties with the PKI (Parti Komunis Indonesia). China was known to be preparing for its first atomic test. In the absence of massive US intervention Ho Chi Minh seemed close to victory in Vietnam. The domino effect looked to be a real possibility—first Vietnam, then Cambodia and Laos, then perhaps Thailand and Malaysia might fall to communism. The Kennedy regime in Washington was wavering and seemed bent on appeasing, rather than confronting Sukarno. In Canberra, Coral Bell was one of the prominent participants in the strategic debate at the time:

A member of the very small intelligence community in Canberra could quite plausibly in those years make a 'worst case' analysis in which the PKI secured ascendancy in Indonesia, and stepped up the confrontation campaign against Malaysia, while Ho Chi Minh's forces took over South Vietnam, with the backing of both China and the Soviet Union, and began to turn their attention to the rest of South-East Asia.

The urgent need for strategic understanding was reflected in the formation of the Strategic and Defence Studies Centre (SDSC) at the Australian National University in 1963. For some analysts the outlook was as bleak as it had been in 1942. Canberra was anxious and hawkish. Decision makers could think only of the big stick as a solution. They were looking to the USA for salvation in the region, while deciding on their own course in Malaysia as part of the Far East Strategic Reserve. It was against Sukarno's incursions that strategic reserve troops were deployed in 1965.

At the height of Confrontation, around 1964, there were eighteen British and Gurkha battalions, and three Malaysian ones, in Borneo, and a total of 65,000 Commonwealth troops committed to security throughout the Federation. Under the Anglo-Malayan Defence Agreement of 1957, the British were committed to the defence of the new state of Malaysia, but the Australians were not part of this arrangement. Menzies was slow to commit troops, although he was invited to do so by the Malaysian government. He was particularly worried that cross-border operations into Kalimantan, the Indonesian part of Borneo, would look like neo-colonialism. The Malaysian government made a second request for Australian troops in January 1965. This time the Australian government agreed to send 3RAR and a squadron from the Special Air Service Regiment (SAS), but a second infantry battalion could not be spared, as troops were about to be committed to Vietnam as well.

The fighting in Borneo was mostly patrol and ambush actions in difficult terrain and an energy-sapping climate, not dissimilar to conditions during the Emergency. There was also the politically sensitive problem of pursuit across the border. These pursuits, 'taking the war to the enemy', were known as Claret operations. They were top secret—Claret was not to be leaked—which meant that the troops involved knew about them, Malaysian generals knew about them, a select few in Canberra knew about them, but most parliamentarians and the general public knew nothing.

The reconnaissance and intelligence gathering work for offensive operations in Kalamantan was carried out by Australian SAS patrols in conjunction with the British SAS. Australia's SAS was created in 1957 following the British model, which had its origins in the dark days of 1940. Its primary role was reconnaissance and surveillance with occasional harassing tasks, its purpose to provide enough information to allow larger, more conventional forces to locate and attack the enemy. SAS patrols in Malaysian Borneo operated along sections of the 1,100 kilometre common border with Kalimantan, mountainous country, so little known that patrol maps bore large blank spaces marked with the words 'No reliable data because of cloud cover all year round'. The patrols were small, four or five men. They carried packs of up to 40 kilograms to maximise self-reliance. In addition to their fourteen days of rations, warm clothing for the nights, bedding, water and M16s, they also carried 100 rounds of ammunition and spare radio batteries, and they shared a load of Claymore mines, white phosphorous grenades, a medical kit, additional explosives and a mini camera. They moved slowly and silently, alert for snakes and scorpions and tiger tracks, regularly stopping to remove leeches, and careful not to disturb orang-outangs, deer or birds that might alert the enemy. The patrols watched rivers, the main method of movement through the jungle, and they sought out the fortified camps from which the Indonesians launched their raids into Malaysian territory. Occasionally they carried out their own ambushes, but mostly their purpose was to locate the enemy, withdraw undetected and provide the intelligence necessary for the brigade commanders to take their men into action.

Most of the Indonesian incursions were small scale, involving groups of less than platoon size. Of 152 incidents in Sarawak and 62 in Sabah, nearly all involved groups of fewer than 40 men and only three exceeded 50. But in Kalimantan, the Indonesian bases were building up to what

On the second day a boat went underneath the ambush position . . . and one of our guys felt that the enemy had seen us. So we pulled back and the next day we shifted the killing ground and went back in again. About six or eight of the enemy came through, so we hit them.

Lieutenant Trevor Roderick, 1 Squadron, SAS

Registering targets with a mortar. Men of 3rd Battalion, 3RAR, at a patrol base in Sarawak, near the Kalimantan border, May 1965.

Heading for the border. Private Kevin Perandis from Chinderan, Tweed River, NSW, May 1965.

Wessex helicopters above HMS *Albion* leaving Borneo with the 3rd Battalion, 3RAR.

Lance Corporal Paul Denehey, 1 Squadron SAS, who was killed by a rogue elephant while on patrol along the Sabah border in Borneo, 6 June 1965.

It had a major impact on the squadron because when we were up there we were all romantic, we were invincible. We were the best that there ever was. And we realised that it didn't have to be the baddies that got you. I mean who would ever have thought that you would get killed by a rogue elephant?

Sergeant Barry Standen, 1 Squadron, SAS

Again, Australian troops would be a bargaining chip in the pursuit of security arrangements.

looked like company-sized incursions, a significant escalation. Australian involvement continued throughout 1965. Troops were engaged in ambushes on both sides of the border, with the utmost secrecy attending to border crossings, and a complete blackout in the press and in unit records. All casualties, it was reported, were incurred on Malaysian territory.

By the time 3RAR was replaced by 4RAR in October 1965, events in Jakarta were taking the heat out of Confrontation. An attempted communist coup on 30 September was followed by the mass slaughter of PKI personnel and tens of thousands of PKI supporters or alleged supporters. The Indonesian army was so preoccupied with the massacre of its own citizens that operations in Malaysia slackened. Confrontation was effectively over, months before a peace treaty was finally signed in Jakarta in August 1966. When it was over, Sukarno was out of power, Suharto was in power and the Indonesian army was content.

Twenty-three Australians died during Confrontation, one killed by a rogue elephant and seven killed in operations. Eight were wounded. The battalion there—now based at permanent headquarters in Butterworth near Penang—switched to new concerns and began to prepare for a very different kind of war in Vietnam. The atomic battlefield was not to be. Borneo has been called a 'refresher course in the demands of low-level intensity conflict', a gruelling tour that called on the high levels of professionalism now present in the Australian regular army.

On the diplomatic front, Canberra was pleased. Australia had managed to keep diplomatic channels with Indonesia open throughout Confrontation, something of an achievement. The new Suharto dictatorship was welcomed. Australian foreign policy had been preoccupied with Sukarno and deeply concerned about Indonesia's potential threat to Australia. The Americans saw it another way but in the end that did not matter. They endorsed the outcome in Indonesia, while it was increasingly clear that Australian and US troops would share a common cause in Vietnam.

Again, Australian troops would be a bargaining chip in the pursuit of security arrangements. And equally, regional security would be an American lever to obtain more Australian troops.

6

PICKING
UP CREDIT

1962 – 1972

VIETNAMIZATION?

STOP THE WAR!
WITHDRAW SUPPORT FOR SAIGON REGIME
BRING TROOPS HOME
VIETNAM MORATORIUM SEPTEMBER 18

Authorised by K.J. McLeod, Sec-Convenor, Vietnam Moratorium Campaign, 232 Castlereagh St, Sydney. Tel. 26 2355   Printed by Comment Publishing Company, 22 Steam Mill Street, Sydney.

The French conquest of Vietnam began with gunboat diplomacy in 1859. In the year that Queensland was created as a colony, just three years after the beginning of responsible government in Australia, a French fleet under the command of Rear Admiral Bonard destroyed Vietnamese forts overlooking the approach to the Dong-nai River, then sailed up the river, set fire to rice stores, razed the fort at Saigon and installed a garrison of its own. A new colony came into the world in a familiar way.

ALMOST a century later, in May 1954, a Vietnamese army defeated the French in the battle of Dien Bien Phu. In July 1954 the Geneva Accords provided for a temporary division of the nation and for elections to be held within two years. It was widely accepted that Ho Chi Minh would easily win a free and fair election. As President Eisenhower put it, he had never talked or corresponded with anyone who was knowledgeable about Indo-China who thought otherwise. Ho was the recognised leader of the anti-colonial struggle, a nationalist who turned to communism after the Treaty of Versailles in 1919.

Ho Chi Minh left Vietnam in 1911, working as a stoker on a French freighter. In London he worked as a chef in the Carlton Hotel and in Paris he took a job in a photographer's studio. Ho was a student of history. He had read the American Declaration of Independence published on 4 July 1776, and had taken it to heart. He believed the Americans would help his people to be free. They had made their declaration and fought a war to free themselves from British colonialism. Those famous words rang in his ears: 'We hold these truths to be self-evident: that all men are created equal and are endowed by their Creator with certain inalienable rights . . .' Ho Chi Minh wanted to petition the great powers to grant his country's independence. He sought entrance to the peace conference at Versailles wearing a hired suit and bowler hat. But with no official certification and no formal standing he was refused admission.

The victors at Versailles were not about to relinquish their colonies. French occupation of Vietnam continued. The people's resistance to it was poorly organised and feeble. As elsewhere in Asia, it was Japanese occupation of French Indo-China during World War II that finally loosened the colonial grip. During the war the French administration was left nominally in control but its visible subordination was a great spur to anti-colonial aspirations. Villagers now observed Japanese soldiers, their long swords clanking on the ground, touching the cheeks of French women to display their power over them. When World War II was over and the Japanese gone, hostilities against the French were renewed with growing popular support, culminating in the battle of Dien Bien Phu.

Men of 3RAR alighting onto the deck of troop carrier HMAS *Sydney* for the return trip to Australia. South Vietnam, 6 October 1971, *previous page.*

Moratorium poster, Melbourne 1970, *opposite.*

'The Spreading Web of Communism', *Bulletin*, July 1950.

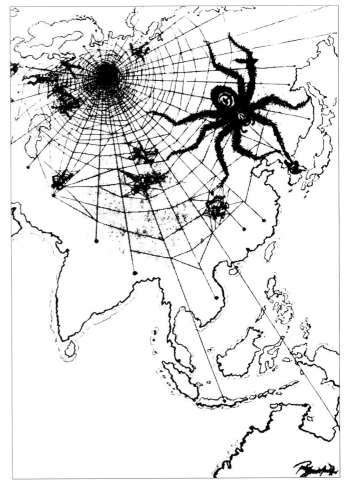

The success of anti-colonial forces in Vietnam caused great alarm in Australia because those forces were led by Ho Chi Minh and the Vietnamese Workers' Party. Menzies was certain that events in Vietnam fitted the Cold War pattern. His ministers routinely spoke of 'floods' and 'tides' and of communism 'lapping on our shores'. In May 1954, two days after the battle of Dien Bien Phu, R.G. Casey addressed a well-heeled crowd in the Peace Memorial Hall in Toorak, Melbourne. He spoke of the 'black cloud of Communist China', the menace at work behind events in Vietnam. 'We must make sure,' he said, 'that our children do not end up pulling rickshaws with hammer and sickle signs on their side.'

Casey was raising the alarm as events in Vietnam went from bad to worse. The elections agreed to in the Geneva Accords never took place. The Accords were denounced by a new leader, Ngo Dinh Diem, installed in the south with the backing of the Western powers. Diem's brutal regime was a major factor in the return of hostilities and by 1960 the resistance to his government had become a civil war in the south.

In Australia the official line presented the war as Chinese-backed expansionism: this was not civil war, it was a North Vietnamese invasion of the South. Speaking in 1962, the Minister for External Affairs, Garfield Barwick, offered his own explanation: 'This war in Vietnam is not a civil war,' he said. 'It is a new form of aggression by means of subversion and insurgency directed and equipped by Communist North Vietnam . . . Recruits are obtained by kidnapping and other coercive measures and sent to North Vietnam for training and indoctrination. Later they come back to form Viet Cong units.' The official position insisted that the conflict had neither local roots nor was it caused by internal discontent. The *Pocketbook* carried by Australian troops in Vietnam followed this line and emphasised the enemy's use of terror and violence not only against government officials but also villagers, civilian schoolteachers and even nurses. Nothing was said of the terror practised by the Diem regime and, as time passed and the Australian involvement became a major military commitment, it was increasingly hard to explain why the battle for hearts and minds was failing.

Communist leadership in North Vietnam did influence the direction of revolutionary forces in the South but those forces, usually referred to as the National Liberation Front (NLF) or the Viet Cong, had an established base of local support. They were well integrated into village life by ties of family, friendship and shared interest. The injustices of the Diem regime had become a rallying point for their struggle.

In his memoir *Ambassador's Journal*, the American economist and diplomat John Kenneth Galbraith described his encounter with the Diem regime in 1961:

It is certainly a can of snakes. I am reasonably accustomed to oriental government and politics, but I was not quite prepared for Diem . . . his surface travel through Saigon requires the taking in of all laundry along the route, the closing of all windows,

North and South Vietnam

an order to the populace to keep their heads in, the clearing of all streets, and a vast bevy of motorcycle outriders to protect him on his dash . . . The political reality is the total stasis which arises from his greater need to protect himself from a coup than to protect the country from the Viet Cong . . . The desire to prolong one's day in office has a certain consistency the world around and someday somebody should explain this to the State Department with pictures.

US officials were aware of Diem's limitations. Privately there was agreement that his rule was dictatorial, repressive and unpopular. Publically he was promoted as the saviour of Vietnam. Australian policy makers took a similar view and routinely misinformed their constituents about the nature of the regime.

In 1960–61 the war escalated. There was armed resistance throughout the South and Diem's forces needed more assistance from outside. During the Kennedy period (1961–63) the number of US military advisers in South Vietnam grew to about 16,000 and the Australian government came under pressure from Washington to make a gesture of support. At an ANZUS Council meeting in 1961 Menzies told Admiral H.D. Felt, commander of the US Pacific fleet, that Australia was willing to supply military advisers. Felt told Menzies that Australian military assistance was not required but a military presence in South Vietnam would be most helpful. The Americans wanted a symbolic contribution. Two weeks later the Minister for Defence announced that Australia was sending a team of 30 military advisers. The Australian contingent was a small gesture, a political response to a political request, but one that suited both parties. It met the American wish to be seen in Vietnam with international support and it met the Australian wish to encourage a US presence in South East Asia as an insurance policy for defence security—without drawing heavily on Australian forces. In Canberra the main fear was not Ho Chi Minh but Sukarno in Indonesia.

Australia was already providing assistance to the Diem regime in the form of communications equipment, barbed wire and other military materials. Now it sent a training team to instruct in jungle warfare, village defence, engineering, signals and other activities.

Warrant Officer L.A. Williams, Khe Sanh, September 1963.

Warrant Officer R.S. Simpson checks the bags of a villager, 1964.

Members of the Team operated throughout the South, acting as advisers to regular South Vietnamese army units and leading them in battle though, officially, Australia was not providing combat troops.

By December 1964 the team, with the formal title of Australian Army Training Team Vietnam (AATTV), had grown to 100 strong. Many were veterans of World War II, Korea, Malaya and the Indonesian Confrontation. They were an elite group of soldiers, mostly Australians, but among them was a smattering of military emigrés from other parts of the Commonwealth (South Africa and Rhodesia), and even from Central Europe. All were seasoned professionals. Their first commanding officer was Colonel Francis Phillip 'Ted' Serong, a Duntroon graduate in 1937, who served on the staff of the 6th Division from 1942 to 1944. After the war he held a number of staff posts at army headquarters until 1955 when he took command of the Jungle Training Centre (JTC) at Canungra. From 1960 to 1962 Serong was an adviser to the Burmese military, training them in the techniques of counterinsurgency, and from there he went to Vietnam to head the AATTV, otherwise known as the Team.

Members of the Team operated throughout the South, acting as advisers to regular South Vietnamese army units and leading them in battle though, officially, Australia was not providing combat troops. They also worked with the Montagnard hill tribes as part of the US Special Forces network and they were heavily involved with the Central Intelligence Agency (CIA) in training South Vietnamese for covert activity against the NLF—infiltration, arrest and assassination—what Casey had referred to as 'dirt boy's stuff'. Brigadier O.D. Jackson, the Team's commander in 1965, described these activities in the *Army Journal* after his return to Australia: 'Team tasks were to identify, locate and destroy the Viet Cong insurgent cadres and infrastructure in contested hamlets and villages and restore them to government control and security.' Members of the Team were awarded many decorations including four Victoria Crosses and a US Presidential Unit Citation. Their standing in military circles, according to one assessment, was 'almost legendary'.

Australian Team members talking with Vietnamese instructors during a training patrol, Phuoc Tuy province, 1964.

With the Montagnards

In August 1963, an Australian army captain flew into Ban-Me-Thuot, capital of Darlac Province in the central highlands of South Vietnam. He was Captain Barry Petersen, a young veteran of Malaya and a member of the Australian Army Training Team in Vietnam. He had been seconded to the CIA and sent to the highlands to train Montagnard tribesmen for the war against the Viet Cong.

The Montagnards were an ethnic minority who maintained deeply felt grievances against both the South Vietnamese government and the displaced Vietnamese refugees flooding into Darlac province. Most of them still lived traditional lives in isolated villages distinguished by communal long houses and bounded by a palisade of fiercely pointed bamboo stakes.

Petersen arrived in Ban-Me-Thuot with a suitcase full of Vietnamese *piastres* (CIA money), a 'vague directive' to organise a guerilla force and instructions to steer clear of English speaking groups, despite the fact that he spoke only English and a little Malay. He took a house beyond the French quarter, a rambling, Vietnamese dwelling surrounded by a walled garden. Extensions were quickly added: a radio room ('manned day and night'), an armoury and accommodation for an eight-man security squad. He inherited peacocks and a monkey from the previous resident—a deposed Vietnamese police chief—and, as time passed, the Montagnard presented him with more living gifts. They gave him deer, gibbons, a young honey bear and a tiger cub.

The Australian captain acquired a staff of three: Jut, an interpreter who spoke English, French, Vietnamese and several Montagnard dialects, Vu, a driver, and H'Pam who became his housekeeper and secretary. H'Pam looked after the accounting for the 'operational fund', typed his reports and occasionally brought a gentle touch to the interrogation of Viet Cong captives. She also bought the household's meat live at the markets and slaughtered it on the premises— a precaution against assassination by poisoning.

Ban-Me-Thuot was a hive of intrigue, a point of convergence for the secret agents of several European nations, the whirlwind tours of CIA men and the retinues of French plantation owners passing through the airport, the hotels and the bars. In the seething streets locals and workers from the hinterland rubbed shoulders with American gunrunners, French Jesuits and evangelical missionaries looking for converts.

Petersen began his work with a force of 100 Montagnard men, which quickly grew to 350. They were organised into small, eight-man teams, each one armed with a light machine gun, two automatic sub-machine guns and an assortment of 30-calibre carbines, sniper rifles and shotguns—cast-offs from the US military that the CIA stored in its Saigon warehouse and distributed to para-military organisations throughout the country.

Petersen disliked American methods. His Montagnard forces operated along Australian lines, relying on stealth, teamwork and deadly impact rather than indiscriminate bombing and massive superiority of firepower. They became skilled in the art of hit-and-run, harrassing the Viet Cong and occasionally uniting for larger operations when they swept through Vietnamese resettlement villages. One of these operations concluded with what Petersen called 'a little tea party'.

The fight had gone well. Enemy dead and wounded were scattered about the village. Every hut with any sign of communist occupation—guns, flags, propaganda or documents—was set on fire. Petersen had a terrified old couple make him some tea. 'I asked him [the old man] about his farming, his children and his home province with my questions couched, I hope, in a humane and concerned way,' he wrote. 'He sipped his tea and answered as best he could, and I could see his terror abating. I thanked them both and we left. It was an odd little tea party—exchanging pleasantries in the wake of war. Yet I hoped that those people could pass on to the other villagers the message I was trying to get across: that we were performing our duties as soldiers, and that they could see we were not ogres.'

But Petersen knew that his presence alone in such operations prevented the Montagnard from taking terrible revenge against the Vietnamese. In one such operation when he was away in Saigon (refilling his suitcase), his troops wiped out an entire village. Montagnard grievances were many. They had lost much of their land to Vietnamese displaced from the lowlands in the 1950s and the influx since then had not ceased. Their rights were few. Vietnamese officials called them *moi* meaning savage and were petty and unjust in their dealings with them.

A year after his arrival in the province, Petersen began to hear rumours of a planned Montagnard uprising against the Vietnamese. The rumours were right. The uprising was a patchwork of ruthless killing in some areas, blundering and indecision in others. For a short time he lost control of his own force to a rebel leader called Y-To Nie. Everywhere, the rebellion was short-lived, but ethnic tensions were now so high that Petersen moved his men to new camps beyond the reach of South Vietnamese artillery in Ban-Me-Thuot.

In March 1965 he learned that the South Vietnamese government no longer trusted him. His force had grown to 1000. It had worked well in the field. His success was his undoing. He was thought too close to the highland people, and too sympathetic to their plight. There was talk of a 'cult of personality'. Some in high places suspected him of being involved in the revolt. His value to the CIA was now much diminished. They tapped his phone and intercepted his mail, raided his safe and confiscated his files. On one of his visits to Saigon his CIA handler asked him to organise 'counter-terror' teams, small groups of professional assassins. Petersen refused. Not long afterwards his posting was cancelled. He was to be replaced by a CIA man.

His departure was marked by elaborate ceremonies conducted by the Montagnard. There were two weeks of farewells, a round of visits to homes and long houses, the beating of buffalo drums and bronze gongs. At the main ceremony, tribal dignitaries and a Montagnard commander made solemn speeches. Chicken, pigs and buffalo were sacrificed in supplication to the spirits in honour of Petersen. Buffalo blood and rice wine was poured over his feet and a live chicken waved in circles above his head, a symbolism he did not understand. He drank from a rice wine jar after one of the Montagnard matriarchs had taken a few sips and beckoned him to follow. Then he sat in state as many came forward bearing small tokens, amber beads and necklaces, bracelets and other configurations of brass piping. The next morning he reviewed his troops. He shook hands with every man assembled and then left for Ban-Me-Thuot. His war alongside the Montagnards was over.

Colonel F.P. (Ted) Serong.

The first Team member was killed in action in July. This death was just two months after President Lyndon B. Johnson's call on 'free world' countries to 'show their flags' in South Vietnam.

A Team member shares a meal with South Vietnamese soldiers, 1964.

Ted Serong, still a British Empire man, claimed in 1972 that 'the Team with its ten years of continuous combat stands as the most highly decorated unit in the annals of the British army'. The AATTV was the first Australian force in Vietnam and the last to leave. Thirty-five members of the Team were still there when the Whitlam government was elected in December 1972.

The Team entered the conflict as the situation in Vietnam deteriorated. The repression of all opposition, not only the NLF, had further isolated the Diem regime. In the countryside that regime was indiscriminately bombing villages allegedly under communist control. As the US Secretary for Defense, Robert McNamara, later put it: 'The net result was that we killed a lot of villagers and there was no rationale for doing this.' In mid 1963 there were demonstrations and riots in Saigon. When Buddhist monks protested against the banning of celebrations for Buddha's birthday, police shot nine dead. Protests calling for the removal of Diem, for the reunification of the country and the removal of the Americans became a regular occurrence. On 11 June 1963, the Western world was aghast at film footage that showed the self-immolation of a Buddhist monk: he sat on a cushion in the midst of a busy Saigon street, motionless in the lotus position, soaked in petrol, as flames devoured him. Over the next ten weeks another six monks sacrificed themselves in the same way. Reports said President Kennedy was very upset. Diem's sister-in-law expressed a Marie Antoinette-like indifference when she publicly referred to these events as 'barbecues'.

Buddhist generals in Diem's army were now plotting his assassination and a coup. There was confusion in the White House: first it acquiesced in the plot to kill Diem, then it demurred, then it switched again and supported the dissident generals. Diem's assassination was discussed in the Kennedy office only weeks before the American President's own assassination. Diem and his brother were shot dead in the coup that followed, and over the next twelve months South Vietnam had a string of presidents and prime ministers.

Permission for the Team to lead troops in combat was relayed from Canberra in June 1964. The first Team member was killed in action in July. This death was just two months after President Lyndon B. Johnson's call on 'free world' countries to 'show their flags' in South Vietnam. He made a specific call upon Australia to boost its commitment with a range of army and air training personnel, pilots, reconnaissance aircraft, forward air controllers and other specialists. The situation in Vietnam and neighbouring Laos was fast deteriorating and Johnson needed Australian help to sway US public opinion in favour of escalation. In Laos, CIA pilots were bombing Pathet Lao guerrillas. In Vietnam, the NLF and regular troops from the North had won control of large parts of the country. The Army of the Republic of (South) Vietnam (ARVN) was losing a battalion a week through battle casualties and desertion.

In November 1964, Menzies announced sweeping defence changes to meet a 'defence emergency'. The problem was not just Vietnam but South East Asia. Troops might be needed in any one, or more, of the Asian hot spots at any one time. Australian forces were operating

In February 1965, American aircraft began bombing strategic locations in North Vietnam with a fire power that only stopped short of nuclear weapons.

It was a frantic time preparing at such short notice. We even got those wraparound First World War leggings, you know, puttees. Puttees for jungle warfare!

Corporal Les McAuley, 1RAR

against Indonesian troops in Borneo and still playing a part in the Far East Strategic Reserve. There was the possibility of conflict with Indonesia on the common border in New Guinea, communists were insurgent in Laos, and now Vietnam could fall. 'We expect a continuing requirement to make forces available for cold war and insurgency tasks,' the Prime Minister told Parliament. The defence statement signalled the largest changes since World War II. The Army was to be increased from 22,750 to 37,500, the Citizens' Military Force (CMF) expanded and conscription reintroduced. Battalions were to be reorganised into smaller, 'lighter, air-portable' divisions to meet the possibility of two or three simultaneous commitments in the region. The Special Air Service (SAS) was to double in size from two to four squadrons and both the air force and the navy were to be re-equipped.

Behind the concern about South East Asia was the paramount objective to bolster credit with the US to ensure Australia's security. Australian foreign policy aimed to achieve such an 'habitual closeness of relations' that support in time of need would be assured, and going into Vietnam alongside the USA was a way of picking up credit for a time of great need. The strategy had worked before when Australia supported the big powers in Korea and Malaya and that it would work again was the thinking behind the commitment to Vietnam. America was now sending combat troops. By April 1964 Australia was ready to send a battalion and was waiting for a spontaneous call for help from the government of South Vietnam. That was organised by US and Australian diplomats in Saigon, allowing Menzies to tell Parliament that he was 'in receipt' of a request for troops, which was not a lie. At the same time, Gallipoli veterans were walking the beach at Anzac Cove. They were on a pilgrimage to mark the 50th anniversary of the landing in 1915, and they were flying home when Menzies announced the commitment of a battalion.

In February 1965, American aircraft began bombing strategic locations in North Vietnam with a fire power that only stopped short of nuclear weapons. In May the 1st Battalion, The Royal Australian Regiment (1RAR) arrived at Vung Tau aboard HMAS *Sydney*.

Sapper Barry Hartford of Broken Hill, NSW, in a Viet Cong tunnel, 25 June 1966.

Vung Tau was on the coast, about 65 kilometres south-east of Saigon. Under French rule it had been called Cap Saint Jacques and had been a fashionable seaside resort for the French from Saigon. In 1965 it was designated the rest and recreation (R & R) centre for the Australians and in 1966 it became their logistics base. There were about 170 bars and 3,000 bar girls in Vung Tau. They entertained soldiers from Australia, New Zealand, the USA, Korea and Thailand. One of the jokes about Vung Tau was that the NLF took their R & R there too.

1RAR was placed under the direct control of the US Army's 173rd Airborne Division at Bien Hoa air base, north of Saigon. The men were driven to the base in buses with windows covered by metal grids to stop grenades being thrown in. Once there, the Americans supplied everything save weapons, some ammunition and uniforms and the Australian government paid the bill. In camp the ram-rod straight, smartly tailored US paratroopers passing an officer snapped a salute and shouted 'Airborne Sir', and the officer's scripted reply was 'All the way'. Further discussion was mostly conducted in a clipped yes-sir, no-sir format. When the US commander in South Vietnam, General William Westmoreland, asked one Digger how he liked the American food he was not expecting a smart-Alec reply, but he got one: 'We can always fall back on dog biscuits.' The Australians, according to the reporter Gerald Stone, seemed like 'ragamuffins' alongside the paratroops, 'slogging around camp in shorts, boots, floppy hats and singlets, or no shirts at all.'

1RAR's preparation for Vietnam had been hampered by short notice and defence misreading. The short notice meant they only had time for one major training exercise before departure. The misreading was the 'invasion from the north' analysis, and it left the troops unprepared for the complexities of the civil war they were about to enter. Cold War preconceptions could not substitute for an accurate briefing. An additional problem was the strain on supplies brought about by this latest commitment in Asia. 1RAR was kitted out in World War II issue boots that were soon falling apart. Some Owen guns were twenty years old, some radio equipment was worn out and there was a shortage of both. In the press in Australia there was an outcry about the low priority accorded to this latest addition to 'forward defence' in Asia.

The battalion was assigned a number of duties—to defend the air base at Bien Hoa, to strike into NLF-held territory to the north and to reinforce ARVN units in combat. Striking north into enemy territory was the most testing duty. The common pattern was for the guerillas to melt away as the Australian troops advanced. The troops would then surround a village and carefully make their way in to find no men at all and women and children staring blankly at the foreigners in their midst.

Operations in enemy territory were also directed at disrupting the rice-gathering activity of the NLF and at assaults on 'fortified hamlets' where the NLF sometimes made a stand. These hamlets contained comprehensive tunnel systems that included firing pits, bunkers, sleeping chambers, conference chambers, kitchens, storage caches for weapons, explosives and rice, concealed trapdoors, panji stake traps, hospital facilities and ventilation shafts. Some of the Australians worked as invaders—'tunnel rats'—one of the most hazardous jobs in the Vietnam assignment.

The danger in those tunnels was only marginally greater than the danger of an attachment to a US brigade. The tactical methods of the US and Australian forces were incompatible and there was a desire among senior officers for the Australians to go it alone. Australian patrolling was small-scale, cautious and stealthy in contrast to the crash-through style of the Americans. The American practice of daily resupply by helicopter gave positions away and the unrestrained use of fire power, while damaging to the enemy, could draw a devastating rejoinder. According to Gerald Stone, 'the Americans are getting ambushed. The Australians, often covering the same ground and running into similar enemy emplacements, are not.'

The Australians preferred to 'go bush'. They kept off tracks and clearings. They worked their way quietly through the varying terrain. They fanned out in all directions, criss-crossing and circling to ensure ground coverage and security. They lived off thin rations. Their tactical preference was to be left out in the jungle for a month, to have supplies dropped once a week, to change position frequently, move at night in some cases and to 'keep those bloody choppers away from us'. Their operational basis was the 30-man platoon. The US (Airborne) was trained for a

A soldier of 1RAR covers villagers during the cordon and search of a village, 24 November 1965. Part of the 'rice denial' campaign.

Once you got down into the tunnel, it was elongated, it was like getting into a coffin . . . I turned right and I looked around the corner and saw two eyes looking at me and I shot back and thought, what's that? So, I put my pistol round the corner and the torch. Saw it was a dog and got a bit frustrated and I put nine rounds into him . . . You just snuck along, nice and careful, and you get your pistol ready . . . they told me there were 5,000 fully armed troops down there. Thank Christ they kept moving.

Ivon Barnett,
Sapper, 3 Field Troop,
Australian Engineers

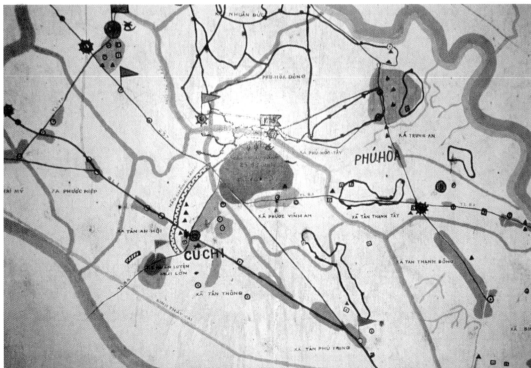

Detail from Cu Chi tunnel system maps showing over 22 km of arterial tunnels (not including branches). Breached by 1RAR in January 1966.

limited conventional war. Its operational basis was the 900-man battalion backed by the lavish use of air power. Between 1964 and 1972, the US used nearly 15 million tonnes of munitions in Vietnam, more than twice the amount it used in World War II, and half of this was delivered by airpower.

The low-profile, intensive style of Australian patrolling kept casualty numbers down, a necessity in a force so small. At the height of Australian involvement in Vietnam, the Australians numbered 8,300. At top strength there were more than 540,000 US soldiers in Vietnam and some Diggers said that American officers were all too ready to expend the lives of their soldiers for minor gains. In April 1966, the *Bulletin* quoted an Australian officer: 'We've seen the Americans go out and in one night lose more than 40 men. That's more than we've lost in ten months.' The small Australian force simply could not sustain high casualties. But it did have to live with the prolonged tensions of jungle warfare. Some patrols were in the jungle for months. From the moment they left their base until they returned they were at great risk. At any time of the day or night a contact was possible. Patrols could take as much as nine hours to sweep a mile of terrain. They would move forward, stop and listen, then move forward again. They operated in a world of silence—of hand signals, whispers and careful footsteps. They were constantly looking for signs and sounds of the enemy. At Pozières in 1916 soldiers were in the line for three days, suffered horrendous casualties, then the survivors were pulled out and replaced. In Vietnam men might go into the jungle for 30 days, or 60, come back for three days to rest and then go out again.

The limits of the Australian–US partnership were set by these tactical differences and led to pressure on the Australian government to field a self-contained force.

Planning for an independent task force began not long after 1RAR arrived in Vietnam and a year later the Task Force was set up in the province of Phuoc Tuy, south-east of Saigon. 1RAR returned home to a rousing welcome in June 1966, to a parade through Sydney's streets. The *Australian* claimed half a million people turned out for this 'excited, emotional heroes' welcome'. R.G. Casey, now Governor-General, took the salute. Crowds lined George Street, three and four deep. Children waved flags, ticker-tape and streamers showered down from office windows, and women threw paper roses in the path of the soldiers. The weight of public opinion was clear. There was one lone protester: a woman whose clothes were covered in red paint ran among the soldiers to smear a few of them with the colour of blood. In court she was reprimanded for improper behaviour and for directing her feelings against gallant men. The magistrate considered a psychiatric examination, decided against it, fined her $6 and put her on a good behaviour bond. Her defiance contrasted with the welcoming crowd and confirmed opinion polls at the time—this was a popular war.

Dramatic gestures were rare, but signs of growing disquiet over the war in Vietnam were not. Until conscription was introduced and then military intervention announced, the peace movement was focussed on atomic weapons and the threat of global war. It was small, marginal, widely condemned and trapped in its own, Soviet-inclined orthodoxies. The Christian and pacifist elements were generally overshadowed by the energy and zeal of trade unionists and intellectuals from the CPA. But at the end of the 1950s there was a thaw. Organisations emerged, more pluralist in their politics and their appeal, rejecting the Cold War model of a world divided into two camps and refusing the choice between two well-defined and rigid ideologies.

Some groups sought the middle ground, toying with non-alignment—an idea already well established in the Third World—and thus thinking in new ways about

The Australians preferred to 'go bush'. They kept off tracks and clearings. They worked their way quietly through the varying terrain.

We were excited, maybe apprehensive. This was a job we'd been trained to do and we wanted to go and do the real thing. It wasn't long before the excitement cooled.

Lieutenant Jim Bourke, 1RAR

On patrol in Bien Hoa, August 1965. Aboriginal serviceman Private Joe Minecome carries the section's M60 machine gun, *opposite*.

Morris West speaking at the first Vietnam War teach-in, Australian National University, Canberra, July 1965.

We feel deeply let down. Just about all of us are mothers of conscripts or mothers of sons in danger of being conscripted. Prime Minister Menzies is ignoring mounting public opinion. Most Australians do not want national servicemen sent overseas. With the war taking so many young men, we must make a stand for all mothers and all families who love their young men.

'Dorothy', member of Save Our Sons

Members of the crowd at the Vietnam War teach-in at ANU.

world politics. Others were concerned with the reintroduction of conscription for overseas service and nothing more. In between, the variations were many. What was important was how these organisations broke the Cold War mould. They were sufficiently small 'l' liberal , and sufficiently respectable, to draw fresh support from young and old. In the early days of this revival, 1964–1966, the peace movement was dominated by the middle-aged whose attitudes to war were shaped by the 1939–1945 conflict and its atomic conclusion. Some of the new leadership had left the CPA in the 1950s. Stephen Murray-Smith, for example, had been a Bren gunner with the 5th Independent Company in New Guinea. He joined the CPA after World War II and left it in 1958, alienated by its Stalinist leadership. He was a leading light in the Australian Peace Council. Respectable writers also joined the cause. The fifty-year-old Morris West spoke against the war at a teach-in at the Australian National University (ANU) in 1965. Another senior figure was the poet A.D. Hope. He was nearly sixty when he challenged the right of one generation to conscript another, younger one for the war in Vietnam:

Linger not, stranger, shed no tear;
Go back to those who sent us here.
We are the young they drafted out
To wars their folly brought about.
Go tell those old men, safe in bed,
We took their orders and are dead.

The mothers of Save Our Sons (SOS) were mostly in their forties. The Youth Campaign Against Conscription (YCAC) was launched at a meeting in Sydney on 29 November 1964 after an address by a prominent ALP figure, Jim Cairns. Cairns was a former shadow squad member of Blamey's Victorian Police Force in the 1930s and an ex-serviceman. His contemporary, Tom Uren, was also working in the peace movement. Uren was a prisoner of war under the Japanese. He saw Nagasaki after the atomic blast.

Fishing boats, fish drying frames and nets, Phuoc Tuy province, 1966. To the right, an Australian soldier on guard.

Calwell was in a dilemma—how to oppose the war without being anti-American.

In New South Wales the full-time secretary of the Association for International Co-operation and Disarmament (AICD) was Geoffrey Anderson, who was awarded the Distinguished Flying Cross during World War II. AICD's foundation committee was made up mostly of educated, middle-class men. It included businessmen, clergy, academics and teachers and five trade unionists. In May 1966 it had a membership of 1,000, of whom 40 were categorised as 'youth and students'.

These outbursts of opposition activity did not win widespread popular support initially as the climate for protest was still inhospitable, but they did begin to free up public debate. Alternative voices could at last be heard and the opportunities to hear them, all of a sudden, were everywhere. There were small marches and demonstrations, vigils of various kinds, teach-ins in universities and colleges, public meetings in country towns, preach-ins in radical churches and rallies in town halls. The federal election planned for November 1966 spurred hope, for some saw the solution in a Labor Party victory. The government was more worried about Jim Cairns than it was about the less eloquent ALP leader, Arthur Calwell. Cairns, said the Minister of Defence, was 'infecting the students'.

Calwell was in a dilemma—how to oppose the war without being anti-American. In the 1950s and early 1960s the ALP had accepted the terms of the Cold War debate. It was pro forward defence; it accepted the paradigm of Chinese expansionism; it was eager for close ties with the US and, until 1965, largely supportive of US intervention in Vietnam. It even accepted the US's decision in February 1965 to bomb North Vietnam to the negotiating table. The change in attitude began when an Australian battalion was committed in April 1965. The time was fast approaching when conscripts might die on foreign soil. Calwell was an ageing Labor leader, an Irish Catholic warhorse steeped in the party's anti-conscription tradition. In 1943 he had been Curtin's most bitter opponent when the geographical limits of conscription for overseas service were extended. Now he promised to bring home the conscripts and the regulars from Vietnam. Donald Horne called him 'an old hulk floating out on the tide', but there was still a lot of fight in Arthur Calwell.

A herdsman and cattle on the edge of Hoa Long, Phuoc Tuy province, 1966.

Labor's primary vote dropped by more than 5 per cent. Some thought the anti-war cause was lost.

Long Dien market place, Phuoc Tuy province, 1969, *opposite*.

On the campaign trail he threw caution to the wind. When a heckler tried to intervene he shouted back: 'You are beyond military age. I will not allow you or Holt or Menzies or anyone to plunge your arthritic hands wrist deep in the blood of Australian youth.' Labor's television advertising followed the same line: one advertisement featured a flag at half mast, the strains of a bugle playing the Last Post and the words 'Should not conscripts be asked if they want to go all the way?'

As the election approached, Calwell's dilemma was ever more visible. When President Johnson visited Australia on the eve of the election, there were effusive toasts and speeches from both sides of parliament. Calwell's welcoming words were perhaps the most memorable of all. He made a point of disagreeing with the policy in Vietnam but he spoke passionately about the American revolution and concluded by reciting the Gettysburg Address from memory in a voice that, several times, quavered and broke. As Ho Chi Minh had once believed, so Calwell believed—at the USA's core there was a glowing nobility.

The election was a great win for the coalition government. Its majority in the House of Representatives rose from 22 to 40. Labor's primary vote dropped by more than 5 per cent. Some thought the anti-war cause was lost. In January 1967, South Vietnam's new Prime Minister, Air Vice-Marshal Nguyen Cao Ky, visited Australia. The timing of Ky's visit was a godsend for the demoralised peace movement. Ky had served in the French air force after 1954. He wore a tailored black flying suit, lavender scarf and dark sunglasses and carried a pearl-handled pistol on his belt. His nickname on the Saigon nightclub circuit was 'The Cowboy'. Much was made of his admiration for Hitler. Anti Ky pamphlets routinely quoted his most infamous saying: 'We need four or five Hitlers in Vietnam.' He was a new rallying point, a focus for demonstrators' outrage. Calwell joined in with the same careless tenacity he had shown in the election. He called Ky 'a little Asian butcher' and 'a little quisling gangster', but apart from Cairns, Uren and other Labor leftists, there were few Labor MPs who joined the demonstrations or backed up Calwell's vitriol—they all seemed to be on holidays or fishing or busy with local business in their own electorates. Their absence confirmed the belief that the movement against the war was flagging.

The 1966 election result was only one measure of change during this transition. The great public inertia of the Cold War period had come to an end. The certainties of a world simplified into good and bad, free and unfree, were diminishing. Public debate finally had gathered pace, authority was challenged and anxious. One of the 'peace parsons', the Reverend David Hope, saw beyond the election result when he said: 'There is a vast, latent subterranean sea of disquiet and disenchantment.' The question was how to tap it.

The signs of this unrest were alarming. In 1966 a breakaway Liberal Reform Group (LRG) headed by a wealthy Sydney businessman, Gordon Barton, campaigned against the war in Vietnam. The LRG argued that Diem and the Americans were jointly responsible for the war for failing to allow elections and

Minister for the Army, Malcolm Fraser, with a .30 calibre carbine during a visit to Vietnam in June 1966.

The situation is about normal. The military have taken control of the government again . . . Yesterday Saigon's civilian air terminal was blown up, and at dawn tomorrow five naughty Chinese war profiteers are to be publicly executed by firing squad in the Central Market. That about sums it up . . .

Neil Davis, Visnews cameraman and correspondent in a letter to his Aunt Lillian in Tasmania

reunification in the mid 1950s. Later in the year the RSL was fractured when a group of ex-servicemen formed the Ex-Services Human Rights Association (ESHRA). It was anti-conscription and anti-war and, though its numbers were small, it soon had branches in Brisbane, Perth, Sydney, Melbourne and Newcastle and its members included veterans of every major war in which Australians had fought since the Boer War. After the 1966 federal election, ESHRA President, Allan Ashbolt, was dismissed from his job at the ABC on the grounds that his political activity 'had limited his usefulness'. At the same time, a schoolboy at Sydney Grammar School refused to participate in war games at a cadet camp. He would not take part in a simulated search and destroy mission in which the enemy was dressed in black with red stars to signify the NLF. The matter became public. An opposition member praised the boy's courage. The Minister for the Army, Malcolm Fraser, quoted an ASIO source, informing the Parliament that the boy's mother was secretary to the NSW branch of the Women's International League for Peace and Freedom and was regarded as a communist fellow traveller.

In the seventeenth century the territory eventually called Phuoc Tuy province was a sparsely populated, heavily forested no-man's land. It was a buffer zone between Khmer-occupied lands to the south in the Mekong delta, and the Cham kingdom of central Vietnam to the north. There are striking parallels between the peopling of the buffer zone and the beginnings of colonial Australia. Early in the seventeenth century, the first settlers from the north, Vietnamese immigrants, began to occupy the territory. They were outlaws, vagabonds and deserters looking for free land. At first the Khmer kings acquiesced, but then they contested the inflow from the north. In reply, the Vietnamese claimed rights of occupation, sent troops, built forts, asserted sovereignty and forced the Khmers in the delta into a westward retreat.

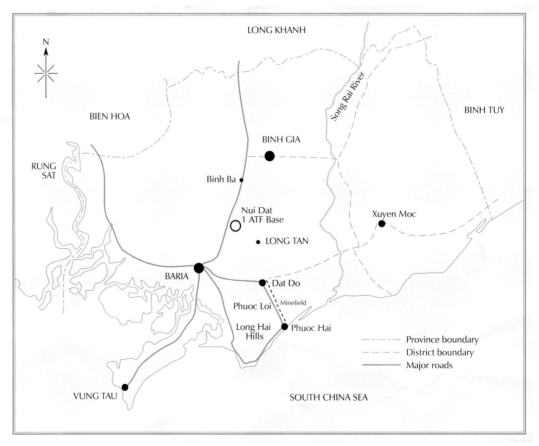

Phuoc Tuy province

Combat Cameraman

Neil Davis on patrol with South Vietnamese troops in the Mekong Delta, Bell and Howell camera in hand, 1967.

The Tasmanian-born cameraman, Neil Davis, won fame for his daring and unconventional coverage of wars in Indo-China. Perhaps his most famous film sequence came at the end of the Vietnam war when he filmed North Vietnamese tank No. 843 crashing through the gates of Independence Palace in Ho Chi Minh City, formerly Saigon, in April 1975. By that time, Davis had been reporting the war for a decade.

Throughout his years in Vietnam Davis did not often go out with Australian troops because he believed that, relatively speaking, they did not do a lot of fighting. The ARVN, on the other hand, were constantly thrown into battle, taking fearful casualties, yet rarely did foreign correspondents bother to cover their operations. Covering the Americans, a correspondent was often assigned his own helicopter, fresh food and water every day. With the ARVN, Davis foot slogged as they did, drank water from the rivers using tablets to purify it, and ate their food—rice, maybe some vegetables and occasionally a small piece of fish.

Davis grew up on a subsistence farm near Nala in southern Tasmania. He left school in 1948 when he was fourteen and began his working life as an office boy with the Tasmanian Government Film Unit. He moved up in that world, trained in the use of a 35 millimetre cinecamera for the Film Unit and, in 1961, became the first ABC cameraman based in Tasmania. Three years later, he moved to Singapore to work for the British Commonwealth International Film Agency, commonly known as Visnews.

From Singapore he shuttled around the region's trouble spots, from Jakarta in Java to Kuching in Sarawak, to Vientiane in Laos and to Saigon, and from these centres to the villages and the 'bush'. It was in the Mekong Delta, south of Saigon, where his career as a combat cameraman began. He wrote: 'I was anxious to get out and see what the war was all about, and of course I had in my mind the example of Damien Parer, the great Australian cameraman from World War II.'

Davis had some military experience. In 1952 when he turned 18 he was conscripted. His weekly routine of work, playing professional football, beer drinking with his mates and betting was interrupted for three months compulsory military training, and then followed by three years part-time service with the Citizens Military Forces (CMF). He wrote later that his survival in this first combat experiences was partly due to luck and partly to his military training in Tasmania. His first patrol in Vietnam made contact at the end of a hard day trudging across rice paddies. 'I remember thinking, I don't want it now, I'm not ready. Why don't they do it in the morning when I'm fresh. But that's not the way it happened.'

Davis felt safer with his chosen ARVN units than he did with the Americans. While US special forces were capable, the regular units, he believed, were a disaster. He called the American forces in the jungle a 'Barnum and Bailey circus'—the Viet Cong called them 'elephants'—with men overloaded, noisy, slow and bearing a distinctive smell of toothpaste, cigarettes and shaving cream. The better ARVN units were lightly equipped, highly mobile and prepared to fight. They moved into Viet Cong territory seeking contact, mostly without aerial or artillery assistance and minimal rations. 'On many occasions it was not a question of defeating the enemy,' wrote Davis, 'it was a victory simply to survive'.

The war cameraman felt an affinity for the Vietnamese on both sides of the conflict. Most of them were 'poor country boys' like himself. 'I never felt a stranger in Asian countries,' he wrote . 'I never had to tell people that I was a farm boy myself. They sensed that and were well disposed towards me.' In his camera work and his tape - recorded narratives, he tried to convey the hardships and humanity of the Vietnamese fighting the war. He wanted to show

that they weren't funny little animals running around, as their allies liked to depict them. I wanted to show them as compassionate people with feeling for their fellow human beings, for their families, and for life itself—and for their own lives, even though they gave those lives courageously on many occasions.

Correspondents died too. Davis estimated that 80 to 90 Western and Asian cameramen, photographers and journalists were killed in Indo-China from 1965 until the fall of Saigon in April 1975. Davis was killed by cross-fire in the streets of Bangkok during an attempted coup on 9 September 1985. Some said he had a death wish, but his survival over so many years of living dangerously put the lie to that. His biographer, Tim Bowden, believed that he had an 'addiction to the sharp realities of a life of action.'

Neil Davis resting with South Vietnamese troops during the Communist spring offensive of 1972.

Sapper Stewart Law of Singleton, NSW, on alert in War Zone D, South Vietnam, 11 March 1966.

By the time I raised the machine gun up to fire he was about a foot and a half from the machine gun. I pulled the trigger, he had about six or seven guys behind him. And when I fired the rounds, I was looking through the sights and they were just pouring into his head, and his head was just exploding. But the fire of this machine gun was actually holding this guy up—it wasn't allowing him to fall onto the ground.

Private Ray Payne, 1RAR

Soldiers of 1RAR in waist-deep water, during a search and destroy sweep to the south west of Saigon.

Then, in the eighteenth century, the Vietnamese set about populating the new province by means of transportation. A troubling surplus from the lower classes—vagabonds, thieves and other unwanteds in the central provinces—were swept up and sent south. The transportees were called 'colons'. They were settled in villages, permitted to select land and by the nineteenth century their descendants were organised into an orderly society. The earlier claimants were gone, driven out. A new rural social order replaced them, traditions were established, sovereignty was assumed, the land was cherished and the new society acquired a history of its own, only to be overlaid by French occupation.

The Australian Task Force arrived at Nui Dat in Phuoc Tuy province in May 1966. The soldiers of 5RAR and 6RAR were supported by Australian and New Zealand artillery units, a squadron of RAAF Iroquois helicopters, armoured personnel carriers and elements of the elite SAS. The two infantry battalions had extensive training and were possibly the most schooled fighters ever to leave Australian shores. They had completed arduous courses in jungle fighting at Canungra in Queensland and also in New Guinea. They had additional training in small arms, and field defences as well as section and platoon coordination. Once 5RAR and 6RAR were in Phuoc Tuy the routine, until late in 1967, was the kind of stealthy, aggressive patrolling that clearly distinguished the Diggers from the Americans, playing no small part in forging their unity and identity, and producing some success. They were also engaged in patrolling and fencing off village populations to isolate the enemy from the people, and associated programs of civic action aimed at winning hearts and minds. These were the main components of what one of their training pamphlets called 'counter-revolutionary warfare'.

The big problem, initially, was a shortage of crucial supplies. Food and ammunition were supplied in abundance by the Americans but otherwise the Australians relied on their own resources and here there were shortfalls. Some of their Owen guns were

World War II vintage, there were not enough weapons and communications equipment and their uniforms were made of a coarse material unsuited to jungle conditions. In the first months at Nui Dat the Australians scrambled for essential equipment in case the base was attacked. One of the battalion officers was charged with stealing five .50 calibre machine guns from the American depot at Vung Tau. Another took slouch hats and shower buckets to Saigon where he bartered them for field telephones. Picks and shovels and tents were also scarce.

For several months companies on patrol had to go short of machine guns to ensure that those left behind at the base could defend themselves. The rationing of radios and telephones was an equally perilous necessity. The low priority given to adequate supply seemed to confirm the notion that the commitment of ground troops was essentially a political exercise. But this was hardly compensation for the men. One 5RAR officer blamed both government and army headquarters and called the negligence 'criminal'. The SAS had similar problems. Their squadron master, Taffy Davis, traded cases of Australian beer for equipment, rations and weapons, and men on leave stocked up on gear in Hong Kong.

Accurate knowledge of the social and political setting in Phuoc Tuy was also in short supply. There were North Vietnamese troops in the province but the NLF was there too, in strength. Local forces, notably the D445 Battalion, had been operating since World War II and had widespread support through the villages. Australian soldiers arriving in Nui Dat were poorly tutored in the complexities linking everyday life to revolutionary warfare in their new surrounds. The NLF had a sophisticated political organisation in most villages in the province; it had strongholds in the hills and mountains. Its fighters were not invaders. They were locals, recruited locally, deeply attached to their terrain, their relatives in the villages, their places of worship, their traditions and their history. Such attachments help to explain a resistance with few parallels and also highlight the difficulties faced by Australian troops and the magnitude of their fighting achievement in that one province.

It would have been safer to set up the base in a coastal area—where the Australians had located their logistic support unit, for example, close to the anchorage and airfield at Vung Tau. From there evacuation and reinforcement would be a relatively simple matter. But the choice of Nui Dat was favoured because it was deep in enemy territory. The location met the Australian desire to 'go bush' and operate independently. It also highlighted the dilemmas facing Australian troops and the limits of what they could achieve.

Australian soldiers arriving in Nui Dat were poorly tutored in the complexities linking everyday life to revolutionary warfare in their new surrounds.

The Australian battalion has been described by war correspondents as the safest combat force in Vietnam . . . it is widely felt the Australians have shown themselves able to give chase to the guerillas without exposing themselves to the lethal ambushes that have claimed so many American dead.

R.J. O'Neill, Intelligence Officer, 5RAR

The Buddhist temple at Long Phuoc, December 1967.

6RAR soldier on guard at Long Phuoc as deserted houses are destroyed, 25 June 1966.

Australian troops took greater risks clearing the village house by house, tunnel by tunnel. Then they burnt it to the ground.

We had a surgeon who was very good at hare lips and did lots of hare lip surgery for the locals. It was quite gratifying because you could see we were doing hare lips and everyone was so glad to have that done.

Carmel Hurst, civilian nurse, Government Surgical Team, Vietnam

A base at Nui Dat required the elimination of nearby villages, the fortified hamlets of Long Phuoc and Long Tan. They were a clear threat to the security of Australian forces. The Australians did not routinely destroy villages as the Americans did, but the erasure of Long Phuoc and Long Tan was a strategic matter. Both were razed and there was no resistance. The village-based NLF had melted away, the remaining villagers were sullen and silent, their allegiances invisible. The Australian journalist Pat Burgess was there when Long Phuoc was emptied and burned.

Long Phuoc was a village of deep, cool wells, of fish ponds shaded by flowering shrubs, of verandahs made for children to play around and to shade the old from the Phuoc Tuy sun. In almost every yard there were wood shavings. It was a village of craftsmen, who made their own furniture, who carved even their own candlesticks. It was a village of subsistence farmers and fishermen. It was also, it turned out, a village of riflemen.

The villagers were told of their fate by means of pamphlet and loudhailer. The American method—napalm and bombing—was rejected. Australian troops took greater risks clearing the village house by house, tunnel by tunnel. Then they burnt it to the ground. Burgess wrote: 'On to the flames they still had to throw the hand-carved candlesticks, the old exercise book, the flimsy parasol, the tiny rubber thong.' Concrete bunkers were blown up, caches of food and weapons were taken away. In all, 537 houses were demolished while beneath them a network of 500 escape tunnels and air-raid shelters was filled in. Like many others, this was a village where resistance predated the Cold War. The charred remains of Long Phuoc became a memory to sustain the struggle as a line from a guerilla diary attests: 'Warriors of the four corners! Revenge Long Phuoc from its devastated scenery.'

Most of the people from Long Phuoc were resettled in Hoa Long, one of several villages in the populous, southern corner of the province where the Australians hoped to both cordon them off, Malayan Emergency style, and build good public relations. Hoa Long became a focus for civic action. The Army built a new market and several dispensaries, roads and wells were renewed, medical care was available and a dentist too. Sometimes the army band played a repertoire of tunes in the market place.

The new market place opened with fanfare late in 1966. An Australian officer presented a scroll to a provincial dignitary:

The Australian Government in cooperation with Free World forces and your National Government in Saigon, respectfully presents this market place to you, the citizens of Hoa Long, with the belief and hope that in a free and open market place, truth will prevail and where truth prevails, men will know themselves and their neighbours.

But the good works of civic action were part of a war and military operations in that war undid some of the goodwill. There were many grievances. The resettlement villages were overcrowded and became more so as smaller communities were uprooted and moved in. At Hoa Long the villagers' access to their crops and orchards (at nearby Long Phuoc) was restricted and, late in 1966, their new home was encircled by barbed wire. The great need to cut the NLF from its life source towered over other priorities.

There was also a need to find out more about the enemy. The Australians and the ARVN (the army of South Vietnam) displayed the bodies of enemy dead in the market place or outside the village office at Hoa Long. They wanted to show their effectiveness, to identify the dead if possible and to observe the reactions of the

The village children of Hoa Long line up to receive combat rations
during a cordon and search operation, 30 October 1966.

Men of 7RAR during
a cordon and search of
Long Phuoc, August 1967.

*Men and
women who
were fishermen or
furniture makers
or schoolteachers
by day were NLF
cadres by night.*

**It's Johnson, McNamara
and Co who kindle
this dirty war of
aggression, who send
you here as gun-fodder
for their interest!**

Viet Cong Propaganda
Leaflet (1967)

people in an effort to learn more about the web of allegiances in the village.

Allegiances were revealed not so much at the market place as in the burial arrangements that followed. Expenses were covered by drawing on the Dao-Tuy, a mutual aid association that provided funeral funds for the burial of members, including dead soldiers. When an NLF defector was killed, however, his family was denied Dao-Tuy support and could not hire a car to take the body to the resting place of their ancestors. The people of Hoa Long ensured the NLF dead were buried with dignity and supported the NLF company operating in the Nui Dinh hills, not far away. It was said there was some form of support activity in the village virtually every night. Men and women who were fishermen or furniture makers or schoolteachers by day were NLF cadres by night.

The Australian soldiers put hard work and sincerity into civic action. The greatest weakness of the program lay beyond its ambit. These good works were supposed to reflect well on the Government of South Vietnam in Saigon, (the GVN), and its officials in the villages. But they did not readily transfer to a better image for a government stricken with inertia and riddled with corruption, bound together by a chain of hand-outs, bribes and inventive taxes that reached into every village. Villages were divided along an invisible fault line, some more evenly than others, with two powers competing for authority, claiming legitimacy and vying for control. The contest even split families where members of the NLF and the ARVN shared blood ties but little else.

What the Australians faced was a 'dual power' situation in which, throughout the province, there was a visible authority and a shadow authority, a visible economy and a shadow economy. Taxes imposed by the GVN had their shadowy equivalent in fund-raising demands that the NLF made of villagers. Not even the rubber plantations were above dual claims upon the purse. Workers on a plantation near Binh Ba paid an annual tax equal to about five days pay. They also gave money to the NLF. The French owners were required to pay up too. They paid taxes to both sides in order to stay in business. The NLF set the terms of economic survival: NLF papers captured in 1971 revealed the outcome of one arrangement: 'The French owners [of the Xuan Son plantation] have requested our permission to resume work. We have agreed and cleared the mined areas so that they can begin.'

The dual power struggle was more costly than mere taxation. The NLF used terror to undermine the government's authority in the countryside. It left notices on the bodies of its victims.

Nguyen Van Bong has been a henchman for the enemy since 1962. Until 1969, he has been the security assistant of [the] Nhon Tri hamlet chief—the subject has captured, beaten and terrorised people . . . He has received three warning letters from [the] People's Liberation Committee. But he did not repent. 1. Bong was judged by his many atrocities. 2. The subject had been warned many times. 3. The subject was judged by the will of the people.

The Battle of Long Tan

The aftermath of the Battle of Long Tan. Private Ken Meredith with a group of signallers awaits further orders.

Just two months after the Australians began operations at Nui Dat, a battle was fought in a rubber plantation north of the derelict village of Long Tan. On 17 August 1966 the Nui Dat base came under attack from mortars and rifle fire from the east, leaving 24 Australians wounded. The next morning, B Company, 6RAR, set out to track the enemy and later that day D Company, led by Major Harry Smith, took over the pursuit. Both groups were unhappy about having to miss the Col Joye and Little Pattie concert back at the base. D Company could hear grabs of sound from the concert as they left the base behind. It was mid afternoon when 11 Platoon clashed with a small squad of about six Viet Cong fighters. The enemy fled eastward. The Australians picked up an AK47 rifle, a Russian weapon not used by local force units, and they noticed the small group was outfitted in khaki, another sign of a 'main force' involvement. The signs were right. A little later, around 4 pm, as the clouds opened with torrential rains, 11 Platoon, a force of 28 men, was ambushed by a combined North Vietnamese–NLF force some 2,500 strong. 11 Platoon was pounded from three sides by small arms fire, rocket-propelled grenades and mortar fire. Within minutes one-third of its strength was gone, dead or wounded, and the radio was out of action. The remaining soldiers fought back. As one of them put it, everything now was simplified—there were no choices to be made, nothing for it but to stay low, stay calm and fire well.

Soon, 10 Platoon arrived in support but was pinned down by devastating fire some 150 metres short of their comrades. By that time 11 Platoon was down to half strength. When its radio was repaired the besieged men were able to direct artillery fire onto enemy positions, but these positions were so close—50 metres away at some points—that a great gamble had to be taken. They called for shelling just 50–100 metres forward of their position. Artillery some 5,000 metres away was to fire on an enemy that was no more than a stone's throw from its own forces. The rain poured down on the gunners of 103 Battery at Nui Dat. The gun crews knew the slim margin for error—each round was potentially lethal to the D Company men. They adjusted their barrage and the firing began, shells scything through the nearest enemy. At these close quarters the effects of accurate artillery was visible to any platoon member, lying prone in the mud, who could get a line of sight. Shells were landing in the heaviest concentration of enemy forces. One attacking wave, said Private Brian Halls, 'disappeared in a howl of artillery fire! At the right time, very close, too close, just what we wanted.' Australians, with very little ammunition left, marvelled at the accuracy of the artillery. 'You would see VC arms and legs flying up in the air,' said one of them. 'Another thing was a VC up a tree. It got hit, and half of this fellow hung up there by a leg, the other half fell out.'

With the radio repaired, Major Harry Smith called for resupply of ammunition, a job for RAAF helicopters, and for the cover of fighters with napalm and bombs. The platoon released smoke bombs to enable the jets to locate them and do their damage clear of the smoke. But they mistakenly threw the smoke bombs forward of their position and, when the smoke did not rise, gave cover to the enemy who now came at them through the haze. In the midst of the battle, as another enemy wave rushed at them, one of the conscripts was talking out loud, audible to soldiers near him, 'up, aim, hold, fire'—it was the drill he had learned in basic training. A little later he was killed.

A Sioux helicopter hovered at a distance and the artillery paused as the jets roared in to do their work but, unable to go low and slow, and hampered by the rain, they were useless. The artillery opened up again. In all, 3,500 rounds were fired. At Nui Dat, as units of 6RAR were scrambling to depart for the battle in armoured personnel carriers (APCs), the artillery was having trouble of its own. After a shell is fired, the fumes are toxic. The rain was tumbling down but there was no wind; the fumes were not dispersing. Gunners were both exhausted from their work and suffering from their own lethal haze.

At the battlefront RAAF helicopters were arriving with ammunition. It was a skilful and daring feat. The enemy was releasing smoke grenades to decoy the helicopters and lure them to destruction, but the grenades were the wrong colour (orange) and so did not work. D Company's smoke was yellow. The ammunition, wrapped in blankets, was dropped from the helicopters through the rubber tree canopy. The combat soldiers took the bullets, the medics took the blankets. Now they were fighting in a quagmire. The rain continued and flashes of lightning lit the scene. They could hear the enemy's bugles; they could see them massing for the next wave-like assault. Someone said: 'All we've gotta do is hit the fuckin' bugler!' Now they had ammunition. But now weapons began to fail from mud and rain and stress; machine guns were jamming.

Then the APCs arrived. 'It was like one of those western movies, when the cavalry turns up,' said a wounded conscript, John Robbins. The artillery paused again as APCs joined the fight, carrying their assault past D Company into the enemy's forming-up places, then returning to join the besieged platoons. Darkness began to fall. Enemy figures could be seen rising up and retreating through the rubber trees. They carried away as many of their casualties as possible but were compelled to leave behind 245 dead. The firing stopped. The battle was over. Seventeen D Company men were dead; nineteen were wounded. There were casualties in the supporting units too and one of these died some days later. Among the survivors there were three men who suffered such severe battle stress that they were sent home. It took the Australians three days to bury the enemy dead.

Constructing the barbed wire perimeter fence along the minefield from Dat Do to the coast, May 1967.

The minefield was intended to be a deadly labour-saving device, much needed because there was never enough infantry.

Australian troops were too few in number to prevent NLF access to the villages. Whatever the enemy's purpose—whether it was to hold a political meeting in the dead of night, to collect food or to kill a GVN official—they were generally able to do this. ARVN troops were frequently no match for NLF forces by day and at night the poorer units routinely shirked their duty. The Australian troops could not be everywhere at one time. One intelligence report in 1967 pointed to the GVN forces as 'completely ineffective'. They readily conceded 'access to the main population centres of Phuoc Tuy, and to the rice, fish, salt and fruit producing region'. The report also mentioned an NLF force coming to Dat Do, a few kilometres south-east of Hoa Long. There the GVN soldiers melted away, allowing the enemy to shop at the town's market, to buy medical supplies, cloth, batteries and numerous other necessities.

For the Australian troops the cross-currents of loyalty in the villages were part of a wider mystery. The enemy had infiltrated every level of administration from the smallest hamlet to the Independence Palace in Saigon. Australian army members were never sure who they were talking to. There were NLF men secreted in the ARVN, in the police force and in other parts of local officialdom. 'To whom do you talk with any degree of confidence?' asked one Australian officer.

In 1967 the Task Force commander made a portentous decision—to lay a minefield reaching southwards from a fortified hill near Dat Do all the way to the sea, a distance of twelve kilometres. The Australians would patrol in a sweep to the north. The minefield would cut NLF access from the east, so they could not reach

Laying the minefield from Dat Do to the coast. Corporal Trent Grall and Lance Corporal Barry O'Brien of 7RAR, May 1967.

this populous and productive, rice and fish-rich corner of the province. The short-hand term was 'rice denial'. The minefield was intended to be a deadly labour-saving device, much needed because there was never enough infantry to guard the base, to patrol near and far from it, to search towns and villages, to move at a moment's notice to engage located enemy, to watch over engineer and logistics activities and to perform innumerable other duties. The minefield would be a big help.

Bulldozers carved out a line from Dat Do through the jungle, past villages and paddies to the sea. A barbed-wire fence was built along the edges of the cleared terrain. About 20,000 mines were laid. One Australian soldier described the work in a letter to his parents.

Just now we are laying our Fence past a village, and right by us are women in the padi and children picking melons. All this goes on side by side with the ceaseless traffic of helicopters, Armoured Personnel Carriers and working infantry. It's a funny life.

But again the flaw was in South Vietnamese government troops. Their job was to patrol and protect the minefield. They did this so poorly that the NLF, with careful probing and study, learnt how to find and lift the mines, carry them away and deploy them against the Australians around their own strongholds and beyond. They dug up thousands of M16 anti-personnel mines, each containing 2 kilograms of explosives. When triggered these mines jumped upwards before detonating, a motion that maximised human damage and gave them the nickname 'jumping jacks'. They could take out six or seven people in a single blast. One Australian commander estimated that from mid 1968 to mid 1970, about 50 per cent of casualties were caused by the stolen mines.

By 1968 all three services were involved in the war. The RAN deployed a guided missile destroyer that operated with the US 7th Fleet in the South China Sea and the Gulf of Tonkin while other ships were engaged in coastal bombardment and interception of enemy craft. A clearance diving team and several naval airmen were attached to US forces. The RAAF was flying Caribou and Hercules transports and a squadron of Iroquois helicopters was flying in support of the army, which had been augmented by another battalion and a squadron of tanks. The helicopters performed many functions. They deployed troops rapidly and kept them supplied with ammunition, rations and water; they evacuated casualties; they delivered captured rice stores to 'liberated' villages; they were kitted out for aerial spraying of insecticide to control mosquitos in the environs of Nui Dat; they were used to destroy enemy crops; and they went on sniffer missions equipped with a device capable of sensing human presence below the jungle canopy. They were also active in psychological warfare, dropping propaganda leaflets on Viet Cong locations whenever possible, but there is no evidence that this was time well spent.

On 31 January 1968 the NLF launched its Tet (Lunar New Year) Offensive throughout the South. Some 80,000 guerilla forces, with limited North Vietnamese support, struck in 36 of 44 provincial capitals and 64 of 242 district towns. The offensive aimed to spark an urban uprising that did not happen, but it did achieve a second goal—it had a profound psychological impact in Washington and it changed the direction of the war. Tet happened everywhere at once. It was a withering act of

Able Seaman Clearance Diver P.C. Kember who was awarded the Distinguished Service Medal in 1967 for his services with Clearance Diving Team No. 3.

Suddenly it appeared as if the whole Australian commitment to Phuoc Tuy had gone for nothing when the Viet Cong occupied the provincial capital [Baria]. In reality, the Viet Cong were quickly ejected and failed to arouse any popular support by their action, but this is not the way in which the incident was viewed by concerned Australians.

Robert O'Neill, Intelligence Officer, 5RAR

Soldiers of 7RAR on guard at the Hotel Canberra in Saigon during the Tet Offensive, February 1968.

The strength, length and intensity of the Tet Offensive was a great shock to defence planners in Washington and to the US public.

defiance and determination, a spectacular display of enemy coordination and resolve. It was not a military victory but it undermined US resolution and it convinced many that the war was unwinnable.

In Saigon a dispersed force of about 4,000 NLF fighters attacked targets all over the city including Tan Son Nhut airport, government ministries and the Independence Palace while a small suicide group laid temporary siege to the US embassy. In Hue, the old imperial citadel was overrun by a North Vietnamese regiment that held on for nearly three weeks, losing more than two-thirds of its 7,500 troops.

In Phuoc Tuy province the offensive focussed on the capital. It began at sunrise on 1 February. About 600 NLF laid seige to Baria and fought a day-long battle against ARVN and US forces, and the 3RAR men who came to assist. The Australians fought their way into the town, clearing buildings, fighting from street to street. The streets of Baria changed hands several times before the NLF withdrew to nearby Long Dien and there the battle was renewed after heavy fighting. The NLF's history of the province, now translated, recalls the day: 'One Australian battalion with the Third Puppet [ARVN] Battalion . . . continuously counterattacked and pressed us in the Long Dien township. Enemy aircraft bombed the hamlets . . . destroying property and killing many of our comrades.'

The strength, length and intensity of the Tet Offensive was a great shock to defence planners in Washington and to the US public. In Australia, a Tanner cartoon pointed to the growing credibility gap between upbeat official statements and the impression that South Vietnam was out of control. Tanner featured a US general outside a shattered and smoking US embassy in Saigon telling a reporter: 'We ARE winning their hearts and minds—yesterday seventeen Viet Cong presented themselves to the US embassy.'

The ABC correspondent in Saigon, Tony Ferguson, told a story that might have been the inspiration for Tanner's cartoon: as the fighting for the US embassy raged, General Westmoreland was waiting in his limousine around the corner. 'As the last one [Viet Cong] died, a siren was heard, and around the corner came Westy with his outriders . . . He immediately held an impromptu press conference in the compound. It was an extraordinary occasion. There were bodies literally everywhere—fellows draped in fountains, some half blown apart. His opening remarks were something to the effect that the enemy had overreached himself, we are in pursuit and we will annihilate him. People couldn't believe it.'

On 31 March 1968, President Johnson declared a halt to the bombing of North Vietnam, announced his support for negotiations with Hanoi (to be held in Paris) and told the American people he would not be a presidential candidate in the forthcoming elections. Australia's Minister of Air, Peter Howson, was in the Melbourne Club when he heard the news. 'A feeling of some apprehension,' he wrote in his diary:

To my mind, it's the first step of the Americans moving out of South-east Asia . . . within a few years . . . there'll be no white faces on the Asian mainland . . . from now on, and to a much greater extent, we shall be isolated and on our own.

Australia's cold warriors lived with the fear of finding themselves in the midst of another great loneliness.

Tet affected everyone involved in Australia's debate over Vietnam. Confidence in American power was shaken—not even the US embassy in Saigon was safe. Editorials in the major dailies wondered what went wrong. The government's strident talk was now compromised by Washington's shift towards negotiation and withdrawal. In the Labor Party, the left believed the war was not only immoral but also unwinnable, while sections of the right now backed withdrawal for pragmatic reasons. In universities and homes across the nation the war's morality was debated but its apparent futility had also become an issue. Two years before, President Johnson had been shaking hands in Sydney streets, his frame hefty, his face tanned, his grin broad and beaming as a million people turned out to welcome him. Television pictures now showed him looking weary, worried and downcast. He had fretted over the possibility of being the first US president to lose a war. He seemed a beaten man.

While 3RAR remained in Phuoc Tuy, the other Task Force battalions, 2RAR and 7RAR, departed to support US troops in the adjacent province of Bien Hoa, north of Saigon. The Australians were patrolling the region as Tet reached a peak of intensity. Their involvement—code-named Operation Coburg—began with their trademark patrolling and a dozen minor clashes in the last week of January in which 22 guerillas were killed. But early in February the nature of these engagements changed as company-size units from the NLF Main Force moved into the area. Another 29 clashes followed in quick succession, at heavy cost to the enemy (66 dead). Later in the month the Australians were reinforced by a

Australia's cold warriors lived with the fear of finding themselves in the midst of another great loneliness.

Troops of 7th Battalion, 7RAR, show special interest in the fold-up bayonet fitted to a Russian-made AK50 automatic assault rifle captured from the Viet Cong during a successful ambush on Operation Coburg. South Vietnam, February 1968.

Private John Hingst applies
grease paint to his face for
camouflage while on patrol,
Bien Hoa province, 1968.

company of 3RAR men and assigned to the defence of Fire Support Base Andersen. This was a concentration of artillery located near a rubber plantation on National Route 1. It was a low, bulldozed hill, nothing but dust and big guns, circled by barbed wire, 'like an ant-hill with the top removed'. Andersen was located across an enemy line of communication and that was enough to draw three major ground assaults in quick succession. All three were repulsed after fierce, close fighting in which the wire perimeter was breached on each occasion.

After Tet the Task Force was briefly back in Phuoc Tuy in strength. D445 Battalion, battered and depleted, had retreated to its base in the Long Hai Hills. The base had been used by the Viet Minh in the war against the French and passed over to the NLF in this war. All earlier attempts to dislodge them from their sanctuary—artillery and aerial bombing and ground sweeps—had failed. But Tet's political impact far outweighed its military achievement. Tet was a heroic military gesture that cost thousands of lives and, for a brief time, made the NLF vulnerable. While this opportunity presented itself the Task Force wanted to press the advantage home, though going into the Long Hai Hills was still a most difficult and dangerous task. The hills were a natural fortress of serrated and rugged ridges, myriad caves, some with concrete or timber floors, ladders connecting one level to another, and subterranean streams. The ground beyond these camps was riddled with M16 mines and booby traps.

The Australian operation was called Pinaroo and it began early in March with a 2RAR and 3RAR cordon and concentrated air and artillery strikes. Infantry, engineers and armoured units then went in to find the enemy had departed. The troops set about the nerve-wracking business of clearing the mines. Much of this work was borne by the engineer combat teams and the battalion's assault pioneers, and the cost in casualties was high. At the highest point in the Long Hai,

Blindfolded North Vietnamese
soldiers captured after heavy
fighting at Fire Support Base
Balmoral, May 1968.

C Company, 3RAR, raised the Australian flag. The Task Force was then able to destroy many of the caves though it was impossible to destroy them all. Thirty tonnes of explosives were used.

The Australian Task Force commander took the view, rightly, that his troops were far too good to be idling as mere garrison troops in the Long Hai. Once the hills were cleaned out ARVN units were charged with keeping them enemy-free. They were to be resupplied at regular intervals by Australian helicopters. The ARVN stayed six weeks.

In May, NLF and North Vietnamese forces launched another offensive aimed at influencing the peace talks in Paris. There were attacks on 119 cities, towns and military targets throughout the south. Thirteen battalions managed to penetrate Saigon and fighting for the streets of the capital went on for a week. The US Command aimed to block withdrawal to the north and Task Force units were deployed in Binh Duong province to help break lines of retreat or resupply. Fire support bases named Coral, Coogee and Balmoral were established to support infantry battalions in the vicinity and units from the Task Force were charged with playing a part in their defence.

The defence of fire support bases was a dramatic change in the nature of Task Force work—from counter-insurgency patrolling to combat along more conventional lines. The human cost was much higher for, while no Australian lives were lost in the week of heavy fighting at Andersen, the toll at Coral and Balmoral was heavy.

The enemy attacked Coral before it was completed. After midnight on 12 May about 400 fighters from the 141st North Vietnamese Regiment rushed the base. They overran a mortar platoon position, killed five and wounded eight of the eighteen in the platoon. Then they seized one of the big field guns but artillerymen turned two other guns on them and fired splintex rounds containing hundreds of small darts, causing terrible execution. The Vietnamese were driven back, leaving 51 dead and one captive. The fighting went on until 8 am with US fixed-wing and helicopter gunships flying in to support the Australians. At 8 am ten Australians were dead and 25 wounded. Four days later a much larger force attacked. The second battle for Coral lasted six hours, cost five Australian lives and nineteen wounded but this time the Australians were better entrenched and North Vietnamese losses were much higher than before.

At Balmoral, later in the month, there was more fierce fighting. 3RAR was entrenched there, backed by an armoured squadron equipped with Centurion tanks from the base at Nui Dat. On 24 May two battalions of North Vietnamese regulars launched a fierce attack across open ground against withering fire, and again the following day. Five more Australians died along with at least 42 North Vietnamese. At home the casualty rates and the change in the Task Force's role were hotly debated. There were charges in the *Bulletin* that leaving Phuoc Tuy undid all the good work there, for the NLF was moving back. The Task Force commander, Brigadier Pearson, countered. He argued that Phuoc Tuy was not the main game. Australian forces were best deployed where they could have the greatest impact— against main unit forces north of Saigon. That meant high casualties. In the fighting during this period, mostly in the conventional battles at Coral and Balmoral, 26 Australians were killed and 110 were wounded.

The weakness of the NLF after Tet created new opportunities for the allies in South Vietnam. A new American commander, General Creighton Adams, ordered a shift in emphasis with greater focus on small-unit patrolling, territorial security and 'pacification' in the villages. The American shift was in keeping with well-established

An unnamed RAAF nurse with Major Michael Boyle of the Royal Australian Army Medical Corps, Vung Tau, 1968.

I had the chance to work with Australian conscripts at Phuoc Tuy. I really didn't know what to expect because I'd heard a lot of them, initially, were not enthusiastic about serving overseas. I have to admit that I was mightily impressed with what I saw, they seemed very soundly trained and most were as good as anyone I'd seen in combat.

Officer, 5RAR

Mortar fire from a gun pit in Bien Hoa province, February 1968.

Bombardier Larry Davenport
and M60 machine gun during
the fighting for Fire Support
Base Coral, May 1968.

*The hills were a
natural fortress
of serrated and
rugged ridges,
myriad caves,
some with concrete
or timber floors,
ladders connecting
one level to another,
and subterranean
streams.*

Supplies come in for 3RAR men during Operation Pinnaroo in the Long Hai Hills, March 1968.

Task Force practice. Late in 1968 the South Vietnamese government moved into step with the new approach. Village chiefs and administrators were given more funds and more powers. Rural investment was raised and in 1970 President Thieu enacted land reform measures that effectively recognised the land distributions of the NLF and compensated landlords for some losses. The battle for hearts and minds went up a notch.

There was another side to pacification. Reform programs were accompanied by recharged military operations against the NLF's political cadres in the villages and renewed efforts to isolate the guerillas from the people. The Americans set up Operation Phoenix to coordinate RVN intelligence, identify NLF cadres and assassinate them. RVN forces in the villages were re-armed and retrained. They were organised into Popular Force platoons and Regional Force companies in the hope that they might eventually give rise to a local militia to be called the People's Self Defence Force. In Phuoc Tuy, the Team was actively involved in this attempt to have local forces shoulder a greater burden in the fight and to turn the tide in the villages. At the time, Ted Serong was still working with the CIA and this new program gave him hope: 'We entered 1969 balanced,' he said later, 'with a proper understanding of the real strategic nature of our commitment, and an enemy who had played himself out.'

This was not the impression at home. The anti-war movement had been changing in response to events far and near. The Americans' diplomatic shift from containment to rapprochement left the Australian government's foreign policy out on a limb and it boosted hope among the war's organised opponents. For nearly twenty years conservative leadership had been purposeful, resolute and seemingly of one mind. Now things were falling apart. In *News Weekly*, Bob Santamaria wrote 'clarity and purpose have vanished'. As if to make that very point, Prime Minister Holt had disappeared in the sea at Cheviot Beach, an hour's drive from Melbourne. His body was never recovered.

Holt's replacement was John Gorton, a former RAAF flight lieutenant whose war in the Pacific ended in 1944 when he was badly wounded. Gorton was something of a maverick Liberal who cared little for forward defence, leaned to an alternative labelled Fortress Australia and perhaps even a return to greater reliance on a civilian militia. His views horrified the old guard and threw the government into a limbo that lasted for more than a year, for Gorton did not act on his inclinations. Defence and foreign policy drew various one-word assessments—'becalmed', 'paralysed', 'non-existent'.

There was more confusion when the new American ambassador, William H. Crook, came to Canberra. Crook had instructions to limit public expressions of Australia's military reliance on the US. He was to tone down Coral Sea Week, a ritual now a quarter of a century old. For keynote speakers, astronauts talking technology were to be preferred to generals talking up the virtues of the military alliance. The Victory Ball disappeared. It was transformed into a dinner dance.

FOUR OUT OF FIVE OF THESE MEN CHOSE THEIR CAREERS

ABOLISH CONSCRIPTION NOW

VIETNAM MORATORIUM SEPTEMBER 18

Anti-conscription poster, 1970.

Conscientious objectors made the news and rallied people around liberal causes of justice and fair play.

All these vanishings charged the anti-war movement with new energy and purpose, but signs of a shift had been evident since Labor's defeat in 1966. That vast 'subterranean sea of disquiet and disenchantment', which the Reverend David Hope sensed in 1966, was now churning up. The disenchantment was driven in part by moral outrage at the nature of a war that involved saturation bombing, napalm and the slaughter of innocents leading to three million people dying, the majority non-combatants. But it was also driven by issues much closer to home. There was disenchantment with the Labor Party. In August 1967 the new leader, Gough Whitlam, abandoned the withdrawal of troops policy and committed Labor to holding operations in South Vietnam. That meant there was no party in parliament working for the withdrawal of Australian forces. The ALP was backpedalling. More people were taking to the streets.

The biggest rallying issue was conscription. Many were driven to the anti-war ranks by the inequality of sacrifice on which conscription was based. Of about 800,000 twenty year olds eligible for call-up between 1965 and 1972, only 63,000 were conscripted into the army. Of these, 17,424 served in Vietnam and 202 died there, the first, Private Errol Noack, was killed in operations with 5RAR in May 1966. Call-up was determined by a six-monthly ballot in which birth dates were drawn from a Tattersall's lottery barrel. This ritual was called Russian roulette, the birthday ballot and later the lottery of death, and the first few draws were televised, turning the event into a bizarre spectacle. The televised ballot was an unusually open gesture and a sign of an administration losing its moral bearings, unable to distinguish good public relations from bad taste. In September 1969, Robert Wilton, the son of Australia's top soldier, General Sir John Wilton, burned his registration papers on the steps of Parliament House in Canberra.

Conscientious objectors made the news and rallied people around liberal causes of justice and fair play. When Desmond Phillipson, 21, sought exemption from the call-up, he was sent to Holsworthy Military Prison in New South Wales. There he was dragged 75 yards along a road when he refused to march to his cell. Guards grabbed him by the hair, wrenched his arms and wrists and raked him along the bitumen on his knees. As he lay on the ground a pin was allegedly jammed into his shoulder but in the court case that followed, after his release, this was disputed. The army insisted the pin was held between Phillipson and a wall to stop him slumping to the ground. People around Australia read about these punishment methods at Holsworthy over breakfast.

Street sign at Nui Dat base, 1966, in honour of Private Errol Noack, the first Australian conscript to be killed in Vietnam.

Early in 1968 a Draft Resisters' Movement was set up. Opposition to conscription shifted from passive resistance to open provocation. Militant student groups aimed to make the system unworkable. They organised raids on government offices, sit-ins and public burnings of registration papers. The first twenty year old to be jailed for non-compliance with the National Service Act was a Melbourne postman, John Zarb, the son of Maltese migrants. As he began his stay in Pentridge Prison, Free John Zarb graffiti spread around the city. The movement now promised not to resist conscription but to wreck it. By March over 100 people had been arrested for inciting refusal to register, Jim Cairns included, and in most capital cities there were Don't Register demonstrations.

In May 1969, Gorton came home from Washington with words of reassurance that later turned into embarrassment. He told Australians that the new President, Richard Nixon, had 'authorised' him to say that the US 'would continue to participate in the Pacific and to strengthen the forces of freedom and progress in Asia'. Three weeks later Nixon announced the first unilateral withdrawal of US troops, 25,000 in all. As the American withdrawal got underway the Australian government cracked down on draft resistance. The movement against the draft was spreading. By the end of June over 500 academics had signed incitement statements urging twenty year olds not to register. A few months later the signatures ran to 8,000.

In August, John Zarb was freed and the *Sydney Morning Herald* ran an editorial in which it compared the courage of draft resisters to the courage of soldiers. The editorial was titled 'Two Kinds of Courage'. Opinion polls now revealed a wider shift and the ALP followed public opinion. A gallup poll in August indicated 55 per cent of Australians favoured bringing Australian troops home. A month after the poll the ALP federal conference took a firmer stand on withdrawal of the Task Force and soon

Men of the 21st National Service intake, 1970.

SAS Ambush

No. 25 patrol, 'F' Troop, 2 Squadron SAS, at Nui Dat, 8 April 1971.

As the Borneo campaign drew to a close in 1966, SAS squadrons were preparing for Vietnam where they would serve on a twelve monthly rotation, sometimes working with soldiers from New Zealand's SAS. The Confrontation experience was to be valuable grounding for Vietnam, though the two exercises were very different. The Borneo patrols had to move through near impenetrable jungle. They were in country where villages were scarce and they were fighting an enemy less skilled, generally less tenacious and fewer in number.

For Ian Conaghan, who was with 2 Squadron in 1966, the transition from one war to another made for exciting times. He got a five day stand down from Borneo, came home to Perth, did a six weeks medics course at Healesville in Victoria, then a further six weeks training in New Guinea, took a brief leave in which he did further weapons training and then flew to Vietnam. 'They were sort of halcyon days,' he said later. 'Your feet never touched the ground. It was all go.'

The SAS squadron was based at Nui Dat and from there patrols were flown deep into enemy territory for long range reconnaissance ('recon') and also 'recon/ambush' missions. Equipping differed for one or the other, notably in the amount of ammunition carried. Soldiers on a recon mission took enough ammunition to 'shoot and scoot' if they had to. Soldiers aiming to ambush the enemy went armed to pour 'volumes of fire' into their chosen killing ground. Equipment also varied depending on the topography, the vegetation or some variation in the objective. If going out to capture a prisoner, a patrol might take a shotgun along with their Armalite rifles and SLRs, the idea being to aim low and wound an enemy in the legs, then patch the legs up while calling in one of the RAAF's Iroquois helicopters for an exit. Nine Squadron RAAF worked closely with the SAS patrols and the choppers were, like the Canberra bombers, one of the aviation workhorses of the Vietnam war.

While the intelligence support for SAS patrols in Borneo had been negligible, in Vietnam there was a surfeit of information for patrol commanders. Planning included the study of air photos, electronic warfare reports, track overlays and Landing Zone (LZ) overlays, prisoner information, the reports of double agents moving with the enemy and, sometimes, previous patrol reports. In Borneo the patrol took a fixed-wing aircraft to a British or Gurkha outpost, then a helicopter to a landing zone near the border and from there walked into Indonesian territory. In Vietnam, as one soldier put it, 'you got the choppers straight into where the bad guys were.' Closing on a target, movement became very slow, with as much time spent standing and listening as moving. Patrols sometimes covered 1,500 metres a day. When contact was near they might hardly move in that time. In the dry season the vegetation thinned out, a problem made worse in some areas by defoliation. This meant the patrol could see further and be seen from greater distances. Dry undergrowth made movement far more difficult too: 'It was like walking on corn flakes.' But rain and the wet season also had its terrors because wet ground left signs and it was impossible to hear anything and far more difficult to see in the midst of a tropical downpour. 'We used to just stop and go into all-round defence,' said 2nd Lieutenant Peter Schuman, 'and hope that the enemy would not come just blundering through the rain.'

The ideal ambush area was a track thickly lined with bamboo on either side, with a good line of sight not far from the track and vegetation such as buttress trees, logs and ant hills for reasonable cover. Soldiers might have to wait for hours and sitting up behind vertical cover helped alertness and offered a better shooting position than prone on the ground. Ideally some sort of natural obstacle across the track helped too—a fallen tree, low branches—slowing and bunching the enemy.

If the patrol's Claymore mines were sited properly, carefully aimed for maximum devastation, there would be little work left to do once they were triggered. The explosive content covered a good sized killing area. The massive blast and the pellets would scythe the enemy to pieces. Further resistance was met with 'volumes of fire' and the patrol then moved in to finish off what was left of the enemy and search the bodies for papers. An AK-47 rifle was a good trophy, but the SAS prized information above all else.

SAS man in high kunai grass, Ho Tram Cape Area, South Vietnam, 1971.

A North Vietnamese captive receives medical attention from Corporal Brian Mills, June 1969.

Mercy, pity,
peace and love,

shop in our
department-store,

the Muzak angels
sang above.

A long way off
was the napalm war.

Judith Wright,
'Christmas Ballad'
(c.1968)

after Whitlam announced a policy of complete withdrawal by June 1970 should the ALP win the election in October 1969. It didn't, but the election cut Gorton's majority by 18 seats.

With Labor still in Opposition, the anti-war movement could only go to the streets. In the US the Moratorium movement drew 250,000 onto the streets of New York and 100,000 onto the streets of Washington. The idea was to put a moratorium on 'business as usual' to show the extent of feeling against the war. A national, anti-war conference held in Canberra planned to do the same in Australian cities. The trade unions began to oppose the war more strongly and the Australian Council of Trade Unions (ACTU) took a stand. Three hundred union officials representing 32 unions met in Melbourne and called on national servicemen to lay down their arms in Vietnam. In the Postal Workers' Union there was an attempt to stop the Christmas mail bound for Nui Dat, and elsewhere a small number of unionists and university students pursued the idea of sending funds to North Vietnam. The slogan 'Punch a Postie on RTA' (return to Australia) was circulating in Vung Tau. But collectively the unions were moderate, cautious supporters. In February 1970, the ACTU voted to support the moratorium. The motion was won by the president's casting vote.

The complexion of the anti-war movement was fast changing. Youth seemed to be taking over. The late 1960s were marked by the ideas of a new and permissive youth culture—an explosion in taste and style, a rebellious spirit, a rejection of conservative drabness and experimentation in sex, drugs and alternative philosophies. The press now talked of a Vietnam generation though activists were probably still a minority among young people and rebellion could just as easily lead not to anti-war activism but to the self-centred sensualism of some drug culture or nomadic surfing along the east coast. The first issue of *Surf International* (1966) suggested the defence budget should be spent on promoting surfing as a way of life. The war was best forgotten, wrote the editor: 'Each time you hear or see the word Vietnam, cancel out the blackness with a picture of a beautiful man-shaped wave, a piece of love-nature. Make waves, not war.' The advice suggested young men should choose apathy not activism. In the next few years the 'Vietnam generation' and many others did the opposite.

In 1969 the Task Force again turned its full attention to the province of Phuoc Tuy. The objective was to support the pacification program and to confront the NLF wherever possible. The dangers and dilemmas remained much the same as before—difficult relationships with allies in the field, the strength of the NLF in the villages and the politically sensitive nature of the war. All three of these problems were evident in two major operations in 1969 and 1970.

The first of these was a Task Force attempt to undermine NLF influence in the Dat Do area. Operations around Dat Do began in May 1969 and were aimed at denying NLF forces from the Long Hai Hills access to fish, rice and salt supplies. The Australians used patrols and ambushes, land-clearing and artillery bombardment to achieve their objective. They encircled the hamlets of Dat Do with a barbed-wire fence and built pillboxes for RVN forces to defend.

The NLF hit back. They used political propaganda against the RVN and the stolen M16 mines against the Australian patrols. The mines were so effective that casualties again became a controversy at home. In June and July alone 5RAR and 6RAR lost a total of nineteen killed and 110 wounded. The twelve-month tour for these two battalions cost 52 lives in all. These enormous casualties, as one commander described them, were partly responsible for the end of the exercise. Another reason for abandoning the exercise was pressure from Washington to opt out of what now, it seemed, was a Vietnamese task. President Nixon was expounding his policy of Vietnamisation and this was making inroads into established Australian strategies. The Australians pulled out of the Dat Do operation, the NLF moved back in, destroyed the pillboxes and drove off the RVN troops. The Long Dat history notes:

> In 1969 the army and people of Long Dat completely defeated the Australian pillbox strategy at Dat Do . . . using Australian mines (lifted from the minefield) to protect the base, and strike the enemy.

Other Vietnamese sources suggest the Australians did have some success. They reveal that while the strategy was in place, the NLF forces dependent on Dat Do were having great trouble feeding themselves—they were living off the jungle and going hungry.

After the Dat Do exercise the Australians renewed their pursuit of the local NLF battalion, the elusive D445. There was some pressure from US military command to go back into the Long Hai Hills but it was resisted because the hills were still riddled with mines and the Australians knew the enemy battalion would only move back once they were gone. But the pressure remained and in February 1970 8RAR troops went into the Long Hai. They were encouraged, early in the operation, by a clash that left 34 D445 fighters dead. Intense patrolling now focussed on the egress routes from the hills. It was known that the enemy battalion was in the area. Sooner or later it would be forced to fight. On 18 February, 8RAR was positioned to engage the enemy in strength but the prelude was to be a B-52 strike, a preliminary that gave D445 the breathing space it needed. The Task Force commander, Brigadier S.P. Weir explained:

> One of the penalties that you pay for a B-52 strike is that you've got to withdraw 3,000 metres. Well, of course, we withdrew 3,000 metres and the VC . . . has got his own intelligence network and because we were having a B-52 strike so close to a populated area you've got to get clearance right down to District level. The Province Chief has got to agree, the District Chief has got to agree; that means if the Chief knows everybody knows . . . We got the B-52 strike and hit the target but the enemy had gone, and, of course, so had we: we'd gone back 3,000 metres and we didn't have enough fellows to cover all the gaps and the VC battalion just melted through.

President Nixon was expounding his policy of Vietnamisation and this was making inroads into established Australian strategies.

We ambushed out in the paddy. It began to pour with rain at 2100 hours and never stopped all night. It wasn't long before we found ourselves with only our webbing and a slight mound to keep our heads above water. By God it was miserable lying in over eight inches of water for the night! No sign of nogs.

Private Frank Wood, 7RAR, 1970

A training session. Corporal Maurie Shaw with South Vietnamese soldiers.

Rosemary Griggs (left) and Mary Gaynor of the Australian Red Cross visiting soldiers at 1st Australian Field Hospital, Vung Tau, 1969.

The first thing I'd say to a badly wounded soldier, as we picked him up to take him back to base hospital, was to stay awake, to keep conscious. Hold on for fifteen minutes and we'll save you. Most of the time it was true.

Nurse, Vietnam

Manning a .50 mm machine gun near Dat Do. Private Dick Bradley on duty with a South Vietnamese soldier, September 1969.

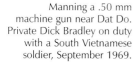

The area was then searched, ammunition caches were found and bunkers destroyed. Australian casualties were light as the men of 8RAR did their work with caution and skill. But ten days later another search headed by an engineer party detonated a booby trap and triggered an M16 mine. Nine Australians were killed and sixteen wounded and again casualties were an issue in Canberra.

The only way to hold the Long Hai was for the Australians to stay there and to do that would be costly in human terms. The Americans now wanted Australian troops to lodge in the Long Hai but the Task Force commander had strong reservations and the Minister for Defence, Malcolm Fraser, ruled it out on advice from the Chief of the General Staff. 8RAR left the Long Hai Hills, the NLF entrenched themselves again and RVN forces were unable to challenge their presence. Australian troops never went back.

Instead they resumed patrolling and ambush duties closer to Nui Dat and they did this with traditional efficiency. There were many clashes. Some took a terrible toll on the enemy. On 18 August 1970 an 8RAR ambush caught an NLF group on a resupply mission to the village of Hoa Long. Eighteen NLF fighters were killed. The war diaries and the area histories of the NLF reveal that the spread and intensity of these patrols had a significant effect on the guerillas' access to food at this time. The Task Force was able to exert a greater control over the main lines of supply to the guerillas and to destroy the NLF's own crops by defoliation. As fast as they were established they were destroyed by aerial spraying of herbicides. The province committee's records for May 1970 indicate the NLF was taking measures to avert starvation. The fighters were living off bush bananas and dried vegetables. There was an acute shortage of rice. An NLF soldier wrote in his diary:

My eyes are staring up somewhere while my stomach is really empty—(I'm starving) and my hands are shaking . . . It is late at night, the more I think of my unit the more I feel my heart bleeding, relating to very sad stories of the war.

Patrol and ambush activity was complemented by the renewed efforts in the area of civic action. By 1970 about 300 men were working full-time with the Civil Affairs Unit. Supply of water and the rebuilding of village markets was a priority. With the downscaling of the war effort and perhaps complete withdrawal on the agenda, it became all the more imperative to win support for the RVN.

In Australia the momentum was now so clearly with the anti-war movement that government spokespeople were showing their anxiety in public. There was talk of the Moratorium on 'business as usual' threatening law and order, of violence in the streets. The Minister for National Service, Billy Snedden, said the Moratorium's leading lights were 'political bikies pack-raping democracy'. His colleague, William McMahon, was far more irresponsible. Four students had been shot dead by National Guardsmen at Kent State University in Ohio. On 7 May 1970, McMahon told the Commonwealth parliament, 'This lesson ought to be taken to heart by all those who are taking part in the Moratorium marches.' The rebellion grew. School students were being suspended for wearing Moratorium badges.

The Moratorium was set for 8 May 1970. Gorton had announced the planned withdrawal of 8RAR only weeks before, but the announcement did not defuse the anti-war momentum. It encouraged the idea that the Moratorium was working even before it happened. When the day came, over 200,000 people took to the streets of the capital cities around Australia, 80,000–100,000 in Melbourne, 20,000–25,000 in Sydney. It was a turnout beyond all the expectations of the organisers. And everywhere it was peaceful. One elderly woman carried a placard that read 'I am a political pack-raping bikie'.

8RAR departed from Vietnam late in 1970 and early in 1971 large areas of Phuoc Tuy were handed over to RVN forces. Australia had followed the USA into Vietnam. Now it was following the USA out. The great quandary was more visible than ever: Australian troops were an able counter-revolutionary force, but their success

Typical of the load carried by Australian soldiers on operations. Sergeant Peter Buckney of 8RAR, January 1970.

When the day came, over 200,000 people took to the streets of the capital cities around Australia

The 1970 Moratorium in Melbourne. Demonstrators sit down at the intersection of Collins and Swanston Streets in the city centre.

A child with a National Liberation Front flag near the steps of the Victorian Parliament, Melbourne Moratorium, 1970.

depended on the ability of local forces to hold the territory. The local forces were frequently unable to fill the gap left by Australian soldiers. The remaining Australian battalions were withdrawn late in 1971, but there were several more battles before the departure and in one of these six more Australians died.

After the Australians had left the province, Phuoc Tuy went the way of all South Vietnam. Although Nixon and his adviser Henry Kissinger had expanded the war with the invasion and bombing of Cambodia in 1970 and the resumption of bombing over North Vietnam in 1972, these last, murderous retaliations achieved no new concessions. The war was lost.

Long after it was over, an Australian veteran, General Peter Gration, summed up the folly of the Vietnam War. Gration had been in Phuoc Tuy province in 1969–1970.

The truth is that we knew very little about the province when we went in—of its long history of struggle against the French, of its history as a Viet Minh stronghold in the war against the French . . . of the almost complete control of the province by the VC in 1966, based on a strongly entrenched political and military organisation and extensive popular support, or of the numerous local accommodations between both villages and government forces . . . and the VC. Some of our own official perceptions of the war as an invasion from the north did not fit this local situation where there was a locally supported revolutionary war in an advanced stage, albeit with support and direction from the north. Many of the people of Phuoc Tuy were the VC and despite our nearly six years of operations in which we had continual and considerable military success, we weakened the local units but never destroyed them or prevented them from recruiting and continuing to regenerate and fight.

Once the troops were coming home, the protest movement evaporated. Those who thought the mass anti-war movement might endure, take up new issues—such as the bombing of Cambodia—and remain a force in Australian society were sorely disappointed. There were second and third moratoriums, but the numbers were nothing like the first and by the time the new Whitlam government abolished conscription on 5 December 1972, anti-war agitation was going the way of the protest movements of Australia's past. Much of the animation and excitement quickly vaporised. But not all the energy disappeared. Some of it shifted to other causes—the environment (built and natural), feminism and land rights—and some of it flowed back into conventional party politics. Protest reconstituted and dispersed into many different causes, but it lacked the national scale of Vietnam agitation and rarely matched it for street drama.

For the soldiers, coming home to a divided nation was a bitter pill. The war was unpopular and the war was lost though the preferred term was 'unwinnable'. Those who came home with their battalion were given rousing welcomes by enthusiastic crowds, both early and late in the war, but once they were back in civilian life the ambivalence and the indifference around them was hard to avoid. Their experience was not validated as was the experience of Diggers in previous wars. Nor was there any certainty about where they fitted into the Anzac legend. Vietnam was judged by many to be a dubious war and its meaning would be challenged for years to come. They even had a new label, an American term that separated them from other Australian soldiers. Formerly Australians who came home from war were returned soldiers. These men were Vietnam veterans.

In 1987, when a recruiting advertisement described Long Tan as a battle in which 100 Australians defeated 2,500 VC at their own game, the veteran activist and

Once the troops were coming home, the protest movement evaporated.

What angered the Task Force was that they could not understand how they could be at war while people in Australia were allowed to parade behind enemy flags, wear enemy badges, shout enemy slogans and collect money for the enemy's support.

Jason, Vietnam veteran

Jim Cairns: a most unusual MP

WE ARE THEM...THEY ARE US...

MORATORIUM!

Moratorium poster, Sydney 1971.

In the midst of a busy and controversial life as a Labor politician, Jim Cairns, the former policeman and Victorian member for Yarra, managed to write books about Asia. This made him a most unusual MP. But as the Vietnam war progressed he acquired another mark of distinction—he was leading protestors, in large numbers, onto the streets.

There was not much time for writing by day. Parliamentary sessions, travel and Party business occupied his time, while his electoral office in Bridge Street, Richmond was host to a constant stream of migrants, pensioners, housewives and other workers in need of help or advice. By night he studied Asian history and American foreign policy. He took his typewriter on holidays. At a time when most politicians knew little or nothing about the disputed colonies and new nations to Australia's north, Cairns produced two substantial works on Asia in four years, *Living With Asia* (1965) and *The Eagle and the Lotus* (1969). The first of these began with the words: 'The most significant recent change in the outlook of Australians is their growing awareness of Asia. We are all aware of Asia. Many of us are afraid of it; few of us understand it.'

Cairns' shared his predecessor Ben Chifley's sympathy for Asian independence movements. He welcomed 'social revolution' saying the peoples of the region had a right to seek social betterment, economic progress and freedom from colonialism. Asia, he argued, was emerging from 'a thousand years of poverty and national impotence' and policies were needed to steer this great trans-formation away from communism. He thought American and Australian foreign policy was fearful, crude and counter-productive. His alternative to 'forward defence' in Vietnam, which he called 'aggression', was land reform, tax relief for hungry peasants, education for their children and a firm stand against brutal governments.

Cairns was a leader in the anti-war movement from the outset. Between 1964 and 1966 he estimated that he addressed about 600 meetings on the subject. He was an able orator who wore his learning lightly. There was a remoteness about him that seemed rather to elevate than to isolate him, to set him above the ranters and factionalists. He became the anti-war movement's outstanding leader, a patron-like figure, able to speak of history, Asia and the complexities of war in Vietnam with great persuasion. He was distinguished, too, by his stand against the left's anti-Americanism. There were two Americas, he argued. One was to be found among the US politicos, bureaucrats and technocrats of the 'military-industrial complex'. The other was to be found in the spirit and values of the American revolution, in particular the belief in sovereignty for nations and progress for all humanity.

In August 1968, four teenagers arrived at his electoral office wanting to talk politics with him. He invited them home for a discussion that evening. One hundred and sixteen teenagers turned up and Cairns chaired the meeting while they talked. They wanted to meet again. Word spread. The next meeting was held at the Jewish Club in East St Kilda. On this occasion, 250 secondary students took part. Cairns chaired the discussion, listened and barely said a word. But he did time the speakers so that all the budding orators could express their views. Events such as these disturbed the advocates of war in Vietnam and alarmed the irrational anti-communists. Cairns was 'infecting the students'. He was called a 'patron of the student underground'.

His analysis of the crisis in Vietnam paid little attention to the particulars of Australian involvement. He was more concerned with American methods of mass destruction. The Americans and their allies in Vietnam were merely the latest in a long line of would-be conquerors, he argued. But the history of invasion, repression and resistance was taking a new turn. This latest war was like no other. It was a war of high technology, a war of indiscriminate killing in vast numbers. This factor created an even greater moral imperative to act. In his third book, *Silence Kills* (1970) he wrote:

You see, if one American soldier aims an M16 rifle at a child in one village and shoots it this may be an atrocity. But what is it if electronic sensors pick up evidence of noise, or perspiration, and beep information into computers that tell B52s to drop one hundred tons of bombs or artillery to fire one hundred shells, and if one hundred children are killed? What is it then?

Yet American technological superiority did not sway him from a firm belief that anti-colonial forces would prevail. He believed America and Australia had 'taken sides in history' against an unstoppable transformation, that anti-war forces in both countries would push on and succeed. He concluded *Silence Kills* with an appendix quoting six American generals and one admiral speaking on the immorality of the US presence in Vietnam. The words of General Matthew Ridgway, former Chief of the General Staff, seemed to sum up Cairns' ultimate faith in America:

It is my firm belief that there is nothing in the present situation or in our code that requires us to bomb a small Asian nation into the Stone Age.

scholar Alex Carey published a response describing the battle as 'primarily a technological slaughter of hundreds of Vietnamese, many of them sons of the local villages, by artillery and armoured carriers. They died, as Vietnamese have died for 2000 years, to free their country from foreign invasion.' Some soldiers wondered if the war of words would ever end.

The war of words had in fact begun before Vietnam. The Anzac tradition was under fire in 1960 when Alan Seymour's play *The One Day of the Year* stirred great controversy. It was to feature at the new Adelaide Festival of Arts but the RSL was outraged and the Festival's Board of Governors banned it for defaming the Anzac tradition because one of the characters, the son of a Digger, was a critical voice. He saw Anzac Day as a mixture of boozing, bigotry and ignorance and the ritual of the day as a glorification of 'bloody wastefulness'. Controversy only fuelled interest in the play, which was more balanced than its critics suggested. It was performed elsewhere with great success. Two years after the ban in Adelaide, *The One Day of the Year* was published. Another two years later it was adapted by the ABC for television. That same year, 1964, the ABC's Four Corners program depicted the RSL as a beery, hidebound organisation ruled by an unthinking anti-communism. Historians began to interrogate the legend too. 'The theme was ripe for history,' wrote Ken Inglis. 'Writers, artists and scholars were converging on the subject.' As the 50th anniversary of Gallipoli approached, that day in 1915—its mythology, its meaning and its legacy—was no longer sacrosanct. As if to make this point, students from the Australian National University secreted themselves in one of the Australian War Memorial's galleries one afternoon in July 1965. They waited till the buildings were locked up, then helped themselves to seven art works by William Dobell valued between £40,000 and £70,000. It was one of the largest art thefts in Australian history. The day after the heist, the art works were found on the university campus and returned unharmed, but the shock of the crime was irreversible. Hitherto the War Memorial had virtually no security—it had not been necessary.

The Vietnam War was more than just another layer of controversy in Australia's experience of war. It produced an opposition with its own counter legend of anti-war literature, art and song. In no previous war had Australian soldiers come home to a nation divided over the merit and the morality of their deeds. The singer Normie Rowe had gone off to Vietnam at the pinnacle of his career and was applauded for his patriotism, but while he was away another pop star, Ronnie Burns, released an anti-war song about a conscript, 'Smiley'. It was in the charts for 20 months, sold 50,000 copies, reached No.2 and won him a gold record. It was still selling when the first Moratorium took place in May 1970. The Moratorium became part of the counter legend too.

Warrant Officer Terence Lyon greeted by his wife and daughters on his return from Vietnam, 21 December 1970.

In no previous war had Australian soldiers come home to a nation divided over the merit and the morality of their deeds.

At the Moratorium I met a Lithuanian girl from a parish where I'd been assistant curate. I realised that when the children of Eastern European refugees, whose parents had fled communism, were turning out to march, then Australia was really changing.

Val Noone,
Vietnam protester

For a small number, perhaps one in ten, suffering after the war became a rallying issue.

For the soldiers, these divisions left their own legacy of bitterness and mistrust, although there were no 'veterans against the war' groups as there were in the US. The veterans here lived with their memories in various ways. Some became full-time campaigners, fighting for compensation, spiritual and financial. Some went back to Vietnam, revisiting battlefields to put demons to rest, and a small number of these found a rewarding camaraderie in meeting former enemies. Some were damaged beyond rescue, while others carried their damage, whether physical or psychological, into productive new lives. Most got on with life, more or less untroubled. The variation was great, but the veterans did seem to have one thing in common—a longing for recognition, for a reconciliation with the society that doubted the merit of their war and seemed indifferent to their deeds and their suffering.

For a small number, perhaps one in ten, suffering after the war became a rallying issue. The Vietnam Veterans' Association (VVA) was formed in 1979 at a time when groups of veterans around Australia were discussing health problems they believed were connected to war service. Their concerns focussed on the effects of toxic chemicals (Agent Orange) used for defoliation during the war and their agitations aimed at an offical inquiry. The new group quarrelled bitterly with both the RSL and the Department of Veterans' Affairs, organisations which opposed an offical inquiry for several reasons. One of these reasons made especially good sense to many veterans—under repatriation legislation at that time there was an onus of proof on the authorities to *disprove* any claims. A negative finding would weaken the claimant's established advantage in law.

There were possibly three times as many Vietnam veterans in the RSL as in the VVA—the latter reached a peak membership of about 5,000 around 1983—but the VVA lobbied hard and used the media to great effect. It had a major influence on the public image of the Vietnam veteran, depicting the homecoming experience

Members of the Vietnam Veterans Motorcycle Club at the opening of the Vietnam Memorial, Anzac Parade, Canberra, 3 October 1992. (Palani Mohan, The Fairfax Photo Library)

A Vietnam veteran in a sea of faces. The Homecoming Parade, Sydney, 3 October 1987. (Brendan Read, The Fairfax Photo Library)

Australian veterans were better treated on return, and were generally less troubled than their American counterparts.

as a thoroughly negative one and the veteran as problem-ridden and somewhat unhinged. The VVA's strident and outspoken style reinforced images of the veteran created by American movies. Australian veterans were better treated on return, and were generally less troubled than their American counterparts, but public perception now merged the two sets of experiences into one.

In the early 1980s, the Agent Orange accusations, propagated by a feisty VVA, became the issue which defined the Vietnam veteran. Elsewhere in the veteran community there was some resentment at the portrayal of returned men as 'sick misfits with damaged children and a head full of bad dreams', but the VVA was successful in so far as it secured limited inquiries into birth defects (1983) and mortality (1984), and a Royal Commission into Agent Orange (1983), chaired by Mr Justice Phillip Evatt.

The results of these inquiries did not support VVA contentions and the organisation attacked all three. But the long and bitter campaign was not lost. It had increased awareness of the plight of veterans, of the health of some and the sense of alienation felt by many. In 1982 the federal government funded counselling centres for Vietnam veterans and their families, and in 1987 a Welcome Home march in Sydney became a major event, a symbolic reinstatement of the men who went to Vietnam.

About 22,000 veterans came together for the occasion and they led a far greater number who joined them to parade through the streets carrying flags to signify the 504 Australian lives lost. Crowds cheered and goodwill abounded. For those who could not get to Sydney, the ABC broadcast the event live to 228 TV stations around the country. Among the veterans were men who wanted to forgive the students, housewives and wharfies, the postal unionists, Labor radicals and others who had made their war more difficult than it might have been. A small number took advantage of the goodwill to reassert right-wing convictions. In the *Australian* Greg Sheridan wrote of 'Left-Liberal anti-South Vietnam, pro-Hanoi forces' who were 'traitors to their own troops'. But Senator Jo Vallentine took a different view. 'Instead of a parade, these people deserve an apology for being sent to fight America's war,' she said. The Welcome Home March was successful enough to be some kind of resolution, but it could not end, nor even hide, the profound differences that once divided the nation and still lingered.

Reconciliation now had momentum. Soon after the Welcome Home march, veterans began a campaign for a memorial. In 1989 the Hawke government donated $250,000 of the $800,000 required. The guidelines drawn up by the official committee established that the memorial was to be in Canberra, in Anzac Parade, the avenue of memorials. It was to be erected in a niche next to Web Gilbert's tribute to the Light Horse and opposite the monument to the Rats of Tobruk, the location fitting the veterans back into the Australian military tradition. The purpose of the memorial was to express 'the link between the Australian Vietnam Forces and the original Anzac Force'. It was to be a memorial 'For all who served, suffered and died'.

The Vietnam monument was unveiled to the delight of a large crowd on 3 October 1992, the fifth anniversary of the Welcome Home march. Only six names appear on the monument which has the look of an open-air temple—the six who went missing in action and were never recovered. The names of the dead are entombed in a granite container suspended overhead and marked with a cross. To see those names the visitor must walk up Anzac Parade to the Australian War Memorial. They are there in bronze, along with tens of thousands of others, on the roll of honour in the cloisters. It is there that the 504 join up with the men of Tobruk, Kokoda, Ypres, Gallipoli and so many other places. And that is what the living veterans want—to be reconciled with their own history and to be part of their nation's military tradition.

The Vietnam Memorial, Anzac Parade, Canberra. (Bluey Thomson, The Fairfax Photo Library)

A moment in the Welcome Home March, Sydney 3 October 1987. (Brendan Read, The Fairfax Photo Library)

7

LIFE EVER
AFTER

CONCLUSION

Of all Australia's conflicts, only one was fought on Australian soil and that—the Aboriginal peoples' struggle with settlers and troopers—was quickly forgotten by most Europeans. Every war since then has been fought in other people's countries, making it harder to discern war's imprint on our own society. In Australia, war has left no devastated cities, no shell-holed landscapes, no napalmed farmlands and forests. It has not changed constitutions, nor redrawn borders, nor incited revolution, nor, with few exceptions, left bodies scattered in the streets.

YET wars have left an indelible mark upon us. They have cut into generations, most brutally in World War I, disrupted family life and gender roles and challenged personal morality, most noticeably in World War II when more than a million American GIs passed through Australia. Wars have changed the economy; they have caused the most bitter conflict on the home-front with conscription; they have given rise to new employment and immigration patterns; and they have transformed the welfare system and shifted power from the states to the Commonwealth. They have also inspired the creative arts, scholarship and public debate, which is the register of our war experience and the record of collective memory.

Most importantly, war gave Australians a national tradition, a set of stories about who we are, about an Australian character and the origins of our nationhood, what anthropologists might call a creation myth. In the absence of any other commemorative moment with the power to draw forth deep emotions, war gave Australians their one day of the year, Anzac Day, when the deeds of the Anzacs, their victories and sacrifices at Gallipoli, then in Palestine and Europe, were remembered. After 1915, journalists and politicians, preachers and others, flung around metaphors of 'birth', 'baptism' and 'coming of age' with great abandon. At last Australia had a national tradition to be proud of and a faith that most, though not all, Australians shared.

What was this faith? According to the storytellers, Australian soldiers were a triumph of social evolution—British in origin, toughened by the pioneering qualities of Australian life, unorthodox, brimming with initiative, full of dash and, for these reasons, exceptional on the battlefield. They were also volunteers and so they had truly *given* their lives for their empire and nation. For many, Anzac became a faith that elevated the ordinary soldier, celebrated loyalty to mates, mocked the alleged effeteness of the English officer class, affirmed that Australian soldiers were decisive in the outcome of the war in Palestine and Europe and found in the Gallipoli venture not failure but moral triumph.

Graves of Australian servicemen who were killed in action in Korea in the United Nations Military Cemetery at Pusan, South Korea, August 1952, *previous page.*

June Vogt walking up the steps of the Shrine of Remembrance, Melbourne, to place a bunch of flowers wrapped in newspaper in memory of her uncle who was killed in World War I. Anzac Day, 1944, *opposite.*

Fallen comrades. Australians visiting the graves in the cemetery between Albert and Becordel, France, January 1917.

In the twentieth century, the nature of war has changed as much as the values that we cherish.

In the twentieth century, the nature of war has changed as much as the values that we cherish. That change has dated the original Anzac legend and reshaped it. Today, few of us, if any, hallow war in the way many of our forebears did. Talk of its purifying and regenerative powers, of war as a proving ground for manhood, race and nation, seems an awful and false creed. The quality of spirited amateurism that was so cherished in our soldiers, and so celebrated and exaggerated by admirers, was losing some of its relevance even as the Australians played their great part in the closing months of World War I. The Anzac legend is a romance of initiative and individuality, of egalitarianism, and above all of character, a romance made all the more powerful by the limits set on these qualities by the nature of modern war. Perhaps that is why it has endured so long. At the heart of our foundation myth is the idea that ordinary Australians can, metaphorically speaking, move mountains. After the war, General Sir John Monash, knighted in the field in that final year on the Western Front, was able to write a book called *The Australian Victories in France, 1918*.

Monash dedicated the book to the Australian soldier who, by his military virtues and by his deeds in battle, earned for himself a place in history that none could change. World War II produced no such finale for the Australians, but it did add new place names to the honour rolls—Bardia, Tobruk, El Alamein, Kokoda, Milne Bay and more. Even the defeats in Greece and Crete could be received as more proof of an indomitable spirit and, like Gallipoli, as triumphs of sorts. Writing in 1943, C.E.W. Bean claimed the new generation of Australian soldiers had renewed the 'Anzac spirit of brotherhood and initiative'.

Yet the legends which grew out of World War II had as much to do with survival in the teeth of privation as they did with fighting prowess. The ordeal of the POWs, tales from Changi, the Burma-Thailand Railway and elsewhere, seized the collective imagination as much as the feats of Bardia, Tobruk and perhaps even Kokoda. And

French children tending the graves of Australians killed in action in the Adelaide Cemetery, Villers-Bretonneux, 26 August 1919.

eventually survivors like Ray Parkin and saints like 'Weary' Dunlop and Vivian Bullwinkel loomed larger than any single warrior or general from that war. The 'Anzac spirit of brotherhood and initiative' was reaffirmed but changed forever by the skeletal Anzacs who had survived the camps and by the tales they brought with them.

There was little or no argument with this reaffirmation after the war but there was an interrogation of its significance. In some quarters Anzac Day acquired a reputation as an excuse for boozing and bad behaviour. A younger generation of teachers and writers was uninspired by the war or sceptical about the civic benefits of war stories. This new scepticism surfaced in 1960, led by playwrights. There was Alan Seymour's *The One Day of the Year* and the less famous *For Valour* written by Ric Throssell, son of Katharine Susannah Pritchard and the light horseman Hugo Throssell VC, who committed suicide in 1931. This play, which contrasted Anzac rhetoric with the confusion and pain of returned soldiers, fitted with the new mood. With hindsight it seems a fitting prelude to the disillusionment surrounding Australia's involvement in the Vietnam War.

The defenders of the Anzac faith hit back throughout the 1960s, deploring attempts to ignore or play down our military history, rejecting the criticisms of Anzac Day's, 'jingoism, cant and glorification of war—whatever that means', as one defender put it, and insisting that it was about 'things like stoicism and fraternalism' and 'national honour and freedom'. As the ranks of Gallipoli veterans thinned, and as the Vietnam War put all things military into question, there were predictions of the end of Anzac Day. These predictions were part of a new debate, a critical revision of our history and a rethinking of Australia's wars.

From the Boer War onwards the notion that all of Australia's wars were fought for noble causes and for Australia's security was widely accepted. But when Vietnam cracked the consensus, new versions of the past conflicts began to emerge. Some wanted to qualify claims about the mightiness of Australian soldiers—the core of the Anzac legend—others debunked the wars in which they had fought. Critics called them 'other people's wars' and argued or implied that Australia would have been better out of them. They gave shape to a new Anzac legend by insisting that although Australians fought well in World War I they were misused by the British military establishment, killed needlessly in a futile Gallipoli campaign and over-worked as shock troops on the Western Front.

The legend of the Anzacs' bravery was still intact but now the young men were victims not victors and their achievements were cut back to human proportions. A new generation of military historians revised the notion of a unique Australian fighting quality and emphasised the importance of training, command, logistics and equipment as much as character.

The new scepticism took another turn when revisionists focussed on World War II. This war, it was argued, was worth fighting, unlike World War I, but this time Britain abandoned Australia and effectively handed the nation over to the US—from one great and powerful friend, as Menzies used to say, to another. The new

Memorial to Australians killed in action, Tobruk, January 1942.

As the ranks of Gallipoli veterans thinned, and as the Vietnam War put all things military into question, there were predictions of the end of Anzac Day.

Anzac Day service at the War Memorial at Herberton, Queensland, 1944. Troops of Headquarters, Sixth Division, are on the left and pupils of St Mary's School are on the right.

But new questions did not diminish the Anzac legend. In revising or challenging it, dissenters created new interest.

interpretation of our military history was dramatised by the films *Breaker Morant* (1980) and *Gallipoli* (1981). Both celebrated the bushman–soldier, cast the British military as callous and unjust, and rendered the Australian soldier as victim.

It was not only the British connection that was questioned, nor just film-makers who were doing the questioning: issues of race, gender, and sexuality also surfaced in the 1980s. Was Australia's colonial presence in New Guinea any less of an invasion than that of the Japanese? How fair was it for Aboriginal servicemen to die for a country whose constitution explicitly stated 'in reckoning the numbers of people of the Commonwealth . . . aboriginal natives shall not be counted'? The suffering of women in wars and the right of gay men and women to join the armed forces also became matters that caused heated disputes and occasional confrontation on Anzac Day.

But new questions did not diminish the Anzac legend. In revising or challenging it, dissenters created new interest. So too did those historians who wrote about war as social history, with an emphasis on the daily life and trials of ordinary servicemen and women. In the greatest of these works, Bill Gammage's *The Broken Years* (1974), the Anzac experience is transformed from epic into tragedy. Around that time there was an outpouring of novels and poetry, as if Vietnam had triggered in artists a belated desire to rethink earlier wars, or perhaps to deal vicariously with the military entanglement of their own time.

The success of the film *Gallipoli* in 1981 ignited an interest in Australia's war experience that was immediately felt at the Australian War Memorial in Canberra. In September that year, the memorial had 83,750 visitors, twice the number in the same month a year before. Since then the memorial has become the most visited of all museums or galleries in Australia. Anzac Day has revived, too, with crowds growing every year from their low point in the 1960s. The rebirth of popular enthusiasm for the rituals of remembrance has been fostered by the media and both sides of parliament, and by numerous pilgrimages and commemorations. In 1994 the government-sponsored Operation Restoration was overwhelmed with requests from around Australia for funding to restore local war memorials.

September 1942. After the battle of Isurava on the Kokoda Track, Lieutenant Colonel Ralph Honner speaks to surviving members of the 39th Battalion.

Mrs Lindorff (left), a mother of four members of the AIF (two of whom died of wounds in World War II) and her friend attending the Anzac Day service, Melbourne 1943.

Time has favoured the resurgence of the Anzac legend. To some extent it has disarmed the critics. Rituals of remembrance have a new found pathos with once formidable soldiers now old men, 'unthreateningly mortal' as Ken Inglis has expressed it. Children today are a new and innocent constituency who have contributed to this resurgence. They have no experience of war in their time and no apprehension of war to come. They can enjoy the freedom to be fascinated by their military history without the shadow of war over them. They can be curious about wars long gone, untouched by the controversies that once surrounded those wars and free to wonder about the men and women who gave their lives for their country. They live in a favoured interim and remain to discover whether that is a blessing or a cruel illusion.

Australia ended the twentieth century as it began it, with its defence forces serving overseas in a hostile environment. But there the similarity ends. In the Boer War, Australians fought as amateur enthusiasts and bit players in a British cause. The INTERFET force that went into East Timor in September 1999 was initiated by Australia, placed under Australian command and predominantly Australian in its make up. Taking the lead in an overseas peacekeeping expedition was a first for Australia and a sign of progress in the nation's long, slow evolution towards separateness.

Lance Corporal Dave Hurrey and Lance Corporal Paul Astbury with Australian Signals Corps, United Nations Transitional Authority in Cambodia, on patrol in the village market, Thbeng Mean, Cambodia, 18 February 1993.

Australian medics watch a soccer match between 1st Battalion, 1RAR and a Somalian team, Somalia, 1 April 1993.

An Australian infantryman carries a cross hewn from forest timber to a forward position to mark the grave of a comrade killed in action, Tsimba area, Bougainville, Papua New Guinea, 27 February 1945, *opposite*.

Over the last 25 years Australia has had to come to terms with a new defence environment. When North Vietnamese tank number 843 crashed through the gates of Independence Palace in Saigon in April 1975, the *Sydney Morning Herald* responded with the front-page headline 'We're So Alone'. For almost 200 years Australians lived in fear of foreign powers and foreign peoples in the region and sought security in close ties with a great power from another part of the world. We were insular and indifferent to the surrounding cultures whose 'otherness' only fired our paranoia and fortified our fears. To guarantee Australia's security in a strange and seemingly hostile world the nation sent soldiers, sailors and airmen to wars far away. Our expeditionary forces were a strategy for survival, a down payment on future protection. That simple equation is the story of Australians at war in the twentieth century.

The new defence environment at the beginning of the twenty-first century calls for a different strategy for survival, one in which integration with our neighbours and familiarity with our region is the principal guarantor of security. Our forward defence must be enlightenment, not armament, our objective to support democracy and economic development throughout the region. The role of the defence forces in this new context is primarily peacekeeping, a down payment of a different kind, which will take the form, as it has in East Timor, of helping to restore peace and security, protecting and supporting United Nations missions and facilitating humanitarian assistance. In the 1990s these new responsibilities placed a heavy burden on the men and women of Australia's armed forces and while East Timor received privileged treatment in the media, much of the traumatic and grizzly work these forces have had to do—in Cambodia, Bougainville, Somalia, Rwanda and elsewhere—went virtually unnoticed.

Some argue that Australia's involvement in East Timor from 1999 has shown that we cannot afford to sustain operations far from our own coastline without the support of a strong ally or a multi-national force. That is the dilemma facing Australia's defence future. It has always been so. Australians have never been keen to support high defence spending in peacetime. The militarisation of our society has always been an unpopular notion. Only in dire circumstances would Australians opt for troops and guns over hospitals, clean water, cars and white goods. In peacetime we continue to rely on a 'core force' concept: that is, a small, highly trained army, navy and air force, hopefully capable of timely expansion in the event of an emergency. This way forward is preferred by most Australians but it is precarious.

In the future the uncertainty of this situation may help to sustain the renewed interest in Australians at war. In the past decade popular support for pilgrimages and commemorations has provided some of the most powerful moments in the nation's ritual history. These moments have marked the anniversaries of terrible battles in places as far apart as Ypres and Kokoda, they have focussed our minds on great suffering and great loss, they have provided a chance for shared contemplation of extraordinary courage and selflessness, and they have reminded us of the values that matter most.

Ceremony for the
Entombment of the
Unknown Soldier,
Hall of Memory,
Australian War Memorial,
11 November 1993.

"We do not know this Australian's name and we never will. We do not know his rank or his battalion. We do not know where he was born, or precisely how and when he died. We do not know where in Australia he made his home or when he left it for the battlefields of Europe. We do not know his age or his circumstances: whether he was from the city or the bush; what occupation he left to become a soldier; what religion, if he had a religion; if he was married or single. We do not know who loved him or whom he loved. If he had children we do not know who they are. His family is lost to us and he was lost to them. We will never know who this Australian was.

Yet he has always been among those we have honoured. We know that he was one of the forty-five thousand Australians who died on the Western Front. One of the 416,000 Australians who volunteered for service in the First World War. One of the 324,000 Australians who served overseas in that war, and one of the sixty thousand Australians who died on foreign soil. One of the 100,000 Australians who have died in wars this century.

He is all of them. And he is one of us.

This Australian and the Australia he knew are like foreign countries. The tide of events since he died has been so dramatic, so vast and all consuming, a world has been created beyond the reach of his imagination. He may have been one of those who believed the Great War would be an adventure too grand to miss. He may have felt that he would never live down the shame of not going. But the chances are that he went for no other reason than that he believed it was his duty – the duty he owed his country and his king.

The Unknown Australian soldier we inter today was one of those who by his deeds proved that real nobility and grandeur belongs not to empires and nations but to the people on whom they, in the last resort, always depend. That is surely at the heart of the Anzac story.

…

This Unknown Australian is not interred here to glorify war over peace; or to assert a soldier's character above a civilian's; or one race or one nation or one religion above another; or men above women; or the war in which he fought and died above any other war; or of one generation above any that has or will come later.

The Unknown Australian honours the memory of all those men and women who laid down their lives for Australia. His tomb is a reminder of what we have lost in war and what we have gained. We have lost more than 100,000 lives, and with them their love of this country and all their hopes and energy. We have gained a legend; a story of bravery and sacrifice and with it a deeper faith in ourselves and our democracy, and a deeper understanding of what it means to be Australian.

It is not too much to hope, therefore, that this Unknown Australiam Soldier might continue to serve his country. He might enshrine a nation's love of peace and remind us that, in the sacrifice of the men and women whose names are recorded here, there is faith enough for all of us."

Prime Minister, Paul Keating, at the Entombment of the Unknown Soldier, 11 November 1993

Jack Buntine with his great-granddaughter, Virginia Holdenson. Jack served in World War I at Gallipoli, the Middle East and the Western Front. (Steven Siewert, *The Last Anzacs*)

Nine year old Tyler Dehn reaches out to shake the hands of passing Diggers during the Anzac Day Parade in George Street, Sydney 2000. (Andrew Meares, The Fairfax Photo Library)

On one of these occasions, in 1993, an unknown soldier from a grave on the battlefields of northern France, was brought home to Australia. A ceremony was planned for his entombment in the Hall of Memory at the Australian War Memorial in Canberra. This body, and its new resting place, was invested with great significance for it would represent the more than 100,000 dead servicemen and women whose bodies lie in foreign lands, far from their loved ones, as well as the dead since the Vietnam War, whose bodies have been brought home.

The unknown soldier was laid to rest on 11 November 1993, the 75th anniversary of Armistice Day 1918. The Governor-General placed a sprig of wattle on the coffin and a World War I veteran, aided by a young soldier, sprinkled a handful of soil from Pozières, the place where in 1916 Australians fell more thickly than on any other battlefield. The Prime Minister spoke words to rival Pericles' funeral oration in ancient Athens or Lincoln's speech at Gettysburg during the American Civil War.

The timing of the entombment was designed so that homage was paid to the original AIF while the last of those Anzacs still lived. But, as the words on the tomb suggest, it was a homage to many more:

AN UNKNOWN AUSTRALIAN SOLDIER KILLED IN
THE WAR OF 1914–1918
HE SYMBOLISES ALL AUSTRALIANS WHO HAVE DIED IN WAR

Somewhere in Australia the name of this unknown soldier—in Kipling's words, 'known only to God'—is probably recorded on a memorial or an honour roll. Perhaps in a country town or a city suburb, perhaps in a school or a workplace or a community hall. With that 'perhaps' we reflect on the names of all who served and died, recorded on memorials around Australia. To think of those memorials, all that sacrifice and all that grieving, is to take a journey deep into the emotional history of our nation.

Bibliography

Unknown, Untried

Amery, L.S. (ed) *The Times History of the War in South Africa, 1899–1902*, Sampson, Low, Marston & Co., London, 1907

Bassett, J. *Guns and Brooches. Australian Army Nursing from the Boer War to the Gulf War*, Oxford University Press, Melbourne, 1992

Belfield, E. *The Boer War*, Leo Cooper, London, 1975

Carnegie, M. & Walsh, F. *In Search of Breaker Morant, Balladist and Bushveldt Carbineer*, National Library of Australia, Canberra, 1979

Chamberlain, M. *The Australians in the South African War, 1899–1902: a map history*, Australian Army History Unit, Canberra, 1999

Coulthard-Clark, C. *Where Australians Fought. The Encyclopaedia of Australia's Battles*, Allen & Unwin, Sydney, 1998

Dennis, P. & Grey, J. (eds) *The Boer War: army, nation and empire*, Australian Army History Unit, Canberra, 2000

Field, L.M. *The Forgotten War. Australian Involvement in the South African Conflict of 1899–1902*, Melbourne University Press, Melbourne, 1979

Hall, R. (ed) *Banjo Paterson. His Poetry and Prose*, Allen & Unwin, Sydney, 1993

Inglis, K. *The Rehearsal: Australians at War in the Sudan 1885*, Rigby, Adelaide, 1985

Roderick, C. *Banjo Paterson. Poet by Accident*, Allen & Unwin, Sydney, 1993

Souter, G. *Lion and Kangaroo: the initiation of Australia*, Sun Books, Sydney, 1992

Spies, S.B. *Methods of Barbarism? Roberts and Kitchener and Civilians in the Boer Republics*, Human and Rousseau, Cape Town, 1977

Wilcox, C. *For Hearths and Homes. Citizen Soldiering in Australia, 1854–1945*, Allen & Unwin, Sydney, 1998

A Chance Scrap of Iron

Bean, C.E.W. *Anzac to Amiens*, Australian War Memorial, Canberra, 1946

Cochrane, P. *Simpson and the Donkey. The Making of a Legend*, Melbourne University Press, Melbourne, 1992

Damousi, J. *The Labour of Loss: mourning, memory and wartime bereavement in Australia*, Cambridge University Press, Melbourne 1999

Dennis, P., Grey, J., Morris, E. & Prior, R. (eds) *Oxford Companion to Australian Military History*, Oxford University Press, Melbourne, 1999

Fitzhardinge, L.F. *The Little Digger, 1914–1952. A Political Biography of William Morris Hughes*, vol.2, Angus & Robertson, Sydney, 1979

Fussell, P. *The Great War and Modern Memory*, Oxford University Press, London, 1977

Gammage, B. *The Broken Years. Australian Soldiers in the Great War*, Australian National University Press, Canberra, 1974

Gerster, R. *Big-Noting. The Heroic Theme in Australian War Writing*, Melbourne University Press, Melbourne, 1987

Grey, J. *A Military History of Australia*, Cambridge University Press, Melbourne, 1990

Hobsbawm, E. *Age of Extremes. The Short Twentieth Century, 1914–1991*, Abacus, London, 1994

Hurley, F. *Hurley at War: the Photographs and Diaries of Frank Hurley in Two World Wars*, Fairfax Library/Damien O'Keefe, Sydney, 1986

Inglis, K. *Anzac Remembered. Selected Writings of K.S. Inglis*, (edited by John Lack) University of Melbourne History Monograph, Melbourne, 1988

Lindstrom, R. 'The Australian Experience of Psychological Casualties in War, 1915–39', Phd thesis (unpublished), Victoria University of Technology, Melbourne, 1997

McCarthy, D. *Gallipoli to the Somme. The Story of CEW Bean*, John Ferguson, Sydney, 1983

McKernan, M. *Here is their Spirit. A History of the Australian War Memorial, 1917–1990*, University of Queensland Press/Australian War Memorial, 1991

McKernan, M. & Browne, M. (eds) *Australia. Two Centuries of War and Peace*, Australian War Memorial/Allen & Unwin, Canberra, 1988

McQueen, H. *Gallipoli to Petrov. Arguing with Australian History*, Allen & Unwin, Sydney, 1984

McMullen, R. *Will Dyson, cartoonist, etcher and Australia's finest war artist*, Angus & Robertson, Sydney, 1984

Reid, R. 'A duty clear before us', Department of Veterans' Affairs, Canberra, 2000

Reid, R. *Beaucoup Australiens ici. The Australian Corps in France, 1918*, Department of Veterans' Affairs, Canberra, 1998

Reid, R. *Just Wanted To Be There. Australian Service Nurses, 1899–1999*, Department of Veterans' Affairs, Canberra, 1999

Serle, G. *John Monash. A Biography*, Melbourne University Press, Melbourne, 1982

Ward, R. *A Nation for a Continent. The History of Australia, 1901–1975*, Heinemann, Melbourne, 1977

White, R. *Inventing Australia. Images and Identity, 1688–1980*, Allen & Unwin, Sydney, 1981

Wilcox, C. (ed) *The Great War. Gains and Losses—ANZAC and Empire*, Australian War Memorial/Australian National University, Canberra, 1995

Young, M. & Gammage, B. (eds) *Hail and Farewell. Letters from Two Brothers Killed in France in 1916*, Kangaroo Press, Sydney, 1995

Business As Usual

Blainey, G *The Steel Master. A Life of Essington Lewis*, Sun Books, Melbourne, 1981

Butlin, S.J. *War Economy, 1939–42*, Australian War Memorial, Canberra, 1955

Chapman, I. *Iven G. Mackay, Citizen and Soldier*, Melway Publishing, Melbourne, 1975

Gill, G.H. *Royal Australian Navy. 1939–1942*, Australian War Memorial, Canberra, 1957

Gordon, H. *The Embarrassing Australian: the story of an Aboriginal warrior*, Lansdowne Press, Melbourne, 1962

Hall, R.A. *The Black Diggers. Aborigines and Torres Strait Islanders in the Second World War*, Allen & Unwin, Sydney, 1989

Hetherington, J. *Blamey. Controversial Soldier*, Australian War Memorial/ Australian Government Publishing Service, Canberra, 1993

Horne, D. *In Search of Billy Hughes*, Macmillan, Melbourne, 1979

Horner, D. *Defence Supremo: Sir Frederick Shedden and the Making of Australian Defence Policy*, Allen & Unwin, Sydney, 2000

Hudson, W.J. *Australian Diplomacy*, Macmillan, Melbourne, 1970

McCarthy, J. *Australia and Imperial Defence, 1918–39. A Study in Air and Sea Power*, University of Queensland Press, St Lucia, 1976

McDonald, N. *War Cameraman. The Story of Damien Parer*, Lothian, Melbourne, 1994

McKernan, M. *All In! Australia During the Second World War*, Thomas Nelson Australia, Melbourne, 1983

Martin, A.W. *Robert Menzies, a life*, Melbourne University Press, Melbourne, 1999

Robertson, J. *Australia at War, 1939–45*, Doubleday, Sydney, 1984

Ross, A.T. *Armed and Ready. The Industrial Development and Defence of Australia, 1900–1945*, Turton & Armstrong, Sydney, 1994

Walker, D. *Anxious Nation. Australia and the Rise of Asia 1850–1939*, University of Queensland Press, St Lucia, 1999

Never More Alone

Austin, V. *To Kokoda and Beyond. The Story of the 39th Battalion, 1939–41*, Melbourne University Press, Melbourne, 1988

Ball, D. *Aborigines in the Defence of Australia*, Australian National University Press, Canberra, 1991

Beaumont, J. *Australia's War, 1939–45*, Allen & Unwin, Sydney, 1996

Brune, P. *Those Ragged Bloody Heroes. From The Kokoda Trail to Gona Beach 1942*, Allen & Unwin, Sydney, 1991

Brune, P. *We Band of Brothers. A Biography of Ralph Honner*, Allen & Unwin, Sydney, 2000

Butlin, S.J. & Schedvin, C.B. *War Economy, 1942–1945*, Australian War Memorial, Canberra, 1977

Callinan, B. *Independent Company. The Australian Army in Portuguese Timor, 1941–3*, William Heinemann, Melbourne, 1953

Charlton, P. *War Against Japan, 1942–45*, Time-Life Books/John Ferguson, Sydney, 1989

Gill, G.H. *Royal Australian Navy 1942–1945*, Australian War Memorial, Canberra, 1968

Greer, G. *Daddy We Hardly Knew You*, Hamish Hamilton, London, 1989

Hall, T. *New Guinea 1942–44*, Methuen Australia, Sydney, 1981

Heseltine, H.P. *Intimate Portraits and other pieces: essays and articles by Vance Palmer*, Cheshire, Melbourne, 1969

Horner, D. *High Command. Australia's Struggle for an Independent War Strategy, 1939–45*, Allen & Unwin, Sydney, 1992

Horner, D. *Inside the War Cabinet. Directing Australia's War Effort, 1939–45*, Allen & Unwin, Sydney, 1996

Johnston, M. *At the Front Line. Experiences of Australian Soldiers in World War II*, Cambridge University Press, Cambridge, 1996

Lloyd, C. & Hall, R. *Backroom Briefing. John Curtin's War*, National Library of Australia, Canberra, 1997

McCarthy, D. *South-West Pacific Area—First Year. Kokoda to Wau*, Australian War Memorial, Canberra, 1959

McKernan, M. *All In! Australia During the Second World War*, Thomas Nelson Australia, Melbourne, 1983

Nelson, H. *Prisoners of War. Australians Under Nippon*, ABC Books, Sydney, 1990

Reid, R. *In Captivity. Australian Prisoners of War in the Twentieth Century*, Department of Veterans' Affairs, Canberra, 1999

Reid, R. *Just Wanted To Be There. Australian Service Nurses, 1899–1999*, Department of Veterans' Affairs, Canberra, 1999

Stevens, D. (ed) *The Royal Australian Navy in World War II*, Allen & Unwin, Sydney, 1996

Wahlert, G. *The Other Enemy? Australian Soldiers and the Military Police*, Oxford University Press, Melbourne, 1999

Walker, R. & Walker, H. *Curtin's Cowboys. Australia's Secret Bush Commandos*, Allen & Unwin, Sydney, 1986

White, O. *Green Armour*, Angus & Robertson, Sydney, 1945

Five Minutes to Midnight

Arnold, L. *A Very Special Relationship. British Atomic Weapons Trials in Australia*, London, 1987

Atkinson, J.J. *The Kapyong Battalion*, NSW Military Historical Society, Sydney, 1977

Bolton, G. *The Oxford History of Australia. Volume 5. 1942–1988. The Middle Way*, Oxford University Press, Melbourne, 1990

Curthoys, A. & Merritt, J. (eds) *Australia's First Cold War. Vol.1. Society, Communism and Culture, 1945–53*, Allen & Unwin, Sydney, 1984

Dennis, P. & Grey, J. *Emergency and Confrontation. Australian Military Operations in Malaya and Borneo 1950–1966*, Allen & Unwin/Australian War Memorial, Sydney, 1996

Deery, P. 'Community Carnival or Cold War Strategy? The 1952 Youth Carnival for Peace and Friendship' in Hood, R. & Markey, R. (eds) *Labour and Community*, University of Wollongong, Wollongong, 1999

Deery, P. *Labour in Conflict. The 1949 Coal Strike*, Australian Society for the Study of Labour History, Canberra, 1978

Edwards, P. (with Pemberton, G.) *Crises and Commitments. The Politics and Diplomacy of Australia's Involvement in Southeast Asian Conflicts, 1948–1965*, Allen & Unwin, Sydney, 1992

Grey, J. *The Commonwealth Armies and the Korean War: an Alliance Study*, Manchester University Press, Manchester, 1988

Hasluck, P. *The Government and the People 1942–1945*, vol.2, Australian War Memorial, Canberra, 1970

Horner, D. 'The Australian Army and Indonesia's Confrontation with Malaysia', *Australian Outlook*, April 1989

Hudson, W.J. *Casey*, Oxford University Press, Melbourne, 1986

Lowe, D. *Menzies and the Great World Struggle. Australia's Cold War, 1948–1954*, University of New South Wales Press, Sydney, 1999

O'Neill, R. *Australia in the Korean War 1950–53. Vol. II Combat Operations*, Australian War Memorial/Australian Government Publishing Service, Canberra, 1985

Rayner, H. *Scherger. A Biography of Airchief Marshal Sir Frederick Scherger*, Australian War Memorial, Canberra, 1984

Picking up Credit

Bowden, T. *One Crowded Hour. Neil Davis, Combat Cameraman*, Collins Australia, Sydney, 1987

Cairns, J. *The Eagle and the Lotus. Western Intervention in Vietnam, 1847–1971*, Lansdowne Press, Melbourne, 1969

Dowsing, I. *Jim Cairns M.H.R.*, Acacia Press, Melbourne, 1971

Edwards, P. *A Nation at War: Australian Politics, Society and Diplomacy during the Vietnam War, 1965–1975*, Allen & Unwin, Sydney, 1997

Frost, F. *Australia's War in Vietnam*, Allen & Unwin, Sydney, 1987

Grey, J. & Doyle, J. (eds) *Vietnam: war, myth and memory. Comparative Perspectives on Australia's War in Vietnam*, Allen & Unwin, Sydney, 1992

Horne, D. *Time of Hope. Australia, 1966–72*, Angus & Robertson, Sydney, 1980

Horner, D. *SAS: phantoms of the jungle. A History of the Australian Special Air Service*, Allen & Unwin, Sydney, 1989

Kiernan, V. *European Empire From Conquest to Collapse, 1815–1960*, Leicester University Press/Fontana, Leicester, 1982

McAulay, L. *The Battle of Long Tan*, Hutchinson, Melbourne, 1986

McKay, G. *Delta Four. Australian Riflemen in Vietnam*, Allen & Unwin, Sydney, 1996

McKay, G. *Sleeping With Your Ears Open. On Patrol with the Australian SAS*, Allen & Unwin, Sydney, 1999

Murphy, J. *Harvest of Fear. A history of Australia's Vietnam War*, Allen & Unwin, Sydney, 1993

O'Brien, M. *Conscripts and Regulars with the Seventh Battalion in Vietnam*, Allen & Unwin, Sydney, 1995

Pemberton, G. (ed) *Vietnam Remembered*, Weldon, Sydney, 1990

Pierce, P., Grey, J. & Doyle, J. (eds) *Vietnam Days. Australia and the Impact of Vietnam*, Penguin, Melbourne, 1991

Life Ever After

Inglis, K. *Sacred Places. War Memorials in the Australian Landscape*, Myegunya Press, Melbourne, 1998

Thomson, A. *Anzac Memories. Living with the Legend*, Oxford University Press, 1994

Australian War Memorial Image Numbers

Unknown, Untried

pp 10-11 P0220/03/01; p 12 129018;
p 13 P0295/843/755; p 14 P1209/62/54;
p 15 P1209/62/41; p 16 P1113/42/32;
p 17 top P0175/462/347, bottom P0187/07/02;
p 18 top P1024/23/21, bottom P0556/02/02;
p 19 P0653/147/054; p 20 top A03687, Johnnie
Boer textbox P1537/16; p 21 top P0492/06/05,
bottom P0044/72/24; p 22 P0413/52/22; p 23
'My God…' textbox A03962; p 24 P0044/72/45;
p 25 top A04292, bottom left P0044/72/51,
bottom right A05154; p 26 top P0295/843/259,
bottom A05168; p 27 top A04298, bottom
P0175/462/007; p 28 top left P1462/04, top right
A05480, bottom left P1580.020; p 30 top
A05311, bottom left A04283, bottom right
P0653/147/024; p 31 P01866.003; p 32 top
P0492/06/01, bottom P0033/01; p 33 A04430;
p 34 P02307.001; p 35 A05315; p 36 top
P0175/462/367, bottom left P0422/20/09,
bottom right A04337; p 37 top P01825.009,
bottom P0474/43/02; p 38 P1051/25/01;
p 39 A04945

A Chance Scrap of Iron

pp 41-42 A02875; p 43 H03358; p 44 top
A00486, bottom J03022; p 45 G00915;
p 46 top H03500, bottom A00830; p 47
G00579; p 48 H15439; p 49 top C00667,
bottom J02401; p 50 top J06392, Wounded
textbox P02119.001; p 51 top A02025, bottom
G00267; p 52 top A02740, bottom G01289;
p 53 top H11613, bottom P0516/05/03; p 54
top P0859/23/18, bottom A00659; p 55 top
P02179.001, bottom P02268.008; p 56 top
H15569, bottom P02171.007; p 57 A03042;
p 58 EZ0147; p 59 H16396; p 60 top EZ0137,
bottom left P02248.001, bottom right
P02248.02; p 61 E00249; p 62 top A03376,
bottom H12763A; p 63 H02211; p 64 E00034;
p 65 top E00081, bottom E00052; p 66 top
H08752, middle P01900.003, bottom left
H11852, bottom right E00454; p 67 top E00403,
bottom P0841/01; p 68 top E00455; bottom
A04728; p 69 A Place textbox E01085; p 70
top left E05429, top right E05988A, bottom
H12635; p 71 top E03864, bottom E00963; p
72 top A00755, bottom H11585; p 73 top
J00360, bottom H13874; p 74 top E02154,
bottom H06708; p 75 top E05495, bottom
E02697; p 76 E02758; p 77 P1695.001; p 78
top H11576, bottom H01894; p 79 H11574;
p 80 top P1102/40/05, bottom P02349.005;
p 81 top A00658, bottom left D00571,
bottom right D00305; p 82 H11563;
p 83 top P1565.003, middle P02406.002,
bottom H03230

Business As Usual

pp 84-85 00459; p 86 158652; p 87 300254;
p 88 top P1617.005, bottom P01817.015;
p 89 top P01862.003, bottom P0604/51/10;
p 90 SUK14895; p 91 P02817.001; p 92 left
141161, right 0003044/14; p 93 top 003068/21,

bottom P02140.002; p 94 002769; p 98, top
044858, Battle textbox 128167; p 99 top
P0631/12/01, bottom 2100; p 100 top left
007394, top right 002088/1, Lady Blamey
textbox 009904; p 101 top 005047, bottom
020048; p 102 13446; p 103 005217;
p 104 009493/21; p 105 top 005230, Post 11
textbox P02473.011; p 106 P1345/16/16;
p 107 top 008788; bottom 008261; p 108 top
P02126.014, bottom 006819; p 109 top
044265, bottom P1166/11; p 110 top 007760,
bottom 007630; p 111 left 006809, right
021941; p 112 top 128425, bottom 087663;
p 113 010426; p 114 P02053.001; p 115 top
069861, bottom P02053.003; p 116 top
306799, bottom 003967; p 117 P02071.005;
p 118 top 010060, bottom 009708;
p 119 bottom, left 005853, bottom right
002619A; p 120 bottom P02825.004;
p 121 top 000008, bottom 010259; p 122
VIC1481; p 123 Tobruk textbox P0034/01/01;
p 124 021037; p 125 top P1260/28/14,
bottom 042826

Never More Alone

pp 126-127 013971; p 129 106588; p 130 top
127903, bottom P1021/01; p 131 128107;
p 132 Perth textbox P0761/52/11; p 133 top
030128/2, bottom 030127/2; p 134 top 011867,
bottom 012672; p 135 030130/5; p 136
136305; p 137 P02018.087; p 138 top 136739,
bottom 012293; p 139 Lend-Lease textbox
029381; p 140 top 011668, bottom 012968;
p 141 Timor textbox 013792; p 142 025626;
p 143 top 012968, Fear textbox 026822;
p 144 P02423.009; p 145 013266; p 146 top
P02312.004, bottom 005638; p 147 013282;
p 148 RAAF textbox, top P02018.128, bottom
026658; p 149 013287; p 150 top 013260,
bottom 013264; p 151 P02038.146; p 152 top
042975, bottom 013238; p 153 top 136379,
bottom 141960; p 154 top 137365, bottom
136882; p 155 'Painting, Ghosts' textbox
UK01175; p 156 ARTV06690; p 157 top
136430, bottom 003870; p 158, 'Fear State'
textbox 013505; p 159 top 026856, bottom
027079; p 160 top 013572, bottom 013598;
p 161 013645; p 162 'Born …'textbox VIC0805;
p 163 top 044866, bottom P01997.009;
p 164 128154; p 166 top 044211, bottom
067887; p 167 Bushcraft textbox P02305.019;
p 168 bottom 052224; p 169 058951; p 170
138698; p 171 058929; p 172 top 063809,
bottom 014378; p 173 War at Sea textbox
300785; p 174 137803; p 175 top 042891,
Canteens textbox P0561/50/23; p 176 top
0G1111, Surrender textbox 115619;
p 177 top 108260, bottom 042813

Five Minutes to Midnight

pp 178-179 P01813.555; p 180 030295/4;
p 181 136741; p 182 top SUK14270,
bottom P0474/43/01; p 183 P0131/60/01;
p 184 P0131/60/41; p 185 304932;

p 186 top 127226, bottom P1144/16/10;
p 187 P1144/16/09; p 188 top P1616.003,
middle P1144/16/13, bottom P1616.006;
p 190 top JK0140, bottom JK10919;
p 191 top P0675/127/018, bottom JK1027;
p 192 146986; p 193 top 147319, middle
147331, bottom JK0966; p 194 Kapyong textbox,
top P01813.744, bottom HOBJ4567; p 195
P01813.532; p 196 HOB/490/MC; p 197 top
304626, bottom P1325/45/12; p 198 Pipeline
Ambush textbox HOB/491/MC; p 199 top
P02222.012, bottom P01858.001; p 200
P1706.003; p 201 044726; p 202 top
P02742.005, bottom CUN/0699/MC;
p 203 CUN/0722/MC; p 204 CUN/0728/MC;
p 205 left P1499/37, right P1399/01

Picking up Credit

pp 206-207 FOD/71/0503/VN;
p 211 top P0963/140/053, bottom
P0963/140/025; p 212 P0963/140/026;
p 214 top P1508/01, bottom P0963/140/046;
p 215 top DNE/65/0114/VN, bottom
P1496/03/01; p 216 CUN/66/0523/VN;
p 217 top P148/01, bottom P1293/25/19;
p 218 DNE/65/0212/VN; p 220 top P02297.008,
bottom P02297.002; p 221 P02354.022;
p 222 P02354.025; p 223 EKN/69/0061/VN;
p 224 FOR/66/0538/VN; p 225, Combat textbox
top P0508/13/03, bottom P0508/13/08;
p 226 top CUN/66/0178/VN, bottom
SHA/66/0006/VN; p 227 P1358/11/02;
p 228 CUN/66/0521/VN; p 229 P1404/24;
p 230 P01783.012; p 231 Long Tan textbox
CUN/66/0704/VN; p 232 top P1582.002,
bottom P01783.003; p 233 P1002/144/121;
p 234 P1539/01; p 235 FOD/71/0255/VN;
p 236 top CRO/68/0076/VN, bottom
CAM/68/0184/VN; p 237 top P02017.023,
bottom CRO/68/0575/VN; p 238 left
ERR/68/0520/VN, right CRO/68/0251/VN;
p 240 top P1014/27/01, bottom P8900/02/01;
p 241 SAS textbox top P0966/97/84, bottom
P0966/97/89; p 242 BEL/69/0383/VN;
p 243 BRO/69/0078/VNS; p 244 top
EKN/69/0166/VN, bottom EKN/69/0102/VN;
p 245 top WAR/70/0026/VN, bottom
P0671/14/11; p 246 P0671/14/06;
p 249 P02650.001

Life Ever After

pp 254-255 JK0359; p 256 140955;
p 257 E00166; p 258 top P0308/12/07,
bottom E05925; p 259 11225; p 260 top 65880,
bottom still P03015.023 from film 01212;
p 261 138723; p 262 top CAMUN93/111/14,
bottom MSU93/207/17; p 263 18176;
p 264 93/197/12A

Index

Page numbers in *italics* refer to photographs